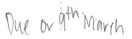
Due on 9th March

MEDIA
AND
SOCIETY

Critical perspectives

GRAEME BURTON

MEDIA AND SOCIETY

Critical perspectives

Open University Press

Open University Press
McGraw-Hill Education
McGraw-Hill House
Shoppenhangers Road
Maidenhead
Berkshire
England
SL6 2QL

email: enquiries@openup.co.uk
world wide web: www.openup.co.uk

and Two Penn Plaza, New York, NY 10121-2289, USA

First published 2005

Editorial Advisor: Stuart Allan

A catalogue record of this book is available from the British Library

ISBN 0 335 20880 0 (pb)   0 335 21589 0 (hb)

Library of Congress Cataloging-in-Publication Data
CIP data applied for

Typeset by RefineCatch Limited, Bungay, Suffolk
Printed in the UK by Bell & Bain Ltd, Glasgow

CONTENTS

3 AUDIENCES AND EFFECTS
Defining audiences and exploring their relationship with texts

4 THE MEDIA AND VIOLENCE
Questioning violence: problems with measuring effects

7 APPROACHES TO FILM
The missing British film industry: audiences, gazing and meanings

8 THE MEDIA AND NEW TECHNOLOGY
The effects and implications of technologies for the media and their consumption

LIST OF FIGURES AND ILLUSTRATIONS

ACKNOWLEDGEMENTS

Acknowledgements may be traditional in book publishing, but they are nonetheless heartfelt on my part. This book has been part of my life for some time, and that life includes people who have helped me make it happen. So I want to thank colleagues in Cultural Studies at the University of the West of England for providing me with an eclectic intellectual atmosphere and with friendship. In particular, I want to thank Stuart Allan, who has been patient and helpful, not least when I have been anxious and doubtful. My thanks to people at the Open University Press, especially Chris Cudmore and Hannah Cooper, who have kept the faith and helped me keep up the pace of production. And a thank you to my family, especially my wife Judy, who has been supportive in times when I was suffering from doubts and lack of vision. Thanks to all of you. This book will not be perfect, but I hope that you feel it has been worth it, and that my readers will feel, to a fair degree, informed, interested and illuminated.

INTRODUCTION

This book is intended to help student readers on degree courses and modules which are concerned with media studies, and, to some extent, with the study of cultures. I want to offer a few remarks about the position that I am coming from, and where I hope you may go to through using this text.

I take a holistic and dynamic view of the relationships between media and society. That is to say, while I present a range of views and debates about the media in this book, I do not really subscribe to pessimistic opinions about the influence of media on society. Nor do I go along with what I regard as over-optimistic views about audience autonomy and power. It seems to me that the media exist in an evolving and difficult relationship with their audiences, and indeed with institutions of the state. The relationship is dynamic in that it is evolving and changing. I also believe that it is possible for different critical positions to coexist. It is possible to be sceptical about the motives and behaviours of economically powerful media institutions. At the same time, it is possible to be optimistic about the effects of regulatory control in Britain, and about the capacity of audiences and society to resist the forces of commodification, and to generate a culture as much as to have it imposed on them.

I feel much the same way about how we should understand and use key concepts. The book is (fairly traditionally) predicated on the importance of institution, text and audience. But I see ideas about ideology, discourse, hegemony, mythologies, genres – to mention only a few examples – as coexisting in the space of 'meaning production'. You will find that this book keeps returning to these concepts, and develops ideas about the relationship between them. It seems to me that every kind of analysis keeps returning one to ways in which ideas and meanings are generated, and then to ideas about the power of these meanings. The media industries are meaning producers. All acts of communication produce meanings. It is the power of these meanings, what we do with them, that shapes relationships, exercises influence, models reality, generates behaviours of domination and feelings of subordination. So major concepts may be equally significant, and exist within a network of relationships with each other.

Media texts are full of representations. Media institutions exist, when it comes down to it, to manufacture representations (and their ideas) which they then turn into cash in a process of material exchange. But, of course, as we consume comics or television programmes, we are also part of a process of cultural exchange. The exchange is indeed one of ideas about the world, about ourselves. In a dynamic model, these keep developing and shifting and moving around. Some ideas are more persistent than others (stereotypes). But it is an exciting world out there, where the media keep generating, recombining, repeating ideas, even if this is mainly in the cause of commerce.

I take a similarly holistic view of the 'big ideas' about connections between the media and ourselves. Firstly, I have tried to give a fair if condensed view of a range of critical positions, in Chapter 2. In many ways I subscribe to a political economy model because it seems to me unarguable that, in the West, we have gone down what is called a capitalist road. Economic factors dominate media institutions, most of all in the ubiquitous presence of marketing. Profitability, competition and other values of the marketplace drive the production of media texts and behaviours in what we call global-ization. In this respect I also feel that the outcomes of Marxist rationales and the validity of the notion of ideology are both important and not to be argued away. But because I am suggesting that ideas exist within a model, I am also saying that, for example, one cannot simply assert that notions of pluralism are nonsense. On balance, I certainly do not think that they prevail. But it is important to me as the writer, that you as readers, take on different views, and think through your own beliefs for your-selves. It is, indeed, part of the development of critical skills not only to evaluate the validity of arguments, but to be able to hold in one's head a variety of arguments and ideas, all of which may have some merit, and all of which may stand in some relationship to one another.

This idea of dynamic relationships also applies to academic disciplines, with which you are involved. No one discipline 'owns' the media, including media schools. So you could be a student of social sciences, with an interest in the media. Because the media are also engines of cultural production you may have an interest in the media among other objects of cultural study. Certainly you will find reference in this book to cultural perspectives and ideas – such as those around identity – which I do not believe it is useful to assign to a kind of discipline ghetto. After this, one could approach the media with all sorts of inflections, from economics to anthropology. So I hope that in reading what follows you will find some sense of reference outwards and across. I have tried to delineate and control areas of enquiry, without seeming to circumscribe some absolute object called media study.

In terms of the structure of this book, you should know that the first three chapters are intended as an overview – of institution, texts and audiences, and their co-relationship. The remaining chapters are kinds of 'case study', which exemplify and develop issues, concepts and debates. They are still predicated on those central terms of institution, text and audience, and on central concerns about the production of meaning and the exercise of power. Although there is a sense in which these later chapters can stand alone, you should realize that reading the whole book is meant to be a process of reinforcement and development. In particular, and apart from key terms such as dis-course, you will find that chapters return to ideas about technologies, gender, representa-tions and globalization. So I think you have to make decisions about using the book in three possible ways: as a whole and developing text, from which you learn by going from beginning to end; as a case study resource in which you can get some ideas and further reading about the given chapter topic by using it on its own; and as a topic resource in which you plunder the index for references across the book to the given topic that you want to find out more about. What I would say is that no book can be the last word on a subject, especially one like this which has a lot of ground to cover. It is meant to give you a overview, mixed with some more in-depth studies of particular topics. But you will need to read more widely. The chapter reading references and the collated bibliography will give you a lot to follow up.

So far as websites are concerned, I take a mixed view of their usefulness. The more specific your object of enquiry, the more useful they are likely to be. But in most cases, the examples that I have given you are meant to be helpful starting points. You need to use your tutors and your learning resource centre for information about sites that are specific to assignments and services such as LexisNexis to which your library will be subscribed.

You will see that illustrations have a small amount of copy with them, explaining why they are in the book, and perhaps inviting you to think about some issues that they raise. You might like to think about the fact that it can be difficult finding such illustrations, and getting copyright at a viable cost. This book and the pictures in it are texts themselves and commodities. They too have a market value, and the producers have to operate within the constraints of market forces that I write about.

I have included what I call major questions near the beginning of each chapter for two reasons. One is that they raise problems and issues for discussion around the chapter topics. The other is that they then inform what follows. However, they are not simply an implied list of topic headings for the sections of the chapter. Discussion of such major questions may take place throughout the chapter. Indeed, these questions, especially those from earlier chapters, will be taken on across chapters, as ideas are developed. Ideas about representations, for example, are developed from Chapter 2 through later chapters about soap operas or sport.

Chapter 1 goes straight into comments about critical perspectives on media institutions, on the grounds that these produce the material that engages the audience, and that there are common concerns about media power when one looks at views on the relationship between media and society. I start with a political economy perspective on this relationship, contrasted with ideas about pluralism and the free market. I have tried to incorporate a reasonable amount of information, as background to the chapters which follow. Indeed, this chapter prefigures later material – for example, on advertising, audiences and technology. Chapter 2 then examines media texts in general, with some emphasis on their deconstruction in order to tease out meanings. I also deal with narratives, representations, realism and genres, which are major areas of study in their own right. These features of text are important to understanding the nature of engagement with the audience, as well as the point at which meanings are produced – meanings which frame how we think about the world, how we conduct social interactions, how we understand our individual and collective identities. Chapter 3 then goes on to look at ourselves as audiences for texts and for the media. I will look at the idea of interaction with the text once more, and take a critical view of assumptions about the effects of media on audiences and on society.

In raising such questions, explaining key terms and laying out issues around the media, I have tried to represent a fair range of established views. These may be alternative, they may coexist, they may conflict. But overall, the idea is to get you thinking, to encourage you to ask your own questions. I stand responsible for the nature of my explanations, and especially for interpretations, comments and views of my own. But you are responsible for your own learning. Writers and tutors are there to help that happen, but never to hand you answers on a plate. I hope that you find all of this book useful for your studies. I hope that you find at least some of it interesting, and better still, provoking. But most of all, I hope that it will support you thinking for yourself, and make you want to find out more about the topics and ideas which you are investigating.

Graeme Burton
Gloucestershire
2004

CHAPTER ONE

MEDIA INSTITUTIONS

Key areas and their implications for understanding media

"A focal question for the political economy of communications is to investigate how changes in the array of forces that exercise control over cultural production and distribution limit or liberate the public sphere.

This directs attention to two key issues. The first is the pattern of ownership of such institutions and the consequences of this pattern for control over their activities. The second is the nature of the relationship between state regulation and communications institutions."

Peter Golding and Graham Murdock (2000) Culture, communications and political economy, in J. Curran and M. Gurevitch *Mass Media and Society* (3rd edn). London: Arnold.

1 Introduction

In addition to the above it may be said that a political economy approach would be interested in

● the production of cultural goods by institutions;

● regulation by those institutions and by government;

● media texts with reference to the relationship between representations and the conditions of production and consumption;

● cultural consumption with relation to cultural and social inequalities.

In this first chapter I want to make connections between elements such as regulation and power, as they relate to the production of meaning, and as they illuminate the relationship between media and society. But we also need to look separately at the nature and operations of media institutions.

Texts and audiences are relatively accessible. Media businesses are not. Information about their policies and financial affairs is hard to come by for reasons of confidentiality. Access to the production needs of their businesses may be denied for the same reason, or because these organizations are suspicious of what academic researchers are going to do and say.

Differing views on the practices and products of media institutions throw up contradictions. For example, if a pluralistic approach proposes diversity of product, then at what point does diversity in fact become cultural fragmentation? May this not simply encourage social fracturing, and work against cultural coherence?

Ralph Negrine (1994) identifies contradictions between statements in support of a free market, and those which then ask for regulation of that market because of the consequences of its becoming 'too free'. He quotes John Keane: 'there is a structural contradiction between freedom of communication and unlimited freedom of the

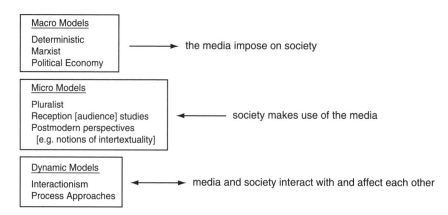

Summary of Models of the Relationship between Media and Society
This mapping of broad critiques of the relationship between media and society represents general truths, but needs particular qualifications.
For example, some political economists veer towards a dynamic model in accepting that there is a complex relationship, in which economic power does not simply determine cultural change. Similarly, Feminist critiques embrace a range of positions, both determinist and audience centred.

market . . . the market liberal ideology of freedom of individual choice in the marketplace of opinions is in fact a justification of the privileging of corporate speech and of giving more choice to investors than to citizens'. Negrine talks of a free market which is 'regulated to allow for freedom, albeit a freedom where market forces dominate, and where, crucially, media content is treated as a commodity rather than a public good'.

In terms of the relationship between media and society, these observations raise questions about different critical approaches, as well as about ideological positions. On the one hand, Western beliefs in democracy and freedom of choice support ideas about a free market and visions of a plurality of media and their materials. On the other hand, the freedom of institutions to produce what they like does not fit other ideological imperatives – to endorse a particular system of social morality and to protect certain social groups, for instance. Nor do such freedoms as are now allowed seem to add up to a genuine freedom of choice for all sections of society. The power of relatively few media institutions to determine what appears in the marketplace equally endorses critiques offered by neo-Marxists and political economists – that society is not best served by the media, least of all in terms of a free market of ideas.

Blair and Bush: Media users, media controllers
How should we understand the media – in terms of economic imperatives – of political regulation? Is media consumption really a matter of choice?
(*Corbis*)

2 Major questions

1 How may we understand the identity, function and significance of media institutions apart from their role as constructors of media product?

2 In what respects may we understand media institutions as being distinct from or similar to other commercial enterprises?

3 How do we understand the relationship of media institutions to other dominant institutions of our society, especially to the advertising industry?

4 What characterizes the relationship between media and government, especially with reference to the regulation of media?

5 How does media policy affect the position of public service broadcasting in particular, as it competes with a free market model?

6 How do media institutions understand their audiences, and what are the implications of this understanding?

7 What do we mean by the phrase 'power of the media'? What is its location, its expression and its significance?

8 How have media institutions changed with the advent of new technology, and with relation to ideas about globalization?

9 Is it possible to conceive alternative models for media institutions?

3 Defining institutions

3.1 When is an institution?

The media do not of course represent one coherent organization, even if one may talk collectively about 'the institution of the media'. Nor can it be supposed that one is talking just about those organizations which are producers of media material. If one is discussing for example

- questions of power;
- the nature of media influence;
- media – social relations;
- the media as public space;

then it is important to realize that the media are about more than the sum of their texts. There may be some things to be inferred about the institution from its texts, but not everything which explains how and why they operate as they do within a social, political and economic context. The production of meaning is about more than the text. Critiques of media – a political economy perspective in particular – are about more than textual production.

Media business covers commercial functions such as finance, distribution, exhibition and retailing, as well as production. The owners of media businesses may be into non-media enterprises. Media institutions may not even be commercial in their foundation –

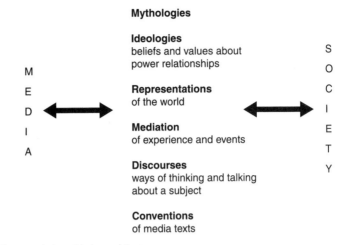

Mythologies

Ideologies
beliefs and values about
power relationships

Representations
of the world

Mediation
of experience and events

Discourses
ways of thinking and talking
about a subject

Conventions
of media texts

Some Key Concepts Linking Media and Society
Media workers and members of society share, for example, ideologies. But media workers have control of
technologies through which to mediate experience in the form of texts. The texts construct representations,
using discourses, and so promote myths and ideologies.
(*Graeme Burton*, 2004)

the BBC is the most obvious example of this, as a non-profit making public service broadcaster with a turnover of millions. Others do not work in a free-for-all market economy. The *Guardian* and *Observer* newspaper groups are run by a trust, which denies control to shareholders or to entrepreneurs buying in to those newspapers. Channel 4 television is constrained by its foundation through an act of Parliament, into providing for minority interests, whatever the commercial implications.

Many media institutions are large and wealthy, without being directly in the business of production and exhibition. WPP is a global advertising agency which designs campaigns and commissions adverts. But it doesn't run the broadcasters or the press that present the ads to us.

Associated Press is a huge press agency that gathers and shapes stories which it sells on to newspapers. The US-owned NTL is, in Britain, a dominant cable operator that distributes the texts made by others. It is a major operator in terms of turnover, and of dominance in its field (though it is still struggling to make a profit). Yet its name is not on the lips of the public because it is not visible as a producer, on screen or in the news-agents. NTL raises another issue about defining media institutions – what one might refer to as associated industries. With texts in mind, one might not regard telecommunication industries as part of the media. But in their operations as distributors or carriers at least, they bring media materials to the audiences.

One may argue that their other operations (for example, telephone) are part of mass communications, as distinct from mass media. But it is a fine distinction to make. The problem with making such a distinction is exemplified by the Net. It is both a carrier of one-to-one communication – email and information from websites – and a distributor of media text – micro cinema or online versions of newspapers. So our object of study is not just about text makers, but also about text enablers and the environment in which text gets made.

The media industries actually comprise interdependent institutions. The links between these are based not least on the outcomes of new technology – about which more later. Even when one considers the interface of texts with audience, there is a tendency to underestimate the scope of the media. So, the sphere of 'the press' is not just about dominant national newspapers but also about the range of regional papers; not just about papers but also about magazines; not just about the public press but also about the trade press; not just about the print press, but also about online newspapers and about e-publishing in general.

3.2 Characteristics of institutions

More accurately one might be talking about the characteristics of dominant media institutions, since the range of business in the media industries in general (see last section) is such that it isn't easy to generalize. This also begs the question of what one means by 'dominance'. But for now I will at least refer to dominance in terms of income/ turnover/expenditure, volume of product/output, size of audience/consumer base. In this case, one may refer to the following:

- degree of vertical integration,
- investment in new technology;
- multi-nationalism;
- conglomeration – lateral integration;
- diversification.

These features are, significantly, not peculiar to media industries. They mark dominance in other industries. In the British media, they mark out those five market leaders (as well as some others) which typically control some 70 per cent of the market concerned. This is the pattern, whether you look at Bertelsmann in Germany, Murdoch's NewsCorp in the USA, Berlusconi's Fininvest in Italy. This pattern represents a capitalist or market model for business, in which competition, profit and return on investments drive the behaviour of the company. It is difficult not to conclude that most media companies operating on these principles work in the interests of owners – as opposed to the interests of audiences or the community at large. Where there are qualifications to this pattern, it is either because of regulation – the BBC – or because the organization is working in a niche market that is of no interest to bigger commercial players.

Vertical integration refers to the pattern of business ownership in which a company buys or sets up other companies which relate to the core business – say, publishing. In particular, big media organizations tend to try and control production, distribution and exhibition/retailing. So when NewsCorp moved into the USA it bought Twentieth Century Fox which is about film production and distribution. These films provide product for Fox TV, which itself was greatly expanded in respect of its production and distribution of TV material. News International also owns a chain of 33 TV stations in major US cities, which gives it some guaranteed exhibition of its product. This integrated power also gives such a media institution the power to cut one-sided deals with apparently independent makers of film and TV.

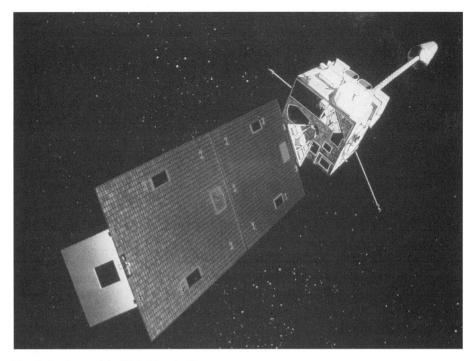

New Technology and the Global Reach of Institutions
NT underpins media power of distribution, across a range of media: films, TV, news production, the Internet, telecommunications.
(*Corbis*)

Multi-nationalism links to globalization and refers to the fact that the largest media companies do business in different countries, have links across national boundaries (co-productions), distribute product across different countries, and have manufacturing bases in different countries. This can make them more difficult to regulate, less easy to tax and generally more difficult to 'challenge' in national and cultural interests.

Conglomeration refers to a tendency to buy into similar businesses in order to meet competition and to dominate the media sector which a given company is in. So in Britain, over the last few years, Granada Television bought controlling interests in Yorkshire, Tyne Tees and London Weekend television companies, and has now merged with the other big player, Carlton, to form ITV plc. To take another example, my local newspaper *The Gloucestershire Gazette* was owned by a group called Southern Newspapers, but the group was taken over by another called Newsquest, which as a conglomerate is now one of the biggest groups in the country (and is itself owned by a US media company called Gannet).

On another scale, the failing French global media business, Vivendi, which owned Universal Pictures, sorted out financial problems (2003–4) by negotiating a merger deal with General Electric, owner of NBC TV, radio and cable.

Lateral integration – refers to a company move sideways, buying across different media. The biggest companies, like NI, provide examples of both vertical and lateral integration. An example of lateral strength would be the Walt Disney Company, which in respect of films owns Miramax and Touchstone, as well as Walt Disney Pictures. In terms of television, it owns the ABC network, as well as Touchstone and Buena Vista television, plus a number of cable channels. In radio, it owns ABC radio networks. In music, it owns Walt Disney and Hollywood records. In publishing it owns, among others, Hyperion books, seven daily newspapers and a variety of magazines.

Croteau and Hoynes (1997) provide good analysis and description of such ownership, including a study of the media conglomerate Bertelsmann, which owns over 350 companies in some 30 countries.

Diversification refers to another version of the lateral process in which a media company is either bought by a business having nothing to do with media, or in which the media company buys into a non-related media business as a way of spreading its financial bets. My regional newspaper *The Bristol Evening Post* is now owned by the Daily Mail and General Trust media organization. Before this, it was mainly owned by the British Electric Traction company.

It may be argued that these characteristics are linked to economic drivers which in turn may be summarized as seeking

- Profitability;
- Economies of scale;
- Control of the market;
- Suppression of competition.

All these commercial practices contribute to the superior market position and power of certain media organizations.

Nicholas Garnham (2000) produces the following definition of media organizations in relation to their economic activity –

1 editorial model – in which individual goods are produced directly for the consumer (such as CDs)

2 press model – in which goods are produced collectively but are also guaranteed repeat sales (such as newspapers)

3 flow model – in which a constant supply of goods is produced (as in broadcasting)

Such models reinforce the idea that media organizations are institutions of commerce, as much as creative sources, cultural enablers or part of a social.

4 Media institutions and finance

What I want to consider here is where the money comes from, where it goes, and the implications. The remarks which follow refer to institutions which are producers, as much as distributors. Grossberg *et al.* (1998) make a useful general description of how media make sales and derive income

1 via direct purchase of the commodity – e.g. the cost of the magazine;

2 via a charge for access to the point of distribution or display – e.g. box office charge at the movie theatre, or the Internet provider charge;

3 via indirect financial support, though the commodity is free at the point of sale – e.g. commercial television;

4 via indirect financial support, plus a cover cost – e.g. advertising in newspapers.

The account which follows amplifies this model and applies mainly to British media.

The BBC is, exceptionally, funded by a licence fee of £121 per annum, payable by all households having a TV set, and bringing in around £2.5 billion a year. In principle it is independent of market forces. In practice it is not. Successive governments, that set the licence fee/income of the BBC, have made it clear that the BBC must compete with the commercial sector in terms of quality, ratings and public approval, not to mention adopting commercial practices.

The rest of British media relies a great deal on advertising. Broadcasting almost entirely depends on this. Newspapers and magazines derive between 30 per cent and 70 per cent of their income from advertising. For example, the *Sun* tabloid newspaper, with sales of around 4 million a day, can charge £50,000 for a full page advertisement. However, one should note that books and CDs, for example, have to make their profits on unit sales. There is also a small amount of money that comes from sponsorship – The Cadbury Group sponsors the successful soap, *Coronation Street*, while HSBC Bank sponsors drama series on ITV.

This dependence on advertising reinforces institutional values which are tied in with a market perspective. It means that the interests of the media become closely identified with the interests of other kinds of business. It underpins the view that media goods come to be treated like any other commodity: that if media products are manifestations of culture, then that culture becomes a collection of commodities, where the media are concerned, at least.

I now want to look at particular examples of media industries.

The film industry (see also Chapter 7)

This is an interesting case in many ways. Firstly, there is no coherent British film industry in the way that radio programmes or books are produced, distributed and sold in Britain. There is a constellation of companies which specialize in things like producing (not making) films, or in support services such as making trailers. Secondly and consequently, there is no large film company which can, from its own turnover and backers, finance movies – least of all for distribution on a global scale. Finance for British films is cobbled together from a variety of sources. Predominantly, money comes from the US majors. Television may also provide some funding. Channel 4 has been a relatively significant supporter of low-budget British films, but by 2004 it has pulled out of this activity. The BBC puts only 1 per cent of its budget into film production. The British National Lottery has also given some money, to be administered through the UK Film Council. Thirdly, what are legally defined as British films (and so eligible for certain tax concessions) may be made largely by British workers, but often are funded by US money – companies such as Miramax. Fourthly, the income of films globally is not derived much from advertising around screening: this goes to the exhibitor, in Britain often one of the US Majors once again. As Doyle (2002) puts it: 'The small size of the domestic UK market and the disaggregated structure of the industry prevent the indigenous production sector from growing beyond a cottage industry.'

But in any case, even globally, few films survive solely on box-office receipts. Video sales are important. So is the income from TV rights – often made in a pre-sales deal which provides cash upfront to pay for the movie being made. And then there are the spin-off product deals – music, games and toys. The fragmented sources of income for movies is partly an expression of the huge sums needed to pay for the most expensive media product of all (if one is considering mainstream film making). Major Hollywood movies cost anything from US$50,000 to US$100,000 on average, to make and promote. But one may also say that the huge sums to be made from such a variety of sources also feeds the ballooning cost of making major feature films. It feeds the profit expectations of film companies. It creates a film producing market in which the divide between global and very local and small scale is marked. It creates a film consuming market in which the worst excesses of mass appeal, mass culture can be realized.

The television industry

In contrast to film, though this makes a lot of money from spin-offs, programme sales, and syndication, it has not inflated the economic balloon to the same extent. If these three sources disappeared tomorrow, there would still be a British TV industry. However, it is also fair to point out how much TV now depends on co-productions – money from US or European networks – to help pay for the really big drama and documentary series, such as *Walking with Beasts* on BBC1.

In 2002, British TV saw a 6.6 per cent increase in the value of programme sales – most of which were to the USA (worth £148 million) and to Canada (£100 million), which £248 million was about half the value of total sales.

So while media institutions derive some income directly from product sales, it is the case that much of their financing and profit comes indirectly from other sources. This is well illustrated as part of the symbiotic relationship of media with one another – the patterns of cross-media ownership. I am talking about ways in which one medium helps finance another. Newspapers advertise on television; television finances some film production; film and television have created the video market; spin-off video games pay a percentage to the film producers and pay for advertising in magazines and on TV.

Cost elements

It follows from the above that, in terms of media expenditure, advertising and promotion is a significant part of any budget. Clearly this may not be the case if one is a provider/distributor like NTL (cable), as opposed to being a major manufacturer of product. But even portal and search engine providers for the Net, such as Yahoo!, not only take income from advertisers, but also have to advertise their merits to attract more users and advertisers. The average feature film will spend between a quarter and a third of its production costs again, in order to promote itself. Quality television drama, such as adaptations of the classics, will cost between £300,000 and £500,000 for 50 minutes on screen. A psychological crime thriller series such as *Wire in the Blood* (ITV) costs £620,000 an episode.

Another significant cost element is labour, including celebrity performers. Of course, specialist workers may command high salaries, not least in operating new technology.

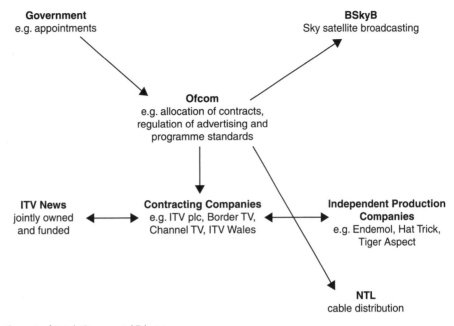

Elements of British Commercial Television
The government set up Ofcom to monitor and regulate the output and commercial behaviour of the contracting companies. Mergers have meant that these are now dominated by ITV plc, and essentially it *is* British commercial terrestrial television. It takes at least 25% of its material from independent production companies. It now effectively controls ITV news, although this is legally a separate body.

Would a model for any one of the media look like this – interdependent organizations, public and private? If so, what are likely to be the consequences for the ways that they operate and for the nature of their media output?
(*Graeme Burton*, 2004)

But the really big cost elements are for those media industries where the star, the celebrity, the personality worker is essential for attracting audiences and income. Film and TV are obvious examples. A British celebrity couple hosting a TV show (Judy Finnegan and Richard Madley) in 2001 took their programme to another station at a cost of £3 million. And no one will have heard of them outside Britain! Media products which depend on individual expertise and recognition have a charge attached to them.

A third major cost element is that of new technology. This is discussed elsewhere. But, in general, there is a huge investment in NT because it may produce:

● economies of scale;

● enhancement of product;

● new products/services or reduction of labour

– and so increase profits and increase competitiveness.

These three elements are the most significant for media institutions. But of course there are many other factors which affect different industries in different ways, and for different reasons. For example, the development of new media which expand the numbers of outlets for advertising and which offer more choices for leisure time activity, has reduced TV advertising revenue (and therefore its capacity to spend) over the past few years. Grossberg *et al.* (1998) report that US Network audience share fell from 91 per cent in 1978–9 to 40 per cent in 1996–7, because of competition from cable and satellite channels. There has been a similar but much less marked pattern in Britain. However, it may be pointed out that the British commercial television system has its own peculiar elements which affect income, costs and profits. In particular, there is the amount that has to be bid in order to get a contract to broadcast in the first place. Then there are taxation costs. In the case of ITV these two cost elements mean that the company pays back to government about 30 per cent of its advertising income. Regulation comes in various guises, and the free market is not, in these respects, as free as it may seem.

5 Media in relation to other institutions

My remarks in the previous section about other industries remind us that media institutions exist within a context of other powerful organizations. Garnham (2000) makes a criticism of at least certain kinds of approach to media when he says – 'media studies . . . tends to focus on things . . . rather than the whole social process which lies behind them'. Media institutions may have particular qualities and a particular position within commerce, society, culture. But they are not pre-eminent. Government uses political and legal power to modify their sphere of operation. Individuals and groups have recourse to the law in order to contain or even redefine what it is acceptable for the media to do. The police may act for the state in a similar process of containment. Education makes the media an object of study and may question its role.

The media also interact with other institutions – say, the military at a time of war through TV news, or the health service in a time of reorganization through an article. They are neither dominant nor submissive in this interaction. But this interaction, this general context, needs to be accounted for in making models of the relationship between media and society. It suggests that whatever influence media may have, this is qualified and modified.

6 Media and audiences (see also Chapter 3)

Discussion of a relationship between media and audiences begs the problem of conceptualizing 'audience' in the first place. Mostly this is discussed in Chapter 5, but it may be summed up in terms of whether one can understand the audience as –

- a disparate collection of individuals who happen to be consuming one text at one time;
- a coherent social group who have in common characteristics outside their consumption;
- a mass group whose identity comes from the very fact of their consumption.

ITV can tell us that it has 45 million viewers a week, and break down these figures by factors such as channel, region and times (2004). Media institutions need to objectify their audiences to satisfy their advertisers. They need to satisfy their advertisers because in most cases they depend on their revenue for survival and profit. In this case they are looking at quantitative research and at ways of measuring what the audiences do with the products. So although given institutions may talk generally about their viewers, listeners or readers, in fact they are thinking about consumers. The raison d'être of the audience is to provide cash for the media organizations to continue to operate. More specific descriptions of audiences emphasize this view. Newspapers refer to readership and circulation figures. Broadcasters refer to ratings. These descriptions translate into numbers. Even where more qualitative descriptions are used – lifestyle identities or psychometric profiles – the bottom line is, how far do these translate into certain numbers of certain kinds of people who are spending, or who are prepared to spend, given amounts of cash on the given media service (and the goods and services that it may be promoting)? So the relationship at the level of policy, of shareholders, of the executive, is a material one.

This detachment and objectification remains generally true at the level of actual media production within the institution. But there are respects in which the audience achieves a greater sense of identity. I am also referring to the fact that media institutions should not be seen as an undifferentiated mass. The size and the ethos of the organization matter, as well as the role of media workers within the institution. At the production level, the institution makes contact with the audience in various ways. So the makers of documentaries or the writers of articles will be going out to the public to gather material. Some media texts figure members of the public. Makeover TV programmes like the gardening-based *Ground Force* (BBC1) does just this. In this sense it is bringing some of its audience to be seen by others. One should not exaggerate the intimacy of the connection, nor the sense of who the audience is, composed of individuals and human beings. But the contact is there. It works at the level of the much repeated account of the Anglian radio producer who conceptualized his typical listener as a housewife named Doreen.

What is true about the media–audience relationship is that it remains unequal, even when audiences are part of the production of the text, as in the case of reality TV. Institutions control access to the media. They define the terms on which audiences may participate. It is obvious in the case of quiz shows, for example, that however participants may be typical of the audience profile, once they are on the show they are no longer the audience. They are not onlookers. And even studio audiences stand in a rather different relationship to textual material than do the audiences at home. What doesn't change is that the institution still controls the role of the players or of the studio audiences – who are also players of a kind. So while it is true that the relationship of institution with audience is rather more complex than a mass audience model asserts, it is still one in which audiences largely lack access to media, and media have the dominant, controlling role in the relationship. This remains true for those media examples where audiences appear to participate through letters, phone-ins and other participative devices.

There are kinds of interaction, but nothing like the social interaction model of everyday life where participants have equal access to the means of communication, and where instant feedback enables genuine negotiation over the production of meaning. The media have established themselves as the producers of texts, which are offered to audiences as made objects, to be taken largely without discussion. Of course, the limitations of technology mean that one cannot achieve a wholly interactive relationship – a kind of public space in the marketplace. And not all audiences want to be made to participate in the play, as it were. But again it can be said that we have lost the kind of responsiveness and participation for which the small town newspaper was once a model – the institution was part of a community, its producers lived in that community, were identifiable, and so were responsive to that community.

The conceptualization of audience in large categories by media producers becomes part of the framework within which the text is made, and therefore meaning is encoded. Such conceptualization, leading to production, leading to encoding, may be seen as an enactment of media power. However, macro and micro studies conceive of audience rather differently. So we need to remember that the macro or broad view of a relationship between media and society will see, if not mass audiences, relatively large numbers of people – whereas micro studies of audience deal in much smaller numbers. And many examples which are described under the heading of audience studies, are in fact micro studies. We may learn a lot about how small numbers of people relate to certain texts. But such studies do not really tell us much about the broader picture of the relationship between institution and audience via texts, and in terms of possible effects.

One may also say that the notion of a free market does not add up to an audience with freedom, in terms of being able to pick and choose among a range of texts and range of meanings. A free market does not give the audiences the economic freedom to be able to pay for, to consume whatever they may want. There is to some extent a correlation in the relationship between institution and audience based on cost and dis-posable income. In turn, this may relate to the costs of and charges for, new technology. The TiVO on top of the TV can give the audience more choice of what to consume and when – if they can afford it. It may be life-enhancing to join the information highway – but lower income groups cannot afford the hardware or the user charges.

However, James Curran takes a more optimistic view of economic factors, and talks down a view of media institutions as operating on the basis of unbridled self-interest.

> The radical media literature is bedevilled by a system logic which assumes that state-controlled media serve the state and corporate-controlled media serve business corpor-ations. This ignores, or downplays, countervailing influences. Privately owned media need to maintain audience interest in order to be profitable; they have to sustain public legitimacy in order to avoid societal retribution; and they can be influenced by the professional concerns of their staff. All these factors potentially work against the sub-ordination of private media to the political commitments and economic interests of their shareholders.

7 Media and advertising (see also Chapter 9)

> To understand the media economy and what is and is not sustainable within it, we need to understand the nature of the advertising market.
>
> **Garnham (2000)**

The relationship between institutions and advertisers is best described as a symbiotic one. The central issue raised is about the degree to which the media depends on advertising revenue. This in turn leads to questions about how far media texts represent the interests of advertisers and the ideology of the marketplace.

The following comments relate to points made under 'Media institutions and finance', above.

Quality newspapers rely on advertising for about two-thirds of their revenue; the tabloid press for about one third. Magazine producers rely on advertising for 50 per cent and more of their income.

Broadcasters rely entirely on advertising, excepting a proportion made from programme sales and spin-offs, and allowing for the special case of the BBC whose main income is derived from a licence fee. Even the BBC raises money through sponsorship deals, providing cash to put on event shows such as the Royal Variety Performance or something like a tour by the Teletubbies (characters from a popular programme for young children). In 2002 these deals were worth £2 million, contributing to the £500 million made by BBC Worldwide, the sales and spin-offs arm of the corporation.

Movies vary – low budget films rely on box office and TV sales for their income. Big budget and mainstream films rely more, though not mainly, on income from product placement deals or spin-off rights. But in both cases the box office take relies a great deal on the amount spent on promotion – advertising and publicity – which might add an additional 20 per cent to the production costs for a low budget movie, to about 50 per cent for a big movie. And, of course, other media examples also need to promote themselves.

So media institutions rely substantially on the work of, or on income from, advertisers. In turn, advertisers depend on media for a vital means of communication with customers. By advertisers I mean any organization behind the advertising text, from consultancies to video outfits shooting an advert, to media brokers doing deals over the cost and placing of the ad, to any business or organization that contracts the ad. But advertisers do have other means of communication apart from obvious examples of mainstream media. One might regard hoardings as part of the media anyway. But the point is that the symbiosis between media and advertiser is not equal and balanced. As ITV, the main British commercial channel has found out, its advertisers can turn to other media, but it has no other means of raising serious revenue. And that revenue has been declining since the late 1990s. Its share of viewers declined to 23.7 per cent in 2003, while that of multi-channel providers rose to the same figure. Between 2000 and 2003, Sky TV's profits rose from £51 million to £283 million.

Advertising as an activity stands for the ideology of the marketplace – commercial competition, company expansion, promotion of product, pleasing consumers, maximizing profits – at any price. It effectively underwrites the tendency of media owners to support the dominant ideology, the security of the status quo and conservative values. The free press in Britain is largely only free within a market economy model. In this model, minimizing production costs and maximizing audience consumption prevails over any genuine pluralism of material or of ideas. So it is that, of its nature, advertising will not support alternative or radical material. And it follows that there is no left-wing national daily newspaper in the UK.

In this respect I am also arguing that the meanings of media texts, the dominant discourses which produce certain kinds of meanings about how the world should be, are a consequence of the patterns of ownership and of the production practices of media owners. They are also the result of a collusive relationship with advertising. This interest in the work of institutions in manufacturing discourses within a text is part of a political economy critique of the media. Whereas approaches which analyse the text and the discourses themselves would come from a more specifically culturalist critique. One may argue that media study should include both kinds of analysis.

8 Media and government

The relationship between the institutions of media and government is similarly one of mutual self-interest, though not entirely one of equals. When the chips are down, it is government that makes law and controls the flow of information vital to media. Mechanisms of regulation (see below) are controlled directly or indirectly by government. Nevertheless, the access of media to the audience means that government often wants to use media to disseminate policy, to promote initiatives, to release information into the public domain, to test reactions to possible new laws, and most of all to present in a public sphere a favourable view of government work.

The attitude of media institutions to government is partly defined by degrees of interference, which are in turn defined by the terms of regulation for a given media industry. It is also partly defined by the ideological position of given media businesses, or even their proprietors, towards the rights of the state, within their own idea of the media–audience relationship. So marketeers such as Rupert Murdoch, refer to the absolute freedom of the press and to the ability of competition in the marketplace to produce the media we want, as valid arguments for government keeping out of media business. Congdon (1995) disagrees and comments with particular relation to news: 'Just as there can be little confidence that unregulated commercial broadcasters are much concerned to maintain pluralism in political debate, so there can be no presumption that the free market will give top priority to the truthfulness of the news or seek an appropriate mix of news and other programmes.'

Broadcasters, even commercial channels, are more inclined to take liberal pluralist positions. Their terms of reference, their executives, their governing bodies, talk more about responsibility and public service. This is built into the statute and charter which allows their existence and which defines the broad terms of their operation. However, although they may chafe at things like restriction on the proportion of cross-media ownership, broadcasters still accept that they should wear the government bridle, if not a muzzle.

One issue which operates at the highest levels is that of mutual self-interest and its consequences for genuinely free media and free opinion. Governments in the West are very conscious of the value of media coverage, of what they assume to be the power of the media to sway public opinion. They also assert the existence of and value of an independent media sector – not least if that independence validates what the media may say positively about government.

However, independence is relative and qualified. The next section will elaborate on this. The media are aware of their supposed influence, but are also aware of the power of government as a prime source of information. Broadcasters are especially aware of the financial implications of government's power to allow or to stop things from happening. What is interesting is the degree of contact between media and government at a high level of management. Meetings between senior media people and members of governments are a matter of record. Government ministers will make pronouncements about what they think the media should or should not do – part of a dance of power between two great institutions. One example would be criticism of news broadcasting of clips from broadcasts on Arab TV channels. Government has expressed concern that such clips showing 'Muslim extremists' may be a vehicle for secret messages (2002). News media are concerned to show the face of 'the enemy'. The negotiation of this conflict of interest takes place partly in the arena of public discussion – government releases information to make this a public issue – but also in negotiations between senior officials.

Politicians in the USA in particular hold media posts and media financial interests while also being members of the Senate or of Congress. In Britain, the requirement to declare interests and other posts held, as well as to avoid conflicts of interest, makes such an overlap less likely but not impossible to a degree.

We are talking about a collusive relationship, which is exemplified by the mutual need of politicians to appear in the media to have a platform for their positions, and that of the media to have the politicians appear so that they may attract an audience by having access to authority figures. The nature of the relationship may be ephemeral and concealed. But, for example, Colin Seymour-Ure reports on former Prime Minister John Major consciously dining out with media moguls such as Conrad Black and Rupert Murdoch, in an attempt to counter bad publicity and to create a better relationship with the press. The Blair governments have made little secret of using a publicity machine to promote government policy and to spin news stories into a favourable angle on government.

9 The regulation of media institutions

 The objective of regulation is to prevent any media controller from gaining excessive powers in the market for ideas.

Robinson (1995)

Any discussion of media regulation raises issues of freedom and responsibility. It raises questions about whose freedom and whose responsibilities. From one point of view, any regulation of organizations' right to be media producers, or of what they produce and how, is a curtailment of liberty in a free society. Libertarianism is behind criticisms of the censorship of media texts. Yet, knowing what you are against does not necessarily explain what you are for. In any case, it is very clear that not just anyone is free to join the ranks of producers, and it is likely that most people would have some objections to some material that might be produced in a free-for-all.

One progresses then to the notion that institutions/producers have a kind of responsibility to the 'public interest'. For pro-regulators, this in turn raises the problem of who defines that interest and how. Media may argue for the public's right to know, when the individual being talked about in the media argues for a right to privacy. Media may argue that public interest requires an article should be printed: government may take the opposite view on the same grounds. In each case one might go on to ask, who is

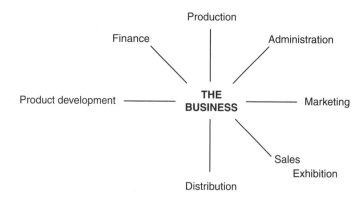

Functions of Media Institutions
Media institutions are businesses like all others, with the same functions. Does their creative output make them different in any way?
(*Graeme Burton*, 2004)

demonstrating what responsibility to whom? Media can purport to serve their audiences, but then we know that in operational practice they serve the interests of their financial backers and of their governing bodies. Governments are at least elected. Yet even here one can easily demonstrate self-interest. For example, in 1991 the US military stopped American reporters from filming flag-draped coffins brought back from the Gulf War. When British troops were sent to Sierra Leone in 2000 to back that government against rebel incursions, it was suggested that the British government's interest was in the arms industry and the oil industry, not the views of the British public. In 2001 there was a furore because a civil servant recommended that the terrorist destruction of the World Trade Center should be used as a distraction and an occasion for the release of politically uncomfortable information. Such examples do not inspire confidence in the idea of government as regulator.

Regulation also invokes ideas about censorship. But the word should not be misused in discussion of what happens to the media. Censorship implies overarching and centralized control of media material – such as is usually only practised by government in war time. The regulatory practices of government on media institutions and their work do not usually emerge in this way. Where the word 'censorship' may seem to be appropriate is if material is removed 'secretly', without this being generally known or understood. So you might consider whether you would describe the practice by TV organizations of cutting films without telling the viewers to be an example of censorship. Similarly, there are those examples where whole programmes have been pulled in response to political pressures, most obviously those about Northern Ireland. Where is the line between censorship and response to concerns about taste, or about the best interests of a political process?

The concept of regulation of media institutions does not only refer to intentional and external forces. If one connects it with the notion of constraints on institutional practices, then there are four main areas in which constraints operate.

1 Law – respects in which the fear of legal action or actual legal intervention constrains the media from 'publishing' anything they please.

2 Finance/the market – lack of resources or concern about performance in the market may constrain media from 'publishing'. This constraint may limit or shape the media product, or even simply stop its production.

3 Professional practices – what media workers have agreed it is OK to 'publish' or not, and in what ways, will in effect constrain what institutions put out, and therefore what we are 'allowed' to have in the public domain.

4 Public responsibility – is also about the beliefs of media workers acting as a constraint. They will share beliefs about the nature of their responsibility to the public and therefore again about what should be 'published'.

Regulation of media is apparently not about intentional and external forces in that in practice much of it is a process of self-regulation. The various categories of media operate either collective and voluntary bodies, or they have internal mechanisms of control. Before one applauds the public-spirited appearance of this condition, it is worth bearing in mind the following points.

- Even self-regulation must be based on institutional values and practices – with which one may not agree, but which one has no control over.
- Part of self-regulation is a response to fear of legal consequences external to the institution.
- Self-regulation is also a response to other external forces
  – what the audience will accept in the marketplace;
  – specific forces such as the government setting the BBC licence fee and therefore their income;
  – what it is understood that the government will accept – or even kinds of government intervention. There have been many examples of ministerial pronouncements that have a weighty intervention in some discussion about for example, TV scheduling.

Examples of British media self-regulating bodies are –
  Movies: the British Board of Film Classification (BBFC)
  Video: the Video Standards Council
  Press: the Press Complaints Commission
  Broadcasting – the Broadcasting Complaints Commission (but also see below)
  Advertising – the Advertising Standards Authority

In broadcasting, the BBC operates an internalized system known as 'referral upwards' (if in doubt about material). The BBC governors establish policy and standards. But this is hardly a voluntary and internalized system because the charter of the BBC establishes ground rules for its behaviour, and because the governors are appointed by the government. Given the fact that a licence is needed to broadcast in the first place (there has been no licence to print since 1697!) it is apparent that radio and television are treated differently from other media.

One major external regulatory body is Ofcom – for the broadcasting industries, which took over (December 2003) the work of the former separate regulators – The Independent Television Commission, The Radio Authority (The Radio Communications Agency which manages radio frequency allocations), the Broadcasting Standards Council and Oftel (the telecommunications industries). In particular, Ofcom has taken over the work of the ITC as an external body for commercial broadcasting, having an overview of programming, advertising and its standards, and responsibility for allocating broadcasting contracts. This may moderate any potential for market excesses on the part of commercial contractors.

It could be argued that there is an illusion of freedom for the media, but many practices of regulation by stealth. Government is partly behind this, but then so are the media themselves. Media practices tend to impinge on the material – the editing of films for broadcasting or for video release. One may also question the effectiveness of such regulation. For instance three policy statements from the Press Complaints Commission assert that

- inaccurate and misleading material should not be published;
- there should be a fair 'right to reply';
- reporters should not misrepresent who they are in order to obtain material.

Some might say that these 'rules' are broken every week.

The law

The law regulates the activities of media institutions in a variety of ways. Some laws relate to the management and operation of the business, as they would to any company. The Health and Safety at Work Act protects employees, for example, in respect of the time spent looking at screens. The Companies Act forces the publication of accounts and a summary of operations, year on year.

It is those laws which affect media material which are seen as being most significant. And it is true that it is the business of media institutions to produce, distribute and publish that material. These regulatory laws are directed at the notion of protection – protection of specific and possibly vulnerable audiences such as the young; protection of the public interest as in the case of security services; protection of the general public as in respect of notions of good taste; protection of the process of law in respect of the notion of a fair trial; protection of the interests of military operations (which are taken to be carried out in the interests of the people).

Examples of such laws in the UK are:

- Laws of defamation of character (Defamation Act 1996) – which cover libel and slander, and are meant to protect the public reputation of individuals. However, it may be argued that the cost of litigation is so great that most people cannot afford to defend their reputation against statements made in the media.
- Obscene Publications Act 1959 – the purpose of which is obvious, but the effects of which are contestable. There cannot be an objectifiable definition of obscenity. So in effect the Act denies some institutions access to some audiences: and denies some audiences the right to read and watch some material to which they may not object. The Act was extended to cover broadcasting in 1991.
- Young Person's Harmful Publications Act 1955 – which covers horrific and otherwise harmful material, particularly in comics and magazines. This raises problems to a degree. For example, 'comics' are no longer a format published for the young. Also there is the question of what is harmful – raised for instance in 1997 when MPs

expressed objections to the new and sexually explicit (if informative) content of magazines for young women, such as *Sugar* and *More*.

- Official Secrets Act 1989 – which in effect covers anything which government decides it does not want known about its security and military operations. The issue of a D notice by someone in the Home Office, covering certain information, is used as a threat merely to invoke the Act. Most obviously this constrains freedom of speech in the press, in broadcast news and documentary. It is the focus of an ideological contradiction between the idea of a free (democratic) society and the practice of state control.

- Prevention of Terrorism Act 1974 – was originally framed mainly to control information about and reporting of the conflict in Northern Ireland. However, it has also in effect constrained discussion of what is going on there and why. It incorporates assumptions about who is a terrorist which, it may be argued, have extended conflict and made a peace process that much more difficult.

- Public Order Act 1986 – has sections which forbid the publication of material which incite racial hatred and unrest.

- Contempt of Court Act 1981 – forbids the publication of anything about a trial in progress which may prejudice its fairness and the outcome. This is why in particular, that one sees drawings of trial events, not photographs.

- Video Recordings Act 1984 – restricts what may be hired from video shops, and imposes categories on films available on video.

This last example, which clearly is a kind of censorship, does remind us that regulation does not merely raise moral issues or those of national security. It also refers to differences of values and of judgement within society – categorizing material on film and video for consumption by different age groups must ultimately be a matter of individual beliefs and values: regulation is ideological in its implications and operation. Male nudity is censored to a degree and in ways that is simply not true for female nudity. There is a whole history of inequity in the disposition of gender power behind this practice.

In this sense, regulation implies cultural norms. In respect of nudity and norms, the British are seen by many other European cultures as being sexually inhibited. Regulation also has a temporal dimension in respect of norms and of ideology: these norms change over time. For example, the word 'fuck' was first used on British TV in 1965 – when it caused an uproar. There was a valid critical context to the use of the word, but still the BBC bowed to the storm and made a public apology. Or there is the example of the early James Bond films which were originally X rated, but have ended up being shown on prime-time television.

One interesting example of self-regulation and of social mores is the sanitized product of US company, Clean Flicks. This runs a successful business releasing DVDs of well-known films, in which most of the sex, violence and 'bad' language has been edited out. There is an as yet unresolved (March 2004) issue of whether they have the right to make such changes without the permission of producers and directors.

In this discussion of regulation and of related issues one must not lose sight of the thrust of market interests (the large media corporations) towards deregulation. Government is sympathetic to this view, while not entirely agreeing with it. In this context, the term 'regulation' is more synonymous with political and economic controls than it is with regulation according to social or cultural norms. The market constructs the term regulation as being opposed to 'freedom' – an evocative and misused term. Such a dichotomy is false. Herbert Schiller (in Tumber 1996) refers with concern to a 'push towards total social unaccountability'. Government remains concerned about accountability, not least if freedom were to undermine governance.

10 Institutions and power

The existence, nature and exercise of institutional power is an issue in itself. The question is raised about what kind of power, exercised in what ways and with what identifiable effects. One may suggest that whatever this power is about, it operates out of a material base, but has ideological implications. For 'power' to have any meaning one has to identify a process in which some kind of force exerted by a given source (institutions) produces some kind of change in the object of its attention (audience).

The material base and source of institutional power may be identified as

- control of financial resources which fund media distribution and production;
- control of technical resources which manufacture media goods;
- control of human resources which develop relevant technology and make specialist production possible;
- control of legal resources which copyright and control the scope of distribution and production, and which amplify profits;
- control of a management centre which holds the reins of ownership, which produces policy, which directs distribution and production.

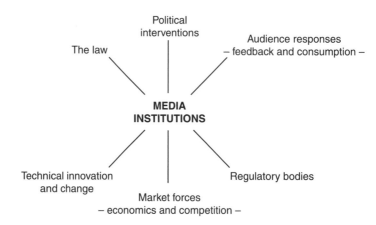

The Media: Power pressures
The media should not necessarily be seen as dispensing influence and exerting power. Media institutions are themselves under pressure from a range of forces, not least those of the varying tastes of their audiences/ consumers.
(*Graeme Burton*, 2004)

The maintenance of this material base depends partly on the ability to generate profit, partly on the production of confidence in the company within the marketplace, partly on the ability to promote the work and products of the media institution concerned. This work may directly produce media goods, and it may enable the production of those goods, and it may enable the distribution of those goods.

The symbolic base of this power and the expression of the power of the material is the media goods/texts which produce meanings and which are the point of contact with the audience. The ideological expression of institutional power is these meanings. This is the focus of possible change. This is the fulcrum of power. If these meanings change the lives and the thinking of the audience in some way which is to the advantage of the institution and to the disadvantage of the audience members, then power becomes real and it matters.

Garnham (2000) refers to two kinds of power –

Structural power: which is about allocation of resources (see Althusser and allocative control) which operates within the institution;
Economic (corporate power): which operates within structural constraints within the marketplace and in the context of regulation.

Power is both potential and actual. By this I mean that the apparent capacity of media to influence the attitudes of audiences is power enough itself. It is this potential which causes politicians to court media appearances. It is the potential which leads to censorship and regulation – as much as actual examples of the exercise, even abuse of power.

At the same time, it is not reasonable to suggest that media power is imaginary. All media industries tend towards monopoly – so that four or five newspaper groups control most of the circulation of daily papers in Britain: the same is true for the control of news agencies. ITV plc owns 12 of the 15 commercial television licences in Britain (granted by Ofcom). Globalization and the need for financial muscle to meet competition leads to larger conglomerates which lead to less competition and therefore to less actual choice. The workings of the market contradict aspirations to healthy pluralism. The numbers of newspapers, the variety of content and the range of audience has closed down as the numbers of owners has decreased.

The power of media owners although exaggerated by some critics is not imaginary. Rupert Murdoch does cut deals. He has built up an American media empire, including Twentieth Century Fox and Fox TV as a credible fourth network in American television. He bought and expanded Star Channel, which satellite broadcasts to 53 countries through 28 channels and in seven languages across much of Asia and the Middle East. Star broadcasts a channel for British Asians as well. He also owns Sky (BSkyB) satellite television in Britain and Europe, plus Japan's Perfect TV. He controls about one third of British press circulation, and more than this in Australia. NewsCorp owns 175 titles across three continents, and publishes a total of 40 million newspapers a week, including *The New York Post* and the *Sun* in Britain. He has acquired control (2003) of the US company DirecTV (satellite and cable), bringing access to 10 million subscribers. He is developing interactive TV. He owns Latin Sky Broadcasting in association with the US telecoms giant AT&T, as well as the major broadcasters Televisa in Mexico, and Globo in Brazil.

David Walker, formerly a journalist with *The Times* in England (writing in Tumber 2000) talks about his experiences of working under the authoritarianism of editors and owners. He describes a feeling of powerlessness and of alienation among journalists, and talks directly of *The Times* being 'compromised by Murdoch's ownership'.

In an article in the *Guardian* (17 February 2003) Roy Greenslade analyses the 'coincidence' of how all NewsCorp papers worldwide backed the war on Iraq. 'He [Murdoch] has an unerring ability to choose editors across the world who think just like him.' Greenslade refers to articles and editorials, as well as taking direct quotations from Murdoch himself, which construct a consistently pro-war line, behind which one may hear clearly the creak of the levers of power being pulled.

Then there is Silvio Berlusconi as an example in Europe, who is Prime Minister of Italy, as well as owner of major TV channels in Italy and newspapers across Europe. Through his company MediaSet he controls 48 per cent of Italian television – Canale 5, Italia 1, Retequattro and La 7. In advertising he owns Publitalia. In publishing he has 30 per cent of the Italian book market plus 50 magazines, through Mondadori. His brother owns the leading Italian daily, *Il Giornale*. He has a 19 per cent stake in Albacom, a telecommunications company. Tobias Jones, in his book, *The Dark Heart of Italy* (2003), says: 'It's impossible to move without inadvertently coming up against his influence. If you watch football matches, or television, try to buy a house, or a book, or a newspaper, rent a video, or else shop in a supermarket, the chances are you're somehow filling the coffers of Il Cavaliere (last estimated to be worth $14 billions).'

In *Mass Media and Society* (3rd edn) (2000), Golding and Murdock refer to the power of the media moguls:

> In the emerging environment, power will lie with those who own the key building blocks of new communications systems, the rights to the key pieces of technology and, even more importantly, the rights to the cultural materials – the films, books, images, sounds, writings – that will be sued to put together the new services . . . the media moguls have a sizeable advantage since they already own a formidable range of the expressive assets that are central to public culture.

In respect of production, power exists materially through the technologies and in the expertise of those who use them. But it also exists conceptually in those workers' view of themselves as professionals. The idea of professionalism is one which endorses expertise and the right to do things in certain ways. People are reluctant to criticize 'the professional'. The good side of professionalism is its attachment to a certain idea of responsibility towards colleagues and towards clients (audiences). Less attractive is a degree of self-regard which leads to uncritical endorsement of production routines and habitual practices. It is well documented that news workers invoke professionalism as a way of endorsing news values and therefore what they do selectively with news material. In fact professionalism becomes part of news ideology. It is a value position which is behind newswork. It is also an instrument of power which supports the authority of the newsworker, what they do, how and why.

It is the case that a relatively small number of media workers collaborate to represent the world to us. One might say that this is analogous to the small number of political workers in the Senate and in Congress, who represent a super power and who also speak for millions. But the media workers are not elected to their positions by even the semblance of a democratic process. They speak to us, but are not entitled to speak for us – though this position, of representing 'the people', is one often adopted by news reporters and newscasters.

If the actuality of media power is its expression through texts and its effects on audiences, then we will look at this in the chapters which follow. This is the power of the production of meaning. The interesting thing is that media material does not have to be politicized to be political, nor does it have to have intentions in order to have effects. Institutions may be blown by the winds of the market economy. This economy may have indirect effects. For instance, in 2001 competitive game shows were proving to be very popular on British television. ITV competed with the BBC for ratings. Its rescheduling of Saturday night programmes had proved to be a failure, and its share of advertising revenue was slipping, so it introduced *Who Wants To Be a Millionaire*, which proved to be very successful. Similarly, the BBC brought in an equally successful programme, *The Weakest Link*, which it later exported to the USA.

The meanings that will be reinforced through a glut of such game shows are, for example, about the value of being competitive, the stigma of being a loser, the desirability of acquiring material goods. This is ideology at work. These meanings are political because they are ideological. They refer to the power of being a winner – and the disempowerment of 'losers'. But these meanings are not intentional. The institutional imperative is to get people watching and to keep them there. This is what power is about as far as the institution is concerned: the power of attraction and absorption. But then media criticism is concerned with unintended but no less real or significant effects.

Dennis McQuail (2000) suggests that key aspects of media power may be summarized as follows:

- attracting and directing public attention;
- persuasion in matters of opinion and belief;
- influencing behaviour;
- structuring definitions of reality;
- conferring status and legitimacy;
- informing quickly and extensively.

One may examine media power in the context of the media imperialism thesis, which relates to globalization, and the next section. It has been proposed that cultures, especially the USA, export an empire of ideas to other countries. They promote their ideology, along with the media product that those countries buy. But again, the prime driver is to sell. This is not a process analogous to evangelical Christianity in the nineteenth-century age of empire. No one is explictly trying to sell Western capitalism to the developing world. Some media critics argue that this may be happening, none the less.

Herbert Schiller (2000), in referring to new technologies and 'new global alliances' talks about control of information. He asserts that 'the world information order remains for the large part still America'. Still, one would have to say that assessment of the effects of control of information flow or of textual production also has to be evaluated in terms of the production of meaning – of understanding at the point of reception. It is not the quantity of material which the USA exports that counts – it is what the receiving cultures make of it, what they do with it in their heads.

Cultures across the world drink Coke and watch US movies, but there is no evidence that they are looking at the world just as US citizens do. The British language has taken on American phrases; British publishing has mostly US owners; the British love most American movies; but peculiarly British speech, books and films are still prevalent. No more have the British become Spanish because millions of them have taken holidays there, nor Australian because of the popularity of some TV soaps from that country. And the British themselves are great exporters of media product to other countries.

Columbia Pictures was owned by a Japanese conglomerate – Matsushita. Now it is owned by a Canadian distillery giant – Seagram. But Columbia product is still distinctively American. I am not saying that there is no power to influence, nor that there are no effects evident. But the imperialism thesis is too simple to account for the complex exchange of media goods across the globe. There may well be large ideological effects at work. It was proposed that the material attractions of the western lifestyle played a part in the collapse of the separate state of East Germany, because many East Germans could pick up western TV. But one could also say that exported South American soaps, telenovellas and light entertainment promotes gender ideology as much as any product from Europe.

The conceptualization of media power and what it does partly depends on the ideological starting position of the critic, and on how this person models society in particular. For example, one might have a consensual model for society – the kind of model generally assumed by news broadcast media. Or one might have a sense of divisions and conflicts, and so model society as an entity defined by social difference and the unequal distribution of resources. The power of the media could be benign – to represent and to hold together a consensus. Or it could be diversionary – to divert attention from divisions and to falsely represent cohesion in their place.

11 Institutions and globalization (see also Chapter 15)

66 99 The maintenance of national sovereignty and identity [is] becoming increasingly difficult as the unities of economic and cultural production and consumption become increasingly transnational.

Collins et al. (1999)

For media institutions globalization means a global reach in terms of range of distribution, range of outlets, scope of the financial base, various audiences/consumers, range of products/texts, range of media owned, and the spread of the ownership/management base. In one sense this global reach does mean more of the same, but on an international rather than a national scale. It does mean similar operations are spread out on a larger stage, and that cash flow works on a larger scale. Bigger sharks swim in larger oceans. The larger base and larger profits can mean more security in the face of competition.

But in another sense global reach means something different. One issue co-relates **cultural imperialism** (see also Chapter 12) and cultural impoverishment. In the first case one sees the predominance of some products from some sources. These products necessarily carry certain ideologies and certain cultural perspectives. Obvious examples are the Hollywood feature film across the world, the Brazilian telenovella/soap across South America, BBC and CNN 24-hour news across the satellite receptive world. The second case is a possible corollary – that the consuming cultures create less of their own product – even that the producing cultures lose out if they are trying to manufacture some kind of common denominator in terms of global genres and global treatments. The USA has around 80 per cent of the TV show sales in the global market. In 1999, Britain exported £440 million worth of programmes. But it imported £843 million worth, mostly from the USA (though it is fair to point out that there has been an increase in local drama production, especially in Germany, France and Japan (IOS, 18 March 2001)).

However, the evidence is that things are not that simple. Certainly the 'developed' world tends to dominate this cultural export business. But there is an increasing amount of exchange which means that it is no longer realistic to argue the US imperialism thesis. And it is evident that indigenous cultures do not 'die on their feet', even if they do change. The Japanese export variations on popular music back to the West, with their own slant on, say, punk rock. It does exemplify the fact that the Japanese young are not spending much time on reinforcing traditional and classic Japanese culture. But equally, forms such as Kabuki theatre have not simply disappeared, even if they have become a minority interest. And it may be said that new forms represent a kind of new cultural energy, which is no bad thing. Similarly, one sees hybrid forms of popular music in South Africa – township music drawing on traditional tribal forms and sounds, which then further develop through contact with jazz, blues and rock.

Global reach also enhances the validity of a political economy perspective on media. The US multinational giant Time Warner-AOL is a model for economic determinants at work, producing political implications and further issues of regulation. The conglomerate has been driven by a need for profit and need to secure its position across media in the face of competition. It controls a range of product – books, comics, TV, films, music, video games, toys, TV news – and a range of distribution – through TV stations, Net portals, satellite channels (CNN), Home Box Office and Cinemax movie channels, the Cartoon Network, and other retail/exhibition networks – as well as the associated range of promotional companies that help secure it in the marketplace. In political terms one may argue that this collectively helps produce a certain view of the world, and controls the means by which contesting views may be debated and presented. This kind of production and control raises questions about terms of reference for regulation – one might talk about the need for checks on the kinds of power referred to above. Such regulation is not forthcoming – the Federal Communications Commission is manifestly weak in its powers and its will to limit the scope of media companies. Many US politicians have interests in media companies. Weak regulation allows the predominance of certain ideological positions through the dominance of certain kinds of institutions operating out of particular principles. This is just as true as saying that over-regulation by given interest groups may lead to the same ideological dominance.

For example, the US Telecommunications Act of 1996 removed even the existing power of the FCC to regulate radio ownership. There is now no limit on the numbers of national stations that can be owned by one company. The guaranteed span of the licence period was extended for both radio and television. As Sterling reports in Tumber (2000), a maelstrom of mergers followed this Act, mostly involving the large telecommunications companies and radio stations. AT&T bought the largest cable operator, TCI. Viacom bought CBS and with it a major US TV and radio network, as well as a music label and advertising sites (it already owned Paramount Pictures, MTV, Blockbuster video and major cable and telecommunications interests). There was a notion to enhance public access to the so-called information highway. The price has been greater concentration of power in fewer hands.

In such respects it is the practices of media production and distribution that lead to a certain kind of globalization, which are as important as debates about cultural imperialism. If there is to be some kind of a hegemony of corporations and of their culture of consumption, then it will be on the back of concentration of control. So far, there is as much evidence of enriching cultural exchange as there is of cultural impoverishment. Small companies survive to distribute world music on the back of new communications systems, in a way that was impossible even 20 years ago. The BBC sells its 'classic dramas' across the globe, and no one talks disparagingly about cultural imperialism in this case.

If there is an area of media in which one should be concerned about the predominance of one view of the world over another, it is in respect of news. It is worrying that a few news agencies – Reuters, Associated Press, for example – have come to determine what news is gathered from where, how it is structured, how it is available and at what price. Their only competitors are the big broadcasting networks. Together they dominate the distribution of product, and therefore of particular ways of looking at events and issues. Smaller newspapers and broadcasters cannot afford to compete and are very dependent on such distributors. Military interventions, refugee aid, trading practices and so on, are all looked at from a first world perspective – put crudely, that what 'we' do and how 'we' do it is right. Ironically, technology makes it very possible to hear about how the world looks from the point of view of the streets of Nairobi, Karachi, Istanbul. But we don't often hear that view.

In talking up the significance of the globalization of news, I am not simply ignoring the potential effect of ideologies embedded in exported media texts. But I am asserting that there is a degree of cultural exchange and kinds of cultural interpretation that contradict any idea that the world is being brainwashed into materialism. The exchange and adaptation of ideas may be a good thing. It is certainly inevitable, unless one conceives of a planet of cultures preserved in splendid isolation from one another. The USA brought a material culture and its technologies to Japan in the later part of the nineteenth century. Indirectly, those contacts laid the foundations for the Second World War in the Far East. But they also brought directly a whole new media in the shape of cinema. Japanese culture was enriched and expressed through its movies. In recent years one can point to concerns about the effects of the Hollywood distribution machine – popular blockbuster films do bring their meanings to the Japanese audience. A film such as *The Last Samurai* (2004) repackages Japanese culture for the West, and sells it back to Japan. On the other hand, indigenous Japanese cinema has developed its own populist forms. And some of these enjoy degrees of popularity in the West, just like the Manga form of comic remade that medium in a Japanese image and sold it abroad.

So the global picture is a complex one, in which access to technology and to means of distribution produces an exchange model of cultural production. But monopoly of production and distribution, produces an 'imperialist' model of cultural imposition. If there is a globalization of culture it is on the back of global distribution (more than in respect of production). But then not everything sells globally, and technology allows cultural diffusion as much as cultural imperialism. Tomlinson in *The Media Reader* (Mackay and O'Sullivan, 1999) proposes something like diffusion, if not actually confusion. At one point he proposes that globalization be defined as Westernization, and that this be opposed to a view of 'Western culture as creole culture'. He argues against exaggeration of the cultural power of the West and refers to 'the myths of Western identity'. He concludes that 'the global future is much more radically open than the discourses of homogenisation and Westernisation suggest'.

12 Institutions and new technologies (see also Chapter 8)

The relationship between so-called new technology and media institutions is one of a kind of mutual self-promotion. The mechanics of contemporary media production and distribution would be inconceivable without the developments in micro-electronics over the last two or three decades. Equally, that which is described as new technology (NT) would not have developed in the ways that it has without the funding from, and the economic self-interest of, media organizations.

The industrially violent move of News International (NI) from Fleet Street to a state-of-the-art Wapping production base in the 1980s has been well documented. The company is dominant in newspaper titles – the *Sun*, *The Times*, the *News of the World*. New technology – word processing for the newspaper industry – already existed. What NI (later Newscorp) did was to face out the print unions (mainly SOGAT), who wanted to move from mechanical to print technology at a price which Murdoch was not prepared to pay. Those who did not move or who went on strike were sacked. New technology was accessible enough that replacement workers could be trained (as indeed they had been, secretly, by NewsCorp). It was easier to compose a newspaper page and to transfer the results to the printing presses, it needed fewer workers, and so held down production costs and helped profits. The Wapping episode and the rush by other newspaper groups to follow NewsCorp (compete or die) meant that the next generations of technology developed at a great pace.

Technologies everywhere tend to develop interactively. One new piece of equipment leads to a dynamic model, creating yet more change. The newspaper industry also saw the advent of electronic processing which made colour illustrations in newspapers commonplace. There was the increasing use of satellite and cable links to send source material, or even composed pages, from one place to another. There was the arrival of lighter and then portable computers, which has made it possible for reporter in the field to compose and send copy down the line, and not have to telephone copy back to base. Even this is only a selective comment on examples of NT which have changed all aspects of the press within a generation.

The existence and implications of NT are so pervasive that it is difficult to prioritize and select from among many issues raised. Let me suggest the following points which relate as much to the ways in which these institutions work, as to their products.

Cost of entry: economies of access

On a large scale, the price of technologies as a prerequisite for becoming a national or global media player is so great that it forces mergers for economies of scale, and shuts out all but the largest companies from joining the big media clubs. But on a smaller scale, it is also true that NT has made possible quality media production for communities and locals areas. In the music business, the performer Baby Bird composed his early hit material in his Sheffield bedroom. Pressure groups produce broadcastable video material, which is occasionally used by the big players.

Information wealth – information poverty

In some respects the media – whether making news or making documentaries, for example – have an unparalleled technical ability to do things like bring live pictures from the bottom of oceans, invent the experience of being in space with computer graphic realism, and bring world events into the living room as they happen. On the other hand, we only see that version of or indeed places in the world, which the media choose to access. The physical geography of the world is quite well provided for, though there are swathes of the planet – China for instance, about which we are information poor. But more to the point, the cultural or ideological geographies of our world are, it may be argued, poorly represented. It is not easy to obtain a perspective on how the world looks and feels if you are living in South Africa or New Zealand – even though the technology exists to attempt to provide that perspective. Media institutions use technology to provide the kind of information in kinds of ways which suit their imperatives – but not necessarily the needs and interests of all possible audiences.

Distributor power: digital convergence

In economic terms technology has enhanced the wealth production of those who control the flow of product, as much as the rewards for those who make media product. Examples of products which are still moved around in a physical form include newspapers to retailers, film cans to cinemas, video cassettes to retailers, CDs to retailers. And even here control of these movements guarantees huge incomes for companies like TNT transport or the distribution/promotion arms of the Hollywood majors. But where the text can be converted to a digital form, then the distribution flow can also take place electronically. This is the dominant practice in broadcasting and is central to debates about the Internet as a distributor. Such debates take place against a background of digital convergence. Increasingly the text is being expressed in the language of number. Digital TV and radio is expanding, not least in Britain, where the BBC spent £300 million on opening new channels, and where the costs of digital radio are plummeting. The first digital cinema has opened in Britain: eventually, movies will be distributed along cables not in containers. The implications for cost reduction are considerable. Films have long been distributed via satellite, and now on disc. It is significant that Viacom (essentially a telecommunications distributor, though it also owns the video retailer Blockbuster) bought Paramount – a producer. It is significant that Time Warner merged with AOL, a distributor. It is significant that companies like Sony and Bertelsmann, while also using copyright law to reclaim exclusive control of their music product, have actually done deals with the Net distributors who were grabbing their product in digital form and making money out of getting it to the audience.

The tendency to vertical integration still predominates, but this process of monopoly may now stem from distributors not producers. Control of text in a digital form, and of the cables and satellites which carry digital text, is behind this move.

Public sphere – private domain: interactivity

NT has, by enabling a global media reach and by offering degrees of interactivity between media and audience, produced the possibility of creating a public sphere. That is an area of information and discussion that may be shared by (even between) members of the audience. It has been argued that the presentation of views via television current affairs programmes creates a kind of public sphere. Certainly there has been a stronger argument for the Web acting as a host to this sphere, given the creation of bulletin boards and chat rooms on the back of digital technology. The curious thing here is that the Web is an exception to the dominant media model in that it is not run by anyone. It is about distribution, not production. No one charges for the distribution. It only distributes some media goods.

The problem with proposing that some media offer a kind of debating chamber for the public good is that in reality most seem to hold on to a private domain operated in the interests of shareholders. The technology offers the possibility of at least more audience participation and intervention. But the reality of things like chat shows is that the media mostly hang on to a model of producing a shaped artefact within a defined space or time slot, as an offering to the audience. Even with the Web, the existing media institutions are perpetuating the closed model, where their sites are generally like retail and publicity outlets. Legal judgements making portal providers responsible for what some users may say works against interactivity, and for the passive model in which those who run the portals and the websites become media owners, and web users become another kind of audience, not participants.

Recasting the output: texts from institutions

It may be argued that NT has had a variety of effects on media texts, and not merely in the most obvious terms – of, say, the fluid graphics in a successful animated film like *Shrek* (2001). For example, NT has not only shrunk the globe in terms of getting stories back, it has also shrunk deadlines in terms of the expectations put upon reporters and editors. In this case it may be argued that the concise and dramatic report has gained precedence over the more reflective and interpretive report or article.

New institutions, new media, new markets

New technology is also capable of using new media in new ways to generate new forms of income. For example, interactive TV, like e-commerce on the Net, is continuing to grow in profitability, in spite of the infamous dotcom crash. Barry Dillers's 'USA Inter-active' is now worth more than Amazon.com. It includes home shopping channels (QVC), an e-travel agency, an accommodation booking service, an e-dating service, and Ticketmaster (for booking sports and concerts), as well as an online lending and mortgage service (IOS, 11 May 2003).

So new technology has in itself created new media, which have given rise to new companies, and have changed the business of old ones. Organizations such as Yahoo! and Hotmail are now familiar names, but have only existed for a few years. The Sony Playstation is a dominant product for a well-established company, but in a fairly new medium – the computer games business. Sky satellite television has existed for barely twenty years, but is already spinning off into the new media of Sky Digital. Its multi-national owner, NewsCorp, also owns Star satellite (now partially available on Sky) which broadcasts across the Far East to 53 countries on 28 channels in seven languages. Mobile phones have become such a tool and an icon of the so-called new communications era that they are being buried along with their deceased owners in Slovakia. The Swedish company Ericsson saw its fortunes transformed through its commitment to this new media business. DVD discs have changed the film business. Handheld computers have transformed the business of companies in a lifetime which has seen the dominance of IBM over company business evaporate in the face of desktop machines and networking. Microsoft's dominance of operating systems and standard software which does the business for many homes and institutions has become so acute within 20 years that it has been the subject of an anti-trust suit – to stop it tying the manufacturers of hardware to its products.

One needs to take account of the fact that the working life of media institutions has been revolutionized by new technology. One cannot just discuss what the audiences can see – computer-assisted technology in animation for movies, or live digicam images from news correspondents in war zones. It is the less glamorous and concealed effects of NT which have changed institutions. Financial forecasting and product development use computer models. Global corporations can only function because of telecommunications. Programme design, even call centres, are outsourced to India. Report writing and financial analysis is outsourced to Germany, while the USA sleeps. Video conferencing enables management discussion and decisions on a global basis. NT even enables new kinds of industrial espionage through which competitors may be outflanked.

Of course, 'new' does not necessarily mean 'good' or 'effective'. Garnham (2000) refers to the phenomenon of 'path dependency' when he points out that the cost/risk/investments features of new technology may mean that industries do not follow the best path of development. The persistence of the QWERTY keyboard, or the stranglehold of the MS-DOS operating program on PC computers are infamous examples of this problem. There is no area of media institutions or their work that is not affected by NT – administration, production, product, distribution, retailing and exhibition. Most of it we are either not aware of, or we rapidly take for granted that which is, for a brief time, remarkable. We do not notice the electronic retouching of magazine images. Neither do we know when commercials have been electronically edited, unless the graphics make it obvious. We take for granted live reports from half a world away. We do not think about downloading music or image files. We become blasé about the digital interactivity which enables us to choose what style of commentary we want with a TV programme such as *Walking with Beasts* (BBC). We will incorporate instant messaging between computers as a part of our lives in the same way that text messaging is no longer remarkable. And this last example reminds one that the line between media as material received and media as material exchanged is becoming very blurred. This is not to ignore the huge volume and value of media product which is still packaged as commodities for the various audiences. But still one has to rethink the nature of media business and media consumption as NT changes the work of media institutions and the kinds of media use by consumers.

McQuail (2000) defines four main categories of 'new media':

1 interpersonal communication media, such as email;

2 interactive play media, such as computer games;

3 information search media, such as Net search engines;

4 participatory media, such as Net chat rooms.

He also points to the changed experience of using such media, compared with the older product/consumption model:

● social presence – a sense of contact with others when using the medium;

● autonomy – a sense of control over the medium;

● interactivity – with the source;

● privacy – of experience when using the medium;

● playfulness – in respect of the enjoyment gained through using the medium as opposed to merely taking things from it.

Things are moving a long way from a media model in which institutions are conceived of as production machines, meanings are thought of as inscribed in fixed texts, and audiences are defined as mass consumers of those texts. NT has made the media–audience relationship more complex. In some respects its ability to expand the range of textual form while also concealing its own artifice makes the audience more subordinate to institutions. But in other ways, the multiplication of media formats and the greater engagement of audience with text in respect of new media forms, gives the audience more power over knowledge production. The institution becomes more of a provider.

There is a question of how far NT produces continuity or change for media institutions. On the one hand, Russell Neuman (1991) inclines to an optimistic view about change. He proposes that

● new media become less expensive and so more available to the audience;

● NT changes the audience view of geographical distance;

● NT increases the speed of communication;

● NT increases the volume of communication;

● There will be more and more channels of communication;

● There will be more interactive communication;

● There will be more control for users;

● There will be increasing interaction of previously separate forms of communication.

On the other hand, Webster (in *the Media Reader*, Mackay and O'Sullivan, 1999) also acknowledges the considerable weight of criticism which sees continuity and the power base of existing media institutions merely being extended. Neo-Marxists like Schiller or political economists like Garnham are placed in the continuity camp, along with discussions of media regulation and the nature of the public sphere.

Webster contrasts these views with those which argue for change and a new kind of society. In this case, one might be looking at the post-modernists and critics such as Baudrillard, at those who argue for a new information society and greater public access to that information.

What the media have to be careful about, commercially, is embracing new technologies with ill-founded enthusiasm. The Time Warner/AOL merger was actually a takeover by AOL, but then the merged company reported a loss of $99 billion for 2002. This astonishing loss was partly due to writing off 'good will' factored into the merger, but happened because, fundamentally, the performance and profitability of the Internet company was much overestimated.

13 Alternative models for media institutions

The first question one needs to ask, is alternative in what way? Presumably, a general answer is anything alternative to the dominant model described above, in which profit and competition drive most institutional developments; and, presumably, something alternative to the capital-heavy, technology-intensive, market-motivated characteristics of multinationals and conglomerates.

Small is not necessarily alternative, if the small organization works on the same principles and economic imperatives as the large ones. With no disrespect intended to the work of the many independent TV production companies in Britain, such as Tiger Aspect (e.g. producer of the *Mr Bean* comedy series), what they produce is largely more of the same. Entertaining as the product may be – documentary or comedy – it does not often challenge the way the material is handled or challenge the way that subjects are thought about. This lack of difference has much to do with the values and material needs of the commissioning organization, with the need to attract large audiences, with the unprofitability of minority audiences. The BBC's backing of the hugely successful comedy series, *The Office*, was largely a producer's act of faith and a risk. It is true that, in the case of television, regulation enforces the commissioning of a 25 per cent quota of 'independent' material. But the BBC and ITV strike hard bargains, which include the rights to sales and marketing in most areas. In 2001, Tiger Aspect made a profit of only £326,000 on a turnover of £34 million.

Economic determinants

What would seem to underpin the possibility of 'alternative' is the source and amount of cash which the institution needs to operate. Large amounts of cash increase the obligations that the alternative organization has to its providers, and the ideological hold which the provider can exert over the work of that organization. What would seem to express alternativeness is something about the philosophy or ideology of the institution.

In raw financial terms, it is difficult, next to impossible, to operate as a totally independent institution. Cash has to come from somewhere, if labour, technology and other cost elements have to be paid for. The source of cash – investors, the state, shareholders, advertisers – is likely to be a constraint. Even when the media material has been produced via, say, the investment of free labour or that of private investors, there are still cash consequences when trying to get the independent film or video or magazine to an audience. Distribution also costs.

Audience factors

In ideological terms, and providing one does not upset the cash providers, it is easier to do things differently, to express minority views. But then the principles of the marketplace also cut in. Who wants to view, listen to or read such views – especially if there is a charge involved? The difficulty with constructing alternative models for media institutions is not merely a material one and to do with a structural status quo – the dominant model of how things are run. It is also a conceptual difficulty and to do with the ideological status quo – in which there is a dominant model of how things are said. If you want to change the way stories are told, what documentaries may tell us, the views that news can bring us, then you not only have to pay for production and distribution, you also have to get someone to stop and listen, even if the material is freely available. Alternative institutions are not much use without audiences of some kind.

The BBC

One considerable model of an alternative approach is that of the BBC, discussed in the next section. Most of its cash comes directly from the public through the compulsory licence fee. It is in principle not beholden to commercial sources. Yet its operation is not unlike that of a private company, and much of its material is hardly alternative in its views. This is partly because the organization wants to prove its 'worth' by showing that it can produce popular material that will plead large audiences. It is also because the politicians who set the licence fee have told it that it must compete with commercial television in terms of ratings. Being 'different' and being independent do not seem to be very compatible with being a large media institution.

Not that one should be too negative in surveying alternativeness. We do have community and hospital radio, which serve individual and community functions. There is micro-cinema on the Net, which gives space to short experimental movies. There is ZeeTV satellite channel for Asian communities. There is *The Voice*, or *New Nation*, weekly newspapers for the black community, though their circulations are only (by estimate, not audit) around 30,000 each, mainly in London. There are regional arts associations and regional film theatres which present film, video and photographic work that would not normally be seen. What has not been constructed is an alternative institutional model in which media producers have access to major channels of distribution and/or have access to significant production funds outside commercial sources. There is some sort of example in the case of Dutch broadcasting. Here, any community organization having membership above a certain threshold does have right of access (and of time, on a sliding scale) to state-supported broadcasting channels. The market model still breaks through, in that the largest organizations (Protestants and Catholics) want to use their considerable rights to time to attract large audiences. So popular genres prevail. Nevertheless, there are some programmes at some times which we would describe as alternative in what they have to say about social and political issues. Perhaps what is important is that alternative models of funding and distribution make possible diversity of opinion which in a sense stops being alternative because that becomes a 'normal' media experience for the audience.

14 The public service debate

The issues raised by the debate over these two models is predicated on the supposed and special influence of broadcasting on the media audience, especially television. It is also the case that when the BBC was established in 1927 it was seen as the only possible broadcaster. So broadcasting was conceived of as a public service. This stopped being the case in 1954 when ITV started. The single **public service** model was broken and the notion of what public service is, was necessarily called into question. The unique funding arrangements for the BBC became questionable once there was another channel funded a different way. The financial issue here becomes a question about why all of the public should pay for some of the service when they don't all watch or listen to the BBC.

The position of the BBC as an exemplar for independent-minded public service broadcasting (PSB) was made worse in the 1980s when the Tory government pushed it further into commercial practices, confirming that it should compete in the marketplace for audience figures. In the early days of ITV, BBC's viewing share had collapsed in the face of the populist and genre attractions of the commercial channel, so it had already moved into competitive commercial behaviour to justify its licence fee to Parliament. But things got worse in the 1980s when licence fee rises were held down and when Channel 4 was created. Just as the BBC was not really free to offer something 'alternative', so Channel 4 did not really have to operate in a free market competitive commercial climate. Indeed it was required to serve minority interests – like BBC2. But it was ensured funding because the government creamed this off the ITV1 Channel 3 profits (until 1991).

Broadcasting regulation, described above, meant that in the first place, no broadcaster ever operated in an entirely free climate. It meant that some channels were positioned by their licences as being more alternative than others. It meant that some element of public service was legislated into the whole system. The more channels were licensed (including radio) to serve more specific audiences, the more the distinction between the BBC as a clear model for wide-ranging public service, and the commercial institutions as a model for populist mainstream provision, was fudged. And it has already been questioned as to whether the BBC, in ideological terms, was ever an alternative institution as it was run by establishment figures and had institutionalized values that fed conservative notions of good taste and cultural norms. One can point to the satirical goosing of politicians through programmes such as *That Was The Week That Was* (1963), under the liberal regime of director general Hugh Carleton Greene. There have been sterling examples of drama such as *Boys From the Black Stuff* (1982), which said a lot about the effects of government policies on the working class. But then its mainstream tendencies were reinforced by the market culture referred to above, and enacted under the managerialist regime of director general John Birt in the 1990s. Indeed, to be fair to the BBC (and Birt) there are ideological contradictions at the heart of the debate about PSB, in the pronouncements of politicians and other commentators. These people wanted a risk-taking, community-serving, creative public service to emerge from a union with market forces. They wanted public service broadcasting to be all things to all people – popular and profitable and yet serving minorities at the same time. The BBC was damned for some for its commercial partnership with the American Flextech (UK Gold) and with Discovery channel, for the considerable profits that it has made from BBC Worldwide. Yet the same people who do not want the BBC to play commercial games with public money because it is in 'public service' also do not want it to serve all of the public if this means that it loses audience share or needs more money.

The Labour government has also appeared to want to face both ways at once. The Charter which gives the BBC a licence to operate in the way that it does, has been renewed only until 2005. The licence fee itself has been renewed only after much debate. The government is keeping its commercial options open with reference to the possibility of BBC funding moving to a kind of commercial subscription system.

It is clear from the above that degrees of public service can be enforced through regulation. Such regulation enforces a degree of service to minorities and communities for all broadcasters; there is the local impact of licences awarded to commercial and BBC radio; these channels do give some voice to local communities, to local issues; they provide local information, and discuss some local problems – while also imitating popular genres and models for talk radio. In particular, Channel 4 has walked a tightrope successfully in providing some populist material, but also screening some challenging film seasons and documentaries which address minority issues.

This takes one back to the contradictions of public policy, in which deregulation of broadcasting has partly driven the broadcasting Acts of the 1990s. At the same time, a recognition that free markets do not actually produce freedom of choice has encouraged government to cling on to kinds of regulation. Negrine (1994) discusses this contradiction, partly with reference to the pronouncements of The Peacock Committee on broadcasting (1985): 'regulatory requirements . . . produce not a free market, but one regulated to allow for freedom, albeit a freedom where market forces dominate'.

What is clear is that the structure of media institutions, and the climate within which they operate, can be enforced by government to satisfy some model of what public service entails. There is no 'natural' base model offered by commercial broadcasting, which then has to be adapted in some way. But neither is the BBC a naturally dominant model. It is possible to use political mechanisms to allow or disallow whatever kind of institutional model we want. What is difficult to do is to determine the kind of service preferred and for what kind of public. Broadcasting to serve the various disabled communities, or immigrant communities, or those who want to question government policy, becomes a political issue. There is no coherent 'public' out there, though there may be larger and smaller communities. But it goes against the grain of dominant political and broadcasting visions to have to accept this and do something about it. In a sense the dominant ideology cannot cope with the vision of a diverse public. Nor can it take on the financial consequences of having to find the money to pay for that public's service. In particular, it is not going to pay for a public voice given to views that might undermine this dominance. Equally, I do not accept that PSB is only, or mainly, about giving a voice to radical and oppositional politics.

The public service debate is not confined to Britain. The conduct and effects of media policies across Europe are a cause for concern to broadcasters and citizens who fear for the erosion of a genuine choice of material and of ideas. These fears are focused on the evident expansion of private ownership and its consequences in market terms for broadcasting: on events such as the selling off of the French TFI public broadcasting network to commercial interests.

Concerns about protecting media so that their output reflects a sense of national identity and serves a real range of audiences takes us back to the beginning of this chapter and to questions about genuine choice for audiences, and about how far we should allow media institutions free rein in a commodified marketplace.

15 Discussion extract

66 99 . . . the special nature of the right to communicate and television's cultural and political role suggest that television cannot be left simply to regulation by the market or competition law. The principles of diversity, pluralism, independence and equality of access that underpin the media's important role in shaping and informing public opinion suggest that, in spite of the promise of bountiful audio-visual services in the future, there are still strong grounds for persisting with regulation. This in turn emphasises the importance of these principles. First, the emergence of powerful transnational alliances to distribute, market and sell digital television not only poses a risk to diversity through fewer suppliers, but may also contribute to less economic competition and ultimately less choice for the consumer if a small number of digital gatekeepers are permitted to control the market. Secondly, conventional analogue broadcasting is likely to remain the dominant force in television for some time to come while digital media become more widely available. This means that safeguarding the plurality of opinion in broadcasting (for example, through stipulations on impartiality in news and current affairs) and regulating access to limited analogue capacity will continue to be regulatory issues until widespread access to digital media allows television to operate more like publishing. Third, the emergence of digital transmission systems will still throw up bottle-necks which require regulation to safeguard diversity and choice (e.g. conditional access systems, electronic programme guides). As the ongoing battles to establish proprietary conditional access have shown, the extent to which companies control access and distribution is much more important than the number of channels they own or the services they offer. This is because network access and control determines how the system will be used and to what extent proprietary standards (through set-top boxes) can be imposed. Regulation then is needed wherever there is a threat of market dominance and a threat to diversity of opinion and choice.

Steemers (1999)

1 Summarize the writer's arguments for regulation of digital broadcasting.

2 How would you explain and amplify the phrase 'television's cultural and political role'?

3 Explain and exemplify different ways in which 'market dominance' may be interpreted.

4 What would be the main differences in attitudes to regulation of media between a liberal pluralist and a political economist?

5 What are the differences between media and their industries which may suggest that there should be differences in the way that they are regulated?

16 Further reading

Curran, J. and Seaton, J. (1997) *Power Without Responsibility – the Press and Broadcasting in Britain* (5th edn). London: Routledge.

Curran, J. (2002) *Media and Power*. London: Routledge.

Grossberg, L., Wartella, E. and Whitney, D.C. (1998) *Media Making – Mass Media in Popular Culture*. London: Sage.

Negrine, R. (1994) *Politics and the Mass Media in Britain* (2nd edn). London: Routledge.

Seymour-Ure, C. (1996) *The British Press and Broadcasting since 1945*. Oxford: Blackwell.

Stokes, J. and Reading, A. (1999) *The Media in Britain – Current Debates and Developments*. Basingstoke: Macmillan.

Tumber, H. (ed.) (2000) *Media Power, Professionals and Policies*. London: Routledge.

CHAPTER TWO

MEDIA TEXTS

Features and deconstructions

"Ideologies are systems of representation materialised in practices.**"**

Stuart Hall (1996) Signification, representation, ideology, in J. Curran, D. Morley and V. Walkerdine, *Communication Studies and Communications.* London: Arnold.

1 Introduction

Media texts are a dominant feature of our environment. They may not be noticed because they are always there. They are taken for granted and may well be treated uncritically. They are commonplace in both domestic and public environments: music in a department store, music in the background in the home; and in some homes, the television is left on, even when unattended. It may be argued that media texts are especially subject to change – street posters come and go. Media texts are continually being produced and renewed. Media texts intend to engage people, to convey some kind of information, and to produce reactions in their audiences which justify their continuing production.

Even when treated as part of the environment they can never been seen as passive in the way that the façade of a building or wallpaper is passive. They are active in their changeability. They are active in their capacity to produce meanings in the minds of the audience. It may be argued that this production of meanings happens whether or not we engage with the text on a conscious level. Even when the text *is* attended to, there are meanings which the reader is conscious of, and yet other meanings which may be produced unconsciously. In this sense the reader of texts is not entirely in control of their engagement with the text. Equally, I am not arguing that the text maker is entirely in control of the production of meaning. The text becomes an interesting place of engagement. Things happen through the text, not all of them predictable or manageable.

2 Major questions

Texts

1 In what respects is the media text both a material object or a set of meanings?

2 How far are those meanings determined by the producer or by the reader of the text?

3 How may we use forms of textual analysis to investigate meanings and their influences, especially with relation to ideology?

4 How may we understand the work of conventions in structuring the text and meaning, in relation to narrative, realism and genre in particular?

Representation

5 How are representations constructed, and what do they construct for us?

6 How do representations naturalize ideology?

7 In whose interests do representations work?

8 How do representations link with the construction and expression of identities?

9 Why are representations attractive to the producers of media texts?

Genre

10 What characterizes genres, and gives them significance among texts?

11 In what respects are genre texts attractive to institutions and audiences?

12 What is distinctive about the relationship between genre texts and their audiences?

13 In what respects are genre texts ideological, and the producers of myths?

14 How do genres relate to determinist and pluralist positions, with relation to debates about media and society?

3 What is a text?

In a broad sense, in relation to the study of culture, anything may be described as a text if people can engage with it to produce meanings about themselves, their society, their beliefs. But media texts are objects produced with the explicit intention of engaging an audience. In some cases (movies in a theatre) they are transient. Even where they are permanent – a copy of a magazine – there is a kind of impermanence in the fact that they are continually being produced – the next edition, the next in the series. In this way, media texts comprise a torrent of materials and produce a flood of meanings. They are a moving target, and textual analysis is in some ways an attempt to stem that flow, and subject it to careful attention.

Media texts also have a variety of forms both within media (publishing – newspapers to novels) and across media (the front page of a website to the titles of a TV programme). This variety has to be taken into account when one engages with what I take to be the central project when studying text – the production of meaning and the process of influence.

Graddol (1994) discusses the nature of text, its range and its materiality. He points out that, even in respect of the original definitions of text, an insistence on written forms excluded other, verbal forms and attributes – spoken and non-verbal. But then he also identifies two kinds of materiality to the wider range of texts (including media). On one level he refers to 'communicative artefacts', to 'commodities which can enter social and economic relations' – these could be DVDs. On another level he talks about 'semiotic materiality'. In this respect he argues that, however **semiotics** seems to be about immaterial meaning, in fact it is also about the material **signifier**. One might refer to the smile of the model on the magazine cover. This then leads on to immaterial factors.

Tolson (1996) talks more about the 'reader' of texts, and about the process of making sense of them: 'meanings are derived from meaning systems to which everyone in our culture has access. The text itself works to structure these meanings', but also the reader 'comes to the text with all sorts of prior knowledge and expectations [. . .] The modern consumer of the media is a reader of many different kinds of text, which inter-relate and feed off one another.'

The constructed text

The familiarity of texts in our lives can divert attention from the fact that they are made objects. This is important because one must then ask questions about who made the text and with what intentions. In whose interest is the existence of the text and its apparent meanings?

Some of the remarks on analysis, which follow – especially those which draw on kinds of structuralist approach – do try to explain the nature of the construction. But one always needs to go beyond the descriptive to the interpretive. A clock is not to be understood by an account of its parts and their workings. It is the idea of 'clock-ness' and of time which matters. It is the effects on our social relations of *having* clocks which are important.

4 Texts and meanings

The relationship of texts to meanings is one that has already been raised, and to which we will continually return, in different ways.

One kind of model tends to assume that the text is a vehicle for meaning. Early effects theory (the hypodermic theory), deterministic media – society models (classic Marxist models), and at least some structuralist analysis, all assume that the text carries messages which are either conveyed into the consciousness of the audience and/or do something to the receiver.

Another kind of model sees the text as a kind of stimulus at the interface between producer and audience. The stimulus may be designed to achieve certain kinds of response, yet may also achieve unexpected reactions. In this respect one may cite Barthes' notion of the **writerly and readerly** text. The readerly text is one in which familiar features (see conventions) make it 'easy' for the reader to make sense of it. It is undemanding. Barthes identifies a narrative feature of such texts – the **hermeneutic code** – which closes down the reader's ability to look for choices of meaning. Genre material, with its strong conventions, and assumptions about how it is to be understood, fits this

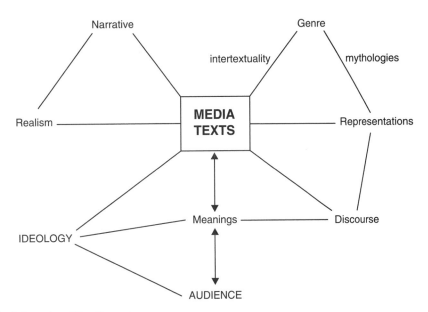

The Relationship of Key Concepts
In terms of the production of meaning, the inter-relationship between notions of text and of audience is so close that one might equally make audience the focus of this model.
(Graeme Burton: *More than meets the eye, 3/e* Arnold, 2001)

version. The writerly text is one in which conventions and predictability do not figure so boldly, and the text may stimulate reflection and alternative meanings for the reader, who in effect becomes a writer of meanings.

A third model is one in which the text is a kind of booty to be plundered by the reader. Meanings are there for the taking. This kind of audience-centred and post-modern analysis is represented by writers such as John Fiske (*Television Culture*, 1987) and Henry Jenkins (*Textual Poachers*, 1992).

Clearly it is reasonable to assert that meanings are ideas which exist only in the minds of people – producers or audiences. But what *kinds* of meanings appear in the reader's mind, and why, is another matter. On the one hand, texts are organized, in various ways for various reasons: so it is not possible to argue that they are neutral goods with which readers can do anything that they please. On the other hand, texts are not so absolutely predictive, and audience members not so lacking in the capacity for critical interpretation, that text makers can produce any kind of meaning/interpretation and impose it.

It would seem that a dynamic model is the most plausible one. Some texts for some audience are more able to determine meaning outcomes than others. Halliday (1996), in discussing **socio-linguistics** and text, produces a useful phrase – 'meaning potential'. Media texts have this potentiality. One might argue that media producers have created the potential, and it is the audience that realizes it.

5 Text and contexts

A criticism of some examples of textual analysis is that they operate in isolation. The text is everything. This may be seen partly as a need, for example, to look at the conditions of production that make the text, or at the nature of the audience in relation to what is made of a text. But even as commodities, texts exist in contexts, as do the readers who produce meanings from the text and who may be influenced by it. This sense of context and its influence is complex and far reaching. Any media text exists in the context of all other media texts, especially those which bear particular comparison with it (see Inter-textuality). Readers have a residual, even unconscious knowledge of at least some of those other texts. They use them to make sense of the text. They are part of a kind of conceptual context.

There is also a *material context* when texts are part of a flow of reading. A news article is a text which is part of larger text – the whole newspaper being read. A TV programme may be part of a flow of programmes in an evening's viewing. There is an *environmental context* in which both text and reader exist. A movie viewed in the home via DVD with others will be viewed differently from the same movie as text viewed individually in a theatre. There is a *social context* which is part of the environment. This is defined in various ways. It is partly a matter of social conventions, in which, if reading a newspaper in a public place, one is not at liberty to turn to a stranger to discuss what is read – as one would be if sitting at home with a partner. It is also a matter of reading conventions, in which one is not expected to engage with a TV programme as intensely in private as one would be in public as part of an audience for a performance of a play.

This social context will affect what is attended to and how. There is an *experiential context* which the audience brings to its understanding of media texts. That is to say, we have an ever expanding experience of texts and of ways of understanding them, which we bring to bear unconsciously on any individual text. Then there is an *ideological context*: the dominant values held by the culture which produces and consumes the text. These values inform the text as it is made and the text as it is read. This is a context of ideas.

6 Deconstructing texts

6.1 Textual analysis

The analysis of texts is a process of deconstruction that investigates the operations of texts, their constructions, the ways they produce meanings, what those meanings may be. Deacon *et al.* (1999) define the approach as one where 'the organisation and meaning of the material itself are the major focus of research'. However, they also warn of the dangers of making assumptions about the validity of any one analytic method – for example, assuming 'a transparency between the structures of media texts and the social meanings made of them'. I would add a rider about the obvious limitations of textual analysis – that in isolation it neither analyses the audience as reader of the text nor the institution as producer.

Thwaites *et al.* (1994), while rather wedded to the methodology of semiotic analysis, make a useful point about texts as 'socially constructed to have certain meanings', and about textual analysis as a way of breaking through a 'façade of naturalness'.

Methods of analysis are various. They have different advantages and disadvantages. They may focus on different features of texts – their conventions of realism, or their endorsement of cultural myths, for example. 'Textual analysis' is a general term which includes various and particular methodologies. For example, *linguistic analysis* might concentrate on the potential effects of style of address. *Content analysis* attends to the repetition and frequency of features, their proportions within the text, and consequent assumptions about significance. The percentage of advertisements of a certain type within a newspaper may, for instance, be significant. *Ideological analysis* of a text would concentrate on meanings about power, and may well seek to reveal contradictions between ideological positions which inform the text. *Narrative analysis* (see following section) has its own kinds of inflection and concerns – structure, or reader positioning.

6.2 Textual codes

The notion of **codes** is one which is especially associated with semiotics and with genres (see below). There is a problem with the rather inconsistent use of the term in critical writing, and it should recognize a set of textual elements that work together according to conventions, which may be loosely understood as kinds of language. The term may be used to describe 'the language' of dress and fashion or the 'technical language' of use of camera, for instance.

What is more helpful in the first place is to grasp the dominant codes or kinds of language which are found in most media texts. These languages speak meanings to us, often working together or striking off one another. They may be summarized as

Written language	the dominant code of this book: much less dominant on television;
Spoken language	a dominant code of radio: otherwise present in film and TV;
Non-verbal language	a dominant code in the case of all representations of people in the media;
Visual language	a dominant code of all 'image media': the language of images in photography, film and TV, which I take to cover features such as use of camera or of composition.

Clearly this account is not inclusive. It does not refer to important codes of number or of music, for example. But it does foreground major areas of attention in any attempt on textual analysis. These languages speak to us from the text. They are significant in the production of meaning.

6.3 Semiotic analysis

This approach regards texts as collections of signs (paradigms) and possible meanings, operating within the bounds of various codes. Its benefit is that it causes one to attend to the question of what actually generates meaning for the reader – the sign – and to the problem of texts having to some degree different meanings for different readers at different times.

A brief survey of key terms and principles now follows, drawn mainly from Barthes' work. The sign is conceived of as having two elements

- the **signifier**, which classes it as a sign with the potential for meaning;
- the **signified**, which stands for its possible meanings. Because there are many possible meanings, one sign may have many signifieds.

The connection between signifier and signified is arbitrary and not absolute. What tends to tie down the meaning of a sign, to make one meaning more probable than others, is context. This context certainly includes the other signs in the text, and would apply most firmly to genre texts. In such cases readers have a lot of textual experience to go on, which in turn includes repeated conventions and strong expectations.

Signs also work on at least two levels, the one more specific, the other more general. This is best understood through example. In written codes, letters are signs which follow rules (conventions) to make up words (rules of spelling). Words may then themselves be described as signs, at a second level. We usually look for meaning in words or strings of words. These strings are themselves bound by conventions of grammar and syntax, to produce phrases and sentences. Similarly, in visual codes the use of colour or camera angle may act as a sign on a primary level. But then the whole image (a collection of primary level signs) may also be described as a sign, on a secondary level. In the case of film and television the image would be a shot, which works in relation to other shots.

Happy Families on Holiday
In semiotic terms, this image denotes a collection of males and females of various ages in a certain place. However, it connotes ideas about the family, pleasures and the holiday. We are positioned as privileged spectators, looking upon this scene.

   The image represents the family on holiday, and works with other such images, from domestic snapshots to television programmes. The representation works to construct meanings (among others) about how the holiday is an approved cultural activity (rather than a commercial transaction): is to be equated with happiness and bonding of the family (rather than a time of stress): is about beaches and sunshine (rather than mountains and walking).
(*Thomas Cook*)

Where one has a string of words or a string of shots which add up to a meaningful unit of narrative, then in formal semiotic terms these would be called a **syntagm** (see also the work of Christian Metz). Less formally one might talk about a phrase in a novel or a sequence in a movie.

   Other books provide effective examples of semiotic analysis, to which you may refer. Among others are Thwaites *et al.* (1994), Tolson (1996) and Bignell (1997). It is Bignell who makes the apt comment that 'There is no perfect analytical method for studying the media since different theoretical approaches define their tasks, the objects they study or the questions they ask in different ways.'

I would also refer you to Barthes' own work, not only for examples of analysis, but also for a wider discussion of two categories of sign referred to through the concepts of **denotation and connotation**. In effect, denotative signs and their meanings would be at a 'first level' which would, for example, refer to those aspects of an image that refer to a real world. These are elements about which one can make apparently objective statements: 'The person is wearing clothes made of a blue fabric.' Connotations are meanings at a second level, which is more subjective and contestable: 'The clothes are fashionable, suggesting that the person has status and wealth.' Two seminal works of Barthes are: *Image, Music, Text* (1977) and *Mythologies* (1973).

6.4 Image analysis

In terms of image analysis, it is important to attend to primary level signs in visual codes, most obviously for examples of still photography. In fact, for all examples of naturalistic imagery, from paintings to advertising images, I would suggest an additional approach to the discussion of textual meaning. This approach categorizes signs in three ways.

(i)   Position: Refers to signs which tell us where we are placed in relation to the content of the image. Mainly, this is signified through the placing of the camera, which then becomes the location from which the spectator is forced to view the content. We may, for example, be placed at an angle to the subject, behind the subject, viewing the subject as if secretly.

(ii) Treatment: Refers to those primary signs, often part of the technique of photography, which are about how the image is made. The uses of colour, of focus, of lighting, for instance, will all contribute to the meanings that we make of the image.

(iii) Content: Refers to objects represented within the image, which may signify to us because of, for example, their symbolic power or because of their composition in relation to each other. For example, one surrealist television advert included the motif of a lion walking through various urban locations – the lion as masculinity and nature. It included a final shot in which a woman is choosing underwear in a department store: the juxtaposition of animal gaze, female gaze and briefs in centre frame creates a whole set of meanings which are greater than the parts of the image.

6.5 Discourse analysis

This is about the recognition of discourses at work within a text, and of the features of language which identify those discourses.

The terms 'discourse' and 'discourse analysis' are somewhat complicated by their histories and by their different uses by different disciplines. For example, 'discourse' originally applied to modes of conversation, and in linguistics one deals with 'units of utterance'. Howarth (2000) provides useful discussion of these differences. He talks of a 'relationship between discourses and the social systems in which they function'. Certainly the ways in which the media 'talk about' social systems helps to define them: equally, our social systems provide a kind of framework within which the media operate.

Howarth describes a kind of Marxist inflection to the understanding of discourse (after Fairclough and Wodak), when he writes: 'The task of discourse analysis is to examine this dialectical relationship' – i.e. between discourse and social systems – 'and to expose the way in which language and meaning are used by the powerful to deceive and oppress the dominated.' Whereas, in terms of post-structuralist and post-Marxist perspectives, Howarth describes a different inflection: 'Discourses constitute symbolic systems and social orders, and the task of discourse analysis is to examine their historical and political construction and functioning.'

What I now propose draws on such views, but hopefully makes understanding and use of the terms more straightforward.

Discourses are linked to ideology and representations, and involve ways of using language – verbal, visual or whatever code – about a subject, so as to produce particular meanings about that subject. Our communication is full of discourses, which shape how we understand our world, how we deal with others, how we make sense of everyday experience. So it is that we talk about parenthood, we talk to parents, we talk as parents, in different terms to those we use towards and about children. Such discourses may well shift from culture to culture, because different cultures think differently about parents and parenting, because they value it in different ways. The essence of a discourse is the 'meanings we have about' its subject. So the discourse of death is not so much about corpses as about 'death-ness'. It is about how we talk dominantly about death; about what death means to most of us in our culture. This talk happens in everyday life, as well as through the media. The meanings that it produces interlock with social practices around death, such as the funeral.

In that the meanings of discourses are about dominant beliefs and values, it follows that discourses are, as it were, ideology in communicative action. Add to this the view that representations do the work of ideology, and you can see how close the connections are between these key terms.

If the discourse lurks within the text, then the language of the discourse is the visible evidence of it – signs which emerge to link us with the invisible discourse and its meanings. To recognize the existence of discourse, the textual reader needs to be conscious that we have 'taken for granted' ways of talking about subjects: this actually means we have 'taken for granted' ways of understanding and thinking about subjects. The selectivity of verbal and visual language can become startlingly obvious if you are able to switch off those assumptions in your head.

For example, the discourse of war is recognizable through language such as 'victory', 'defeat', 'outflank', 'skirmish', 'manoeuvre', 'troops'. The meanings of the discourse derived from the use of these words refers to ideas about 'aggression', 'conflict', 'winning'. Now look at ways in which your newspaper talks about politics or economics or football. The odds are that you will find this discourse of war used in an account of a match or of disagreement between political parties. You are so used to it that you do not notice this is happening. But it certainly skews our thinking about the activity called 'sport', or about the process called 'politics'.

The language of discourse is in some ways the word association that we make with the subject – what we think of first – because it is so embedded in the way we talk and think. Gender is a powerful example, in which many words are, for instance, associated with the female subject – 'soft', 'emotional', 'intuitive', 'caring', 'illogical', 'maternal' and so on. Similarly, we take it for granted that images of women may use soft focus, position the lens/viewing eye to look at their breasts, or show women crying. This selective language (selective use of signs) produces selective meanings about how females think about themselves and about how they are thought about by others.

The discourse is also marked by what it is not, by what it is opposed to. Just as war is opposed to peace, so female is opposed to male. The words and images I mention are not used for males. Indeed, they are seen in opposition to being male, to ideas about masculinity.

So texts may also throw up discourses and their meanings if you attend to what are called **binary oppositions**. Textual analysis from the work of Barthes and Lévi-Strauss onwards has referred to patterns of opposing meanings in various ways. Lévi-Strauss noticed that tribal myths contained within stories were often centred on the opposition between characters, and by the association of ideas about what was good as opposed to what was evil. Other narrative analysis has exploited this opposition in terms of motifs, or themes, or dramatic conflict. The approval of a given ideological position may be reinforced through evident disapproval of an opposing view, and vice versa.

So the discourse of war used in political news stories tells us that politics should be competitive. The discourse of masculinity used in the same stories may also tell us that winning is everything, that men are assertive and 'right': conversely that to admit you are wrong is unmasculine and weak.

A given text may contain a number of discourses. Some may oppose one another. And the language of a discourse, however dominant in a culture, may not be entirely consistent. Ideological positions vary. Ideologies are not self-perpetuating, unvarying sets of beliefs, however slowly shifts can take place. So one kind of text and its discourse about the subject of nature may be dominated by meanings about beauty and sentiment, while another may be dominated by meanings about loss and the need to preserve species. In this case, what is also interesting is, for example, to see how nature is generally talked about now, compared with language about nature used, say, a hundred years ago. Then, nature was about 'plenty', now it is about 'endangered species'; then it was about 'exploration' and 'adventure', now it is as much about 'conservation' and 'protection'.

Discourse analysis, then, is the analysis of a text through identification of language, so as to reveal its discourses and to comment on their meanings. It is also about the revelation of the ideology behind the text. It is about certain understandings of the subject of the discourse.

7 Texts and narration

Media texts tell stories; they have a narrative. Narratives are about story telling and story meaning. As with previous discussion of meaning, it may be argued that the narrative and its meanings are in the shaping of the text, and then work on the reader. But they are also in the mind of the reader because of what that reader does with the text.

A **structuralist approach** will demonstrate that there are features of a text which present an order, a form, cues to the reader, all of which give shape to that thing called narrative. Those features lead to meanings. A more audience-centred, even cognitive approach, will look at the audience as the active element in the construction of meaning. The audience draws on knowledge of conventions, of other texts, to construct things like storyline and the significance of the narrative. The idea of 'a narrative' is a construct in our minds, it is the product of a set of textual features. Narrative itself is made up of ideas such as place, time, character and relationship. Often the function of narrative is to generate these elements in such a way that engaging with the text is an experience in which a kind of reality is created. Different **modes of narrative** create an illusion of reality for as long as we are textual readers. They do not have to imitate life experience to work. We can go along with flashbacks or jumps in the action, so long as the narrative is consistent to itself – to the rules of the game which it has set up, and with which we are familiar because of our history of reading texts. Most narratives are dominated by two significant features. One is the unfolding of events (plot). The other is the unfolding of emotional states and of ideas (drama), through the representation of characters and relationships, and through the device of the authorial voice.

One needs to take on the idea that there is no such thing as *the* story. There are indeed some texts where readers will probably make pretty much the same story and the same meanings (genres). But there are others where they will not. We tend to assume that the narrative is an object to be uncovered, to which the reader stands in some relation. This is not true. Rather, it is a set of ideas to be put together (by the reader), and the way that they are put together sets up an imagined relationship with the reader. We may feel that there is a story out there, to which we relate differently, for example, if it is autobiographical rather than conventional third person. But there is no story out there. And the sense of authorial voice is just a trick. We are persuaded that we have some position in relation to a truth, but it is an illusion. The sense of a narrative or of a reader relationship, gives substance to the illusion of events actually taking place. Indeed this helps create the **diegesis**, or self-contained reality of the story. It kids us that we as individuals have a privileged and intimate view of that reality. It enhances a sense of the truth, of the validity of what we experience – but it is just a story, just a set of representations. In fact the illusion is just another kind of meaning produced by the words and images. A sense of truth and actuality may serve only to convince the reader of other meanings to be drawn from a given narrative – the nobility of the human spirit, the power of love, the rightness of a given social order. Such meanings may in fact equally be arrived at through semiotic analysis or discourse analysis. They are also ideological.

I am not saying that the sense of a narrative, the sense of a reader relationship, the very pleasure of reading, is not significant. The experience may well be valued. But still it is important to establish that a narrative is a conceptual construction, and has no materiality, however it may refer to material objects such as places and people. Narratives are common, in most texts, in all media. Narratives may be read in factual as well as fictional material. They may be read in still images as much as in sequences of images. We tend to think of them as emerging from fictional, naturalistic material – of which there is a lot in the media. But there are very few examples of media communication of which one may say – no one can make a story out of that. A television documentary orders its material to produce a line of argument, to introduce and conclude its subject, perhaps even to impose some dramatic development on the subject. This is no different to a television news item or to a drama. We look at still photographs, especially those dominated by human figures, and construct a story around the scene, the people. This narrative may be limited in extent, compared with a whole movie, but it is narrative none the less.

One may argue that people have an inclination to make narrative out of most experiences, not least media experiences: that we take pleasure in following the cues of media material to make narratives. In a sense narrative is a consequence of the particular cognitive skills of our species. We have a sense of time: we conceive before, now and after. We have a sense of place: we conceive here, there, elsewhere. So we conceptualize where and when. We also construct motive: we have a notion of human psychology, of the reasons for and consequences of people's actions. We may not always be right about people. But we do it. Time, place, motive, cause and effect dominate all narratives. The text does not have to supply the narrative. We can do that. A photograph of an old couple sitting on a park bench leads to narrative speculation. What happens next? Why are they there? What is being said about the elderly? The possibilities of narrating are in our heads, not just locked in the text. Narratives – documentary or fiction – are not just artful imitations of some kind of reality. They also signify meanings about their subjects, about society and about the times in which they are created. They are inevitably ideological.

Narrative structures

Narratives have shape and structure. This is much related to order of events and the arrangement of dramatic episodes and resolution. With relation to binary oppositions, I have already referred to one kind of structure. This might emerge through pairs of people, opposing sets of characteristics, pairs of places, and certainly through sets of ideas. The most common narrative structure may be described as mainstream narrative or as the **classic realist text**. It has become a benchmark by which other kinds of narrative, other evocations of reality are measured. This is characterized by a progression of events through time, by conflict between characters, by problems for the protagonist(s), by a series of dramatic moments. Events move forward towards an eventual denouement, a resolution of the problems. Such a narrative structure has closure – it is tied up at the end – as opposed to being open-ended. It is the work that the narrative does, as a vehicle for ideas, which makes the structure significant.

Mainstream narrative imitates our lived sense of things moving forward, our beliefs in the linkage between events in our lives, our need to resolve problems. And in this mixing of experience and endorsement of how we feel life is lived, so also such a narrative structure endorses the plausibility of its own ideas. The same may be said of other structures and structural devices. *Circular narratives*, in which the beginning of a story is its end, are a kind of reflection on how we reach points in our lives. The main body of such a narrative is an extended flashback, a disquisition on our belief that our past affects our present. *Parallel narratives* are those in which two or more plot lines are dealt with alternately and eventually brought together. These construct an imitation of our recognition that events coexist in our lives, that coincidences happen, that we live within a context of simultaneous and related events and people. Parallel narrative reflects on the significance of one part of our life story to another.

Narrative structures and various features of narrative are largely invisible to the average reader because they are so familiar and conventionalized. The rules or **conventions** by which plot is organized, drama is evoked, time and place are understood, are so well understood by media producers and audiences that the construction called narrative is invisible. It is a corollary of the power of these conventions that narrative which disobeys the usual rules of story development or of keeping the other invisible (for example) may described as 'alternative'. We notice the rules when they are broken. Such conventions may work against an effect of naturalism, against plausibility, against narrative as a reproduction of lived experience. For instance, movies will, by convention, abridge time and place. The story does not move forward at the pace of real time. Bits are 'missed out'. Screen time is not realtime. Certain conventions or narrative cues may well help us understand, unconsciously, what is going on. In a movie a character will announce that they have to see someone: then we jump forward to another place and to that meeting. But we do not see that as bizarre or unrealistic because we have been cued to expect it. No more do we crib about the sound of music appearing from nowhere (perhaps to induce emotions that relate to the drama). In fact the music would be described as non-diegetic, or outside the scope of the actual story (the diegesis).

If narrative is also a feature of representation, then we become all the more aware of its constructedness. It is just another way of ordering and evoking meanings. Narrative is so often validated critically in terms of its ability to imitate experience of a physical world, or of the psychology of character and relationships. But in fact what it is really about is comment upon and meanings about our material and conceptual worlds. Analysis of narrative features, and of their significance, leads to meaning and to visions of how the world is.

Reader positioning

Our recognition that there is a construction called narrative depends to an extent on reader positioning. I have already referred to that mode of narrative called autobiography. This addresses the reader directly. It constructs the idea of there being a narrator. It helps authenticate that which is being talked about. It contrasts with the more frequent third person form, in which that which we call 'the story' is apparently told by an invisible narrator, neutrally, as a given thing. But, of course, the idea that there is a narrator is in itself just a device, another aspect of narrative. The narrator is actually a function of the text. The idea that the reader is positioned is more accurately about how the text influences the reader's understanding of what the text means. *Identification* describes the effect of involving the reader with the story, of constructing it as truth. It produces a meaning of truth – a belief in the validity of the text and of all the other meanings that we make from it. *Alienation* is about devices of disengagement from the story – positioning us 'outside' it, as opposed to feeling we are 'inside'. Brechtian alienation in theatrical terms was a self-conscious narrative device intended by the playwright to draw attention to the fact that something called narrative does exist and is manipulative. But alienation may exist only at the level of a degree of detachment for the reader. Such detachment may be useful when, for example, the producers want to moderate the possible effect of emotionally charged material. If one moves the camera (and, therefore, the spectator) to an apparently concealed position in some bloody battle scene, then this can make violence more bearable.

The positioning to which I refer has spatial, temporal and psychological dimensions. In a movie like *Gladiator* (2002), one may be positioned in relation to the action in the arena, in relation to the Roman times of the story, and in relation to the protagonist and his feelings about combat. Feuer (1995) refers to a level on which this relationship may be seen in terms of a whole medium, as much as the individual text – 'television's foremost illusion is that it is an interactive medium, not that we are peering into a self-enclosed diegetic space' (as is true for many movies). So narrative and the act of narrating is a core feature of many media texts, and this dominates the output of most media.

8 Texts and realism

It may be argued that realism is a function of narrative – the way the story is told – not a separate textual feature. But again it may be argued that where narrative includes content (an account of material elements in some kind of order or relationship with one another), realism is only about form (how that account takes place).

As a notion about the quality and value of some text, of some medium of representation, realism has its own creative and critical history. The nineteenth century, especially in respect of art and the novel, was dominated by aspirations to make paintings 'true to life'. What 'true' and 'life' mean is another matter. As Furst (1992) says,

The Royle Family on Television: Media reconstruct life so that media reality fuses with social reality
In what respects may one argue that the media either bring us the world or give us the world?
(BBC)

in relation to the novel, 'realism cannot . . . vouchsafe access to an innocent, uncoded or objective experience of an independently existing real world'. Nor is it the case, of course, that all texts even propose manufacturing a 'real world'. Certainly in media studies we would understand that all media are only forms of communication which represent something. That thing may not be life as it is experienced, it may be an experience which is only imagined. And in any case one has to acknowledge the 'problem' of **mediation**, in which the act of communication must in some way transform the 'event' which it seeks to represent.

There are a number of reasons why realism is much discussed in relation to media texts. There is that kind of *material analysis* which is intrigued with the illusion of reality – the kind of text which convinces its reader of the authenticity of character or place – naturalism. The fascination is with language used in such a way as to construct an apparent material or behavioural truth. The discussion is about how it is done.

But then, perhaps along with such analysis, is the validation of the text on the grounds of its qualities of realism – *value analysis*. There has been a strong tradition in Western representational systems of striving after actuality, and of proposing the creative superiority of such texts. The traditions of Victorian naturalistic painting, then of photography, followed by film and television, are all media in which realism as actuality has predominated (though by no means suppressed other modes of realism). In this case the debate is about the merit of what has been achieved – the approval of one mode of representation above others.

Then there is a kind of *philosophical analysis* which is concerned with the very concept of reality, as well as the style of realism which purports to achieve this reality. The quality of seeming real may be as much to do with a sense of truths about human relationships, or about the characteristics of a healthy society, for example, as it is to do with what seems to be authentic or probable. This is about ideas, not form. It is about the representation of an immaterial world. The notion of reality as truth links with the realism that achieves truthfulness. So it may be that a treatment of the text which we describe as surreal, for instance, is as effective in achieving truth as is naturalism. Formalist styles such as Expressionism in the 1920s or film noir in the 1940s may not be 'realistic' but they are about realism. They draw attention to the form of the text, but also point symbolically to truths about the darkness in the human soul, to the truth that evil matters.

If one follows this argument that the form links with the matter of the text, then it is fair to say that to discover the qualities of realism in a text is also to discover meanings about realism. If we say that a scene in some TV drama seems to be realistic because the interaction of the characters is plausible, then we are also saying that one meaning of realism is 'the mimicking of everyday life'. However, another drama in some formalist style might not have naturalistic interaction. But it could still be validated as, for example, 'getting at real truths about how people can play power games with one another'.

This leads one to the idea that one can also talk about something like *ideological realism*, following on from the notion of truth. The audience/reader might well approve the realism of a given text because it expressed what they took to be valid ideological positions. But in ideological terms, that which seems valid often also seems to be the truth because ideology generally works to exclude other ways of looking at its subjects.

A narrative which describes a man being manipulated by a woman may be seen as having realism and as expressing a truth about gender behaviour – if the reader believes that view of the world which sees women as being manipulative in relationships and men as being incompetent to deal with such manipulation.

In this respect it may be said that the importance of realism in relation to media texts lies in the views of the world which it endorses. Even a text which is marked by authenticity and naturalism is significant not just for its appearance, its ability to reproduce the physical world (or even the social world). It is significant because it endorses beliefs about that social world, about the value systems behind the material appearance.

So realism is a feature of a text. It is one measure by which that text is validated in its own right. It is a measure by which it may be valued in comparison with other texts. Indeed Hallam and Marshment (2000) argue that one can only define realist styles by comparison with other styles, given that there is no absolute style of realism to act as a reference point. The criteria for that realism operate both out of what we know of the real world, as well as out of the constructed world of the text. This is realism as 'part of discursive struggle to make sense of our realities' (Hallam and Marshment).

We may use the real world as a measure for the authenticity of the appearance of objects and places. We may use real world experience by which to measure the plausibility of human behaviour, or the probability of character motivation. Real world experience may determine our judgement on the probability of plot and on the nature of coincidence. But those same measures also depend on our experience of the text in question and of other texts. The text being judged can produce its own set of rules, which in turn relate to what we see as its mode of realism, what we should expect. In adventure, action or horror movies we expect some improbability in terms of the real world. But we suspend this relative judgement in the cause of genre pleasures, and go along with what is possible in the film world. In other words, realism is indeed relative, not absolute. Realism may be at work even in texts which on a relative scale of values we might describe as being unrealistic – a number of genre films, such as horror.

Bordwell (1988) points out that 'intertextual motivation' in genres means that part of their realism for the viewer actually demands that they should include, for example, a stock situation like the shoot-out. But this expectation, this repetition and its satisfaction is in another sense unrealistic. Similarly, Bordwell's notion of 'artistic motivation' suggests that the shoot-out can happen in slow motion or with much intercutting. We could expect this and feel that it is consistent to the genre. Yet, in its artifice, in that the medium draws attention to itself, one may say that such a device makes the movie unrealistic. It is only in terms of genre and its own rules that one has a sense of realism.

Other media texts become a measure of realism because they supply us with other information, depictions of other places, possible patterns of behaviour. We may not have been to Chicago, but, even subconsciously, we will judge the realism of some depiction of Chicago of the basis of other things we have seen or read about the city. Indeed, it may be argued that we are inclined to forget that many sources of information are merely representations, not first-hand experience, and that they can become as 'true' for us as any real-life experience.

It may be said that realism is nothing but a combination of conventions within the text. Some of these combinations form what are called modes of realism: they are kinds of category. We may use specific terms to describe these – documentary, fiction, fantasy.

This categorization, as with genre, sets up expectations of the nature of the text. Such expectations are useful for media producers – for example in scheduling TV programmes by type, or in marketing books. They also help the reader to make mental adjustments in terms of how they will interpret and value the text. There is a kind of axis of realism, with the most factual material at one end and the most fantastic treatments at the other. On the one hand the real world of social experience and material objects becomes a benchmark. On the other, improbability and impossibility become accepted hallmarks.

What we need to remember is that texts are only kinds of representation. So television news may be relatively more real than a satirical novel about the future. But neither is it reality. Because it brings us real-time images of people and places does not make its meanings true. Equally, the novel may be unrealistic in a material sense, but truthful in an ideological sense.

9 Texts, representations, ideology, identity

The idea of representation is central to understanding the production of meaning through texts. Texts are nothing but representations in both a material and an ideological sense. In the material sense the text is a made thing, a product of technology, an image on a screen, a set of marks on the page. In semiotic terms, the signs stand for what is represented, objects or ideas. But they are not the thing itself. In an ideological sense, texts do indeed represent ideas. The reader interacts with the text. The interaction produces the ideas, perhaps preferred by the producer, perhaps more critically manufactured through the mental work of the reader.

The car in a magazine advert is a mental construct produced via a process of perception, using representational features such as hue, shade and outline. And, of course, that construct includes concepts represented about the nature of the car, the desirability of the car, its place in our lives.

Debates about representation in part centre around alternative notions of reflection or of construction. With visual media there is a temptation to follow the 'mirror of reality' approach because of iconographic nature of images in photography, film and television. The pictures look like what they are meant to refer to in the real world (see the idea of denotation). Such 'reflectionist' arguments also link with certain notions of realism. The visual text may be praised for its invocation of physical authenticity (an aesthetic judgement). The text may also be 'approved' of for its representation of, for example, 'natural' social behaviour, or for the 'truth' of lifestyles and attitudes. This kind of value judgement is still very apparent in press reviews of film and television. As Sturken and Cartwright (2001) say: 'Despite the subjective aspects of the act of taking a picture, the aura of machine objectivity clings to mechanical and electronic images.'

Barsam (1974) is part of the critical history of this approach when he speaks approvingly of the qualities of free cinema or of cinema verité documentary film movements – 'the camera work is intimate, often giving the viewer the immediate sense that he is "there" ' – and of a particular film – 'a beautiful study of ordinary people in ordinary jobs'. But of course representation is anything but ordinary. The 'constructionist

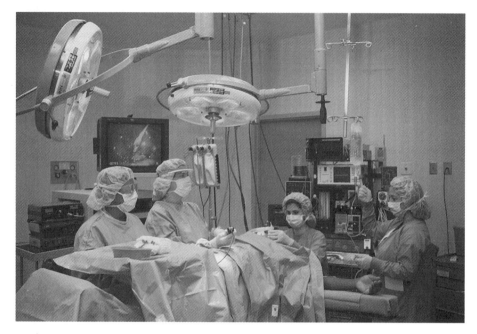

Female Surgeons
This image raises questions about how the media represent society to itself, and about how identities for social groups are constructed. Specifically, one may ask how common it is to see images in which surgeons (as opposed to nurses) are female, not male, or even from non-Western ethnic backgrounds.
(*Corbis*)

approach' emphasizes the illusion of the representation, and falsity of a number of the ideas which it may propose about people and society.

Corner (1996) robustly critiques the idea of documentary as a 'referential record'. He talks of a critique 'interested in questions of representational form' 'which aims to "uncouple" the relationship between putative reality, pro-filmic reality and screened reality which much documentary depends upon.'

Stereotypes and ideologies

When representation is discussed in terms of social groups and images of people, its significance is not simply about appearance. It is about the substance of ideas invoked about that group. This is in no way to dismiss the significance of stereotypes, or of the examination of images of people. But one does need to get beyond discussion of things like physical characteristics or even patterns of behaviour for their own sake, and get to the ideas that are represented. For instance, the femme fatale as a female type goes back to texts from the beginning of the twentieth century, to Georg Pabst's 1920s film vamp, Lulu, for example. But in examining such a type it is inadequate merely to catalogue features such as dark hair or dark clothes; to identify characteristic behaviours such as a seductive manner; or even to describe conventional plot functions such as temptation of the hero. What matters is the representation of ideas about women, perhaps especially in the context of the era in which the text is made.

These ideas are ideological. Representations give substance to ideology. Textual analysis reveals ideology in action. The femme fatale is about gender and power. It is about the male fear of being 'unmanned' by the sexual power of the woman, a fear of 'losing control'. In the 1950s, representations of such a type would include condemnation (sexuality was allied with murderous tendencies) and retribution (such characters were likely to die or to end up alone, without a man). By the 1990s, the films of John Dahl, for example (*The Last Seduction* or *Red Rock West*), represent the femme fatale as strong, and the male often as weak or indecisive or pointlessly violent. The woman is not necessarily punished, sometimes not even for a crime.

Representations tend to reflect the ideological positions of the times in which they are created. They tend to be most conservatively ideological in genre material. Sometimes those reflections are of contradictions between one ideological position and another, or of kinds of challenge to the ideological status quo. Considering the contradictions between the various role expectations of women, it wouldn't be surprising if media representations reflected good examples of those contradictions – e.g. woman as passive beauty object versus woman as active earner. 'Ideological analysis is . . . about recognising the semiotic and discursive contradictions and tensions within a representation [. . .] at the core of these contradictions and tensions is the potential to challenge particular power relations and concepts of identity' (Ferguson, 1998).

And Gunter (1995a) says of the representation of women on television: there is a gross under-representation of women in action-drama shows in terms of actual numbers relative to the presence of men . . . even when women do appear, they tend to be portrayed only in a very narrow range of roles.

These comments suggest that representations reveal their negative ideological credentials through who is presented (or not), and how they are shown. The contradictions between the world on screen and the world as we experience it, reveal ideology at work, display a partial view of social relations and dispositions of power.

Social types

Representations of people involve a typology of repeated surface characteristics – appearance and behaviour – that through repetition reinforce ideas about the type and/ or group depicted. This typology falls into three main categories, marked by the intensity of recognition, and depth of cultural history.

Archetypes are characters which are recognizable across genres, have few but very dominant features and characteristics. They are in effect a distillation of ideas about gender, or possibly about well-known occupations. For instance, the heroic male adventurer who is physically powerful and irresistible to women, repeatedly emerges in popular texts. He is Caucasian in appearance and marked by loyalty in male bonding and persistence in pursuing quests. His provenance is legendary – Theseus or King Arthur. Such archetypes tend to emerge in texts set in a more fantasy mode of realism. But the impact of the ideas is no less significant for this. Notably he appears in novels and films made from novels – James Bond, Luke Skywalker, *Total Recall*, *Lord of the Rings*, *Diehard*. The heroic male adventurer is almost always a protagonist, rather than a supporting character. He very much links with genre myths and with a cultural idealization of masculinity.

Stereotypes are equally recognizable, but rather less mythic. They tend to belong to genres rather than to cross them. They may distil the characteristics of specific social roles, or of more contemporary occupations. But they also generate meanings about the stereotype which come out of conservative and dominant aspects of ideology. The stereo-typical barmaid has big boobs and a big heart. What she stands for are ideas about sex without danger for the male, listening without criticism, the boosting of self-esteem, and above all a female who knows her place in a male universe.

Types are the least distinctive category, perhaps because they are also the most sketchily drawn, the least represented and so the least reinforced. They are supporting players. One must acknowledge a degree of subjectivity in how characters are judged in this respect. But examples might be the stupid gang member – parodied in *Bugsy Malone*: the bucolic farm worker, as represented in a television adaptation of H. E. Bates's *The Darling Buds of May*: or the sharp young party-goer, who appears in material such as *Bridget Jones' Diaries*.

In terms of meanings about social groups being constructed through representations, it is worth noting that what is *not* said about the type may be significant. It could be said that these 'meanings by omission' also emerge through analysis which looks for binary oppositions. So racism may emerge in texts firstly through roles which the subject is not given – how many actors from non-white groups appear in mainstream television drama? Barnard (2000) comments that even in a non-visual medium – 'it is the lack of black and Asian voices on mainstream, daytime radio that reflects least kindly on British radio's representation of non-white listeners'.

Secondly, this kind of prejudice by default could be shown through representations of race in association with crime: if, say, black comes to equal criminal through representations, then what it does not equal, by implication, is 'law-abiding'.

It will have become apparent that much concern about textual representation is about its negativity. Travellers are often constructed as feckless and deviant. Such constructions also imply the opposing norms of behaviour and belief. Again, one is looking at ideological statements. To be nomadic is to be deviant, to be settled is to be normal. To have no fixed address means one can evade some state controls: this is threatening to the state.

Naturalization

The notion of norms also links to the idea that representations are given force through a process of **naturalization**. This means that it is seen as natural that a given social group should be represented in a certain way. It is seen as natural that the representation should carry particular ideas about that group – and not other ideas. It makes negative ideas seem normal and unchallengeable. In fact it makes those ideas invisible. This naturalization also underpins hegemony and the uncritical acceptance of the attitudes and values of the dominant ideology. Indeed one may also hear appeals to 'nature' in terms of genetic inheritance when even casual social judgements are made. Women, so goes the popular myth, are 'known' not to be good drivers – they cannot park a car properly, which is to do with their lack of spatial awareness. To represent women in this way ignores three things. Parking a car is not 'natural' but a learnt skill. The premise about spatial awareness is a false one. Good driving is defined in many other ways – for example, women generally drive more carefully than men, because they are less inclined to take risks.

Media representations of social groups purport to show to others what those groups are 'really' like. They also in fact show to members of the subject group both how they may be seen by others and how they 'should' be seen. This could mean that black teenagers are

- seen as being likely involved with crime and drugs;
- believe that they are seen by others as being so involved;
- believe that it is normal to be seen like this.

Subjects of representation

Finally one needs to recognize that the subjects of representation are not only social groups. The term applies to a much wider range of subjects. At its most basic, representation is 'construction of ideas about a subject' through some means of communication. One can talk about representations of institutions or even of social practices. So TV hospital dramas such as *ER* in the USA or *Holby City* in Britain represent not only an occupational group called nurses, but also the institution of the hospital, and the collection of practices known as medicine. Investigative documentaries and news reports will, for example, contribute to the accumulative process of representation, as much as fiction drama. There is *The Trust* (Channel 4, 2002) about the institution of a large British regional health authority and its hospitals; or *How to Build a Human* (BBC2, 2002) about genetics and the possibilities of medicine. And the range of media that construct representations such as the one whose subject is medicine, extends beyond television – newspaper articles on the health service – advertisements for 'health products'. There is a symbiotic relationship between representation and discourse, in which the former takes on a range of discourses to help make meanings about its subjects – nursing or hospitals or medicine – just as it may be said that the discourses contribute to the representation. For instance, whatever the subject of hospitals (and their representation) means to us includes discourses of gender, technology and sickness – to mention only three. Discourses are kept alive through the continued use of language which rehearses their meanings.

Identities through texts

Representations of social groups help create identities for their subjects. The concept of identity is one that is often examined within the sphere of cultural studies. However, at least some comment is appropriate at this point. One can start from the point that representations not only create meanings for the media audience as onlookers, but also for the audience as individuals and as subjects of the representation. Representation is something that is about us, not just about other people. It constructs a sense of identity for us individually, as well as about others. Identity has many dimensions beyond that of mere appearance. I have already referred to characteristic behaviours – what is inferred as being typical: and those which are characterized *for* the group – what is assigned as typical, whether that is true or not. Then there are the 'meanings about' which refer to assumptions about personality, emotional make-up, and attributes – the mean, dour Scotsman with a liking for whisky! There are the 'meanings about' which refer to beliefs, attitudes and values. This point intersects with ideology. Our Scot believes in being frugal, has contempt for Sassenachs, and is very patriotic.

But more than these dimensions are those which focus on a sense of common culture, of belonging, of being distinctive and different. These aspects of identity are those felt by the subject, not by others. They are taken on by the Scot as subject – not assigned by others, because others cannot feel the force and meaning of such identity dimensions. For the Scot, one might be talking about things like: a Presbyterian background; a sense of place (Highlands or 'classical' Edinburgh); a feeling for clan; a sense of history (awareness of the Highland clearances or of emigration pressures); a sense of class.

So identity has a number of dimensions. It may be about a sense of place – belonging to a community in a certain city or country. It may be about history – having a certain shared background of events and experiences, which go back to the past of previous generations – being a New Yorker, or being a Polish person in New York. It may also be about family and history – the stories around a dead grandmother and where she came from. It may be about cultural practices – from the observance of religious occasions to the rituals of family holidays. It may be about role and relationship – taking on the experiences and obligations of fatherhood. It could be about occupation. It is most likely to be about a combination of some or all of these factors.

Most intangibly, identity has been described in terms of being part of a **diaspora** – a sense of belonging to cultural practices and an ethnic background which seems to transcend place and time. One might talk about a Jewish diaspora to which many people, not necessarily practising Jews, feel spiritually attached.

The notion of identity is linked to ideas about personality. There is a debate around the traditional view of a core personality (or fixed identity) and the opposing view that personality and identity is much more mobile. It is unfixed or flexible. Barker (1999) talks about 'the de-centred subject, the self as made up of multiple and changeable identities'.

There may be dominant personality traits, but otherwise personality is actually a response to different social situations. The idea of a fixed identity has attractions because it is securing, it provides a stable view of people. But in truth all we know of people is to do with their behaviour. Personality and identity is to do with their inner lives. These are ideas which we construct from the evidence of behaviour. Identity is something which we feel we have, it is to do with how we see ourselves, but it is also something which is ascribed to us by others. The identity which others believe we have may not be the kind of identity which we ourselves believe in. Representations are very much about ascribing identities to others.

The terms in which one talks about representation and identity continue to overlap in many respects. One may feel positive or negative about one's sense of identity and difference. The onlooker may see the identity in a positive or negative light. Much critical work focuses on negative constructions, not least in trying to explain prejudice, social divisions, social conflict. But this negativity should be qualified by recognition of all the positive views of identities, in which people take pride in their culture, take pleasure in their sense of place, place value on their own social practices. It is not always true that social groups or ethnic groups see themselves as being diminished and less worthy by comparison with some other dominant culture (and dominant ideology). It could be argued that the media notably add to the possibility of feeling diminished because they carry the images, information and ideas of powerful cultures. They diminish global isolation, yet make more possible global comparisons – perhaps to the disadvantage of some cultures. Yet it is possible to have celebration as much as denigration. The multiplying channels of broadcasting make it very possible to present multi-cultural material and to address a range of audiences. In Britain there are, for instance, satellite channels that address Asian communities.

Gilroy (1996) talks about the high profile of identity issues and identity politics because of the proliferation of media material. He refers to 'the increased saliency of identity as a problem played out in everyday life, and . . . identity as it is managed and administered in the cultural industries of mass communication that have transformed understanding of the world and the place of individual possessors of identity within it'.

It remains true that in critical studies the concepts of **difference** and of **otherness** are often used to emphasize the negative: 'sameness and difference are marked both symbolically through representational systems, and socially through the inclusion or exclusion of certain groups of people' (Woodward, 1997).

The concern is that the representation constructs detrimental ideas about the difference of the subject from others: constructs feelings of being 'other' in the sense of being less. When the subject is looked upon it is seen as the other and not as worthy or 'normal' as the onlooker and their identity. The gay person and the state of being gay is often represented in this negative way. This may be done crudely by exaggerating the appearance and mannerisms of the opposite gender in the subject: to emphasize the idea of not-man or not-woman. It may be done through the representation of relationships, in which the subject is shown to be unhappy with their sexuality or unable to have a happy same-sex relationship. It may be done through narrative resolutions in which the gay character ends up alone or hurt in some way. Of course, by implication, all this says a lot about what one 'should' be like in gender terms, how one should behave, how one will achieve a happy life. It implies the absent opposite – those cultural norms which 'should' prevail.

It is possible to celebrate difference and the challenge norms by in effect exposing the discourses. So it is that black activists of the 1970s used the slogan, 'Black is Beautiful', and gay rights activists of the 1990s publicized the phrase 'Proud to be Gay'. Campaigning drew attention to social inequality. How far such slogans caused most people to think again about difference in its negative sense is less certain.

10 Genre texts

Genre texts dominate media output. Some genres have enjoyed a lot of attention – most obviously news. Film studies has been seminal in exploring the characteristics of certain genres – the western or film noir – and in exploring their ideological implications. There is a fair range of material on TV genres such as soaps and crime thrillers. In general, there is a lot said about the features of genres, and to some extent about what these repeated features may signify. But not so much is written on ideas about genre as a concept, not so much development of the idea of genre itself.

Genre texts are in fact very interesting because they clearly yoke institution and audience around text. Genre texts satisfy the market interests of media institutions, as well as the private interests and pleasures of audiences. They can be intensely conservative in ideological terms, and yet sometimes adroitly subversive of the dominant ideology. They run against that Western tradition of individual artistic achievement as mass product, and yet can occasionally achieve originality. They raise the hackles of those supporting an aesthetic valuation of texts, because they are seen as the creatures of commerce. And yet those same self-interested commercial enterprises have sometimes nurtured genre texts which have been acclaimed as something called Art. They work on principles of repetitive conventions, and yet much of the time manage to reinvent themselves before reader exhaustion sets in. They would appear to resist social change and yet can provide a map of this, as well as sometimes exploring the possibilities for that change.

10.1 The formula

We have already established that genres are full of representations, with all that implies about the production of meaning. The repetitious nature of genre elements is at one with the repetition of types in genres.

Many accounts of genre start by establishing repetition, conventions and the formula. I am assuming that this is largely familiar to the reader, probably in terms of particular genre examples. It is worth emphasizing the idea of formula, which tran-scends genres, and which provides a perspective on the building blocks of narrative. I am talking about the elements of hero and villain; stock characters; stock situations; iconic objects, characters and background features; mainstream narrative plot structure. The idea of formula is the idea of an overarching blueprint. This blueprint – remembering structuralist approaches – does seem to pivot on opposing elements where oppositions have to be resolved, and on a developmental narrative in which progression, learning and the classic Todorovian equilibrium have to be achieved (for an account of Todorov's ideas about narrative and generic structures, see Hawkes, 1977).

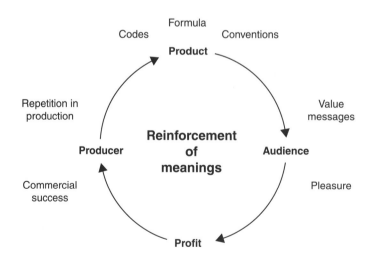

Genre: The circle of repetition and reinforcement
Pleasures for the audience and profits for the institutions help maintain a continuous relationship between the two, as well as reinforcing both conventions and their meanings.
(Graeme Burton: *Talking Television: An Introduction to the Study of Television*, Arnold, 2000)

Of course the exact nature of the elements and of their combination is so varied that the formula can be satisfied (and the audience), without the progress and outcome being entirely predictable. The formula is dominated by fictional examples, but is not peculiar to fiction. The very existence, the life of the formula is prolonged and made known to the audience precisely because the media use it so much. Even game shows work to this formula: the quiz master is a narrator; the contestants are protagonists in opposition to one another; the studio set is iconic; sometimes the contestants (personalities who return week after week) become stock characters; the plot line resolves with one team winning but everyone going away as friends.

The formula and its patterns satisfy in the audience a need for predictability, for security: variations on the formula satisfy a need for some excitement, for risk and the unexpected within a safe framework. Neale (1995) emphasizes the point that the formula creates repetition, yet also frees up a genre creatively so that it can be different: 'genres are best understood as processes. These processes may, for sure, be dominated by repetition, but they are also marked fundamentally by difference, variation and change.'

Problems of genre

The formula becomes a way of identifying a genre – perhaps where this is not immediately obvious. It links to Barthes' readerly texts, where textual patterns and meaning are, at least in the first place, familiar and easy for the reader. Implicitly it identifies those texts which are not genres: the writerly texts where the audience has to work harder on the material to produce meanings. What is not useful, I suggest, is to engage in debates of the 'when is a genre not a genre' variety. I happen to think that film noir is a style, to be found in a range of genres, but mainly yoked with crime thrillers. Similarly, I would argue that melodrama can most easily be seen as a mode of realism and as a matter of style. It is not formulaic in the way that a soap is. I find it confusing when people talk about autobiography as a genre, when it has only one dominant feature, or about children's programmes, which have nothing predictable in common. They are generic in terms of being a category, but not a genre as such. But in the end, what we define as genre formulaic material is significant for *what* it is, rather than for *how* it is. What matters is what genres reveal about industrial practices, about the process of audience reading, about its representations of social reality, about its relationship to ideas such as hegemony or identity.

These comments pick up some of the 'problems' of genre study. As Feuer points out (1992) much genre study has been partly an exercise in taxonomy, partly a critical attempt to promote the value of one genre, or of certain examples of genre texts above others. Film criticism in particular has a tradition of talking up the worth of popular genre material (e.g. Warshow, Sobchack, Maltby) and its industrial origins, in opposition to an aesthetic tradition which (put simply) valued the art film and the work of the auteur.

Feuer usefully summarizes three approaches to genre study

1 'The aesthetic approach includes all attempts to define genre in terms of a system of conventions that permits artistic expression.'

2 'The ritual approach sees genre as an exchange between industry and audience, an exchange through which a culture speaks to itself.'

3 'The ideological approach views genres as an instrument of control . . . genres are ideological insofar as they serve to reproduce the dominant ideology . . .'

There is also the question of genre critiques which are either inflected by the medium analysed, or by the critical approach imported to inform that criticism. So, one may argue that looking at TV genres is not the same as looking at film because of the different nature of the industries involved and because of the different nature of the audience – text relationship. Similarly, it matters if one uses a specific critical approach through which to analyse a given TV genre.

For example, Mary Ellen Brown (1990) writes of soap operas firstly in terms of their generic characteristics as a product of TV in particular, 'whereas traditional literary narratives have a beginning, a middle and an end, soap opera consists of an ever-expanding middle'. But then Brown chooses to interrogate the genre in terms of feminine discourse and the notion of 'carnival'. Among other points, she concludes that whereas dominant discourse represents the position of mothers in society as unproblematic, in soaps the feminine discourse 'plays with conventions' and recognizes problems. Bakhtin's ideas about 'carnival' are invoked in relation to an argument that female viewers are invited to 'participate' in the world of the soaps, and perhaps to challenge the conditions of the world in which they live.

Brown is interested in texts as they are 'read', not in isolation. This is also the case for Gauntlett and Hill (1999), in a piece on gender and television. What is interesting is their reference to 'history' and to 'change', for both TV genres and their audiences. One is not talking about a static form – 'the soap operas that were largely shunned by 1970s men were clearly different in content from the soap formulas which have become relatively popular with men today. Therefore the percentage of "men who watch soap operas" actually has *a different meaning*'. The writers argue that a study of gender representations from a TV genre text broadcast many years ago does not have much relevance to a contemporary study, least of all in respect of influence and gender formation. In this sense, genre study must be ongoing and updated.

10.2 Expectations

Producers and audience are linked by their knowledge of the formula. Sometimes this relationship is even self-conscious, as with the Wes Craven series of *Scream* movies, which partly depend on viewer knowledge of other horror movies and of what has gone before in the series.

Expectation becomes a creative advantage when the producers know that there are some things they do not have to explain. So the formula is both a cage within which the producer must operate and a framework within which the producer can build different versions. It is both a trap for the imagination of the reader and a structure on which that imagination can build. It closes down some meanings, yet opens up others. It depends on producing preferred readings about the genre in general, but allows for oppositional readings. So in the case of a film like *Black Hawk Down* (2002), expectations are ideologically satisfied in terms of reading ideas about masculinity, heroism and patriotism. But, oppositionally, military authority and the state behind it may be read as being seriously incompetent.

Expectation turns into a commercial tool when marketing campaigns are designed to raise hopes and tap into prior knowledge, to create anticipation of fresh pleasures to come on the basis of past pleasures enjoyed. Expectation satisfied through the text, through the anticipation of the formula and the challenge of the unexpected, turns into an audience pleasure that depends on the fact of the material being genre.

10.3 Conventions

What is expected are the conventions which rule the construction of the genre. The elements of the formula are conventions: the ways that they are used can also be called conventions. So the car chase is not only a conventional piece of content, of plotting, in a crime thriller. Its use in showing off the quality of the hero, or pitting hero against villain, is also a convention. In addition, one may argue that creating the excitement of the chase by using the squeal of tyres on the soundtrack is a convention of form.

So this prior knowledge of the 'rules' of genre helps the reader anticipate what will happen and how. It helps the reader to make sense of the text. It both closes down meanings and yet also gives the producer a clear foundation on which to compose the text. The operation of conventions in genres is comparable to the formal definition of conventions within semiotics – rules about the combination and use of signs which help make sense of them. It opens up the same debates about how far textual meaning is predictable and can be the preference of the producer (a closed text), and how far texts may be genuinely **polysemic** and open to the preferences of the reader (an open text). Conventions have to be strong enough that some meaning is possible, and so that a degree of social sharing of meaning is possible. Genres take this sharing on to a central area of common ground, where beliefs and values as meanings have a pretty wide currency. There is, as it were, an ideological consensus which is appealed to and re-affirmed, about such subjects as masculinity, heterosexuality, loyalty, social roles. But also from this common ground, from the security of this consensus, genres are also able to question and re-evaluate some subjects.

Conventions are powerful in the way that they frame meaning and make some meanings predictable. They give power to the producer to play games with the audience's understanding of the text. They give power to the producer as a marketer of texts: conventional and iconic elements of genres tap into beliefs and pleasures of the reader. So they are part of the influence of the marketing devices which sell novels or movies by referring to these elements. Audiences are brought to want to consume the text because they want to revisit the emotional turmoil of a battle scene or of a love affair, for instance.

They also give a kind of power to the reader, the power to predict some of the meanings that the text will propose. The reader can predict some content and narrative development, and is left freer to attend to how these things are handled. This position on reader power implicitly says that media producers do not absolutely dominate just because they make the texts in which the conventions appear. The idea of conventions, the idea of 'genre-ness', is something which lives in a cultural space. It is not an object like a spring washer, to be copyrighted and controlled by the source of production, and which can only be used in a particular way. Convention is more like a force which producer and reader can tap into. At the same time, one has to accept that the relationship between producers and readers is unequal, in that this force is contained by the producers in the first place, within the construction called the text. Reader power depends on accessing the force of conventions and re-using it.

10.4 Intertextuality and post-modernism

The idea of the reader using the text, even playing with it, is one part of post-modern views on genres. In one sense, this idea has been around for some time through the example material like the murder mystery thriller series or the action hero comics. In these cases, the 'writers' know that they have a fan base which enjoys being teased by thwarted expectations, which enjoys meeting familiar characters. The fans write in to the producers about questions of continuity, probability, scientific possibility. This exchange cannot take place in real time because of the nature of the medium, the mechanics of production and distribution. But there is an intensity about the relationship, through the genre material, which pushes towards the quality of a live, real-time conversation. The writer plays with the reader: the reader knows that the writer is doing this: the writer knows that the reader knows. The writer invites the reader to enjoy their shared world.

In this shared world (as with a soap opera) one text about Inspector Morse or Spiderman is understood with reference to another. This cross-referencing is what intertextuality is about. It works on many levels of generality or particularity. It works both on an unconscious level in the mind of the reader, but also consciously, as with the example just given. Unconsciously, one may cross-refer an archetypal protagonist in one genre with the hero in another genre. One may understand the importance of a chase scene in a road movie with reference to a similar scene in a spy thriller. But then the references may operate within the genre – kinds of robot in science fiction. The references may operate temporally, when scenes or characters refer back to earlier examples. This intertextuality, it is argued, has a special intensity in defining post-modern texts. Pam Grier was used as an actress in Tarantino's film *Jackie Brown* partly because she had previously appeared in Blaxploitation thrillers of the 1960s and 1970s.

Not all post-modern texts are genres, but genre has always depended on referentiality. So it lends itself to this intertextual intensity, where form and style lead over content and structure. Even back in 1978 a film like Walter Hill's *The Driver* was a distillation of other heist/crime movies. This film self-consciously did not name its characters because they referred to generic types in other movies. And if the quality of irony includes a certain cynicism about the world, plus juxtaposition of characters and events to create this ambience, then again genre films lend themselves to this quality of post-modernism. A film like Hill's *Last Man Standing* is intertextual in its debt to Kurosawa's movie *Yojimbo*; it also contains ironic comment on the quality of heroism and the lack of integrity in human nature.

Intertextual qualities can reduce a text to an anorak's game of 'spot the reference'. But they can also add resonance and layers of meaning. Genres lend themselves to intertextuality because the audience already knows the essentials of plot and character. It is also true that at least some of the audience for a given genre form a committed fan

Posh and Becks: Alastair McGowan and Ronnie Ancona – satire and intertextuality
What other examples of media text can you think of, which depend on the audience knowing about the source(s) which it refers to?
What may this say about the 'problem of meaning' and about the part that popular culture plays in our lives?
(*BBC*)

base, and this means that they have the intensive knowledge of, say, gothic horror or romantic melodrama which is there to be woven into the text.

10.5 Myths, discourses and ideologies

Generic texts are at the heart of popular culture. They have become generic because they are popular. The TV presentation of a football match works to a formula, as much as a magazine for young women. They are popular because they tell the stories we want to hear. They give us characters we can fit into our view of the world. They give us a view of relationships, motivation, a moral universe, a structure of beliefs which also fits this view of the world. In fact, they give us a view of the world. More than this, they have already given us such a view: we grow up with genres. So if genres contain ideas about who we are, how we should live, what kind of moral and social structure we should inhabit, then they have generated, repeated and reinforced those ideas. Genres are not, of course, the only influence on people as they develop. But, in the context of information about time spent on viewing and reading genre material, then they are at least significant in helping form the ideas by which we live. The very fact of repetition and reinforcement, the inclination to consume genres and their ideas because they are pleasurable, makes them significant among other texts.

Genres are ideological because, for instance, they naturalize ideas about social role, they endorse ideas about social, economic and political power, they promote ideas about what is true and what is false. They are central to a dynamic relationship between media and society in which genre reflect and promote ideological positions. One might say that they draw on what is 'out there' and reshape it to some extent. At the same time, society consumes genres and draws on their representations in a process of reinforcing its ideas (but also evaluating them to some extent). There is a complexity to this view of exchange and transformation – dynamic interaction. A simple model of media reflecting society or of a helpless society being shaped by the media will not do.

In the mafioso television series *The Sopranos*, Tony Soprano is on the one hand a traditional model for the audience of masculine physicality, aggression, social power and paternalism. On the other hand, the motif of his visits to the psychiatrist (with his own reflections on his behaviour), come from a social world in which masculine identity is being questioned. The dynamic, the uncertainty, plays off the genre framework. Traditionally the mafiosi were certain of their place in the world, of the rightness of their values. Tony – indeed a number of characters – are both certain and uncertain at the

The Cowboy as Media Icon of a Culture and of Ideology
What does this image say about the following: the use of conventions in genre material; the history and cultural persistence of genre material; the presence of mythologies about masculinity?
(*Corbis*)

same time. The genre framework gives a point of reference from which the questioning can begin. *The Sopranos* is about ideological divisions. If genres are ideological then they are also full of discourses. In *The Sopranos* these are dominant discourses of gender, family and crime. And discourses help construct myths.

Myths are dominant ideas produced by discourses, about culture and society. Myths centre around dominant ideological positions on their subject, and may be focused through characters and roles. For example, the 'whore with the heart of gold' focuses the myth (also seen in other kinds of female character) that there are women 'out there' who are – into sex for its own sake; can give (the man, of course) sex without responsibility; and will also be kind and non-judgemental. This kind of myth is altogether convenient for and unthreatening to the male.

Myths have deep cultural roots and are part of the history of a given genre. Dracula is clearly a figure of masculine power – the ravisher – yet also an expression of deeper fears about general cultural invasion – evil taking over the world. *Star Trek* draws on the myth of frontiers and discovery, of uncomplicated codes of conduct, beliefs in order and loyalty – a world where everyone knows their place, and in the end assimilates the universe into that world. 'Myths and genres are universal forms . . . they represent "the way in which a particular culture has embodied both mythical archetypes and its own preoccupations in narrative form" ' (Real, 1989).

One should be clear that here one is talking about something that is partly to do with Barthean mythologies in semiotics, but which is also to do with wider definitions of mythologizing. Cultural myths structure the text, yet are concealed within it – made invisible by the language of discourse, which naturalizes views about its subject so that one cannot think about them in any other way. So any media text may refer to myths. In Barthean terms one might refer, for instance, to the fact that it is quite common for advertisements to invoke the myth of status linked to the acquisition of certain goods or commodities. As a myth it is merely an idea. Part of its falsity lies in the fact that, for example, wearing a Rolex watch is not a guarantee of status. The myth of status may well be invoked in a piece of genre material, but genres go further into mythologizing, through their repetitions and the development of their histories. They create 'stories about' social roles, gender roles, ways of living. They promote myths favourable to the dominant ideology and to a culture's view of itself. A collection of such myths in American culture has been about how 'we won the West', 'we won the war', 'we are winning the fight against crime'.

What should also be apparent is that myths are about illusion and falsity, while not necessarily being simply invalid. We want to believe the ideas that form the myths in genres, even if they aren't true. Part of the popularity of genres is precisely because they contain this quota of wish-fulfilment. Romantic novels perpetuate the possibility of the caring, sensitive male – not to mention the primacy of life-long, committed relationships. There is nothing invalid about either of these ideas. What is mythological is the romantic world in which this man, this relationship, is idealized and out of step with the messy and problematic realities of the world which the reader actually inhabits.

History

These comments also remind us that genres do indeed have a history, on which producers and audience may also draw for understanding. It is a history in which the genre develops its repertoire of conventions and renews itself (or not), perhaps be creating new sub-genres. But that history is not a matter of truth and document. War films like *Saving Private Ryan* (1998) may be about actual events, and may indeed be praised for their verisimilitude. But that genre also has its own history of manufacturing heroes, of revisionism in the cause of favouring Western ideology, of negative representations of real or imagined former enemies. Similarly, the history of US gangsters is 'rewritten' through the development of the genre to explore the anti-hero, to exploit violence, to investigate the line between legitimate enterprise and illegitimate crime. Facts are changed and personalities are mythologized as the genre develops. And some genres do not have even the semblance of historical fact to secure their narrative. Notably, the horror film draws on cultural myths and seminal texts (usually novels) to build a fictional history that makes yet more myths out of the original fantasies. So the history of genres can tell us a lot about the times in which the texts were made, but not about historical 'truth' as such.

Genres often fall into groups of films – cycles in their history – which in retrospect represent prevailing concerns and beliefs of the period in which they were made. Television series such as *The Sweeney* or *Starsky and Hutch*, from the 1970s, represent an implied contemporary desire to find action heroes who would deal boldly with crime. Crime was seen as more violent and more of a problem than it was in, say, the 1950s.

'Genre serves as a barometer of the social and cultural concerns of cinema-going audiences' (Hayward, 2000). As a 'barometer' of society, genres cannot help but be profoundly ideological. They may have the power to subvert or challenge, within their traditional form and structure; but they also have that tradition. It would not strike a chord with the audience if it was not about established ways of understanding the world. So, much genre material reinforces traditional gender roles, reinforces traditional ideas about maintaining order in society. Indeed many story lines are about ideological differences, about threats to the status quo and about the restoration of order.

> Different genres possess . . . their own ways of resolving the ideological issues with which they deal. The science fiction film is set in the future and deals with the intrusion of 'others'; the gangster film is set in the present and deals with the contradictions that stem from striving for social and financial success; and the western is set in the past and deals with the ethics of violence.
>
> **Neale (2000)**

It should also be said that Neale balances ideas about ideologically determinist readings of genres with comment on the variety of genre material, and on the complexity of genre background – history and industrial processes. In other words, not all genres are simply vehicles for a dominant ideology.

10.6 Genre and the political economy

Genre material is not only attractive to audiences because of its pleasures and its approvable ideological positions, it is also attractive to institutions because of its predictability and because of its economies of scale.

The fact of the formula means that the production side of genre material is relatively predictable. The production team has at least some prior understanding of how schemes may be handled, what materials may be used, how the elements may be put together. Its predictability means that it is easier to budget for costs. Its predictability means that it is more possible to predict success in the marketplace – this applies to generic forms such as the series, the serial and the sequel, as well. The familiar profile of genre material, especially iconic elements, means that it is easier to market than one-off, individual texts. It is no quirk of fashion the British television broadcasts fewer original single dramas than it did 15 years ago, but produces far more examples of genres and of series.

Of course, the drive for success (profit and beating the competition), sharpened by the considerable cost of production (in movies most of all) means that economic imperatives favour genres, yet do them no favours. This means that the 'play safe' syndrome favours another series of the television soap *Neighbours* so long as the ratings hold up, but is reluctant to take a risk on a pilot for an unknown series (even one that is within a known genre). This means that more and more genre material is needed. This is especially true for television, where the number of channels continues to expand. What cannot be bought is the creative impulse which produces new versions of genres. What has happened is that economic imperatives undermine genre when they exhaust them.

Genres become the weapons of the global corporations as they fight in the marketplace for audience share and for the approval of the advertisers. Syndication, spin-off products, different media versions of the text, add to the economic lustre of the original, successful genre text.

It may also be argued that, with reference to politics and regulation, that genres are often ideologically conservative or, if subversive, they cloak their opposition with the familiarity of the formula. Not that I am suggesting that genres are always uncontroversial. But the controversy usually relates to sex, violence and 'bad language'. Government seeks to regulate this in the public interest, but institutions seek to exploit it in the interests of marketing. Controversy can become free publicity. The two great institutions of media and government dance around one another, negotiating their interests. Government invokes criteria of 'taste', media invoke criteria of realism or of creative freedom. But neither seriously challenges what some might see as the tyranny of the marketplace, which to a fair extent denies the audience alternative texts. So one might argue that the depiction and presence of violence in many genre texts is not so much a 'problem', as is, for example, the implicit endorsement of to whom the violence is done. The idea of regulating out of texts violence done to women, or to other nationalities, or even to criminals, would become a lot more controversial because it is ideological.

10.7 Genre and the illusion of pluralism

The commercial success of generic forms multiplies the amount of media material in circulation. Genres such as news, and looser categories such as children's programmes, now occupy whole channels of broadcasting. But there is little or no evidence that this expansion of material brings about exploration of the form. We have news or children's programmes done in much the same way as before, only there are more of them. This is not consumer choice, nor is it pluralism except by numbers. If pluralism is to mean anything then it must involve plurality of forms for a plurality of audiences. It should mean plurality of points of view. It should serve minorities as well as majorities.

A successful genre text in any medium is likely to produce replications of the text or spun-off additions based on the core text. But again, more is the same. Similarly, a successful text will induce imitations with the same characteristics. The novel *Longitude* was followed by any number of dramatized science factual stories. This is not to argue that all imitations are without merit, but that the extension of generic forms produces only an illusion of pluralism.

The debate about what constitutes pluralism takes an interesting twist when one reflects that the commercial response to criticism is, 'it is what people want, and it sells, and it keeps some people in work'. Such a material argument neatly avoids any reflection on questions such as: Why do people want such material? How do they come to have such wants? Which people don't want it? Which people might enjoy texts that are denied production support? How does anyone know what they want if they can't see what might be on offer? Who really decides what we do or don't want, anyway?

In terms of genres, one might say that a media model in which the market rules, produces false pluralism – economies of production, targeting of the most profitable audiences (of whatever size), play-safe production decisions, repetition of formulaic material. A model in which there is disinterested regulation and the protection of experimental and challenging producers and texts, should produce some exploratory and innovative genre material. Genre can provide a shelter under which some ideological goosing of dominant views and of the establishment can take place. Genre formulas can provide a reference point for experiments with form or with the representation of character types. This would be the kind of pluralistic environment in which choice and variety is not just an illusion.

The question is, how may we create that kind of environment, in which multinationals do not determine our choice of texts, and in which we may easily obtain that choice of texts and those points of view which indeed serve a multi-cultural and varied society?

11 Discussion extract

66 99 In general terms, if semiology provides a way of analysing meanings, and ideology provides a way of talking about the relationship between meanings and social structures, what discourse theory has achieved is a way of re-thinking that relationship. At the heart of the matter is the question of social power. ... Ideology theory talks about the imposition of dominant meaning systems, and is interested in the way people are

recruited to, and possibly resist, those dominant systems. But the power that establishes the dominance of these systems is, in ideology theory, an external social power; it might, in simple Marxist accounts, be the ruling class that has this power; in more complex versions, dominant ideologies are reproduced by the social system. In discourse theory, however, power is not external but internal to meaning systems; meaning systems themselves are powerful. This is because meaning systems are now seen, not simply as systems (structured like language), but also as signifying practices. And it is not simply that meanings are embedded within social practices (as they are in Althusser's theory of ideology); meaning and practice are now indistinguishable. Meaning *is* practice, in discourse theory. The particular theory of discourse I am introducing here derives from the work of Michel Foucault.

and referring to Janice Winship's analysis of the ideology of sex and sexuality in the magazine *Cosmopolitan*. . . .

Moreover, like other women's magazines, *Cosmopolitan* is generally obsessed with sex, both in terms of the amount of space it devotes to sexual technique and to the discussion of sexual problems. But this can be seen as one instance of a more general phenomenon, discussed by Foucault in *The History of Sexuality* (Vol. 1). Here he is interested in the fact that, despite the alleged 'Victorian' repression of sex, western societies, since the eighteenth century, appear to have been continuously preoccupied with sexuality and sexual 'problems'. Sex has become a subject for scientific and social investigation; but, more generally, it has become a popular cultural obsession . . .

Foucault argues that it [sex] performs some important and useful 'governmental' functions. Sexual orientation can be used to classify individuals; alleged sexual 'perversions' can justify forms of 'treatment'; but, more generally, the pursuit of sexual fulfilment is a major way in which people 'discipline' themselves. In our culture, happiness is defined by sexual goals, which in turn require appropriate forms of living (for example as heterosexual couples). In Foucault's general perspective, this is one way in which social populations are 'policed'.

Andrew Tolson (1996)

1 Explain in your own words how Tolson sees the difference between discourse theory and ideology theory with relation to ideas about power.

2 What is Foucault's view of the significance of 'sexual obsession' in our culture?

3 With relation to discourses of the male or the female, discuss the idea that 'meaning and practice are now indistinguishable'.

12 Further reading

Allen, R. (ed.) (1992) *Channels of Discourse Reassembled*. London: Routledge.
Bignell, J. (1997) *Media Semiotics*. Manchester: Manchester University Press.
Bordwell, D. (1988) *Narrative in the Fiction Film*. London: Routledge.
Doyle, G. (2002) *Media Economics*. London: Sage.
Graddol, D. and Boyd-Barrett, O. (1994) *Media Texts – Authors and Readers*. OU/Multilingual Matters: Clevedon.

Hall, S. (ed.) (1997) *Representation – Cultural Representations and Signifying Practices.* London and Buckingham: Sage/Open University.

Hallam, J. with Marshment, M. (2000) *Realism and Popular Cinema.* Manchester: Manchester University Press.

Lacey, N. (2000) *Narrative and Genre.* Basingstoke: Palgrave.

Neale, S. (2000) *Genre and Hollywood.* London: Routledge.

Thwaites, T., Davies, L., and Mules, W. (1994) *Tools for Cultural Studies.* Melbourne: Macmillan.

Tolson, A. (1996) *Mediations – Text and Discourse in Media Studies.* London: Arnold.

Wasko, J. (2003) *How Hollywood Works.* London: Sage.

CHAPTER THREE

AUDIENCES AND EFFECTS

Defining audiences and exploring their relationships with texts

❝ . . . we note five main traditions of research in this area: (1) effects research, (2) uses and gratifications research, (3) literary criticism, (4) cultural studies, (5) reception analysis . . .

In simplified terms, the sets of theories available in the area may be divided into the humanistic type and the social-science type . . .

The social-science type theories have been developed mainly within the traditions of effects research and U & G research, often on the basis of more general psychological, social-psychological and sociological theories. They are usually transformed into graphical and statistical models of processes of influence whose elements and inter-relations may be tested by formalized procedures. The humanistic type theories, in their turn, derive mainly from the traditions of literary criticism and cultural studies. They are systematic but as a rule not formalizable descriptions of how content structures – media discourses – come to carry specific meanings for recipients in a particular social context. In reception analysis, attempts are being made to combine the two types of theories. ❞

Klaus Jensen and Karl Rosengren (1990) Five traditions in search of the audience, in Blumler, J.G. et al. *European Journal of Communication*, Vol. 5, nos 2–3. London: Sage.

1 Introduction

In one sense, having followed a sequence of chapters, from institutions to audiences, it may seem as if we are following a **transmission model** for media. I want to dispel that notion. It is true that in textual terms, one can see one kind of sequential process model in which the text is conceived, manufactured, distributed and finally consumed by the audience. The model works for the individual text, up to a point. But in terms of the relationship between the media in general and the audience as members of society, I would like to remind you of that dynamic process model, in which the parts stand in a more equal relationship with one another. This is a model in which the media industries are simultaneously institutions of society, proposers of information to society, and drawers of material from society. This is a relationship in which, as manufacturers of representations, the media variously and simultaneously remake versions of society, but also are themselves shaped by forces within that society.

Rather than choose between critical positions summarized in terms of 'the media do things to people' or 'people do things with the media', I want to propose that both views are true. You will remember that I have already suggested that while it may be true that institutions produce texts within which certain devices prefer certain kinds of under-standing, it is also true that the audience reads the text. The text has the potential for meaning, and perhaps the potential for selective and partial meanings. But this potential is not realized until some process of cognition in the mind of the audience/reader actually 'makes sense' of that text.

I also want to remind you that behind this debate about the relationship between three core concepts is the further debate about the general relationship between media and society. In this case and in connection with ideas about influence, one is referring back to determinist and pluralist positions. I would remind you of issues around these positions.

- Do the media determine the nature of that relationship, and is the operation of the media itself determined by dominant forces such as those of economics?
- Or are the media so plural in their institutions and texts that no such determining influence is possible?
- Does this plurality mean that the relationship is one in which the audience can make choices not just about what it consumes, but also about the meaning it makes from this consumption?

There is a dominant critical tradition within the media – audience debates that assumes 'an effect on' those audiences. But there is also a newer tradition – ethnographic survey/reception analysis – which sidesteps this to examine 'the relationship between' media and audience. I would point out that the nature of relationships affects both elements, so one cannot simply hit the effects debate out of court. But it is true that, even having ideology within one's terms of reference, looking at how things happen, rather than assigning a determining power to the media producer alone, seems to offer a less assumptive, more openly enquiring approach to audience study.

2 Major questions

So major questions about audience in the context of media study which one needs to address are to do with who it is exactly that we are talking about when we use the term 'audience', and with how that audience stands in relation to both media texts and the producers of texts.

1 How do we understand the term 'audience', given the difference between the actuality of the reader as an individual, and the notion of audiences as coherent groups?

2 How should we understand audiences in terms of the marketplace?

3 How may audiences be understood as being 'active' in their engagement with texts, and how far does any such activity give audiences power over the production of meaning?

4 How may we understand the process of audiences reading texts?

5 In respect of visual media, how should we understand the act of looking, in relation to representation, and especially with regard to gender?

6 What do we mean by audience pleasure in the text? In what respects might one validate such pleasures, and in what ways may they be an expression of the producers' hold over the audience?

7 In what ways can we see the audience as having access to a public sphere created by the media, in which debates take place?

8 What are the dominant views of the process of media influence on the audience? What factors modify such views?

9 What evidence is there for various kinds of media effect on the audience? What are the problems with researching such effects?

10 How may we recognize gender differences in audience relationships with given media texts?

3 Concepts of audiences

The term 'audience' is problematic. There are assumptions made about it which do not stand up to examination. For example, the idea of audience as a collection of people experiencing a performance may be true for live theatre, but is not true for magazine readers. There is not even a collection of people in one place at one time. The idea of mass audience is hardly valid, only on a relative scale of numbers. The significance of any audience may lie in its composition as much as in its numbers. The scale may run from tens of thousands to millions. I am not saying that media audiences are insignificant for their size. It is difficult not to assume some process or degree of influence in this case. But it is also difficult to define or prove this influence. Certainly the conditions under which Marxist critiques of mass audience and mass culture were formed, no longer exist. In the past 50 years the number of media and the range of media texts has increased immeasurably. This has not just expanded the numbers of the audience, but has also fragmented it. We should not ignore the 15 million or so viewers for peak-time popular TV programmes, but we should also understand that one has moved from the dominance of broadcasting to more **narrowcasting**. In the 1940s, mass media were dominantly the press, cinema and radio, with the music industry rapidly expanding in size. There is no longer this coherence and focus, not least if one considers what new technologies have done to expanding the range of media. The very idea of audience in relation to the Internet or to multi-functional mobile phones is problematic, though not totally invalid. Just as film is no longer all about movie theatres, so music is no longer all about sales of discs. Just as film is no longer dominated by a mass audience attending by the week, so music is no longer about a few dominant genres and mass purchase in specialist stores. This further undermines the notion of audience as a coherent term. Now there are both large and small audiences, general and specialized audiences.

It is also arguable that the social and cultural coherence of audiences has changed greatly in the past 50 years. The demarcation between a working class marked by lack of mobility and dependence on employment in manufacturing, and a middle class with a markedly greater income no longer holds true. Class still exists, but in different terms. And anyway the media industries are only interested in spending power. Now,

Family Watching TV
This image of the family gathered in front of the television set, intently watching a programme, is not supported by audience/reception studies.
    In what ways do television viewing practices differ from this image?
(*Corbis*)

a school-age person can save up to spend £200 on Playstation 2. In the 1950s, they would save to spend the price of a bag of sweets on a cinema ticket – very possibly to see the same film that their parents would go out to see. Now the movie-going audience is fragmented into categories of consumption – youth, family, 'adult', art-cinema goers. For the industries these are niche markets. For the critic this relates to the arrival of 'narrowcasting' – specialist magazines, dedicated channels.

The more closely one examines the characteristics of those who watch a programme or who read a newspaper, the more differentiated the audience members become. This increasing differentiation also increases the variables in any assessment of effects and influence. The more variables, the less easy it is to say that a given text is likely to affect its audience in a distinctive manner.

But the 'opposite problem' is that, in terms of reception studies, while looking at very specific audiences may reveal the 'truth' of individual response, it undermines the possibility of generalization about influence. This is the disadvantage of detailed ethnographic surveys. 'Much audience theory remains over-concerned with the microscopic worldview of socially dispersed viewers, readers and listener' (Stevenson, 2002).

One needs to juggle the quantitative evidence of research into macro-audience preferences with the more qualitative evidence of micro-audience research into detailed pleasures, responses and behaviours. Knowing how a selected group of women enjoy some soap operas does not prove that women in general are influenced by most soaps. Equally, knowing the viewing figures by age and gender for given soaps says little about the meanings which specific groups of female viewers may construct into their lives.

'Audience' is also complicated by having to allow for, in the case of television, the presence of both primary and secondary audiences. The former would be the studio audience for the chat show, the fans at the outside broadcast (OB) of a rock concert, the crowd on screen at a football match; the latter will be the audience at home. The experience of the programme as event is clearly different for each of the primary and secondary audiences. So also the meanings are different.

4 The commodified audience

Audiences are defined as commodities by the media because those industries want to objectify their natures and their existence. They want to quantify the idea of audience.

The audience may be fragmented into categories by interest, e.g. for video – sport, 'keep fit', drama, porn. The media industries have a vested interest in validating the idea of audience as a meaningful and coherent term. If they can't define their audiences in terms which validate investment by backers and expenditure by advertisers, then they don't have a business.

Audiences are defined and delivered in terms of number – reader figures, circulation figures, box-office figures, viewing figures and so on. These numbers are worth money, not least for those media where their output is sold by the unit (for example, magazines, CDs). Quantity analysis may be refined by such factors as region of sale or time of viewing. It may be further defined as in the case of television where television ratings (TVRs) measure the numbers of the target audience for the programme who are

The Weakest Link: Multiple audiences
The audience at home looks on the audience in the studio, which in turn looks on the entertainment taking place before it. The studio audience becomes part of that entertainment.
        What does this do for our understanding of the term 'audience'?
(BBC)

watching at the time of broadcast. This is as distinct from the total audience, and may include features such as gender and occupation.

In such terms does the audience itself become a commodity to be bought and sold. Indeed, it may be argued that the media manufacture audiences: they do not discover them. These audiences have a value in the marketplace of rate cards, circulation managers and media brokers. The success of the media producer is measured in terms of 'audience as goods' as much as on the basis of any critical estimation.

For the media producer, audiences may be defined as 'audience profile', which is in turn defined by features such as age, gender and disposable income. What matters is the producers' ability to target the audience and its purchasing power. Audiences may also be defined in terms of the product type which they prefer, which in turn relates to their interests. This is why marketing devices such as The National Households Survey are used, to try and define such interests. This is a generic audience: the readers of computer magazines or of romantic fiction. More specifically, one could define audiences by the particular product consumed: the audience for *The Washington Evening Post* or for *Harpers* or for *The David Letterman Show*. Similarly, broadcast channels seek to identify and attract their 'type' of audience. The more specific the material broadcast, the more specific the audience identity is – from Discovery Channel to local radio.

And even where qualitative elements appear in descriptions of audiences by the media, it is always an adjunct to quantity. Lifestyle or psychographic descriptions of audiences' character and social behaviour is ultimately linked to factors such as disposable income, purchasing habits and the numbers in the group so defined. The media

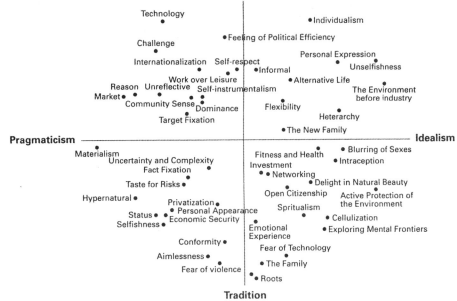

Innovation

Technology
• Individualism
• Feeling of Political Efficiency
Challenge
Personal Expression
Internationalization Self-respect
• Unselfishness
•Informal
Work over Leisure
• Alternative Life
Reason Unreflective Self-instrumentalism
The Environment
Market •
before industry
Community Sense
Dominance
Flexibility
Target Fixation
Heterarchy
• The New Family

Pragmaticism ———————————————————— **Idealism**

Materialism
• Blurring of Sexes
Uncertainty and Complexity
Fitness and Health
• Intraception
Fact Fixation
Investment
• Networking
Taste for Risks •
• Delight in Natural Beauty
Hypernatural •
Open Citizenship Active Protection of
Privatization•
the Environment
Status • • Personal Appearance
Spritualism
Selfishness • Economic Security
• Cellulization
Emotional
• Exploring Mental Frontiers
Experience
Conformity •
Fear of Technology
Aimlessness •
• The Family
Fear of violence
• Roots

Tradition

RISC Chart of Values
Research into Social Change attempts to segment people as audience or consumers, according to their
preferred life values. Research via interviews and questionnaires may deal with groups as small as a single
family. These groups can be placed on the chart and described in terms of the main values they espouse, and
in terms of the four key qualities which make up the axes of the chart. The numbers of groups from an area and
their placing helps identify a kind of consumer in that target area.
(Reprinted by permission of Sage Publications Ltd from 'The best of both worlds? Media audience research
between rival paradigms' by Kim Christian Schrøder in *Rethinking the Media Audience* edited by Pertti
Alasuutari, 1999)

want to be able to categorize people, for commercial reasons. This does not mean to say
that these categories are valid.

And, of course, all this commodification rides on the back of the related industry of
market research. Generally speaking media industries sub-contract their audience
investigation, description and measurement to others who then also have a vested interest in the commodification of audience and the validity of their findings. In Britain there
is the Broadcasters' Audience Research Board or the National Readership Survey.

This commodified audience may be seen as the audience which is 'spoken at' by the
institution and through the text. It is in effect addressed as an object, as constructed
groups, within the terms of reference of the market. This is the target audience as
conceived by the producers, the audience of the advertisers' world. It is not the more
complex audience of a real world, as it lives, and as it is studied through critical audience
approaches to the media.

It may also be seen as the 'audience in the text'. In this case one has to understand
how media texts find ways of putting into themselves the kind of audience at which they
are aimed. Generally, one only has to ask 'what is it about the text that causes one to
believe that it is aimed at a particular audience, and why?' to identify how that audience
is written into that text.

Part of the writing of the audience into the text may be in the representation of the audience as an ideal type within that text. So TV ads for cars aimed at women include a kind of female whom the target audience might like to be – independent, romantic, assertive. The representation is not a reflection but an idealization, a stereotype. It is an idea about the audience which both producer and viewer would like to be true.

5 The active audience

This is the audience conceived in terms of how it deals with the media. This is about taking a perspective which starts from the view of the audience, not the view of the institution. It is about how the audience engages with the text. The notion of activity draws attention to the part of the audience in making choices, making sense of the text. It allows for the audience being a producer of meanings. The activity referred to is both about the intellectual work of the audience and about kinds of physical reaction around the text.

For example, in terms of context, audiences do not passively engage with media. They use radio as an adjunct to activities such as driving a car or household work. It has been shown that audiences engage in all sorts of activities while 'watching' television – from playing a musical instrument, to forms of housework. Newspapers and magazines may encourage active engagement with quizzes or crosswords, which have nothing to do with news or reading articles.

It is also true to say that audiences can be active in making choices (channel hopping) and in using technology (selectively recording programmes). Indeed, one form of 'resistance' which audiences can now practise against TV is to buy and use various hard-disk recording devices. These can, for instance, screen out advertisements: not good news for the US networks and for British ITV, both of which are slowly but steadily losing audiences and advertising revenue.

The very act of reading requires a process of cognition – constructive cerebral activity to make sense of the text. Of course this kind of activity may vary in its nature and in its intensity, from emotional response, to analysis and reflection. Sonia Livingstone (1990) warns against idealizing the active reader, and might refer to the 'dangers' of readerly genre texts when she says that 'Activity may refer to . . . the more mindless process of fitting the text into familiar frameworks or habits.'

Post-modernist and audience-centred critiques see the audience as taking charge of the production of meaning and as taking their pleasures from the text. In this respect, they argue against the audience as an unresisting victim of the text. Rather, the audience may resist the underlying commercial intentions of the producer.

This inclination to allow the audience autonomy in the production of meaning is best exemplified by John Fiske (*Television Culture*, 1987), in which he makes much of the notion of the 'producerly text'. He argues that television texts 'delegate the production of meaning to the viewer–producer'. But against this critical swing to endorsing the power of the audience in the 1980s one must set the evidence of textual analysis which demonstrates that not all TV material is that malleable in terms of meaning. Programmes are not necessarily 'open texts', though some may be more open than others.

As Morley (1996b) argues, 'the power of the viewer to reinterpret meanings is hardly equivalent to the discursive power of centralised media institutions to construct the texts which the viewer then interprets'. I have already suggested that one should see the audience more as a kind of collaborator in making meanings. It is not possible to demonstrate that audiences resist all the effects potential of media texts.

Wayne (1994) is also against an uncritical view of audience power when he says –

> Problems within the mass culture tradition are more than balanced by the blind spots of popular traditions which come through strongly in audience studies. Here, there has been a tendency to conceive the popular as a realm of cultural self-making where 'the people' reconstruct their identities and their sense of place in the world at will. Thus questions of power and ideology are suppressed by methods which celebrate audience creativity and/or dissolve the text as an object with any effectivity.

Uses and gratifications

One fairly traditional perspective on the audience as a user of text (which also is part of the effects debate) is described as the uses and gratifications approach. In this case it has been assumed that people are motivated by kinds of 'need' in their engagement with the text, as with their engagement with others in social interactions. I will summarize these as

- informational needs;
- personal needs such as maintenance of identity;
- social needs, not least for forms of interaction;
- entertainment needs, including the need for kinds of diversion.

In such cases one might say that a given audience member will take from a text what it says about a personal issue of moral principle, or how it describes social behaviours that are of interest to that individual. The audience is actively selecting aspects of the text for its own use: it is using that material actively to work through interests and concerns. This approach, although it includes the idea of the collective needs of an audience, also tends to emphasize the audience as an individual. This again runs counter to an institutional conception of audiences as coherent, consuming groups.

Ethnography – reception studies

The notion of the active audience relates to a tradition of audience-centred media studies, which has, since the 1980s at least, tried to talk up the importance of the interaction of specific audience members with specific texts. We are back to a struggle over the ownership of the power to produce meanings. Ethnographic research in particular has been used as a way of addressing the qualitative nature of 'audience'. It investigates reception in its context and as a social activity. This approach may include conversational engagement with respondents rather than questionnaires, Ang (1991) says; 'the ethnographer . . . conceptualises media audience-hood as lived experience'.

6 The reading audience

This is the audience in a state of engagement with the text. This conception of audience is about it being engaged in an activity. But audiences as readers are not necessarily understood to be entirely in control of the process of the production of meaning.

Indeed, one approach used by Morley (1989) (drawing from Hall and before that from Parkin's ideas about three 'meaning systems') describes the audience in terms of three different relationships with the text. In each case the audience has more or less autonomy in terms of the sense they make of the material.

- The **preferred reading** is about that meaning which is preferred by the producer, inscribed in the text, and likely to be taken from the text by the reader because the use of various conventions and devices close down other ways of understanding it.
- The **alternative reading** is one that produces meanings which were not intended by the producer but which do not seriously challenge the dominant meaning.
- The **oppositional reading** is one which does so challenge that dominance, and implies a degree of intellectual autonomy in the reader. This kind of analysis also tends to deal in ideology, so that dominant meanings are also about the dominant ideology.

Taking the popular press coverage of the death of Princess Margaret in Britain (2002) as an example, one would say that the preferred reading of this event was in terms of an expected but tragic event of a statusful public figure. Alternatively, it might have been read as the regrettable passing of a life, but of little relevance to the lives of most British citizens. Oppositionally, a reader might have understood it to be a matter of relief that the death of an old-guard member of an anti-democratic institution (the monarchy) made it a little more likely that the abolition of that institution could take place.

The question remains, to what extent is the audience free to resist preferred readings? The answer seems to have a lot to do with the cultural background of the audience member, and with their particular beliefs, attitudes and values within that cultural nexus. Liebes and Katz (1993) have demonstrated that a text may be understood in different ways by those coming to it with different sets of values and priorities.

Silverstone (1994) comments on their work: 'results suggested that cultural and ethnic identity do provide a significant determinant of different relationships to the texts, differences which are an expression of those groups culturally and politically in the wider society'. However, he also disputes that differences of understanding, of moral judgement for example, necessarily mean that the 'ideological force' of the text is blocked. 'Viewers can be critical but still accept the basic, dominant or structural meanings offered by the text.' Yet again the jury stays out on attempts to demonstrate media influence, though the importance of conditioning factors remains pretty clear.

In the initial flush of a structuralist period of media criticism, Hall conceptualized 'audience as reader' as decoders of material. We have to recognize the codes and conventions within a text in order to make sense of the text. He was interested in the relationship between producers and audience in terms of the amount of common ground there was between them (or not). They would share for example knowledge of the codes of news. They would share the ideological background to that news. They would even share understanding of the technologies which produce that news – the use of camera or of satellite links. What concerned him was the extent to which that sharing might close down the possible meaning of a text, the extent to which there was a closed circle of encoding and decoding. Again, this concern was ideological in basis. If drama or news encodes crime as a problem with an inflection of race, then what chance is there for the audience to decode crime as perhaps a problem of selective representation, or perhaps as a problem of how police deal with crime?

At the same time as attention was turning from the text alone to the audience, and to what was entailed in reading, there was also a recognition of the polysemic nature of visual texts in particular. So again, there was a conceptual struggle between the notion of the text closing down meanings for the reader, and the ambiguities of texts (some more than others) which offer more opportunities for different readers to open up different meanings. By the same token, whatever influence is proposed becomes less certain, less specific, more problematic.

The notion of the 'audience as reader' does at least get rid of early critical notions of audiences as some kind of receptacle into which ideas might be poured by the media. But then, even when one understands that audiences do have some part to play in the production of meaning, still there is the question of how that part is conceptualized. Critical views still tend to fall into the model of audience as either victim or as hero. What we need to remember is that, if texts cannot be neutral – and some may be less neutral than others – so too audiences as readers bring their own experiential and ideological baggage to that process of reading. In saying this, I am not suggesting that there is some kind of absolutely truthful reading out there of the film or magazine. But I am drawing attention to the fact that readers may be 'influenced' by factors other than devices in the text, or their experience of the media in general.

The variability of audience experience and attitudes has been used in what Curran (1996) has called 'New Revisionism', which argues that the media do not influence the audience in any consistent or meaningful way. He cites research by Meyer (1976) as typifying findings about the variability of response to the media: 'different types of children, bringing different beliefs, attitudes and values to the viewing of the show as a result of different socialisation processes, are affected in different ways'. Such evidence has been used to talk down media influence and to talk up the importance of the text and of the 'audience as reader' (not as victim). This approach is about reception analysis, not analysis of influence as such. This kind of analysis has been used to emphasize the power of reading, the possibility of making oppositional readings. It argues for ways in which the reader reuses media materials to affirm cultural identity, to resist subordination to that same material.

However, this kind of use and its immediate context (in micro-studies of audience) is also open to the criticism that it fails to take account of a larger industrial and political context to 'use'. Murdock and Golding (2000) criticize the 'romantic celebration of subversive consumption' (see also section 8, Taking pleasure).

7 Gazing and looking (see also Chapter 7)

These terms are relevant to the nature of the audience's engagement with visual texts.

In the first place, some of that engagement may be understood within the context of narrative theory. Ideas about spectator positioning not only relate the audience to the 'narrative as an idea of story' but also to events depicted on the screen. In this respect positioning is about camera placement, and, therefore, where the spectator is placed spatially in relation to the action. That placement also influences the viewer's understanding to the story. So if one's view of a scene is via a camera placed half behind some object, then one is positioned as some kind of spy. If the subject of that scene is some kind of private moment or romantic encounter, then the spectator is positioned as a voyeur. Indeed, the spectator becomes subjectively involved in that thing called 'the story'. The same thing applies if those conventions of camera and editing are used which cause the viewer to adopt the gaze of, and understanding of, one of the characters in the story (subjective camera). Usually the camera/spectator position is something more neutral, in which one is, as it were, just looking in on the scene, at the characters. This is objective camera, or third-person narrative. This kind of spectator position may also be seen in still images. Again, the camera positions the spectator in relation to the subject within the image. This is especially relevant if the subject represents a person. The position helps construct meaning. It is commonplace that a low-angle point of view on a figure produces a sense of the dominance of that figure, especially if that figure is looking down at one, as the viewer.

There is also the matter of the nature of the look. It is not just camera position that causes us to look at certain subjects in certain texts in certain ways. It is to do with the cultural experience that we bring to looking, and to specific media experience which has encouraged certain ways of looking. Looking is not neutral. What we attend to in the image, what sense we make of that image, is an active process. The use of the word 'gaze' in critical theory has intended to replace the falsely neutral sense of the word 'look'. Gaze has been related to gender critiques of media texts in particular. There is the notion (Mulvey *et al.*) that there is a peculiarly male gaze which regards images of woman in a voyeuristic and sexual fashion. It is a gaze which constructs the woman as a sexual being, which objectifies her. This process of objectification may be magnified by camera movement which surveys the woman's body as if it were an object of pleasure, as if it were a man looking. It may be magnified by the selective close-up (common in advertising), which attends to parts of the women's body, making her less than a whole human being. This male gaze, it is theorized, is one which may even be adopted by the female viewer of the image of a woman. It is the female, as it were, taking the man's part, because she has learned that her 'natural' gender role includes being looked at by men. 'The determining male gaze projects its fantasy onto the female figure, which is styled accordingly. In their traditional exhibitionist role women are simultaneously looked at and displayed, with their appearance coded for strong visual and erotic impact so that they can be said to connote *to-be-looked-at-ness*' (Mulvey, 1989).

This same kind of gender positioning is put forward as a way of making sense of the woman who gazes out of the photograph. Many magazine and advertising images of women look at us, the viewer. It is proposed that the female reader may identify with a woman in the image but, as that person, conceive herself as being looked at by men. In the case of sexually provocative looks, it is clear that the women in the picture are encoding messages for the supposed male viewer. But even in the women's magazine, where the viewer may be assumed to be female, still it is suggested that the viewer sees herself as the picture woman who is seeing herself in terms of the male gaze – a kind of indirect engagement.

'*Men act* and *women appear*. Men look at women. Women watch themselves being looked at. This determines not only most relations between men and women but also the relation of women to themselves. The surveyor of woman in herself is male: the surveyed female. Thus she turns herself into an object – and most particularly an object of vision: a sight' (Berger, 1972).

The concept of gaze has also been associated with the idea of an intensity of attention to the image, which is assumed for the film viewing audience in particular. Indeed, John Ellis (1992) coined the term 'glance' to describe how, he believes, television is looked at differently. He argues that television is a less intense experience, in which the audience may be distracted by friends and family, by doing other things at the same time, by practices such as channel hopping. However, I would point out that it has also been shown that audiences watch some television intently, that they are not necessarily very reflective about all movie viewing, and that anyway we gaze upon a wider variety of visual texts. The idea of gaze should be associated not so much with degrees of intentionality, as in terms of how it relates to the production of meaning, the manufacture of identity, and the conduct of social relations.

8 Taking pleasure

The notion of audiences taking pleasure from texts is one which is associated with post-modernism, with feminist critiques and with audience-centred studies. In the first place one may look back to the last section, in terms of the male gaze and the sexual pleasure of voyeurism. Cinema has provided some notorious examples of this kind of gaze and pleasure, including De Palma's *Dressed To Kill* (1980). This included a shower scene much criticized for lengthy gratuitous shots of the female protagonist victim. But then the shower has become a stock setting in its own right for this kind of gaze and pleasure (see promotional shots in mail-order catalogues).

In terms of post-modernism and popular culture texts, the idea of audience pleasure has been set up as both a kind of gratification from that text, and as a kind of validation of the text. So the idea is partly that pleasure is a valid response, but also that this validity transfers to the text. It may be populist, but that is acceptable because it is enjoyed. In one sense this is partly a reaction against that kind of analysis that has seen the text as worthy only in relation to its seriousness of purpose. It is also something of a reaction against a post-modernist and Marxist analysis which goes for the ideological nature of a text and what it imposes on the audience. So in terms of audience studies, validating pleasure is also a way of winning back power for the audience.

Fiske (1993) discusses the pleasure of 'playing with' the text. The referentiality of post-modern texts encourages this. The construction of computer games like *Monkey*

Island Two actually makes this play mandatory. Unless one plays with the choices given and reacts to the 'problems' thrown up, there is no text. Take pleasure, play the game – or there is no game. Fiske argues that audiences enjoy ways in which texts both confirm that there are rules, but also take the audience along on narrative journeys that challenge and break those rules. We can experience death – but outside the trauma of social reality. This is where genres in particular can 'have it both ways'. They depend on intertextuality for their understanding and enjoyment. But precisely because their base material is so well known, it is possible to work off this, to be inventive and challenging.

The taking of pleasure can work on different levels. In the case of game shows, there is a studio audience that is directly involved with the performance. They can enjoy the spectacle, the challenge, the right to respond, at first hand. But then there is the domestic audience, taking pleasure at a distance. There is pleasure in the ritual of the genre – a ritual which is controlled by that lord of misrule, the host. There is pleasure in the possibility of unruly behaviour: the form is largely unscripted. Fiske (1987) – himself drawing on ideas from Bahktin about carnival and excess – sees this kind of populist material as resisting the meanings that might have been imposed by the producer through the text. He talks about 'a theory of pleasure that centres on the power to make meanings rather than on the meanings that are made'. However, Bourdieu (1984) argues against this kind of autonomy. He proposes the notion of 'habitus', in which people are predisposed to respond to experiences in certain ways because they have been so culturalized. We are back to questions about what or who shapes the meanings that come from the experience of engaging with any text. We are circling round the notion of ideology, which lurks behind such ideas about predispositions or about kinds of resistance.

I suggest that, however the post-modernist position tries to marginalize and efface either the presence of ideology or the possible influence of textual features, this is not sensible because it does not actually deal with these two factors. In any case, interests in the working of ideology and the working of audiences on texts do not have to be mutually exclusive.

In terms of feminism in particular, there is literature from Radway through to McRobbie that speaks for the female audience in various ways. Not surprisingly, this criticism addresses what are known as dominantly female texts – the romantic novel, girls' magazines, television soap operas. The female-ness of the texts and of the pleasures is defined in terms of female subject matter and ways of making sense of this. The pleasure is in, for example, the expression and negotiation of emotion and of relationship within the narrative. The pleasure is in identification with character and situation. In terms of uses and gratifications, the pleasures are about satisfying personal and social needs. Sometimes the pleasure is solitary – Radway's readers escaping domestic duty in the world of the novel. Sometimes it is shared – Silverstone's soap viewers talking about how problems in the soap world relate to problems in their own lives, working through problems indirectly by talking about the soap. The problem remains as to whether pleasures are taken or given.

Curiously, the notion of pleasure in texts provides an argument for saying that post-modernism eats itself. So there may indeed be pleasures in the ironies and referentiality of post-modernist form, in the fractured or shadowy narratives of a supposedly typical post-modern text. But the most popular texts – murder mystery thrillers or soaps, for example – are still resolutely modernist in their structures. The grand narratives are still with us. Reports of the death of modernism or indeed of realism, have been greatly exaggerated.

9 Audiences and the public sphere

The notion of a public sphere was proposed by Jurgen Habermas and defined in terms of a 'space' where information could be exchanged and public debate could take place. It may be said that this space could be provided by the media. In terms of politics and democracy, the idea becomes attractive as a kind of electronic substitute for the direct interaction between citizens in the agora of the classical Greek city state (my meta-phor, not Habermas's). The idea is also an attempt to redefine the functions and activities of the media. That is to say, generally speaking, media have been seen (and set up) as a mechanism for broadcasting to an audience. They distribute material for which people pay. Audience members do not generally interact with one another, even in examples such as stage and movie theatres where they literally inhabit the same space. So if the media could become more interactive and more genuinely plural, then something like a public sphere would be created. Ironically, and since Habermas pro-posed his ideas, the Internet has offered a new working model for such a sphere. Bulletin boards and chat rooms attached to 'political' websites offer a discussion space for the Net-connected and Net-literate. But this does not include all citizens, and it does not much affect the conduct of conventional politics. In other words, it is a sphere only adjacent to the lives of many citizens and only tangential to the dominant political process.

The problem is that citizens are not in the end equally free to participate in this public sphere, whatever its form may be. Historically, the evidence is that 'public debate' in fact involved a limited range of literate citizens with access to the media of the time. As Gripsrud (2002) says of the nineteenth century: 'Discussions in the public sphere were to aim for *consensus*. The principles of the public sphere were primarily *the bourgeoisie's understanding of itself*.' One could argue that nothing much has changed, looking at the value placed on consensus in the discourse of contemporary news and current affairs in television.

Curran discusses the work of Newcomb and Hirsch and their analysis of television fiction as 'a forum of normative debate' (Curran, 1996). He refers to what they say about 'the way in which television fiction potentially informs the collective dialogue of society' (ibid). This is an interesting extension to the scope of the public sphere and the arena of debate. Livingstone (1990) also argues that her research fits in with Newcomb and Hirsch's findings, showing that 'television provides a "cultural forum"'. But as Curran points out, it is a fallacy to suppose that television 'reflects the full diversity of society' which would make such 'collective dialogue' in such a 'cultural forum' at all meaningful. It is true that some fiction represents some discussion of issues which are of public concern. But the terms of reference of this discussion are another matter. This kind of argument is dangerously like that which proposes that the media reflect society to itself,

Media Consumption in a Public Place
Media technologies of entertainment and communication are available everywhere, in public and in private.
     What are the possible consequences of this, in terms of social interactions?
(*Corbis*)

and so everything is right with the world – uncritical pluralism. If there is 'normative debate' in this kind of public sphere, then one would want to ask whose norms are in play, and whose are ruled out, and by whom?

The media which the public dominantly experience – and television is pre-eminent here in terms of hours spent – often purport to speak for the public, but do not often let the public speak. When the public does speak, it is usually under terms and conditions which the broadcasters control. So discussion and current affairs programmes are controlled up-front by personalities. Those who do appear are allowed to do so by producers. Their appearance is allowed in relation to ideas about balance and audience interest. Access to the media, to a public sphere which all might at least switch on to, is not free, is not guaranteed and in fact only takes place according to ground rules defined by the media themselves. Broadcasters always reserve to themselves the power of editorial control. The relevant kinds of programmes are placed in off-peak schedules or minority channels, so that the 'sphere', such as it is, is set up for minorities. Equally, one should not sound too strident a note about lack of audience access to a public sphere constructed by the media, where 'the people' might have a voice. The voice of some people might be less welcome than that of others. There are few of us who would like any person or group to have absolute right of access to the media.

Silverstone (1994) discusses 'a suburbanisation of the public sphere' in which he argues for two things. The first is that there has been (and still is, to an extent) a 'coherence' that broadcasting has offered to 'the community of suburbs'. Secondly, he suggests that this suburbanized public sphere is fragmenting, as new technologies multiply and divide means of distribution, channels and audiences. He describes the politics of this kind of public sphere as 'a domestic politics of self interest, conformity and exclusion'. But the real power play happens elsewhere. 'Participation of a kind may have been substantially enhanced by the mediation of national and international agendas . . . but the terms of that participation and the possibilities for its realisation are very much in question.'

So in effect the media continue to be consumed in the private sphere of the home for the most part. The material which is distributed is dominantly that of entertainment. Audiences are treated as deindividualized groups of consumers. The dominant pattern of relationship is between audience members and producers. There is a financial charge on that relationship. Audience members may interact in terms of private discussion about what they have seen in the cinema or have heard on the radio. But this discussion does not take place in a public sphere. The audience is unable to make an impact on the conduct of public affairs, whether these are to do with the management of the media or with the conduct of political decisions. At this point one might remember the issues surrounding a public service model of the media. Who defines what kind of service for what kind of public?

It seems that the service does not include the creation of a genuinely public sphere. This has a particular irony in that the Labour government (2004) is very fond of proclaiming the need for 'a genuine debate' on given issues of the moment. The problem is that, apart from the floor of the House of Commons, the only place for that debate is in the pages and the programmes of the media. And that sphere remains privatized and commercialized.

There is also an issue as to whether we can identify a clear distinction between public and private spheres, given the place of broadcasting in domestic life. However, this does not deal with the previous question about whether or not there are real debates in whatever public sphere we may have – real interactions between those who move the levers of power, and those who live with the consequences of this leverage. There also needs to be a questioning of what, it is assumed, 'belongs' to each sphere, especially on gender grounds. News practices represent a difference between hard news and soft news: between masculinized reports that bear on power politics and conflict 'out there', and feminized reports that bear on health and family issues, on social relations and celebrity behaviour. But one needs to question the assumptions that refer such feminized reports into a private/domestic sphere. Andrea Press (2000) refers to the 'customary division between these spheres'. With reference to her own work (with Elizabeth Cole) on abortion, she points out that the debates about this do take place out there in a public and politicized arena. An Irish referendum on abortion (2002) may have reflected on what goes in a private sphere, but the media debate was fierce, and out there in the public sphere, with no sense that the issues had been assimilated into some 'less worthy' feminized soft news reporting.

10 Influences and effects

There is a long-running debate about the possible influence of the media on certain audiences, via certain material, under certain circumstances. There is also a popular mythology around the idea that media effects are proven and that they are pernicious.

This is not so, even with relation to the effects of violent material in the media (see Chapter 4). One significant source of negative views lies intellectually in the work of the Frankfurt school and the writing of members such as Adorno, Horkheimer and Benjamin, in the 1930s and 1940s. Their critique, relating in effect to popular music and cinema, described a new kind of mass culture, generating a new mass audience, and undermining the values of a genuine culture of the people. This 'genuine' culture is conceived as something like 'folk culture'. Another negative and critical impetus appeared in the 1950s, with the arrival of television. Its material was deprecated by a number of critics, including Richard Hoggart of the Birmingham Centre for Cultural Studies, essentially on the grounds that it would undermine and supplant the values of 'high culture' (as Raymond Williams described it). Criticism of violence in such American crime genre series as *Dragnet* followed on this more general argument against television and for its negative effects. Ironically, the main vehicle for views about the negative influence of the media has been the media themselves. They have been the means through which intellectual and political opinion and debate filters through to the general public. They have been (and still are) the sometime agents of moral panic, which typically might relate to the release of some film or video which supposedly influences the minds of the public at large or of the young in particular. The media and especially the press, can be said to be motivated in this criticism by two things. One is the urge to create controversy which sells product, the other may be to gain kudos as the champion of public 'safety' by attacking another medium. This would have been especially true in the 1940s through to the 1970s, when television viewing figures rose steadily, as newspaper circulation declined.

All this debate goes back to models of the relationship between media and society, between texts and audiences. The conservative position returns to an argument that the media do things to people, that audiences may be passive, and that the media producers have a power which audiences cannot resist. This book has so far argued that none of these things is true, or has not been conclusively demonstrated. Truth is more complicated.

It may be useful to summarize a few points about media influence, which do seem to hold true.

- media effects may be benign as much as malign;
- the influence of media is collective rather than operating through any one medium or text;
- the media collectively operate within a range of other cultural and social factors which also condition possible influence;
- the influence of media is conditioned by a range of personal and social factors for the individual audience member, including their social upbringing and their immediate personal circumstances;
- influence is conditioned by the context of reception;
- influence is more likely if the media text speaks of attitudes and values already held by the audience;
- one may recognize behavioural response to, for example, a charity campaign: but this does not demonstrate attitudinal change.

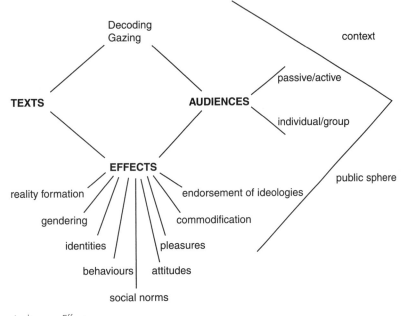

Audiences: Effects
The interaction of audiences and texts, within given contexts, produces a range of possible effects.
(*Graeme Burton*, 2004)

So the influence of the media is a subject which most people have opinions about, but which is so hedged about with conditional factors that it may be difficult to sustain those opinions. The kind of influence which invokes most concern relates to attitudinal changes. It is assumed that favourable attitudes are behind people's decision to behave in certain ways. In this case it is not surprising that research and debate weighs most heavily in certain areas: violent behaviour, voting behaviour, purchasing behaviour. The first has to do with public order and the security of the state. The second has to do with the mechanism which transfers power from people to politicians. The third has to do with the consumption on which our capitalist system depends. So there has been a certain emphasis of research resources to the possible benefit of those who exert political and economic power.

Previous discussion of media power and ideology has already suggested that the media may be seen as a site of struggle for the dominance of one set of ideas over another (Gramsci), or as a kind of ideological state apparatus, a Trojan horse for the dominant ideology (Althusser). But propositions about how ideology reproduces itself, or how it exerts consensual control, are only propositions. John Thompson (1990) disagrees with the notion of the ideologically subjugated audience. 'It cannot be assumed that the individuals who receive media messages will, by the fact of receiving them, be impelled to act in an imitative and conforming way and thereby be bound to the social order which their actions, and the messages which allegedly impel them, serve to reproduce.'

Curran and Seaton (1997) say much the same thing on a broader basis which still reflects on effects and influence: 'there is no adequate vocabulary to describe the relationships between the media, individuals and society'.

Nevertheless, convictions about the effects of the media remain, and research abounds. There are various propositions about effects, how they work and therefore about that relationship between audience and media.

- *hypodermic effects* propose that the media directly influence people, largely adversely, 'injecting' them with views and behaviours;

- *copycat effects* propose a variation on this theme, which is about imitation of media behaviours;

- *innoculation theory* proposes that audiences become desensitized to the adverse qualities of media material through repetitive exposure to that material;

- *two-step flow theory* proposes that media influence is indirect, mediated through opinion makers in the media and through opinion leaders in the social groups inhabited by a given audience member (see Katz and Lazarfeld, 1995);

- *uses and gratifications theory* proposes that audience needs influence their choice and use of media material (see above);

- *cultivation theory* proposes that repetitive consumption of certain kinds of media material accumulatively cultivates certain kinds of attitudes and values.

Propositions about media influence have also been set up along a short-term/long-term axis. Short-term effects are sometimes known as hypodermic theories (above). However, over the past 50 or so years, it has not been shown that media in any area can simply inject people with ideas and behaviours, with immediate results. So most cautious propositions about media influence now hinge on the idea of long-term attitudinal change.

What are also important in this respect are attitudes to a whole range of social groups and social behaviours. One may ask what part the media play, for example, in forming attitudes towards ethnic minorities, or towards situations such as single-parenthood. One may ask whether they have changed or hardened existing attitudes. One could argue that they have failed to bring about change when it needed to happen (for example, in the treatment of gay people in the popular press). It is difficult to believe that the media have nothing to do with the way we view others and construct our beliefs. On the other hand, it is in the end impossible to demonstrate conclusively that this influence is there. This kind of problem is relevant to discussion of negative representations of social groups. It seems reasonable to assert that those representations of young people that treat them as 'a problem' will tend to confirm prejudices, and to help ensure that they are a problem. But, even when respondents in research articulate negative attitudes on the basis of what they have seen or read, still it is hard to connect what some people say they think with what they or others actually do.

It is also the case that there are positive representations around. One can find examples of the media offering a constructive lead in thinking about such subjects as 'race' or 'crime' or 'youth'. So how does this fit into the equation? The most certain thing that research throws up is that people tend to use media material selectively to reinforce what they already believe. But, of course, what they already believe may itself be a product of prior media use.

In terms of outcome – as opposed to the process of effect – there are a number of dominant propositions which dominate conclusions about effects. One version is summarized by McQuail (2000) in terms of the influence on beliefs and opinions held by the audience –

- causes intended change (conversion of views);
- causes unintended changes;
- causes minor changes (perhaps in the form of views held, or in their intensity);
- facilitates change of views (whether intended or not);
- reinforces existing views;
- prevents a change in views.

His categories refer to whether or not change happens, and in what ways. Media influence may lead to attitude change, not necessarily of great significance or by any calculation on the part of the producers. Equally, it may either reinforce what people already believe, or even work against people shifting their beliefs. So evidence is in some respects contradictory.

Burton (2002), on the other hand, describes influence in terms of types of change, and of broader effects on society and on social groups.

- *attitude change*: effects on people's orientation towards or against certain ideas or behaviours – what one is for or against;
- *cognitive change*: effects on people's values and beliefs – how one thinks about a subject;
- *affective (emotional) change*: effects on the emotional state of the audience: this may include the production of an emotional frame of reference for or against such subjects as social groups or commodities – what one feels about a subject;
- *agenda setting*: especially through news material, constructing a prioritized set of issues for the public sphere, and denying the importance of other issues;
- *moral panics*: inducing unfounded anxieties about given social groups, social behaviours or social phenomena;
- *socialization*: in terms of persuading audiences that certain norms, certain kinds of behaviour, certain kinds of social relationship should be adopted (in preference to any others);
- *reality formation*: producing a set of ideas about what constitutes 'the real', especially in relation to social reality and social norms;
- *social control*: acting a mechanism for the production of a consensus about the 'proper' relationship between social groups, between the state and society, with an emphasis on particular ideas about law and order;
- *endorsement of ideology*: reinforcement of a dominant set of values which add up to a certain way of looking at and thinking about the world: this includes reinforcement of views about power relationships between social grounds and about difference between groups.

Ideas about the process and outcome of effects are themselves dependent on given research methodologies, which are also open to question, for various reasons. One may refer to Gauntlett (1995) for a blunt critique of research methodologies in relation to television (which are much applicable to other media).

A few comments, at least, will indicate the scope of 'the problem'.

1 If one is trying to identify attitudinal effects, then one has to find a method and evidence that unambiguously points to that internal state which we call 'attitude'. In particular, surveys are only as good as the questions they ask. They depend on the ability of respondents to express 'truthful' answers, and on the objectivity of the researcher in correlating the comments and information drawn out. Examples here would be the questions asked of and records kept by respondents in research done by the Broadcast Audience Research Board or by National Readership Surveys.

2 If one is trying to identify behavioural effects, then one has to be able to describe distinctive behaviours, and distinguish an unambiguous connection between that behaviour and given media material.

3 If one is trying to fasten on media material as being the key variable in the context being researched, then it has to be distinguished from possible influences outside the media, from influences of other media, from influences of other material within the medium being examined. This is a tall order.

4 If one conducts any 'hands-on' research, then by definition there is a kind of intervention which means that the experience of consumption is no longer 'natural'.

5 If one conducts research into textual material alone (e.g. content analysis) then any statements about effect are conjectural (however, they may seem to be probable) because the engagement of audience with text has been ignored. Similarly, correlation studies assume that there is a connection between two exceptional items of statistical information, and they assume that this connection is causal. Neither may be true.

6 If one conducts experiments with large audience numbers, then one is likely to come up with generalizations about effects, at best. And these generalizations will appear less true the more one looks at specific sections of the audience.

7 If one looks at individuals or small audience groups – ethnographic surveys – then the specific information elicited will not necessarily be true for larger audience groups.

11 Gender modelling

There is a quantity of material on audiences, which is concerned with gender differences between and within audiences. This interest attends to audience preferences and audience reading of texts. It looks for ways of modelling these audiences.

Christine Geraghty (1996a) has considered ways in which women are constructed as an audience and operate as consumers, in relation to a proposed difference between how the viewing of film has been understood, as opposed to television. In the case of television she points to an emphasis on the context of viewing for the female audience. With regard to film she refers to an emphasis on spectator positions and psychoanalytic discourses. She comments on other critiques which draw attention to the way in which the female viewer of film is often modelled as being passive, whereas the viewer of television is often described as ' "active", "conscious" and "optimistic" '. She discusses the representation of mothers, in particular. There are accounts of various views on the nature of identification with mother characters, for the female audience. Psychoanalytic positions seem to be more pessimistic about women reading disempowering meanings into, for example, melodramas. Whereas a more post-modern analysis is fairly positive about pleasures gained and about a sense of resistance to social strictures being generated. There is also comment on the process of viewing – perhaps a shared experience in the case of TV, in which women will talk about and assimilate material collaboratively.

Such comments on viewing tend to be confirmed by the work of Silverstone (1994) and Morley (1992), for example. They comment on the fact that male viewers of TV prefer not to be interrupted, whereas female viewers may view spasmodically, and prefer to talk about material on screen. On the other hand, their research suggests that males more than females will control the machinery of viewing, and therefore the material that is actually watched. It should also be pointed out that such gendered behaviours and preferences operate in a context – that of family life. Other kinds of media consumption may take place in other contexts, with other implications for gender. For example, males and females will go to see a movie as a shared and social experience, not just for the film. The choice of the film could depend on either male or female preferences.

So the context of that lived experience is not just about the domestic sphere. And even where it is, gender roles may vary from one type of household to another and over a period of time. So, for example, Hobson (1982), like Morley, found that female viewers of the then early evening soap, *Crossroads*, experienced interrupted viewing because they were trying to watch, prepare a meal and deal with children. But twenty years on and more one would have to say, what about that majority of households that do not contain children? What about the impact of the VCR and the possibility of deferred viewing? What about the impact of the microwave and ready meals? What about different households of different socio-economic groups, with different incomes?

So, one might now question the validity of work by people like Morley, on the basis of the comparatively narrow cross-section investigated and of the possibility that social behaviours and relationships are changing, even since such research was carried out. Certainly the British prime-time TV schedules are increasingly full of drama material that contains themes and characters of relevance to women's lives, and which are sometimes treated in what might loosely be termed 'soap style'. One example was the third series of a drama called *Clocking Off* (2002), based around a northern textiles factory. The storylines focus on both male and female characters, but they are very much concerned with relationships and emotional dilemmas. The series *Playing the Field* is about a women's football team, but is dominantly about what goes on the protagonists' lives, not about matches. Episodes contain multiple storylines and a cross-section of female types, much like a soap. An example of 'women's themes' would be *The Cry* (2002), a two-parter, in which the female protagonist is a social worker who has to deal with suspected child abuse and with the trauma of her own miscarriage.

Similarly, it is noticeable that movie releases contain a fair proportion of material which is clearly aimed at a specifically female audience. *Bridget Jones's Diary* has topped both novel and film best-sellers' lists. The novel and film *About a Boy* contains male protagonists but appeals to female readers/viewers because of its exploration of emotion and relationship. One also has to be careful about explaining a gendered audience in terms of material supposedly tailored for female viewers. For a start, there will be differences between what younger and older females will prefer. Indeed, the whole notion of a 'female audience' implies a coherence of interest, of background, of gender definition, which hardly stands up to examination, and which is in its own way demeaning. Not much better is the assumption that material supposedly for a female audience contains nothing of interest and value for men. I would also argue that audiences may not and should not be differentiated by gender without good evidence. The audience for David Fincher's *Panic Room* (2002) was as much female as male. Horror material in all media is very attractive to a young female audience. Or a film like *24 Hour Party People* (2002) is sold on its cultural attractions and references, within which gender is largely irrelevant.

It is interesting to take, somewhat at random, exit reviews of the film *Bend it Like Beckham* directed by Gurinder Chadha (in the *Independent on Sunday* 14 April 2002). This film is partly about football, but also about gender behaviour. It is enjoyed by the audience partly for this reason, but not because of their gender. A 39-year-old male reviewed it as 'really exciting and had all the right moments and emotions you want in a film'. A 25-year-old female said, 'I don't know anything about soccer, but that didn't matter because the interracial differences came across well.'

Where there has been explicit identification of a female-gendered audience one may argue that it has something to do with those ideological shifts related to feminism, and a lot to do with economic changes that have given women more leisure and more spending power.

One notable US TV series, *Cagney & Lacey*, starring two female cops, started out as a made-for-TV film pilot in 1981. It was conceived as material for women, and explicitly pursued this end over a number of years, covering, rather like a soap, specific issues including sexuality, abortion, gender orientation and marriage. There is an excellent discussion of this series as a case study by Julie D'Acci (2000).

A contrasting, but equally interesting example refers to a gardening programme on British television. The researcher/writer Jacqui Gabb (1999) suggests that the audience for such programmes is dominantly female, on the basis that

- she received an exclusively female response to an open letter asking for responses,

- a 1998 live arena show of the programme (*Gardeners' World*) was attended by a clear majority of women,

- the presenter would overtly address a female audience.

Gabb draws attention to the gender-oriented language about gardening used in the programme. She refers to the myths of nature, of mothering and nurturing, which are clearly invoked. She is clear that the text speaks through a female discourse to a female audience. 'Within *Gardeners' World*, the dialogue between the feminine text and the female subject is not passive discourse, but requires that "she" actively construct the narrative. [. . .] The female subject . . . is encouraged to inhabit subject positions and scenarios that she would not assume in real life, experience an emotional intensity that she is usually denied.' Gabb also argues that the original presenter, hugely popular until his death in 1996: 'represented a complex blend of patriarchal authority and feminine (maternal) power, singularly embodied within a male physique'.

This kind of study, of a personal relationship between audience members and specific texts, is an example not only of the use of a feminist perspective, but also of a kind of micro-study. This contrasts with the broader macro-studies that try to generalize about large audiences, even about society as a whole. Clearly there are a range of problems in understanding audiences, both in terms of defining their composition and in respect of explaining how they engage with media texts. In spite of widespread beliefs about media influence, it is easier to show how and why media are unlikely to affect audiences, than to prove that they do. We may categorize kinds of influence, and propose how this may work. But the evidence for effects on the audience is tentative, given the complexity of contextual factors at work.

I now want to move on to looking at particular aspects of specific media, with some emphasis on gender, technology and globalization. However, you will find that the scope of these chapters continues to be defined by the key areas of institution, text and audience. I will hold on to an interest in the production of meanings and the work of ideology. You should find that these case studies build up that picture of media and society which has been sketched out in these first three chapters.

12 Discussion extract

The pleasure of these viewers (women watching soap opera) in playing with the relationship between the representation and the real, questions the power of the programme to control the representational illusion and is a way of exercising control over their own viewing practices. Their active choice of whom to 'identify' with and their choice to identify or not in the process that I have called 'implication-extrication' are both examples of exerting control through play.

The play may not in itself be resistive or subversive, but the control or empowerment that it entails produces a self-esteem in the subordinate that at least makes resistance or subversion possible. Radway (1984) has found that some women readers of romance novels reported that they chose to read the novels in the face of husbandly disapproval and found meanings in them that supported feminine values and criticized masculine ones. This choice and this validation of a subordinated value system gave them the self-confidence to assert themselves more strongly and to resist the patriarchal power of the male in the family.

. . . Rules have inscribed within them both the power they convey and its origin. Gilligan (1982) makes the point that men in patriarchy think and work through rules, because rules allow them to dominate; the women playing with the system of representation in soap opera are like children playing, in that both subordinated 'classes' are using play to question the rules that maintain their subordination. Rules, then work in a similar way to ideology to maintain the power base in its current location. Like ideology, they emanate from a sociocentral source and attempt to construct social identities.

. . . Barthes' . . . centrifugal model of pleasure allows for a diversity of pleasure 'around the circumference' and suggests a line of force in active opposition to the centripetal force that attempts to centre control at a point of ideological and social unity. So Barthes moves away from seeking to explain a text by referring to its singular ideology towards the plurality of pleasures it can offer in its moments of reading. Pleasure may be provoked by the text, but it can only be experienced by the reader in the reading. It can thus differ from reader to reader, and even from reading to reading. Barthes suggests that any one reader reading any one text at different times may experience different pleasures, or none, at each reading. Whilst this notion locates pleasure in the reader rather than the text and emphasises difference rather than homogeneity, it does imply randomness which is of little help in explaining the process.

John Fiske (1994)

1 In what ways does this extract suggest that taking pleasure as a reader is an empowering experience?

2 What is said about gendered difference in the audience /reader with relation to 'rules'?

3 How do Barthes' ideas about reading reflect on problems with defining the idea of audience?

4 What are the arguments (in the extract and elsewhere) for suggesting that audiences are subordinated by ideology both directly to the text experienced and indirectly to the institution that produces the texts?

13 Further reading

Dickinson, R., Harindranath, R. and Linne, O. (eds) (1998) *Approaches to Audiences – A Reader*. London: Arnold.
Gauntlett, D. (1995) *Moving Experiences – Understanding Television's Influences and Effects*. London: John Libbey.
Morley, D. (1992) *Television Audiences & Cultural Studies*. London: Routledge.
Moores, S. (1993) *Interpreting Audiences*. London: Sage.
Ruddock, A. (2001) *Understanding Audiences*. London: Sage.
Seiter, E., Borchers, H., Kreutzner, G. and Warth, E. (eds) (1989) *Remote Control*. London: Routledge.

CHAPTER FOUR

THE MEDIA AND VIOLENCE

Questioning violence: problems with measuring effects

66 The ubiquity of crime and violence in the mass media has stimulated a whole host of debates about how far the media may encourage anxieties, shape attitudes, define values or excite behaviour in the public. Not surprisingly the most persistent concern has been the mass media violence causes violence in society . . . Andison's (1977) calculation that 77% of the studies claim that media violence causes violence in real life probably still holds true . . . Nevertheless, in most respects the research has been quite inadequate and on close examination simply does not concur in the way most reviews argue. 99

Guy Cumberbatch (1989) Violence and the mass media, in G. Cumberbatch and D. Howitt,
A Measure of Uncertainty: The Effects of the Mass Media. London: John Libbey.

1 Introduction

It is a truth often proposed that the media contain 'too much' violence, and that this violence is in some way to blame for violent social behaviours. But what has been proposed has not been demonstrated. This is not to say that there is no relationship between media depictions of violence and social behaviours and attitudes, but say that the nature of that relationship is complex, and that it certainly has not been demonstrated that the media directly cause violence. 'The mass media have long provided convenient scapegoats for the most glaring of society's ills, and the visual communications systems have been especially popular as objects of blame' (Howe, 1977).

One might suggest that, rather as we are prone to attribute blame to others, it is easy to blame the media for violent behaviour. It is harder to accept that social environment and aspects of individual upbringing have been shown to be a more consistent factor that correlate with violent behaviour. It is easier to look for single causes to problems (if indeed there is a problem), than it is to deal with multiple and interacting causes: 'the causes of violence and crime seem much more likely to be found in poverty, unemployment, homelessness, abuse, frustration, personality traits and psychological background, than in television programmes' (Gauntlett, 1995).

Critics of film and television in particular have made large assertions about the influence of those media, without producing the evidence to back the rhetoric. Michael Medved (1992) is an example of this rhetorical and sincere approach, in which evidence is used selectively and uncritically.

Gunter (1985) referred to assumptions and to the unsupported use of terms: 'The terms "violence" or "aggression" receive almost indiscriminate use, not simply by journalists with reference to television portrayals, but also by ordinary people in everyday life.'

The problem with talking about media effects and media violence does not just start with embedded social assumptions about the media doing things to people. There are other problems to do with differing definitions of violence, the differing nature of media (for example, the written word as opposed to the visual image), and different socio-cultural factors which will affect how representations of violence are understood.

This does not mean that we should be unconcerned about representations of violent acts and attitudes. Neither does it mean that one abandons investigation of the relationship between media and society, between text and audience. But it does mean that generalizations, assertions and scaremongering are not acceptable. One should recognize that, for all the reservations laid out in this chapter, some media analysts are still convinced that (with qualifications) the media can generate violent effects. For example, Potter (1999) says

> We are certain that violent portrayals are pervasive in the media, especially the most dominant medium, television. We know that people use the cues in the portrayal of violence to construct meaning. Scholars strongly agree that exposure to media violence leads to negative effects both immediately during exposure and over the long term of continuous exposure. We also know that certain types of portrayals of violence, certain types of viewers, and certain environments increase the probability of negative effects.

Though it is simply not true that 'scholars strongly agree'. However, the position is one that deserves expression in this debate. And it is the undoubted concern about media and violence that has produced such strength of contesting views.

Ironically, it is sections of the media that are themselves significantly responsible for arousing public anxiety and for making uncritical assertions about violence. More will be said about this in relation to moral panics. But it can be said now that the media, especially the press, and especially news, have made themselves the arena for debate. Violent and unexpected events such as the Columbine High School massacre become the catalyst for commentary. What is said on the news or in current affairs programmes is in no way simply a reflection of conversation in pubs, homes and cafes, but it certainly feeds back into these everyday discussions. I am saying that the existence, the nature and the perception of the level of violence is in itself something to be questioned. I am not saying that violence is not a social problem. But how we recognize and frame such problems has a lot to do with the media. The media transmit information, arouse anxieties, set agendas – without necessarily being a cause of violence as such.

There is evidence that media cause people to believe that there is more violence occurring in society than is actually the case. People worry about violence happening to them and to their relatives. This concern causes those people to adopt particular lifestyles or patterns of behaviour (see Gunter's reporting of British crime surveys in 1981 and 1983, in Gunter, 1987).

An example of pretty much ongoing criticism – reported of course in the media – was that contained in a Broadcasting Standards Commission report (May 2002). This expressed concern about violence in soaps, especially because they are broadcast pre-watershed. It referred to stories about assault, prostitution and rape. The report was based on research surveying the attitudes of 2,100 people. It did not in fact provide evidence that any great number of those surveyed condemned the representation of violence in soaps; but it did provide evidence that 23 per cent thought that soap material should be suitable for family viewing. However, newspaper articles interpreted this as condemnation.

One should also reflect on models for media and society. That is to say, if one accepts determinist models, in which it is believed that the media do things to their audiences, then it is easy to accept that one of those 'things' is at least making them think about violence in a particular way. On the other hand, if one takes a more post-modernist view, then one is disinclined to believe in a big picture of cause and effect. The 'violent text' is just a fragmented experience. It may be enjoyed for its irony. It may be appreciated for its reference to other violent texts. The question then would be, does one see the media world as one apart from a social world, or do their realities merge? In other words, our pre-existing views about the relationship between media and society in general will affect our particular views about whatever we see as violence in the media.

In reading the rest of this chapter you should refer to the penultimate section of the previous chapter, which summarizes views about the nature of effects and models to explain these. The fact that many of my comments refer to the medium of television reflects the dominant interests of those researching the effects of media violence on audiences.

2 Major questions

1 How may one define violence in the media in any consistent and meaningful way, especially across the range of media?

2 How do representations relate to an understanding of violence and its possible effects?

3 What types of effect may we propose or demonstrate?

4 What is the relationship betwen institution, text and audience, and the understanding of media violence?

5 Does regulation tell us anything about the perception of violent representations?

6 What research approaches (and problems with these) may we identify?

7 What models can we construct to suggest a process of influence which causes violence?

8 What are the problems with these models?

3 Defining violence

Media violence is often discussed in relation to acts of harm done to the body, depicted on television or film, and in the context of fictional material. It is more complicated and problematic than this.

Those conducting content analysis of violent material have had to distinguish between different acts of violence. Clearly a bullet through the heart is different from a knife in the arm, which is different from a punch on the jaw. There are different effects on the victim. More importantly, we have different emotional responses to, and cultural judgements about, the kind of harm that is inflicted through varying means on another person. These responses and judgements mean that one act of violence can never be equivalent to another. Research which simply tots up such acts within a given period of time is missing an important point.

Again, violence is not just physical. People inflict psychological and emotional damage on others. Episodes in which someone is reduced to tears, humiliated or simply made fearful (perhaps by the threat of violence) are still violent. Their emotional charge and possible effects on the audience are different from, but not demonstrably less than, an episode in which someone is shot dead. Indeed it is easy to show that material which is considered violent is in fact about implication and a climate of violence, as much as about explicit scenes of physical violence. The black-humoured accidental shooting in the car in *Pulp Fiction* does not show the death. But it shows the mess it makes. One could also argue that the casual attitude to violence within this film is more important when constructing a critique of violence, than are the acts of violence themselves.

Gunter (1985) suggests four categories of violence:

- instrumental violence – used to achieve a goal;
- expressive violence – committed in a state of anger;
- intentional violence – intended to do harm to another;
- unintended violence – not knowing that another would be harmed.

Images of Conflict
Public debates about the effects of violent material tends to show more concern about physical acts of violence, and less about the psychological effects of verbal and emotional violence.
     What do you think about this?
(*Corbis*)

Potter (1999) reviews the nature of violence in terms of aggression, and refers to litera-ture which discusses this. For example, he quotes Berkowitz in saying that aggression is 'any form of behaviour that is intended to injure someone physically or psychologically'. He refers to Berkowitz's comment that violence is an extreme form of aggression. He also picks up that notion that violence can be verbal as much as physical in referring to seven dimensions of aggression (Velicer *et al.* 1985):

1 assault (physical violence against others);

2 indirect aggression (malicious gossip, slamming doors, temper tantrums);

3 irritability (grouchiness, rudeness, bad temper);

4 negativism (oppositional behaviour, usually against authority figures);

5 resentment (jealousy and hatred of others, especially related to mistreatment);

6 suspicion (projection of hostility onto others, distrustfulness);

7 verbal aggression (arguing, shouting, including threats and curses).

If the nature of violence is variable, so are its contexts, causes and effects. Violence committed within a domestic context, one on one, will be understood differently from violence that happens in war, or violence which happens because of some unexpected natural event. These differences relate to ideas about the personal or the impersonal, to degrees of reader identification – and once more to differences in the nature of effect.

Perpetrators and victims also vary. The shooting of a criminal by a cop in the street is likely to be seen as legitimized violence. The strangling of a wife by a husband in the home will be seen as illegitimate, and understood in a different way. At this point one also needs to bear in mind that we already have frameworks of understanding in our heads, through which we deal with these media experiences. One may refer to ideology or discourse in this case.

Another variable which helps define violence in our minds is the medium itself. It is no accident that the violence debate tends to centre on visual media. There is an assumption made about the emotional impact of graphic representations.

But what about violence in comics, in novels, on radio, in computer games, on the Internet? There is a difference. The decoding of a violent image in a comic is more immediate than the decoding of words. But that does not mean that what is written about violence may not have a significant effect on attitudes towards it. Alternatively, it may be argued that the comic visual is inherently less realistic than the film image. But one cannot assert that it is therefore less significant, especially when one takes into account factors such as the private and intense consumption of the comic image, as opposed to the public and shared consumption of a movie, where there may be a chance to talk through a shared experience of the violent images after the event.

So the inherently different nature of media becomes yet another variable. But then again, media do not exist in isolation. So our understanding of what is violent behaviour, the formation of our attitudes towards violence, happens through a collected and accumulated experience of various media (and various texts). This notion is what underpins Gerbner's 'Cultivation Theory', which suggests that complacent attitudes towards violence grow over a period of time and through experience of the range of media.

Violence is not a single act of a single text within a single medium. Violence, whatever it is exactly, is a composite of experiences across media. And media not only have inherent characteristics that help define the nature and significance of violence; the individual text may also handle the individual act in a variety of ways which also skew that definition. Violence is different when seen from a subjective rather than an objective view. Violence is different in close-up. Violence is different if dwelt on. Violence seems different according to its consequences. Violence may be signalled and anticipated, or it may be unexpected.

3.1 Violence as representation

Violence is something that is perceived and judged through its representation. Features of the violence cause it to be rated in different ways. For example, Gunter (1985) found that TV viewers judged the severity of violence according to a number of factors:

1 the physical nature or type of violence perpetrated;

2 the kind of weapon used (cutting weapons were seen as the 'worst');

3 the degree of harm done to the victim(s) of the violence;

4 the nature of the physical context in which the violence takes place;

5 the realism of the setting for the violence;

6 societal norms, themselves relating to which character perpetrates or is victim of the violence.

We need to remind ourselves of essential truths about the nature of representation. Violence in the media is only a constructed version of that which it pretends to represent. It is not 'real' violence. But as a representation, it also necessarily constructs ideas about violence. So media violence is simultaneously invalidated in one sense as a substitute for experience in our social world, yet also validated as a source of ideas about how we may understand and deal with that experience. This duality reflects on views of effects. The media experience is one which we may separate from everyday life. We know that a film about organized crime is an artifice and that watching it is an experience separate from everyday living (in which for most of us, organized crime does not figure). Such a separation argues against the representation having any effects on us. On the other hand, that movie may produce ideas about violence in the mind of the movie-goer. If so, then there has been some effect. So the degree of separation or of overlap between our media lives and our social lives is important to arguments about media effects.

Fact and fiction

Such distinctions are further complicated by ways in which we may categorize texts as fact or fiction. A great deal of effects research has related to fictional material. In one sense this is valid because of the huge public appetite for kinds of drama in any medium. There is also that argument which suggests that violence in genre material, widely repeated and disseminated, must have a particular significance in arguing the case for effects. However, one may equally argue that audiences are only too aware of the constructed nature of this material, and therefore are less likely to be affected by it. Whereas factual material, especially news, however it is still actually constructed and still only a matter of representations, has a kind of plausibility. It may show violence, perhaps associated with war, which has the validity of depicting authentic events. This violence may be second-hand experience in news, but we know it has been first-hand experience for some people. And in terms of taking on its ideas we will be further persuaded by the discourse of news, which is in our heads and which speaks to us of the truth-telling properties of news.

There is a sense in which, curiously, we allow news more latitude than drama in bringing us verbal and visual accounts of violent events. The curiosity of this distinction is accounted for by the extent to which we have been taken in by news discourse. If anything, we should be the more disturbed by 'reading' about violent events precisely because we believe they are true. But in fact audiences do, to a degree, suspend their criticism of possible effects of violence in news by invoking a kind moral justification. This kind of debate defined discussion of the effects of a news photograph showing an incinerated Iraqi soldier, during the Gulf War of 1991.

The contradiction is that news is little different from drama in principle. Both involve production teams of media workers, scripting and editorial choices. Television news, like drama, has its code of practice regarding the depiction of violence – because of its possible effects on the audience. In general, close-ups on dead bodies are edited out of broadcast material. On the other hand, there were still disturbing scenes of the 1999 Omagh bombing in Northern Ireland which made it onto screen.

News is, arguably, also like drama in respect of the degree of violence selected into its material. Schlesinger and Tumber (1994) point out that newspapers do not report crime and violence in proportion to the actual incidence of crimes. They quote Doris Graber's research in the USA (1980): 'an exaggerated picture is presented of the incidence of the most violent types of crime, while the incidence of lesser crimes is minimised'. They refer to British research which 'tends towards the same conclusion'. They refer to an analysis of Scottish newspapers (Ditton and Duffy, 1983) in which violent and sexual crime constituted 45.8 per cent of all crime news, where the police statistics measure such crime as 2.4 per cent of crimes committed. They found similar results from their own research, including a distinct increase in the amount of violent crime reported as one moved from analysis of the quality to the popular press.

This kind of selectivity not only undermines the idea of objectivity in news, but also relates to the idea that representation of violent crime may lead to a fear of crime, as much as to violent behaviour. In this case, one also has to take into account the idea that violent news items are part of a marketing strategy of news providers seeking to appeal to the audience and to please their advertisers. This view would be endorsed by Hamilton (1998), who discusses the commercial advantages of broadcasting violence. He quotes a US senator as saying 'programmers, producers and advertisers have discovered the axiom that violence is nearly a sure-fire ratings booster. It moves the numbers.' Similarly, he refers to a journalist's observation that 'violence boosts TV news ratings; the gorier the pictures, the higher the ratings and thus the ad rates'.

So we see some material as being more or less constructed than others, and some materials as having a more or less reliable connection with life experience than others.

4 Institutions – violence

Determinist and instrumental views of the media see them as purveyors of violence. I suggest that one should, rather, see them as mediators. Either way, we are talking about a context to the effects debate, rather than providing conclusive evidence about the nature and extent of any effects.

Of course, as producers, the media institutions are implicated as a source of violent experience, albeit merely in the form of representations. It is true that many people may only experience violent death through the media. But again, violent talk and some violent behaviour is a part of social experience, starting, for instance, with bullying at school. It is uncritical to discuss the effects of media violence as if it is a unique source of such experience.

The apparatus of media institutions, regulated by internal and external bodies, acts as a kind of mediator of possible and actual violent experiences. The debate about violent effects should not be framed in solely negative terms. Texts give readers the chance to experience mediated violence, rather than to suffer the effects of first-hand violence. Institutions stand between the audience and a huge array of experience out there in the world – some of it violent and unpleasant. Texts may manufacture violence as a kind of 'what if' fictional experience – but it is only a story. This is not to manufacture a blanket apologia for all kinds of media violence – to take the discussion off the map. But one has to recognize the various and coexisting positions of criticism, in which institutions can be both providers of representations that conceal ideology and their interests, and mediators via representations that may allow experience without suffering.

I have already referred to the idea that media institutions use violent material as a way of responding to economic imperatives.

> The media industries are in the business of constructing audiences that can be rented to advertisers. Therefore, programmers are under pressure to select material that will appeal to the greatest number of people within a desired audience segment. The most desired audience segment is people 18 to 34 years old, because advertisers heavily target this group. Advertisers want to get their message in front of these people, because these are the consumers with the highest needs as they set up their own households and establish brand loyalties.
>
> People in the industry believe that violence is an essential tool in building audiences, especially younger audiences.
>
> **Potter (1999)**

Hamilton (1998) produces a similar argument:

> Economics determines the supply and demand of violent images in American television programming. The portrayal of violence is used as a competitive tool in both entertainment and news shows to attract particular viewing audiences. The likelihood that a television program will contain any violent acts and the type of violence portrayed depend on a number of economic factors: the size and demographic composition of the potential viewing audience; the distribution of tastes for violent programming; the values placed by advertisers on viewing audiences and the willingness of viewers to pay for programming; the costs of different types of show; the number of networks and stations in a viewing area; the market for different types of US programs abroad; and the interactions among the theatrical, video, cable, network broadcast, and syndicated television markets . . .
>
> Economics explains television violence as the product of rational, self-interested decisions made by viewers and television programmers. The top consumers of television violence are males aged 18 to 34, followed by females aged 18 to 34. Advertisers are willing to pay a premium for these viewers, which means that some programmers will face incentives to offer violent shows.

A political economy perspective on the media would suggests that if media violence may have effects on audiences, it is the marketplace and its economic imperatives which are responsible for producing the violence.

5 Texts – violence

Clearly the content and treatment of a given text shapes its potential effect on the audience. So do judgements by those who regulate our media. I have already pointed out that the mode of realism – fact or fiction – is influential in this respect. The degree of plausibility or of naturalism in the treatment of violence is likely to affect the seriousness with which it is taken by the audience. The fantasy violence of Hollywood thrillers or action movies is of less concern than, say, emotional violence depicted through some TV docu-drama.

The textual narrative, within which the represented violence is produced, also matters. In particular, narrative outcomes construct a view of whatever violence has taken place. Violent acts and violent characters may be implicitly condemned or explicitly punished by the end of a story. The questions one then has to ask are:

- How far may any emotional impact of such violence be mitigated by such outcomes?
- How far is it possible for narrative to define the effect of violence on the audience?
- Can these outcomes shape attitudes towards violence, towards approval or disapproval?
- Or is the power of the audience to take a view stronger than the power of the text to shape a view?

Violence in Computer Games
As computer graphics achieve more naturalism in their representation, is it possible that perceptions of the effects of their violence will also change?
(*Digicollage.com*)

You will see that, in effect, these are debates about the relative power of producer, text or audience being revisited from earlier chapters.

Mythologies and ideologies

One may also revisit ideas about the positioning of the spectator and the production of mythologies. Of course, with reference to the question of the location of meaning, the work of discourses or of signs in invoking mythologies about violence is not all done by the text. As has been said before, we bring prior knowledge and ways of thinking to a text. The producers of texts may well tap into this knowledge. But still we may remind ourselves that the possible effects of violent material are at least partly dependent on the ideas that a text refers to.

For example, we are predisposed to believe that females, children and the elderly, will be victims of violence. They have already been cast in this role by the prevailing mythologies which inhabit texts. We are disinclined to believe that women or children will commit violence. We are persuaded that violence committed by forces of law and of authority is legitimate. We will be affected in different ways by the textual experience of either violence committed as part of war and assumed patriotic duty, or violence committed for personal gain. Mythologies about who 'should' or 'should not' commit violence, about legitimate and illegitimate roles in violent episodes, are of course about beliefs and values. They are also inevitably ideological, since violence is an expression of power, and ideology is at least in part about differentials in the exercise of power within society.

The likely effect of invoking myths is to reinforce beliefs about violence. The effect of violent episodes works within the context of the beliefs and values which may be both inscribed in the text and carried in the minds of the audiences. There is a sense in which the effect of violence in texts is relative to the ideology of its time. Violence used (sometimes) to subordinate black people in films of the 1930s is no longer acceptable. The effect of such scenes then was different to the effect that would be produced now.

In making such comments one is not dealing with the question of whether violent material does have an effect or not. One is dealing with factors which clearly would condition such effects.

Moral panics

The issues involved with news texts and moral panics are similar, in that we can see how items about the given subject rapidly accumulate in the news. We can see how the subject is being treated partially. But the effect of these texts on the readers is less clear. It seems reasonable to talk about the development of a climate of anxiety. But once more, it is not so easy to distinguish the media as a cause of that anxiety.

In this case we are talking about news and current affairs, and we are talking about those panics which are often to do with crime and the fear of violence. The classic study in this respect was made by Hall *et al.* (1978) with regard to the wave of reporting on young black muggers as perpetrators of crime and violence, especially on white people. Their work was itself a development of an earlier study by Cohen (1973), examining youth groups and the representation of 'moral panics' about them in the press. It is arguable that this kind of panic (and inaccuracy) is actually a response to other social factors which are felt as much as articulated (see Sparks, 1992). In this case a new generation of black Britons was growing up, less deferential than their parents, more visible as numbers were swelled relatively by immigration from Indian and Bangladeshi Asians. At the same time, both television drama and news media in general had been producing stories that foregrounded violent crime and raised questions about the competence of police forces to deal with this. Previous mythologies of the avuncular policeman and a police force that was 'in control' were undermined. So it may be said that the media were both responding to a general anxiety about crime and violence, and creating a more specific panic about being mugged by black people.

Schlesinger and Tumber (1994) would, however, argue that 'the evidence on the relationships between media coverage and fear of crime is far from clear-cut'. They point to a number of demographic variables which affect how certain kinds of audience read material involving crime and violence. They point out that different media and indeed different newspapers can be shown to cover such material in different ways.

Moral panics about crime and violence are also generated by the production practices of news media, that feed off one another, borrow and promote stories that seem to have currency and popularity. In 2000 we saw a panic about 'the child molester living near you'. One newspaper actually took it upon itself to seize some kind of moral high ground, and to publish the location of paedophiles who had returned into communities. The resulting mob behaviour and civil unrest is an example of an unintended media effect, and of the danger of generating anxieties that have no proper foundation.

The now infamous case of the murder of James Bulger (1993) was an example of where moral panic and accusations of imitative behaviour merged. Press claims that the killers had been inspired by watching the film *Child's Play Three* on video were untrue. What is most interesting (in the case of such one-off cause célèbre cases) is the lack of attention paid to the fact that thousands of children who had seen the film (released on satellite and video) did not commit any violent acts. What price effects here?

Clearly texts do have an important part to play in the generation of effects on and among their audiences. Yet the nature of these effects is not predictable. Nor do media texts operate in isolation from other social or cultural factors. Texts do not exist in isolation from one another (see genre and intertextuality). So often debates about violence centre on a particular example. But critical studies need to take account of collections and accumulations of texts. Any influence that violence may have is in the context of the whole of textual experience, however distinctive a given text may seem to be. In any case, texts have to be read to have meaning and impact.

6 Audiences – violence

The profile of the audience makes a difference to the propositions and assumptions that are presented about the effects of violent material. Profiles may be affected by medium. For example, television is freely available in the home, and may be assumed often to have a family audience of all ages. Whereas in the case of movies the audience has to decide to go to the cinema to view a text, which to a degree selects a preferred audience. The effects of violent material in a domestic environment as opposed to a theatrical environment, and on different kinds of audience, are likely to be different. Violence in children's comics which can be bought in a local store is different by medium (and availability) from that in an adult comic which can only be bought in a specialist outlet.

What is evident here is that a number of factors come together. The audience is to an extent defined by the nature of the medium. But the medium is also defined partly by its means of distribution. And then, regulation affects the audience use of the medium. TV scheduling or cinema release patterns refer to the assumed age of the viewer. The same is not true for books. In principle a 10-year-old can buy a novel full of violent behaviours without being challenged. The audience profile varies according to medium (and distribution).

Regulation embodies assumptions about media violence having effects, but unequally, with reference to audience profile and medium. It assumes that the printed word is less effective than the image. It assumes that children (to be defined) do not watch TV after the 'watershed' of 9.00 p.m. It assumes that 'children' do not get into cinemas to see movies that are 'too old' for them.

The child audience

We are now talking about audience profile by age – yet another definition and another minefield. There is a lot of difference between a 7-year-old, an 11-year-old and a 15-year-old. Emotional and critical development varies between individuals, and is contingent on various backgrounds and experiences. We are simply not clear as to the effects of various kinds of violent material on these various kinds of children. Indeed, it would be by definition impossible to research children's responses to violent material, when legal regulations and cultural rules forbid us to expose children to that material in the first place. We do know that children are disturbed by exposure to kinds of first-hand violence – by experience of war, social aggression and killing in Northern Ireland or Sierra Leone, for example. But then media life is not real life. One is back to that uncertainty about the power of representations.

Even just to talk about 'children' as an audience is to invoke a discourse of childhood, sets of ideas. As Livingstone (1996) says: 'the concern over children and television may reflect cultural pressure towards constructing childhood as a period of innocence, as a private sphere of protected and uncontaminated leisure in which children can acquire the moral strength to deal with society and in which adults can ground their values and ideals . . .'

So in trying to discuss the effects of violent media material on children, we have a problem stemming from our preconceptions about 'children' and 'childhood'.

One also has to take account of the real patterns of children's viewing, which, depending on the age of the young person involved, can vary considerably. Hamilton (1998) for example, points out that in the USA children aged 2 to 11 spend an average of 23 hours a week watching TV. But he also found that, in a sample of viewing made in 1993, more children watched prime-time sitcoms than programmes for children. He also asserts that considerable numbers of children watch violent material that is not intended for them. For example, he says that the most violent movies shown on prime-time network TV in 1993 were seen by a total audience which included 1.3 million children aged 2 to 11.

When considering the adult audience, one may also raise a number of other questions. Regulation does not distinguish by gender. But one may reasonably ask whether the female audience is affected by experiencing an accumulation of dramas in which, whatever the narrative outcome, women are shown to be the victims of criminal and domestic violence. Are they caused to be more anxious than men, as some studies suggest (Schlesinger *et al.*, 1992)? Does media material enhance a fear of violence among the elderly, by privileging reports of attacks on the elderly. Because these are seen to be the socially reprehensible and exceptional (rated within news values) they get a higher profile in news media. At the same time, many of the elderly are aware of being more physically vulnerable than those who are fit and capable. This segment of the audience is not protected by regulation. But it may be affected differently to a degree by violent material.

The further one interrogates the nature of audience, the more variables even this one concept seems to throw up. For example, a younger more street-wise audience may read post-modern ironic violence as entertaining and deft, where an older audience reads the violence as gratuitous and unpleasant. Here one is talking about the textual and perhaps the social experience of the reader. Identifying what is likely to make a difference to effects does not make it certain what those effects will be.

Finally, there is the question of how the audience engages with a given text. Here you will need to refer back to Chapters 2 and 3. In this case, one reframes the debates and issues in terms of, for example, what kinds of meaning the audience constructs about violence from the text. There may be a short-term emotional jolt taken from decoding the violent event. Indeed, just as many studies point to violence creating a state of arousal, so too they point to the audience actually enjoying a state of fear – up to a point. This is another kind of reader pleasure. Children have also said that they like being frightened by material – again only up to a point. Such audience comments are evidence of a kind of short-term effect, but not the kind that leads directly to anti-social behaviour.

In terms of effects I suggest that what is more significant are the longer-term meanings about violence. We return to questions about what kind of violence is acceptable or not, committed by who, on whom? There are those problems raised by ideas about active and selective audience reading of texts. What about readers who skip to the exciting bits of sex and violence in a novel? They could be enhancing negative effects, not least if they miss out passages which put violence in a context.

Audiences bring their experience to a text. A drama involving road deaths will affect someone who has experienced this first-hand differently from others. There is the context in which reading takes place. A child reading under the covers by torchlight gets a different experience and meaning about violence from one who goes to the cinema with his or her friends. So there is the matter of whether the audience reads material as being violent in the first place. Then there is the matter of what is done with that reading.

- How is the reading assimilated into the reader's sense of how the world works?

- To what extent is the violence approved or condemned within some moral structure?

- Is the violence taken into some mental construct of social reality, or is it placed within some media frame of reference, apart from social reality?

- Does the violence affect the reader's attitudes and values, or not?

- In what ways do any such effects matter?
- In terms of ideas about reading positions, can one demonstrate that the text prefers a certain kind of reading about the violence?
- Is the reader capable of making an autonomous alternative or even oppositional reading?

These are questions which media research attempts to deal with, about which it has formulated propositions, but to which it has found few conclusive answers.

In particular one may recognize the context both of the text and of reception as being a significant variable when trying to make sense of the effects of violence. For example, the use of humour and of kinds of realism clearly affects interpretation of violence. One of the most obvious examples here is the cartoon aimed at children. Extreme violence may be a feature of this material – for instance, Tom and Jerry. But the comedy of the format, indeed the literal absurdity of many of the violent events and the miraculous recovery of characters from violence, places the violence and its likely effects well away from those of, say, realist drama. Potter (1999) identifies seven factors relating to text and surrounding the portrayal of violence which, he argues need to be evaluated when assessing the possible effects of violent representations. That is – rewards and punishments in the narrative, harmful consequences, motives, justification, realism, identification and humour.

7 Research methodologies and their problems

The point of this section is not to diminish the efforts of research into violence and effects, over many decades. A great deal has been learned from these efforts. But every approach to research does have its problems which work against drawing absolute conclusions about media influence and violence. There is a difference between believing that media have long-term attitudinal effects on their audiences, and setting this up as a hypothesis to be proven. And a further problem is that given audiences are not society as a whole. Nor are individuals who may be influenced separate from the audience as a whole. Part of the problem may well be that as yet we are simply not up to the kind of theorizing needed to argue and proved such affects: 'there is no adequate vocabulary to describe the relationships between the media, individuals, and society' (Curran and Seaton, 1997).

Here are some brief critiques of research approaches by way of example.

7.1 Content analysis

This depends on assumptions about how one defines violence in a given medium, how one categorizes types of violence and then on how one measures incidents – by number, for example, or by time/space given to them.

The kind of study carried out by Cumberbatch in 1989 for the BBC used elaborate categories, and in the end indicated that the incidence of violence on television had gone down over the previous ten years, even though this might not have fitted with public perceptions.

But in any case the key assumption behind this methodology is that the number of incidents will be significant and necessarily implies an effect on the audience. In fact this does not follow. One might read violent novels all day and every day without this proving anything about how the material is made sense of, or affects the reader.

In a summary of content findings Potter (1999) asserts among others, the following content findings about TV violence

- rates of violence fluctuate across different types of programmes;
- rates are higher for verbal violence than for physical violence;
- violent crime is much more frequent on TV than in real life;
- most perpetrators are white, middle-aged and male;
- a high proportion of violence is committed by 'good' characters;
- consequences for victims are rarely shown;
- weapons are often found in violent acts;
- much of the violence is portrayed in a humorous context.

In elaboration on these points he comments on the fact that white characters are more likely to be portrayed as police officers, whereas African American and Latino characters are more likely to be portrayed as criminal suspects. He refers to the fact that the serious physical, emotional and psychological consequences of violence are rarely portrayed. Again, one's concern for the implied consequences of this kind of representation need to be modified by uncertainty as to how, in any given examples, such features may or may not be taken seriously by the audience. The difficulty lies in uncertainty about how various audience members may or may not incorporate such 'facts' within their world views. As Gunter (1985) put it: 'Major problems arise when moving from statements about what the content implies, as assessed by objective analysis of its inherent structures, to how it is actually perceived and interpreted by the audience.'

7.2 Laboratory experiments

These are inherently 'unreal' because they take place under artificially controlled conditions. They remove the influence of everyday surroundings and influences – the context of life.

The well-known Bandura experiments of the 1960s with Bobo the doll were said to have demonstrated how violence could be transferred from play to social behaviour in children (and it may be argued that media consumption is a kind of play). However, and apart from the fact that not all the children showed this transfer, the experimental conditions removed normal social constraints on violent behaviour. Also, they arguably set up the children in a frame of mind where they would behave in ways which they could see might please the researchers (Bandura, 1973; Bandura et al., 1963).

7.3 Field experiments

These are only as effective and significant as the quality of their questions and the reliability of their respondents – let alone the validity of what sense the researcher makes of a given set of responses.

Belson (1978) produced a widely reported piece of research which seemed to proved that heavy television viewing and violent behaviour were connected in respect of teenage males. One problem among others was that the work depended on the recall of respondents. It is a common experience for researchers to find the people's memory is selective and erratic. There is also the question of the backgrounds of respondents, and how far these correlate with a preference for violent material. In this case, 38 per cent of boys from working-class homes admitted to violent social behaviour, as opposed to 13 per cent from non-manual working social groups. And indeed, the boys who committed most aggressive acts in life were in fact only moderate viewers of violence.

Barker and Petley (2001) have demonstrated that children will lie to researchers (in this case about videos which they could not have seen because they did not exist). Questions and discussions which depend on recall of violent material are suspect, to the extent that our ability to remember things is selective and fallible. Research can be seen as tendentious if, for example, it has preselected and predefined its material as being violent – 'here are some violent videos, I want you to talk about them'. And research involving children may contain its own sets of fallacies. For example, we tend to generalize about how we define children and what they are like as a category. In fact, there are many ways of distinguishing categories under the heading of 'child' – all of which may change understanding of media effects.

8 Effects models and their problems

Effects models are inherently problematic because they are hypothetical. Do they arise as a result of carrying out experiments (which we have just said will have their own drawbacks)? Or are they propositions prior to experimentation? (In which case they are just a notion, but one which will influence how experimentation is carried out.)

8.1 Hypodermic models – short term and behavioural

These models are about short-term cause and effect, and include so-called copycat killings. They are discredited, in spite of having a hold on the popular press and the popular imagination because it has never been demonstrated that media violence leads to violent behaviour. Even copycat killings have been shown to exist in certain kinds of context – usually of the social environment – which render them exceptional rather than usual. However, they may be a response to some media behaviour. In any case, a number of such examples have revealed false claims and blame on the media. For example, in September 2000, in a well-publicized court case, a 15-year-old Florida male blamed his abuse of his 8-year-old sister on ideas presented in an edition of the *Jerry Springer Show*. He lied: the show was blameless.

PERPETRATOR
age, gender, motivation

VICTIM
age, gender, response

AUDIENCE
age, gender, socialization
frequency of exposure
peer group values

REALISM OF REPRESENTATION
relative to conventions and nature of text

discussion of representation

NATURE OF MEDIUM
e.g. novel or film
written or visual codes

EFFECTS OF

VIOLENCE

NATURE OF TEXT
e.g. comedy or drama or news

NATURE OF ACT
wounding, harming, killing
physical – verbal
weapon used

OUTCOMES OF ACT
physical, psychological
harm, death

CONTEXT OF ACT
Textual – within narration
Societal – attitudes towards
act: where experienced
e.g. home or cinema

Media Representations of Violence: Conditions surrounding effects
This great array of factors relates to the social and media experience of individual members of an audience, as well as to characteristics of media and of their texts. Such a variety of conditioning factors makes it difficult (some would say impossible) to distinguish particular effects of exposure to representations of media violence – let alone to determine particular causes of any effects which may be proposed.
(*Graeme Burton*, 2004)

8.2 Cultivation model – long term and attitudinal

The cultivation model of accumulated media effects leading to an internalized 'climate' of violence is also imperfect, though attractive in its willingness to look at long-term effects and at attitude change as much as at behaviours [see Gerbner *et al.*, 1986]. It suggests that heavy television viewing cultivates a negative view of the world as being a violent place. Refinements of the theory through research over a period of time have added notions such as that of the general or mainstream television view of violence, among other effects areas. It has also been suggested that effects vary between different social groups.

One problem is that it relies quite heavily on content analysis, of television in particular (see above). It also assumes that 'heavy' users of television are more likely to be influenced than are 'light' users. This does not necessarily follow, and ignores other factors which might in fact cause a light user to be influenced (first-hand experience of violence, for example). It assumes that television viewing is as much a passive as an active experience.

Other approaches to long-term effects have looked at children in particular. Some research has suggested that childhood viewing of violence may be related to aggressive behaviour in adulthood. However, the evidence is not conclusive, given the range of socializing influences that may produce such an effect.

There is no space here to offer a more lengthy critique, which has in any case been well done by others. But examples of other models which have led to inconclusive or negative results when tested in experiments include.

8.3 Innoculation theory

This proposes that experience of media violence leads to desensitization and toleration of violent behaviour. This has been no more proven than Aristotle's theory of catharsis, which proposes the opposite – that experience of violence (through drama) purges violent thoughts and impulses in the audience. Feshback and Singer (1971) in particular have explored the idea that violence on TV can make some viewers less likely to commit violence in life.

8.4 Uses and gratifications theory

This proposes that we use media material to gratify certain internalized needs that drive our behaviours in general. Apart from the fact that this model has been little used to evaluate violent material and violent behaviours, persuasive as it is, it is predicated on the fact that such needs actually exist. Their existence as an internal mental structure is itself predicated on categorizing human behaviours. So far as violence may be related to this model, it would seem to fit in with a need for diversion and entertainment. But then there is nothing in the model that suggests, for instance, that reading crime thrillers with violent incidents in them has any influence on behaviour or on attitudes to violence. If anything, the effect is to make the reader feel better for having been diverted.

It would seem that a general problem with research into media and violence is selectivity of approach and a failure to take whole views of problems, methodologies and the range of work in the field.

66 99 . . . if research of the 2000s is to better comprehend the import of media violence and achieve more practical results, it must be directed by an overall view, that is, it must theoretically embrace media violence as well as the power of culture, the active audience, and the economy, power relations, and media technology in society. It must, therefore, combine teleological understanding and causal explanations, and quantitative and qualitative methodology. It must also leave the simplified notion of 'entertainment violence' aside and realise that the borderlines between fictional and non-fictional media violence are often blurred and sometimes non-existent, and that all kinds of media violence are cultural or symbolic constructions.

Von Feilitzen (1998)

9 The implications of regulation

Again one needs to refer back briefly to a previous section on regulation which brings out implications for establishment and social attitudes towards media violence. In other words, regulatory statements by bodies which in some respects censor the media, tell us a great deal about what is assumed by them concerning the relationship between media and audience.

It is assumed that some media are more influential than others – broadcasting more than publishing. It is assumed that some acts of violence in some media do have some effect on the audience – the BBFC censors violent scenes from US movies which have already been passed by their censors. It is assumed that some audiences are more suscep-tible than others – there are industrial codes of practice, legal obligations in broadcasting and other statutes (Young Person's Harmful Publications Act) which control the content and treatment of violent material offered to young people. It is assumed that the elderly, or those who have just achieved the legal age of adult responsibility are not likely to be adversely influenced by most violent material. It assumes that some media industries should not be left to regulate themselves.

One may also notice various indirect effects of regulation on the presence and consumption of violent material. For example, the imposition of a 'high' rating on a movie at its time of release may simultaneously shut out a certain younger audience yet also make it more attractive to potential viewers because it is assumed to be 'more exciting'. In the case of television material, if violence requires some kind of viewer warning, then this may affect the willingness of advertisers to spend money on slots – certainly for goods and services which relate to a family audience. Conversely, advertisers of sport and alcohol may even be attracted to more violent material. It all depends on the audience profile, which is defined by what is shown and how it is regulated. Potter argues that in the USA this situation works against the networks being willing to place warnings on violent material. He demonstrates that the loss of even a small percentage of potential advertising over a period of time because of such regulation can add up to the loss of millions of dollars of income to the networks.

10 Effects and conclusions

The jury is still out on the matter of the media influencing violent attitudes and behaviours. Concern about the possibility of influence remains. However, one also needs to recognize that public concern is itself to some extent a consequence of media influ-ence. Similarly, it is the media that dominantly report this public concern, once it is aroused. So it is easier to demonstrate that the media cause worry about levels of vio-lence, than it is to prove that they cause the violence itself. One can prove that in some cases media exaggerate the nature and frequency of kinds of violence. One can be pretty clear about ways in which violence is treated, about the nature of representation, the use of discourse. What is less clear is the precise effect of such representations on audiences, however much one may feel that the accumulative effects of some representations must be adverse. Equally, we should recognize that neither has it been proved that media have no effects at all. 'Undoubtedly, many viewers choose selectively to watch violent or stereo-typed programmes . . . However, it does not necessarily follow that there are no effects of viewing such programmes or that motivated viewers can successfully undermine any possible effects' (Livingstone, 1996).

Effects are not necessarily clear and direct, or even those one might have expected.

For example, it was reported that sales of child toddler reins went up after the notorious abduction and murder of a young child (James Bulger) by two older children, in 1993. The increase in sales is a clear effect. An increase in parental anxiety levels is a probable effect, which can only be inferred. But the effect on our understanding of and attitudes towards violence cannot even be guessed at.

In discussing the issues raised around violence in the media, one needs to account for the fact that debates and actions related to this are generated by public and political organizations. Media violence (or even crime and violence) is not an issue which spontaneously gets people out on the streets. There is one respect in which bodies like Ofcom both feel a public responsibility, but also have it thrust upon them by politicians. I suggest that one reason for the political impetus to the debate is that violence is about disorder, and disorder is something the state fears.

So far as the media are concerned, while they may at times raise concerns about violence in the media within a framework of public responsibility, I suggest that their dominant underlying agenda is that of the market. Violence sells; and nothing sells news in particular so much as bad news.

One may reasonably be concerned about effects on younger people, who are unarguably in a phase of development – moral, social, and in terms of identity. But we do not have agreed and secure models for that phase, let alone for dealing with the problem that people develop in different respects, at different rates, under a whole range of different influences.

In an ongoing discussion about whether the media reflect or refract social attitudes and behaviours through their texts, it is impossible to determine where media reflection of existing behaviours ends, and the refraction of those behaviours into something else, into a matter of concern, begins. A single example would be the story strand in a soap opera, *EastEnders* (2003), in which two female characters have been the victims of violence by the same man. We know about the levels of domestic violence against women. These exist without media intervention. But now that this programme, with up to 16 million viewers an episode, has intervened, it is unavoidable that public consciousness has been raised. There has been some effect. People talk. But one cannot make any firm statements about a change in public attitudes towards women as victims of domestic violence – other than perhaps to see how legal judgements have shifted towards recognition of the problem and towards liberal judgements. How much soap operas or the media in general have anything to do with this shift is impossible to measure.

In conclusion, it may be useful to look at Gunter's account (1994) of seven categories of primary effects, which he draws from his work and from the critical literature in general. These are

- catharsis – media violence purges the reader of violent feelings;

- arousal – violence excites the reader;

- disinhibition – violence lowers inhibitions against approving of or even against committing violence;

- imitation – violence encourages the copying of such violent acts;

- desensitization – accumulated experience of violence makes the reader less sensitive to its implications and effects;

- cultivation – violence experienced over a period of time encourages a climate of acceptance towards and even approval of some kinds of violent acts (see also Gerbner);
- fear – people are frightened by the experience of violence through the media.

These effects are at one and the same time, propositions and conclusions about the effects of media violence. Either way, they have to be proven. They are not true because they are proposed. They are not valid conclusions if the research methodology is flawed or if the evidence does not support them.

There is no firm evidence that the media uniquely cause violent behaviour or engender violent attitudes. They may be part of a social and cultural context which predisposes some individuals towards approval of such attitudes and behaviours.

11 Discussion extract

Television has been hypothesised to influence its audiences at a number of levels, principally, cognitive, affective (or emotional), and behavioural. These effects have tended to be investigated quite separately. This pattern has probably been shaped to a great extent by the particular specialities and interest of the researchers concerned. Either the focus of study has been the cognitive effects of media messages, or their effects on usually short-term emotional responses or their short-term and long-term, behavioural effects. Yet, it is entirely reasonable to assume . . . that the same media messages may have an influence at more than one level. Furthermore, audience responses at these different psychological levels could even be interdependent. It has been fairly clearly established that audience reactions to television and film content are often mediated by intervening factors. The latter factors may be behavioural, relating to the amount of exposure to a media item, or cognitive, comprising some sort of judgmental response in which the media content is classified in some way by its audience or compared with information from another source. The way in which media audiences weigh up media content has a crucial part to play in their subsequent response to it. Thus, television violence which occurs in a fantasy setting will be perceived differently from that which occurs in a contemporary drama setting much closer to life. This kind of perception will influence the nature of any further cognitive response (shift in belief or knowledge), affective response (fright reaction), or behavioural response (increased aggressiveness). It could also be the case, however, that the emotional or behavioural responses will also be contingent, at least in part, on the cognitive response. For instance, viewers who watch a great deal of television violence, it could be argued, may become more aware of violence in real life or believe that real-life violence is more commonplace than it really is. In consequence, they also develop a greater fear of falling victim to violence.

. . . The use of media does not occur in a vacuum. Media-related behaviours occur alongside other activities that occupy our time each day. We also have access to other sources of information about the world comprising direct experience and interpersonal experience through conversations and interactions with other people. The role of these social forces in the cultivation of norms and values that govern how we think, feel, and behave cannot and should not be ignored. Understanding the influence of the media on social attitudes and behaviour cannot therefore be divorced from the broader social context in which individuals are brought up.

Barrie Gunter (1994)

1 How do some of the comments in this extract relate to the criticisms offered by Gauntlett (above)?

2 How is it suggested that audience reactions to violent material may be mediated via a number of contingent factors?

3 How, in your view, might comment on types of effect and on the difficulties of constructing research methodologies, apply to examples of violence in media other than television and cinema?

12 Further reading

Barker, M. and Petley, J. (eds) (2001) *Ill Effects* (2nd edn). London: Routledge.

Carter, C. and Kay Weaver, C. (2003) *Violence and the Media*. Buckingham: Open University Press.

Gauntlett, D. (1995) *Moving Experiences: Understanding Television's Influences and Effects*. London: John Libbey.

Gunter, B. (1994) The question of media violence, in J. Bryant and D. Zillmann, *Media Effects, Advances in Theory and Research*. Hillsdale, NJ: Lawrence Erlbaum Associates.

Potter, W.J. (1999) *On Media Violence*. London: Sage.

Von Feilitzen, C. (1998) Media violence: four research perspectives, in R. Dickinson, H. Harindranath and O. Linne, *Approaches to Audiences: A Reader*. London: Arnold.

CHAPTER FIVE

WOMEN'S MAGAZINES

Manufacturing a gendered space: questions of guilt and pleasure

❝Women's magazines offer their readers particular definitions and understandings of what it is to be female.❞

Ballaster, R., Beetham, M., Frazer, E. and Hebron, S. (1991)
Women's Worlds – Ideology, Femininity and the Woman's Magazine. Basingstoke: Macmillan.

1 Introduction

In this chapter I want to take a look at magazines produced for a female audience, in terms of how they define themselves as gendered texts, and of how that audience may make sense of these texts. These magazines seem to open doors to a special, even secret, and feminized world, in which the state of being a girl or a woman is celebrated. Pleasure are offered and shared.

Women's magazines have a long history (see White, 1969), in contrast with the lack of any kind of equivalent magazine for males. Having magazines that are read predominantly by males, not least those in specialist hobby areas such as computing, is not the same as having a 'men's magazine'. Nor do the British 'lads' mags' of the 1990s – *Loaded* or *FHM* – really fit this definition. This difference is significant, not least because it can be explained in terms of culture and ideology. Put simply, men's world is 'the world' – it needs no further explanation or definition. But the woman's world is defined in relation to this 'naturally' dominant model. Women's magazines have helped a process of demarcation and distinction – the working of difference. This contrast is underlined by the range of magazines for women, by their long history, and by their selection in terms of the age of the audience. The market recognizes and defines their female readers from the age of 12 upwards (arguably earlier). Before that even, there are comics (or picture mags) doing the work of socialization, defining what it is to be female and what is a female place in the world.

Women's magazines assume that women exist as a coherent readership. They construct women as a largely 'homogenous group': they address them as if they are a 'naturally occurring group' (Ballaster *et al.*).

Women recognize what is going on in these media products. The expansion of formal education together with a certain level of public awareness about media production and marketing, has contributed to a much reported tension in female readers

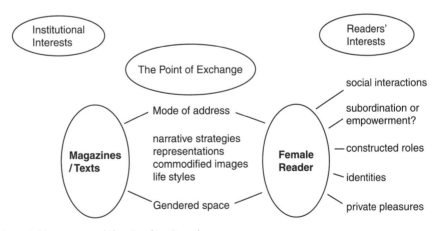

Women's Magazines and Their Readers: Some key terms
The constructed and commodified world of women's magazines works in the commercial interests of media producers. But does that mean that it works entirely against the interests of a female audience? Is there an outcome in the readers' interests that undercuts the force of ideology, at the same time as this force subordinates women in social, political and economic terms?
(*Graeme Burton, 2004*)

between guilt and pleasure. Many women enjoy reading these magazines, yet realize that they are being levered into certain roles, and into being concerned for their appearance in the eye of the male gaze.

There is now some degree of equivalence to this in the lads' mags, but this is a recent cultural phenomenon. So they do help carry the messages of the twenty-first century 'cosmetics-for-males' industry. They do have articles on appearance, fitness and so being attractive to women. But they still contain images and articles that place women as sex objects. They have a small readership among the male population as a whole. They tacitly assume a culture of male dominance and privilege. They are nothing like the world of women's magazines, which females grow up with, and which clearly promote billion pound industries concerned with fashion, cosmetics, domestic and child-care products.

As an aside, and with relation to what will be a critique of the ideological work of women's magazines, it is worth remembering that half of the women in Britain do not read these magazines at all.

Women's magazines represent women to themselves in certain ways, bringing together social interaction and consumption. They incorporate assumptions about women in terms of their biology, their career aspirations, their roles models, their emotional lives. They can be sexist by stealth, ideological in what they do not say, and sometimes racist and ageist by implication. They naturalize and so endorse heterosexual definitions of sexuality as being 'normal'. But still a range of women enjoy reading them – and this needs to be elucidated, from both post-modernist and hegemonic perspectives.

Apart from looking at these magazines as gendered texts, as vehicles for representations, I also want to pay some attention to their narratives. In a larger sense they tell a story about becoming and being a woman. In a particular sense, they contain narratives – in features or readers' letters or short stories – which incline to certain concerns and certain outcomes. This is what McCracken (1993) refers to as 'the ostensibly authoritative grand narrative of reality developed month after month'.

2 Major questions

1 What do we understand to be distinctive about this genre defined as 'the women's magazine'?

2 What is the nature of the relationship set up through the magazine and its mode of address, which works on the reader?

3 What meanings may derived through the narratives and the representations of these magazines?

4 How may one understand these magazines in the context of debates about the relationship between producer, text and audience?

5 In particular, how may one evaluate alternative positions which justify texts as pleasurable and condemn them as being trivial and ideological?

6 What do these magazines say about female roles, female space and 'the feminine'?

3 Genre features – convention, expectation and fulfilment

> Given that there are more than eighty magazines for women on the news-stands, it is surprising how similar groups of them are.
>
> McKay (2000)

Women's magazines have consistency of type of content and treatment, across their sub-divisions and even across a long period of time. This consistency both creates a certain kind of relationship with the reader, based on expectations, and it imposes a certain kind of understanding or interpretation of the text. This consistency and continuity also stands for kinds of ideological verity about women's place in a constructed order of things. These magazines both stand for, and help maintain that construction, to varying degrees. The features that we anticipate – that have become conventional – focus on appearance, domestic work, relationships, romance. These may be couched in various modes – letters, features, fiction, true-life stories, advertisements and ad features.

They may be framed by various narrative devices – the problem, the autobiography, the call for help, the counsellor's advice. They may have a varying emphasis from age group to age group (and maybe from magazine to magazine). So magazines for young women are strong on forming relationships, on sex information, on leisure adventure: those for older women place more weight on maintaining relationships, dealing with loss, operating in the domestic sphere, among other topics. This genre world is still largely white and heterosexual. What is not represented or discussed is significant by its absence. Genres by definition of their mass appeal, are poor at recognizing minority interests. So women's magazines are socially normative, or ideologically conservative. They use a repetitive format and a confined range of subjects to please a majority audience, and to satisfy the economic interests of advertisers.

As with all media genres, women's magazines exist on an economic basis that makes profit from the pleasures of its audiences. The circuit of profit and pleasure predicates repetition and reinforcement. Genre features are reinforced, as are the ideological positions endorsed by the text. This reinforcement is adjacent to the process of naturalization through which the world of women's magazines is made to seem 'normal'.

The presence of advertising has become a normal feature of the magazines – as normal as the commercials embedded within TV programmes. What is exceptional is the sheer volume of promotional material. Not only is 50 per cent or more of the page space likely to be occupied by paid-for advertising, but also a great deal of other material is promotional. Feature articles are not always neutral. They may, for example, review or sample products – a device which in fact draws attention to those products. The primacy of promotion has become an unsurprising feature of the genre. It is not surprising to learn that on average 39 per cent of magazine revenue comes from advertising (Braithwaite, in Briggs and Cobley (1998)). When *Glamour* magazine was launched in Britain in 1991 (having been a success in the USA, it had an advertising launch budget of £5 million), it had a tie-in promotion deal with L'Oreal cosmetics and an in-store sales agreement with the Dorothy Perkins chain of clothing stores (*Independent on Sunday*, 17 June 2001).

So far as one can distinguish sub-genres under the heading of 'women's magazines', the differences are about the goods on offer, the lifestyle with which these goods are offered, and the life position of the reader. It is clear that *J-17* is aimed at free young females embarking on relationships, whereas *Woman's Own* is speaking to older home-makers and mothers. *Homes & Gardens* refers to class, aspiration and disposable income. *Stitches* refers to a very specific but female/domestic located interest. I would argue that while there are these variations on a theme, the theme is definitely there – beauty, fashion, relationships, sex, the home – these are the parameters of the world of women, or so it seems.

The genre features of the magazine are, it may be argued, attractive in the reassurance they give of a consistent world, a way of making sense of life. Indeed, the routine content – horoscopes, letters, features, advice, fashion – becomes a part of everyday life routine for the reader. Of course, it is dangerous to generalize about such routines – many women do not have children, for example. But in any case, media use is both part of and a break from this routine. And the short and varied elements which make up such magazines are good for slotting into routines. They can be picked up and put down without having to lose a narrative thread.

Certainly this is what Hermes (1995) argues for through her research. She takes an ethnographic approach in which she interviews Dutch women across an age range from 20s to 60s, attending to how, when and where they read, as much as to what they read. It appears that her respondents adapted media use to the rhythms of their days. This research also refers to two particular genre elements – things practical and things emotional. Her respondents were positive about what were seen as useful tips for making things, and about advice for coping emotionally with the various crises in life. Hermes herself is less convinced about the values of such material.

She sees the magazines (and their producers) as balancing the need to be slotted into everyday life, to be able to be put down, with a need to be diverting enough to be picked up in the first place – dispensable and yet indispensable. Hermes also talks about the 'repertoires' which she suggests that readers use to make sense of material. So, there is the repertoire of 'connected knowing', which 'addresses crisis situations'. This might, for example, relate to a feature about dealing with children on drugs – and becomes a way of securing life against change and threats. Or there is, for example, the repertoire of 'melodrama', which 'recognises the tragic quality of life'. This could also be related to the child/drugs example, which would then become all the more powerful as a text. What Hermes (1995) does not develop, but which seems pretty clear, is that these repertoires 'for making sense of' are equally characteristic genre features. They are in the text as well as in the reader.

In both historical and contemporary terms, one can see generic features in relation to the wider debate about media and society. For example, one might argue from a liberal pluralist view that the genre has developed in response to women's needs, and as a reflection of the changing conditions of women's lives. From a neo-Marxist view, the genre has developed as an expression of the class system, and recognizes mainly those women with disposable time and income. Also, it expresses the interest of capital and the process of commodification – much of the material is about selling goods. From one feminist view, the genre expresses indirectly the interests of patriarchy – from the male-dominated, multi-national owners of the magazines, to the implicit male in the text whose interest is in woman as beauty object and domestic labourer.

My own position is not to be trapped by labels, but is one which asserts that ideology is alive and kicking. So, although this chapter refers mainly to text and audience, one should also see the genre in the context of the political economy. There is room for allowing degrees of audience autonomy, while also asserting that the genre and its salient features work against the interests of women (and their autonomy).

In talking about girls' magazines in the early half of the twentieth century, Tinkler (1995) observes that 'the form and content of magazines represented the articulation of capital's concern to exploit girls as consumers, with patriarchal interests in the hetero-sexual development and orientation of girls as a necessary precondition of their accept-ance of unequal gender relations and a subordinate position within marriage.' One needs to question how far this situation has fundamentally changed in the meantime. In other words, the genre has developed in response to economic and ideological forces, not as a kind of mirror for the 'natural interests' of females.

4 Mode of address – positioning the reader

Magazines for females employ a familiar mode of address through which they engage the reader and set up a relationship. The tone and effect of this address assumes a complicity in a 'woman's world', in which the priority of certain interests is assumed – affairs of the body and affairs of the heart predominating. This mode of address contrives to gloss over the industrial and economic base which manufactures pleasurable words and images. It helps make the pleasures and the meanings unproblematic. It depends on its own history and on the related network of discourses about gender which are out there, being lived day to day. It is this history which has constructed the idea of 'a woman's world', that has made it self-evident who these magazines are for.

There is a degree of difference between magazines for various ages and interest groups. Publications aimed at the younger teenager, such as *Bliss* or *Sugar*, have more intimacy than detachment. They use argot and idiom of a supposedly cool nature – youth not adult. The graphics are full of fun/action and pink hues. The general tone and role position of the editorial or the features is that of big sister. Sexuality is acknowledged – intelligently in some cases. But this is a world in which girls have fun, boys are for fun, and domestic and economic responsibility does not figure much.

Publications aimed at the older woman address them as friends and equals, and never in that rather authoritative manner adopted by magazines of fifty years ago and more, which had more than a touch of 'mother knows best'. Still the woman is hailed as a partner in a gendered universe whose prison bars are out of focus, whose landscape of domestic activity, social performance and cultural improvement is very much in focus. Some magazines – say, the high fashion-oriented *Vogue* – are not even on the same planet so far as most women are concerned. But mainstream examples such as *Woman's Own* or *Cosmopolitan* have that largely conversational mode of address, which seeks to corner the market as a woman's friend.

The address, whether verbal or visual, positions the reader within a kind of role. That role position is partly measured against the role of the narrator/writer – whatever element of the magazine one is talking about. It is also a position that predicates a kind of relationship – one that doesn't really exist, but which may become real in the mind of the reader. So dipping into a women's magazine becomes rather like having conversations, it becomes a social experience – to this extent it becomes attractive and possibly addictive. It is an entirely false relationship. Most of all the reader is positioned in terms of reading the material – making meanings from the text. One may argue that the female reader feels well disposed towards pronouncements on ageing or advice on kinds of domestic improvement because she has been drawn into the position of listening to a friend who understands her life and its predicaments. The idea that this kind of media text may be partly responsible for weaving the threads of her life and of her gender understanding in the first place, is suppressed by the warmth and familiarity set up by this mode of address, and by the fact that magazine reading becomes part of her life's patterns.

The skill, the pleasure, even the addictiveness generated by the mode of address, is that the female reader feels addressed both individually and as part of a female community. She feels validated as an individual – she has a friend – she is 'understood'. But she also is led to feel that her problems, her concerns, her needs, are shared by a larger female community which is kept in touch through the pages of the magazine. What is so seductive and suspect about this address is that it is both an artifice and yet relates to social experience. It is acknowledged that many women do network, share problems, give priority to issues surrounding relationships. Magazines did not create this nuance of gendered social behaviour. On the other hand, the 'address' of these magazines is something constructed by commercial organizations with commercial ends in mind.

Hermes argues that media use, including magazine reading, does not have to be particularly meaningful. But then, nothing is meaningless. Humans are meaning-makers. So one has to deal with a debate in which on the one hand there is an argument against placing too much weight on the significance of popular media texts: but on the other hand, meaning may be created even from what is deemed trivial and transitory. Again, there is the issue of who determines what is more or less meaningful. Who is the media critic to tell the female reader that what she reads is lacking in influence because it appears to be 'insignificant'?

Critics have commented on the history of this mode of address and of generic patterns in terms of their consistency over three hundred years. It is in this context that it is hard not to see address as fulfilling an ideological function – 'the pleasures of the magazine for its women readers cannot be understood as "innocent", nor separated from their ideological function in women's lives' (Ballaster *et al.*, 1991). The women's magazine may sometimes recognize female subjectivity as a problem – one which it purports to solve. But in fact the magazines are reproducing the very contradictions that they appear to sort out. Any numbers of articles on assertiveness do not deal with the dominant meanings of advertising material, which 'teaches' subordination, passivity and objectification. The inherent contradictions of material which (like soaps) contain elements of social realism alongside the fantasy and unrealistic aspirations, remain unresolved.

5 Representations

The very phrase 'women's magazines' incorporates an assumption about the coherence of a group of people labelled 'women' who can be represented collectively, spoken for as a recognizable group. This coherence shuts down, if not actually eliminates, the possibility of variation in conceptualizing categories of women and their different needs and interests. It is a coherence that both informs the representations and is manufactured by them. It is a coherence that has been manufactured by decades of publications holding on to and constructing an audience. This representation of women may in part be inspired by cultural assumptions and attitudes – stereotypes are never simply invented by the media. But it is also in part a creature of market forces. Familiar and understood representations, invoking familiar sets of values, help sell magazines.

Many of the faces on the covers smile at us in close-up. This is the look that engages our attention, which is close and familiar. This is the face that the reader has to attend to because it is a role model in its appearance – both friendly and flawless of skin. Inside the magazines, women are presented as camera conscious (gaze aware), posing to show off the clothes. They are represented as people for whom appearance is of prime importance. The space in the magazines is dominated by such images – not by articles on economic management. The material representation (words and images) is bound up with attractiveness, idealization, the beauty myth. Connotatively, these representations still speak predominantly of passivity, social performance, domestic activity, and not of power.

One also notices – speaking of women's magazines in general and in terms of circulation figures – that some women are not represented. Those who look old are largely absent. Those who do not fit implied definitions of attractiveness are absent.

Those who belong to minorities such as the disabled or ethnic groups are (largely) absent, as indeed are those belonging to sexual minorities such as gays or transgendered groups. So the representations which purport to speak to and about all women, actually do not. And in so far as they do speak about women, they are extremely partial.

McCracken (1993) talks up the importance of the covers of women's magazines, as an advertisement in itself, as a genre identifier, as a semiotic system: 'the interplay of the photographic, verbal and chromatic texts on each cover creates a series of value-laden cultural significations, but is primarily intended to attract revenue from advertisers and increase circulation'. She sees the cover as window to a future self, which the woman aspires to attain but which is never quite attainable. McCracken discusses the representation of women on covers in terms borrowed from Irving Goffman. They may be signalling emotional display (the bright smile of delight and engagement); or signs of subordination (lowered gaze or head); or appeasement; or inner states (the distant gaze); or 'licensed withdrawal' (hands over face or mouth).

Ballaster *et al.* refer to 'a set of images and representations which construct an imaginary world and an imaginary reader'. This world is circumscribed by the generic elements already referred to. The reader is also assumed within this generic text. This reader construction is simultaneously generalized and differentiated. 'Woman' is represented as being universally concerned with things like attractiveness [*sic*] and social behaviour – and yet is to a degree separated into domestic woman, career woman, young single woman and the like. Both the generalization and the differentiation fail to deal with the genuine diversity of the readers. Images from ethnic minorities, where they exist, are westernized. Class is ignored. Ageing is suppressed, resisted and denied.

6 Narrative strategies

To some extent the devices used in these magazines to narrate a story about 'woman-ness' may be conflated with what has been said under mode of address. The narration is also about positioning the reader.

But in this case, I am talking about two areas. One is narration within the generic parts of a magazine. The other is about narration in the larger sense of discourse and meaning – the story that is told through the magazines in general – the story that is actually the constructed meaning of gender – the gendered world as the magazine sees it.

An ideologically informed approach to this narrative construction must take account of the ubiquitous ads and ad features that are common in women's magazines. The 'story' of what it is to be female and to behave as a woman, depends on consumption. Many of the pleasures that are promised – to be an object of affection and approval – depend on consumption. Many commodities are to do with the body, skin, adornment, tactile experiences. But they may also be to do with manufacturing a female environ-ment – very possible in the woman's spaces of bedroom and kitchen – but not always. There is also the performance of being a woman in public spaces – perhaps other places given over to bodily pleasures such as the restaurant or the gym. In any event, the story is that something has to be bought. It is a never-ending story because the narrative can never be resolved. It is about living. It is about ageing. It is about the arrival and departure of others in one's life, in the story. McCracken talks about a 'double narrative strategy' in which the reading experience offers one level of narrative and pleasure (perhaps the story about the improved kitchen). But on another level the reader has to 're-enact the narrative in the public sphere by purchasing goods and services'. The story is never ending because 'the commodity resolutions can only offer temporary pleasures'. What she does not point out is that there are problems in the stories, underlying the pleasures, and which themselves can only be resolved through commodities. The problems are themselves ideological constructions. One's appearance, or ageing, or one's kitchen, or one's state of health, or even one's relationships are not a problem unless one believes they are. So the narratives of women's magazines are as much about raising problems as resolving them, as much about making pleasure a problem that requires further action, as of being an end in itself.

7 Roles

66 99 There is a strong strand of feminist criticism which argues that by their very nature magazines aimed at women do acquire roles as shapers and definers of what women are and how they are perceived (Ferguson, 1983; Greer, 1999; Macdonald, 1995 and

many others). If that's so then it does matter what images of women are provided by these publications and what social roles women and girls are seen to play in them.

McKay (2000)

In terms of models for social performance and cultural positioning, women's magazines offer their readers a suite of roles to occupy. These roles are part of the representations. I have already pointed to the place of role in terms of reader positioning – the female reader as confidante. But it is the social models that help to define a woman's place in the ideological order of things. Dominant models in the history of women's magazines are the roles of wife and mother. The woman is seen as a nurturer and carer – of children and of men. She is a manager and a purchaser – within the domestic sphere.

Tinkler (1995) in magazines of the 1930s in which even stories about married relations positioned the young wife in a maternal role vis-à-vis her husband – no sex, but she could pull his troubled head to her bosom. Tinkler mainly explores roles within girls' magazines – as friend, daughter and schoolgirl, with a demarcation between the middle-class, and working-class girls who would leave home to work and had some money to spend. She observes that the distinction between class/social roles of the audience continues to be in evidence in the later twentieth century (shown through McRobbie's analysis of adolescent female readers of the magazine *Jackie*, in the 1970s). Tinkler refers to this class difference in terms of the emphasis on fiction (entertainment) for working-class girls, and wider range of education/information for the middle-class audience.

Class roles in terms of magazine content and implied audience are now much less explicit, as is the identification of marriage as major life goal. But romance, fun and being in a long-term heterosexual relationship remain the staple fare.

Magazines did become more explicit about romance and the heart (in relation to the goal of marriage). But then, as the teenager/girls' market opened up from the 1960s onwards, and adulthood defined only as work/marriage was further deferred, catching a man was transcribed into dating a boy. The role of fiancée was for more formal times and preparation for the more inevitable and dominant role of wife. But increasingly the young female was allowed to be girlfriend, and her sexuality has been acknowledged. Yet, either way, one is looking at another set of roles which are fundamentally defined in relation to males. As a critic, one is in a difficult position on the surface – the glum face at the party, which appears to deny fun. So the point here is not to diminish the emotional value of romance and its place in a pleasurable social fabric. The criticism is about the subordinated nature of the female in such roles. It is about the commodification of romance when it is contextualized within the material trappings of the date or (still, sometimes) the wedding. This commodification may be connoted not just by any references within an article but within advertising in the magazine, that speaks of a lifestyle, a story of romance, that relies on spending and giving material objects.

Of course one has to qualify these generally valid statements with particular qualifications. Some magazines for young women in some articles do talk up ideas about being in control. They do not always talk up the goal of marriage. Nor do they see the date as a prelude to engagement. There has been some kind of change in the way that women's magazines handle sex and romance, but there has not been an absolute ideological shift. And one does have to consider not only women's magazines in general, but also the related cultural and media context. I am referring for example to the wedding supplements in papers and magazines, to wedding exhibitions, to the romantic novel, to the discourse of fictions in other media. All these provide a context to the reading of women's magazines, and provide fuel for the discourse in general.

Returning to kinds of role, another kind of qualification needs to take account of those magazines of the past 20 years that have come to recognize the changing social roles and positions of women. There are more women out at work than ever before. Women do marry later in life. Women do juggle careers and families. So to an extent magazines like *Cosmopolitan* and revamped traditional magazines do present women in the role of worker or single achiever. However, what these magazines or articles also often do is to qualify this role in terms of discussion of appearance or of lifestyle/ leisure activities or of cultural development. There is still this pull back into issues of appearance, not achievement, of the domestic sphere not the public sphere, of self-improvement. The roles in this modern woman's world are still tied to dressing up, to leisure activities, to domestic work.

The over-arching role constructed through women's magazines is that of the feminine. This construction (as Ballaster and others have pointed out) happens because of a history in which the women's magazine has itself developed a role as 'friend, adviser, narrator'. The magazines define what it is to be feminine in appearance and behaviour, in a domestic or a public sphere, in relation to family or men, sexually or romantically. Most of all, in their own commercialized interests, the magazines imply that the readers are still learning and developing their role: that they lack something – that is, femininity. The magazines' advice, and their products in particular, can satisfy this lack. But, of course, it is never quite satisfied – one can always read more, become just that bit more feminine and complete. 'Femininity, therefore, becomes both a source of anxiety and a source of pleasure because it can never be fully achieved' (Ballaster *et al.*, 1991).

Magazines can be bound up with a woman's changing life role as well as with her sense of identity – for example, teens to young singles to young marrieds to middle aged – 'your self-identity as a married or a single woman is tied up with your choice of magazines' – 'identity is achieved through consumption' (Ballaster *et al.*, 1991).

So the magazine both reflects changing roles, yet also contrives to shape and define them. It becomes a lifestyle accoutrement. It is part of living, of the woman's very reality. Pictures of women become kinds of recipe for femininity.

Ferguson (1983) sees the acquisition of a feminine role as being a kind of religious initiation ceremony. Through magazines (and other cultural sources) females learn how to anoint their skin, perform nightly and morning rituals of cleansing, don the right robes in the right way, learn the secrets of menstruation, sexuality, birth.

8 Social interactions

Similarly, the interactions represented in women's magazines are circumscribed, obviously with relation to roles. Interaction are referred to within the home, in leisure situations, in relation to children and loved males, in relation to friends, in relation to professionals who are helping them with health issues chiefly and then possibly with matters such as divorce.

The interactions have significant emotional dimensions. They may be expressed in terms of how the woman is regarded by others. They have a lot to do with the woman achieving the approval of others, and in terms of her own self-esteem.

Articles which refer to women in the public sphere still often drag the agenda back into line. The woman concerned is talked of, or talks for herself, in terms of things like coping with family and work, dressing up for work, leisure in contrast to work or dealing with people at work. That which is highlighted is given value. Certain kinds of interaction are placed within the woman's sphere. What is not dealt with is unimportant by omission – public performance, public achievement, economic competence, the exercise of power in the public sphere.

Equally, there is a cutting double-edge in this argument. To deplore the relative lack of material for and about women in powerful public roles risks appearing to denigrate the interactions and domestic roles just referred to. This is not valid either. One is caught between condoning the commodification of women's lives, the equation of material and emotional living, and recognizing the value of 'women's talk'. So often this talk – not least in magazines, sections of newspapers, and even in broadcast programmes – is categorized as gossip (men never gossip, of course!). But then there is a deal of difference between an article which leads on the dating patterns and home decor of some TV personality, and a feature (or short story) which leads on the negotiation of relationships. Emotional intelligence is valuable. It is the scope and context of interaction in women's magazines which is perhaps the issue.

9 The ever-present male

The point has already been made about ways in which role, interaction and representation in women's magazines contains a male dimension. I want to further draw out this point that his apparently self-contained world, which is both *of* women, and *for* women, is in fact, like the female discourse, defined to a fair extent in relation to a male world.

This is most obvious in respect of the images. Fashion pictures in particular, often with stylized poses, expect the gaze of a female reader, but covertly assume that the gaze which is posed for is that of a male. This is the female who expects to be the object of attention. This is the female who learns to perform for the male gaze. Some advertising images have even explicitly contained the gazing male. But in any case, it is the camera position which gives away the male gaze. If the lens centre is directed at the model's body, or the camera was placed in some voyeuristic location (behind an object, or to one side of the model), then the range and history of visual forms makes it clear that this is masculine looking.

The male figure also 'watches' from other margins of the magazine. My argument about appearance, performance and gaze clearly relates to all other materials which are about clothes and cosmetics. But then the male also lurks as the significant other who is boyfriend, partner, husband, or even celebrity.

'Men are a constant reference point', 'women's activity (in magazines) is directed towards . . . responding suitably to men's anti-social behaviour' (Ballaster *et al.*). These authors also comment that 'the work of maintaining healthy personal relationships is women's work'. They point out that even when referring to magazines aimed at the young single market – 'the "single" state (without a man) is a temporary condition. In the more traditional magazines, being single is usually understood to be a problem.' So the woman's space is always defined by having a male in it, or one waiting on the sidelines.

10 Contradictions

Drawing from the previous section, one of the many contradictions in women's magazines is the pretence that this is a self-contained woman's space, when in fact it is defined to a fair extent by the male. It is what the male world is not. Its preoccupations are at least to a fair extent with the implied male who provides the motive for many of the activities drawn out through features, letters, fictions and life dramas which are a staple of content.

- There is the contradiction which exercises critical work on women's magazines – they purport to speak for the needs and situation of women, yet their connotations work against the interests of women.
- There is the contradiction that, generally speaking, they articulate opposing discourses of male and female, yet appear to speak of cohesion and harmony and satisfactory relationships. This is not a world in which men and women appear on equal terms. Yet the magazines will refer to equal opportunities and the status of women. It is a world of conflicting appearance and reality.
- There is a contradiction in that the reader is identified as a woman, but is addressed as if she is still learning to be a woman, so is not yet in fact the woman identified.
- There are wider contradictions between elements of magazines which talk up stable relationships and the domestic sphere, and those which allude to sexual autonomy and erotic affairs. In this respect, the very nature of the romantic genre is in itself contradictory – immediate gratification vies with deferred pleasures.
- There is a contradiction between the appearance of entertainment in domestic activities (often with relation to food), and the reality of routine domestic labour.
- There is a contradiction between the largely middle-class labour represented (when work in the public sphere is mentioned at all), and the actuality of repetitive part-time jobs which is the real experience of many women.
- There is a contradiction in the way that beauty/appearance is framed in terms of the natural, when in fact it is constructed and an artifice.
- There is a contradiction between the representation of home as a place of leisure (perhaps a place to be beautified), and the fact that it is the location of labour.
- And there is the oldest contradiction of all – in which women are simultaneously sexual and on display, yet also represented as being chaste and loyal.

11 Pleasure and a woman's space

Discussion of text and reader in this case has to take account of the huge sales figures for, and the well-evidenced pleasures gained from reading these magazines. One cannot talk simply in terms of hegemony at work, of women as a mass being hoodwinked by the machinations of capitalist institutions. Clearly women's magazines do, after all the critiques are made, offer kinds of reward and satisfaction in the reading.

Whatever the forces that create the particular social environment for women, their magazines do deal with that environment as it is. The process of reading offers a leisure space. The structure of the magazines offers the chance to dive into the pool for a quick dip. The process of reading is undemanding and it offers a chance to engage with material that women have already learned is part of 'their province'. So there is the pleasure of entering a special place that is integrated with one's female identity, that gives one distinction and satisfaction, that somehow sets one apart.

Many critics address the 'problem' of guilt and pleasure (as they see it), in which the pleasure of reading vies with guilt at involving themselves with material that is sometimes trivial and certainly ideological. A post-modernist view might try to settle the problem by arguing for reader power – one takes what one wants, and one uses rather than being used.

Hermes (1995) certainly concludes from her research that this is the case, according to the 80 readers interviewed. They say that the material is forgettable, the pleasure is transitory, and that there are no profound meanings. But then one has to ask how far these readers can be aware of the internal processes through which meanings may be accrued. One has to relate their responses to those other comments about guilt in reading such material – they would say that it doesn't mean much, or influence them, wouldn't they? And one has to account for the reasons why those loyal female readers keep coming back for more of their favourite magazines.

But a political economy analysis, or indeed audience analysis that still acknowledges ideology and hegemony, would be asking questions about how far the 'woman's space' is simply a gender trap, a gilded cage at least partly constructed by the material of women's magazines.

McCracken invokes different critics in an attempt to explain the seductive pleasures of mass media texts. She refers to Jameson in terms of a compensatory exchange in which the pleasures and gratifications of mass culture become a kind of pay-off for passive consent behaviour in political terms. She refers to Modleski in relation to romance fiction and soap operas – the idea that these forms help women manage the real problems and injustices of their own lives, so that the pleasure is bittersweet and purposeful. She refers to Radway in relation to readers of romantic fiction – the idea that the pleasure is about identification, self-recognition and developing a sense of self-worth through reading. She herself refers to findings from her own research, which indicate that some readers in some way enhance their own identity simply by being the reader of a certain magazine that speaks of a certain kind of woman with a certain kind of lifestyle.

The very structure of a women's magazine makes for a kind of pleasure, and at least the illusion of control of the text. The reader chooses to buy it. It can be dipped into or explored at greater length. It offers tips as well as cultural gossip, so it may afford the moral satisfaction (and justification) of providing useful ideas for providing meals for the family, for 'improving' one's environment, for 'improving' one's public image.

Yet pleasure, like the magazine itself, is a constructed thing. The very notion of 'natural' pleasures is itself ideological. It relates especially to ideas about 'nature' and the female discourse. In different ways, various elements of magazines encourage women to be 'natural' (and free), to express their 'natural femininity', to enjoy the pleasures of 'being natural'. But this pleasure, this naturalness, this freedom, is often constructed (and purchased) through commodities such as skin products, tampons, shampoos, detergents and clothing. Similarly, beauty is also a myth and a construction. It too is often equated with the natural – that which pre-exists and is revealed through the beauty product. But, of course, it does not exist at all. As an idea it is defined and constructed by the commodities sold through the magazines.

So the experience of reading women's magazines may well be a pleasure, but the reader may or may not recognize those mechanisms which construct the illusion of a valid, gendered social world.

12 Discussion extract

First, I believe that magazines do wield a strong influence over their readers. I base this on common sense, my own experience and, much more convincingly, on the research undertaken by publishers and advertisers. Second, I am firmly on the side of Cynthia White who argued in her Royal Commission Report that magazines should cover a much wider range of subjects the better to prepare girls and women for life in a real world instead of one which is bounded by agonising over how they look and how to cope with domestic drudgery. She was writing in the mid-70s but her conclusions are, regrettably, still valid.

Third, I take what might be called a traditional feminist position in that I find the picture of women's lives to be gleaned from reading many women's magazines disheartening as well as unrealistic even allowing for a bit of fantasy and plenty of light-hearted fun. The underlying assumptions of so many publications is that women are obsessed by their appearance and with good reason as that is what will define them in the eyes if the world. The argument here is also commercial as American feminist editor Gloria Steinem described in *Sex, Lies and Advertising* (Steinem, 1995): lack of confidence about looks leads to expenditure on clothes and cosmetics, without which consumer magazines would not exist . . . Romance and marriage have been pushed aside since White was writing, it is true, but they have been more than replaced by sex dressed up in various guises on the problem pages, the fashion pages, the general features and the health pages. Nothing wrong with that if people want to read about it, but it is the fact that there is so little in the way of debate about anything vaguely contentious (as opposed to prurient) that gives rise to criticism.

McKay, J. (2000)

1 What is the writer's argument about the nature and effect of material in women's magazines?

2 What research methodology would you construct to evidence assertions about a shift of emphasis in women's magazines from romance to sex?

3 What kind of 'life' do you find is represented in given women's magazines, and what kind of relationship do these magazines appear to construct with their readers?

13 Further reading

Ballaster, R., Beetham, M., Frazer, E. and Hebron, S. (1991) *Women's Worlds – Ideology, Femininity and the Woman's Magazine*. Basingstoke: Macmillan.

Hermes, J. (1995) *Reading Women's Magazines*. Cambridge: Polity Press.

McCracken, E. (1993) *Decoding Women's Magazines*. Basingstoke: Macmillan.

McKay, J. (2000) *The Magazines Handbook*. London: Routledge.

CHAPTER SIX

POPULAR MUSIC

Questioning the popular, questioning control, questioning the global

66 Popular music is a primary . . . leisure resource in late modern society. 99

66 Popular music . . . functions at a collective level. 99

Bennett, A. (2002) *Cultures of Popular Music*. Buckingham: Open University Press.

1 Introduction

Popular music excites emotions and inspires devotion in fans. It brings together large and active audiences at festival events. It sidesteps the demands of written and spoken languages. It has an appeal that crosses national and continental boundaries.

Examination of popular music (PM) raises some interesting questions and problems about the nature of the beast and about how one makes sense of the object of study.

What exactly is popular, and with whom? Is music about lyrics or melodies or rhythms or all of these? How can one, indeed should one, separate music from its context? Vivaldi is popular with a certain audience – possibly as popular in terms of numbers listening as is a group such as the Scissor Sisters. Andrew Lloyd Webber's music is popular with another audience – some of whom experience it only as part of the spectacle of a theatrical performances. Spectacle is an inseparable part of the experience of most popular music performances.

Again, it hardly makes sense to talk about music without referring to the global multi-nationals that still dominate the volume of production of CDs which bring music to huge audiences. But equally, music of the people (that is, grass-roots material) is actually about small, independent production, small audiences, alternative sounds. This is popular, in another sense of the term. This could mean the politically conscious work of Billy Bragg, or the musically eclectic work of the Welsh group, Super Furry Animals. And in terms of audiences one has to take account of a huge range, from those on the dance scene from the 1980s onwards, to the newer consumers of Americana.

It is also the case that critics and critiques come from different academic directions, all valid in their own way. For example, there is a strong sociological tradition of examining youth cultures and subcultures, for whom music may be a strong part of their expressive behaviour. There are musicologists who have commented on the construction and effects of sound. There is a literary tradition which has picked up on lyrics, their effects and meanings. There are film critics who have taken an interest in the visual encodings and meanings to be derived from music video and music in film. There are the culturalists who have examined the nature of consumption, the importance of performance, the sense of identity which may be built through consumption of and participation in music material and music events. And there are media critics who are interested in questions about the industrial/marketing base to popular music, about music genres and their reception, about the kinds of meaning that audiences may derive from whatever one can agree is the text.

Shuker (2001) identifies six critical 'points of entry' in the critical literature about popular music:

1 a high cultural, conservative critique – in which by definition pop music is low culture, transitory and of little value. Where this approach would place the scored, orchestrated and complex music of someone like Duke Ellington is an interesting question.

2 The mass culture critique of the Frankfurt School (see Adorno) – which criticizes popular music as a product of industrialization, leading to mass culture and to a loss of the true culture of 'the people'. In this case, one wonders what one is meant to make of the rich variety of Indie music and specialist vinyl pressings.

3 The political economy perspective – which would examine features such as regulation of music/lyrics (for example So Solid Crew) which were deemed offensive by 'authority': or would look at cultural control and exploitation of cultural capital by large media corporations. This approach would now have to accommodate strategies of 'resistance' by artists such as David Bowie, who are bypassing corporations to release and control their material via the Web.

4 The structuralist-oriented approach of musicologists and literary critics – which makes formal analysis of music or lyrics in order to explain the production of meaning and of effect on the audience. This approach may have the limitations of a textually biased approach to media, ignoring, for example, contexts in which music is experienced. Dance culture in Agia Napa experiences music in a very different way from audiences at a benefit gig for some political cause.

5 Culturalist perspectives including subcultural analysis – in which the construction of cultural identities or resistance to dominant forms of culture may be discussed. This approach has to account for qualifying factors such as the complexity of multiple identities, the temporary nature of weekend clubbing fans, or the consumption of music by loose constituencies in the population (such as youth in general or older women in general).

6 The post-modern perspective – in which PM may be discussed as something which is appropriated and reused, or as being typically fragmented and only to be made sense of in terms of the engagement of particular consumers with particular examples of music at particular times. Critiques of post-modernism also apply here – it is not valid simply to abandon that part of critical work which considers ownership and control or the relationship between media and society. What fans experience at an event such as the Fleadh cannot simply be disassociated from the way Mean Fiddler acts as the controlling organization, or from considerations of performing rights.

I am going to approach a set of questions, problems and critical observations in this brief chapter, with relation mainly to institution, text and audience. But as always in this book I am consciously trying to make you aware that subject or discipline boundaries can be unhelpful, and that indeed cross-disciplinary interrogation may be useful, even more exciting. In terms of media studies, one is interested in the production of meaning, in that whole process which co-relates industries, audiences and the musical experience as text. A holistic approach is echoed by Hesmondhalgh and Negus (2002): 'A distinctive feature of popular music studies has been the willingness of participants to address the relations between musical meaning, social power and cultural value.'

2 Major questions

1 How may one define the term 'popular music'?

2 How does context affect the way we experience popular music?

3 In terms of institution, in what respects may one see PM as just another industrialized example of media?

4 What is the relationship between institutional production, and the exploitation of musical forms and their existence as a minority interest?

5 How does PM fit with notions about globalization?

6 What is the relationship between music genres, music industries and audiences?

7 In what ways do the different kinds of consumption of PM change our ideas about the nature of audience?

8 In what respects is music production, performance, distribution and consumption affected by technology?

9 In what ways may audience consumption relate to ideas about hegemony and resistance?

10 What do we understand about PM and a gendered audience?

3 Defining popular music (PM)

There is a general understanding of the term in western society which relates to industry-created charts of popularity and to what is easily available on the radio. There is a question of whether 'popular' should refer to that which is attractive to large numbers of audience/consumers, or whether it should refer to that music which is generated and consumed by 'the people'. The latter definition might have nothing to do with mass media and numbers. It might have everything to do with, for example, Klezmer music of the Jewish diaspora or the Marrabenta rhythms of Mozambique.

Either way, popular music is also something which is often experienced with others – in concert, in dance, with social ceremonies, as an adjunct to a whole range of social practices. In this respect one is talking culture as much as media. In the narrow space available, let me offer a few definitions of the term, which may productively open up questions about the object and methods of study.

- *PM is the sum of its genres* – Americana, Soul, Drum 'n' Bass and so on – which attract large audiences and generate large sales of CDs. Further discussion of genre will follow, but one might already see problems with debates about what is included or excluded, about just how large 'large' has to be to equal popular. Genres are to an extent industry-generated categories used as marketing tools. There was a time when Acid House was very popular – with a certain section of the (mainly young) population. But until raves made it into the press, the music was relatively unknown, and was certainly not an industry genre.

- *PM is that which appears in the charts.* But then British chart sales in a given week or month are small compared with, say, the sales of Country and Western over a year. And is chart music seen as popular simply because it is understood to be bought mainly by the young, whereas C&W has an older audience and does not have the kind of cool image that HipHop based music does? Also, the ever diminishing number of single CDs sold undermines the claim of these charts to represent the popular.

- *PM is the experience of the everyday.* This might itself be defined in terms of what is easily available on radio stations. But it could also include the music we hear in stores

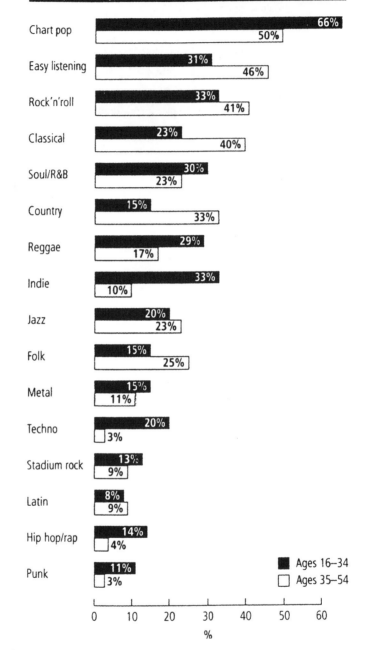

Which of these types of music do you enjoy listening to?

Genre	Ages 16–34	Ages 35–54
Chart pop	66%	50%
Easy listening	31%	46%
Rock'n'roll	33%	41%
Classical	23%	40%
Soul/R&B	30%	23%
Country	15%	33%
Reggae	29%	17%
Indie	33%	10%
Jazz	20%	23%
Folk	15%	25%
Metal	15%	11%
Techno	20%	3%
Stadium rock	13%	9%
Latin	8%	9%
Hip hop/rap	14%	4%
Punk	11%	3%

■ Ages 16–34
□ Ages 35–54

Enjoyment of Music by Categories and Age
This chart illustrates the variety of music genres available, as well as the tendency for hybrids to appear, all on a global scale.

In whose interests is it to have such categories?
(Graeme Burton: Media and Popular Culture, Hodder and Stoughton, 1999)

or other commercial venues. It might exclude a variety of music which is not so easily available.

- *PM is the music of youth.* This might include the material of TV coverage – *Top of the Pops* in Britain, or MTV. But this clearly does not do the job because 'youth' is demographically a declining proportion of the population. And there is a huge older audience for a variety of genres, from classic rock to 'easy listening'. This sign of the times is in the burgeoning audiences for BBC Radio 2 – the 'oldies' – and the static audiences of BBC Radio 1 – the 'kids'.

- *PM is the stuff of commercial mass production.* Certainly this addresses the idea of popularity defined by audience numbers. It also opens up the idea that the popular may be that which is attractive to mass audiences because it has been marketed with that effect. But such comments ignore the 'pull' of popularity which is genuinely inspired from the audience end of the equation. It also gets one into fruitless arguments about just how many sales/how big an audience it needs before one passes the popularity test – a numbers game.

- *PM is of the people, as opposed to commercial interests* – the difference between Grunge emerging on the West Coast, and the 'manufacture' of groups such as S Club Seven. But this definition also falls apart in a number of ways. For example, singers who emerge from talent shows such as *Pop Idol* and top the charts are nevertheless, it may be argued, genuinely popular with the disc-buying public. Or, one may argue that classical music (especially the main-stream classical pushed by Classic FM radio) is more popular with more people than are versions of Jungle. And anyway, 'the people' might include 'folkies', US urban-street cultures and an ageing middle class which enjoys Frank Sinatra and Kenny Rogers.

One might observe that attempts to tie a definition to the use of technology also fall apart, given ways in which musicians of all kinds – even those who produce music which is not popular in the commercial sense – create music through technologies. Similarly, one cannot go along with definitions which try to invoke performance, given the central place that forms of recorded music now have in popular culture.

One might also engage with the problem of how 'music' is to be defined. Early rock was seen as being not 'proper music' by its critics. Music is modified by technologies so that it is not just about instruments. Music as genre is continually changing, not least because of the capacity of global society to circulate and modify that music.

Toynbee (2000) argues that 'popular music differs from both folk and classical in that it developed historically in and through the mass media'. This attempt to define PM in terms of what it is not, has a degree of validity. But then there is a more recent history to folk and classical music which is also tied in with mass media. These forms or genres now owe as much as any other to media marketing, to institutional production techniques, to mass distribution and to creative input which also depends on global media. Equally and oppositely, one needs to recognize that PM also develops through grass-roots creative musicianship, through the sharing of music on a global scale, which has nothing to do with the efforts of the music majors. Indeed, it is Toynbee who discusses the 'cycles' theory of PM development, in which it is creative independents (working apart from the majors) who set off new styles and genres which may well then be taken up by the majors in a commercial sense. This is equally true of Punk in the 1970s and HipHop in the 1990s. As Negus says (1999) 'industry produces culture and culture produces an industry'.

Longhurst (1995) discusses Adorno's critique of popular music, and a contrast set up between popular and serious music. Longhurst refers to the 'standardised and routinised responses' of Adorno's listener, to the 'superficial and false' pleasure derived from listening to the standardized product produced by an industrialized music system. The contrast is a rerun of the high culture–low culture debate. Longhurst's chart of contrasting features (p. 9) is interesting in its attempts to invoke judgements based on complexity–simplicity: what Barthes would have called writerly–readerly texts. But, at the risk of sounding condescending, the nature, production and reception of music which is popular has so far changed since the time when Adorno was writing, that discussion in his terms has become at least partially irrelevant. This is not to say that his larger arguments about the nature and possible effects of a then new phenomenon called mass culture are not still relevant. What Adorno would have made of the music of Michael Nyman or Philip Glass, let alone their relation to the popular medium of film, is a matter for productive reflection.

In an article in *The Times Higher Education Supplement* (27 June 2003), John Richardson argues that from one view, that the manufactured animation band, Gorillaz is 'Adorno's malevolent "culture industry" incarnate'. But he also points out that in ironic post-modern terms, Gorillaz is a kind of thumb in the eye to commodification, controlled as it is by real musicians and a cartoonist.

4 Experiencing popular music

As a way of defining the object of attention – as a cultural experience – this is as important as trying to define PM by form: those kinds of songs which appear in the Pepsi Chart of the most popular CD singles. PM permeates both the public and the private spheres of our existence. It may be foregrounded or in the background. It becomes part of experience and helps give identity to moments, to relationships, to events. It is technology that makes that experience possible – the iPod on one's belt, the CD player in the car. To this extent a lot of PM is sourced as a recording rather than as live performance. Live performances at a local level are still prevalent, yet the line between 'live' and 'recorded' is now blurred, with the use of prerecorded tracks in public performances.

- *PM is a major feature of radio broadcasting.* Radio accompanies us everywhere – in the home, in the car and as background at work or even when shopping. Here, it may be an individual or a shared experience. But in this case the media choose the music.

    PM is a considerable feature of TV broadcasting. This is not just about the music programmes or the music channels or about talent shows, but about the insistent use of PM in a variety of contexts. Songs accompany adverts or form part of programme titles sequences. They are heard in the background as part of a scene in drama. They may set the mood or the time for some documentary.

- *PM may be a more personal, individually chosen experience,* via a music centre in the home or the personal player that one carries around, or the CD that is played while working at a computer, or material downloaded from the Internet.

- *PM is an ubiquitous part of the retail environment in the public sphere* – muzak and copy material in stores. But it also inhabits other parts of this public sphere – elevator music, mall music and bars. Indeed, it is so common that some English pubs actually advertise the fact that they do not play recorded music.

- *PM is experienced as a leisure activity in the public sphere* – perhaps shopping and browsing for material, but also as a live experience – part of clubbing, concert-going and festivals. Live music may be part of the pub repertoire. It is something that a lot of people make as well as listen to.

- *PM is an adjunct to any number of activities and experiences* – from the fitness centre to the telephone-hold music.

All this contributes to a meaning of PM in the experience of most people. The meaning may be about the ambience of shopping, the pleasure of intense listening, the emotional charge of a meeting in a public place. In many respects, PM has become a 'taken for granted' emotional colouring to the processes of everyday living, a part of social practices. It becomes noticeable when it is not there. Many of these examples are about the music from the corporations. A definition of what is popular is manufactured through reinforcement of particular tracks and particular sounds. To this

Mall Music
Forms of popular music have become ubiquitous in public places such as the shopping mall, so that music is part of everyday life.
What role does popular music play in the texts of other media?
(*The Bentall Centre*)

extent, selective purchase, selective listening at home, selective clubbing, is a kind of resistance to this dominance.

From the above, and especially in relation to audience reception studies, it will be understood that the context of the reception of music is crucial to ways in which it is understood, used and responded to by an audience.

Mall music is designed as a mood enhancer and a device to make a large public space seem more personal and private. Its style is anodyne because it wishes to be all things to all people. *Music in a music store* is designed to arouse the emotional levels and the interest of the shopper. It acts as a showcase for the product. Stores will even set up their own in-house pseudo radio station, to engage with and reassure the shopper. It is, like mall music, part of a social practice and the exchange of commodities. *Music in a club* is part of dance and social interaction. It helps define taste and lifestyle. It forms part of a cultural practice, of social interactions, of identity formation.

Bedroom music, by contrast, is not chosen by others and may be a solitary experience. It may be part of asserting space and territory, especially as practised by young people. If others are invited into the space then it may be a way of asserting group identity, as well as being a part of social interaction.

In a given context, music may be more or less actively responded to, it will be one part of social activities and cultural experience, it will evoke an emotional response, it will likely place the listener somewhere in the cultural landscape in terms of norms or of resistance.

5 Institutions and change

In talking about the dominant institutions in the PM industry, one is addressing central issues about how far they manufacture the nature of PM and control its availability. Certainly the characteristics of the most publicly accessible and familiar kinds of PM are to do with the talent spotting, production practices distribution systems and marketing strategies of the dominant multi-national players – BMG (Bertelsmann Music Group), Warner Music, EMI Music, Sony Music and Universal Music Group. These groups are themselves a part of larger media conglomerates. Shuker observes that the US media are dominated by six such corporations, and the global media economy by 12 multi-nationals. Implications of this kind of ownership are in terms of synergy between parts of these groups. Sony, for example (which also owns CBS Records), will be interested in promoting sound tracks from its films (it owns Columbia Pictures as well as Columbia records).

One is addressing questions about how far 'the popular' has been defined in terms of the political economy, and has been taken out of the hands of 'the people'. Yet at the same time one is also looking at ways in which cultural production still exists at social grass-roots level, at the level of the Indies: at ways in which 'institution' does not simply refer to corporate monoliths.

How far are social meanings and the process of consumption of music defined by the corporations, and how far do audiences have the ability to determine their own patterns of consumption and production of meanings? Is PM all about studio audiences for *Top of the Pops* jigging about and responding to cue cards, in a programme which is a showcase for the industry-defined top twenty and for marketing the industry? Or is at all about the 2002 Rave on the Beach at Brighton, in which an unexpectedly large audience of over 100,000 temporarily took over the centre of a town for music which was not out of the charts?

To an extent the history of, and changes in, PM industries match those of the rest of the media – a process of takeovers and concentration of power, of global power and marketing, of the value of copyright/property. On the other hand, changes are also marked by situations peculiar to PM. For example, at least some of the most popular musicians have a position not matched even by the box-office power of Hollywood stars. Madonna is a miniature industry in her own right. The George Michael case, in which the singer successfully argued his way out of an 'oppressive' contract, signified another change, and reinforced the peculiar power of his position. There is something distinctively emotional about the effect of music and about the relationship between the music makers and their fans, which is not matched by the press or television industries, for instance. Music is a form which is felt as much as perceived. In terms of lyrics or of notation, it is much harder to analyse and to understand in terms of textual features, compared with, say, a TV-news programme. PM is a distinctively creative cultural industry, depending on individuals or small groups for its inspiration and force. So institutions have never been able to control or industrialize its production and reception in the way that Hollywood has achieved for cinema. 'The media or music industry cannot simply "construct" a market, produce a type of consumer, nor determine an artist's meaning' (Negus, 1999). There isn't, as Toynbee (2000) says, 'a unified commodity form' for the music industry, comparable with the production and distribution of that text labelled 'a film'.

5.1 Ownership and control of the popular

> The recording industry establishes specific control strategies and dominant agendas while a considerable amount of musical production, distribution and consumption is beyond the immediate influence and understanding of the corporations.
>
> **Negus (1999)**

So one is caught between arguments advancing the power of the corporate strategies used by the entertainment conglomerates, and those arguing for the influence and survival of music made and distributed beyond the reach of the corporations. There is the question of how far any musicians can be entirely beyond such 'reach'. In one sense, if the 'music pool' uses the technology of the business or listens to CDs produced by the majors, then they are touched by that power of ownership – even if they do not sign a recording contract. As with other media, it is almost impossible to remain truly independent in terms of musical innovation, production and distribution.

To the extent that multi-nationals do control PM, it is not in respect of the creative base so much as in respect of distribution. From a commercial point of view, PM is about the numbers of units shifted. Institutionally, PM is about that which sells, that which is on the CDs, that which can be categorized into markets, and that which is marketable. The nature of the creative core of PM also means that for institutions there is a high cost/risk involved in signing musicians and producing material. It costs relatively little to run off the CDs, so volume is also important – the more one sells, the more profit rises in relation to production costs. This is another argument for hanging on to control of distribution. This is why Warners and others fought Napster into extinction and off the Internet. This is why CD piracy causes high anxiety in music corporation boardrooms.

In April 2001, worldwide music sales started to fall for the first time. The value of sales for that year dropped by 1.3 per cent to $36.9 billion (International Federation of the Phonographic Industry). In 2003 the IFPI reported an average 10.9 per cent fall in worldwide music sales for the first half of the year, twice as much in the USA (12 per cent) as in Britain. The value of these sales had dropped to $12.7 billion for the half year.

Cheap CD production and the Internet work against a centralized industry and in favour of independence. Even domestic computers can burn music CDs at a rate which, for instance, is impossible with videotape copying. And the Internet is still a significant source of music material. It cannot be controlled in the way that, for instance, broadcasting is. So we have a situation of tension in which the definition of what popular music is, and the availability of PM in a reproduced form, is both in the control of commodity capitalism and yet also outside this, in the hands of individuals and small groups.

To an extent, this tension of scale, of control and of individual inspiration is paralleled in the availability of live music performances. Only certain high profile organizations with access to serious capital, can provide the venues, events and infrastructure to support a Rolling Stones' tour or a major music festival. In Britain, Mean Fiddler dominates the festival scene, now including a major stake in Glastonbury. There is no point in trying to play the Birmingham Centre unless you can guarantee an audience of thousands. On the other hand, there are thousands of musicians playing thousands of small venues every week. There are hundreds of groups who have never made the charts who are out there with boxes of CDs for sale.

And whatever the power of the music majors to foreground certain genres of music, manufacture opportunities for certain groups, make certain songs/tunes part of everyday experience, still they do not have the power to make the music popular. 'There is no point-to-point correlation between controlling the market-place economically and controlling the form, content and meaning of music' (Garofalo, 1986).

This lack of control over something called 'creativity', and indeed 'popularity', may explain conflicting models of the music industry.

A *Neo-Marxist model* might foreground centralized control and the role of the majors. In this case one might look at the comments on vertical integration made by Peterson and Berger (1990). It is also Simon Frith (1992) who, in assessing different perspectives, articulates a classic Marxist/commodity critique of the popular music industry: 'Pop is a classic case of what Marx called alienation: something human is taken from us and returned in the form of a commodity. Songs and singers are fetishised, made magical, and we can only reclaim them through possession, via cash transaction in the marketplace.'

On the other hand, a *pluralist model* talking up consumer choice might foreground smaller institutions and the range of producers – a history of creativity which includes examples such as Stax Records, 2 Tone, Island and Rough Trade.

A *political economy model* might recognize both majors and Indies, and their interdependence, satisfying both mass and niche markets. Certainly Negus (1992) pointed out that majors would scout and eventually purchase from the innovative work of small companies. And those companies live interdependently with the majors (and major retailers), sometimes doing distribution deals with them, sometimes being taken over by them. It is a kind of symbiotic relationship which calls into question the degree and nature of independence. This situation and issue is analogous, for example, to the TV industry, where a nominally independent production company such as HatTrick has a limited range of distributor/broadcasters to whom it can sell.

Negus (1999) discusses ways in which the music industries try to control what is actually a very uncertain business (in terms of hits and profits) by trying to introduce order, predictability and accountability into the process of seeking, signing, nurturing, promoting and profiting from talent. He summarizes four corporate strategies as (somewhat paraphrased):

- throw enough mud at the wall and it sticks (i.e. put out enough material and some will succeed);
- wait until an Indie finds the next big artist, group, sound and then jump on the bandwagon;
- what goes round comes round, so wait for the next profitable music cycle to turn up;
- genius will out, so natural talent will emerge from your acquisitions.

What is clear is that music businesses, like Hollywood, work on the portfolio principle of spreading risks and assuming that only a few of your signings will generate big money. Negus also points out that control of distribution means that the companies get market information feedback about what is popular and is selling out there. This advantage is to an extent contradicted by a desire to shift big units and a failure to deal with small retailers and small numbers of units. Music corporations are good at selling what is already recognized, selling large numbers of CDs, and promoting successful bands and trends.

Note that all these comments place PM as a commodity and measure its success in terms of profit. This says nothing about the value placed on it by musicians or audience in terms of emotional satisfaction or of its being part of forms of social resistance. We are talking here about creativity and musicianship and recordings as having a commercial value, a price placed on them. As with all media industries this is based on the notion of copyright, of ownership, of a price placed on use. There is a price paid for recording someone's music (mechanical rights); for using a recording or for using someone's music (performing rights). There are in Britain groups such as The Mechanical Copyright Protection Society set up to monitor use and to collect money for the record companies and artists. Most of the money goes back to the companies.

There is a struggle between two kinds of culture and ethos. On the one hand commerce seeks to codify, control and materially benefit from the creative and social experience of music. On the other hand, musicians and social groups seek cultural ownership and sharing of their music. This is not a simple dichotomy between art and commerce. The companies get (recorded) music to those who would otherwise never hear it. They do lose a lot of money nurturing some talent that never hits the button. And musicians often aspire to the fame and cash that a deal can bring them.

5.2 Globalization and technologies

There are also opposing positions that one may take, over the interaction of technology with popular music making and reception, and with processes of globalization. These two factors have both encouraged a kind of cultural imperialism in, for example, the global spread of rock music as a format, and yet have also opened up Western music to all sorts of traditions and influences. Born and Hesmondhalgh (2003) take a pessimistic view when speaking of corporate expansionism:

> The movement of musical styles and instruments across the world is nothing new, as the diasporic nature of African American music itself suggests. This mobility has intensified in the twentieth century, in part because of the activities of transnational corporations seeking markets for musical reproduction equipment and for recordings abroad. One result has been a spectacular inequality in the economic rewards and prestige accorded to western pop products outside the West when compared with how non-western recordings are viewed and rewarded in the West.

Yet they also acknowledge the creative possibilities in global music flows:

> Given music's suitability to mass, global commodification, and given the profitability of the music industry, the stakes in the exploitation of indigenous and marginalised groups' cultural properties are very high. At the same time, due to commodified music's bound-less capacity to create and corral desire, the capacity of these other musics to generate new aesthetic forms of identification, new modes of the global imaginary, are also great.

Western music industries have gone multi-national and have global distribution power. Yet the technology of CD production (for example) has brought what is loosely categorized as World Music to new audiences around the world. Major music groups which have come out of the pop industry put on hugely expensive world tours. But at the same time musicians from developing countries come to Britain to play local venues. Globalization has not brought economic or creative domination of PM. It has indeed extended the influence and profits of the corporations and the mega groups. It has internationalized certain genres and styles of music; but it has also given life to independents and it has brought two-way traffic around the world.

One also has to question *Determinist or Neo-Marxist models* which assume the imposition of cultural artefacts on unwilling communities and audiences. Rock music has a global (not universal) audience. Without taking post-modern arguments about audience power to the other extreme, it is fair to say that youth in many countries such as Japan took to rock because it resonated in mood and attitude. They also took rock and did something with it, within their own musical sensibilities and needs for social resistance.

Negus (1996) argues that 'the productive powers of imperial corporations cannot directly determine consumption'. We cannot be talking about the simple imposition of commodities and predetermined meanings. He takes the view that 'the convergence of cultural practices and social activities is making it difficult to identify any power that might be directing such movements'.

In terms of geographies and location, Negus also takes issue with the tendency to try and pinpoint place and 'ownership' of musical styles. Grunge was identified with Seattle in the 1980s, but is it really accurate to say that the entire style came out of one city? Clearly not. He is not trying to deny cultural geographies in locating music on a global scale – the souk, for example. But he is saying that the 'ownership' and location of music has always been complex. One could go on to say that it has been made all the more fuzzy through the interactions of global travel, global electronic exchange, global practices in broadcasting and global distribution systems.

There are senses in which technology is explicitly global. I have already referred to the Internet as a global distribution system. Electrified instruments have produced for example, distinctive guitar sounds in South Africa, new accordion sounds in Scandinavia. Cheap tape and CD duplication has spread the sound of indigenous music within national and regional borders. As in Britain, there is no evidence that the spread of recorded sound has killed off live performance. Fela Kuti and then his son Femi, in Nigeria, have used a mixture of western and indigenous instruments, have maintained a tradition of dance performed with music, have maintained a tradition of protest songs, have borrowed from jazz and reggae, have generated the style of Afrobeat and moved on through hiphop.

'In technological terms anyway the world is becoming the local and the global: the national level no longer matters when every household has access to the global flow . . .' (Frith, 1993). Clearly technology has changed the sound of music performed and recorded, has made recorded sound commonplace, has made the experience of music a recorded rather than a live one for most audiences – but it has not simply made popular music the creature of corporations. Here, the technologically determinist argument has no credibility. Rather there is an interaction between people and machines. Drummers play to click tracks. Drum machines have facilities to make them sound less mechanistically regular than their originals. Toynbee (2000) argues that there is now a disappearing distinction between musicianship and 'technician-ship', that some groups do not contain musicians in the conventional sense. He talks about a shift from 'the documentation of a performed song to the construction of a song-sound' – clearly thinking of the reformed role of the DJ, as well as of groups like the Chemical Brothers. Technology allows the borrowing, reworking, construction of sounds and beats which are a long way from the straight performance of three guitars and a drummer sound of the 1960s.

Toynbee (in Hesmondhalgh and Negus, 2002) also argues for 'global networks and forms of affiliation' which 'transcend the preceding organisation of mainstream hegemony'. In this view, globalization is about nothing so simple as multi-nationals or the use made of technologies. He is talking about music and global audience responses, in three areas, or global formations.

1 *world music* – a dialogical network which mixes traditional and western sounds, and which uses technology as it pleases.

2 *rap and reggae* – another network in music of specific origins that has been borrowed and reworked across the globe. Toynbee also describes these forms as adaptable and attractive in their association with cultures of resistance.

3 *market blocs* that have emerged in addition to Anglo-American – Mandarin and

Cantonese pop; Spanish language in the Americas; pan-European music, especially a dance repertoire.

Andy Bennett (2001) also talks about globalization in terms of interaction of musical styles and of commonalty in moods of resistance. He refers to ways in which Punk in the 1970s and 1980s was colonized by other countries as a form of protest – by 'a globally situated youth culture whose music and stylistic shock tactics have become bound up with highly particularised local conditions and circumstances'. He talks in much the same way about rap and hiphop: 'Rap and hip hop are now re-worked in ways that reflect and engage with local issues in different cities and regions around the world.'

Chris Wood (*Times Higher Education Supplement*, 16 August 2002) discusses music as a tool of political resistance. He quotes examples from Scotland to Tibet to East Timor: 'political song is alive and well and being used to express disapproval of bureaucratic incompetence as well as to foster nationalist movements'.

Negus (1999) on the other hand, remains more concerned about the local dimension being lost as the economic importance of a world market grows. He refers to an interview with the then president of Sony Music in 1996, who argued that the cost of signing, recording and promoting a new artist was even then so great ($1 million), that one had to sell in a world market to make a profit. But as Negus points out, this world market is not a given thing. The music industry is creating it. Cultural and technological factors such as the reach of satellite TV, the common format of the tape or CD and the spread of English as a common language, all help this manufacture of a global business for music trading in dominant genres – whose dominance is also partly a result of marketing practices. Also, this new world order in music is very selective in its markets. The multi-nationals actually prefer to develop markets where copyright is enforced and they have measures of control. So Japan is significant in their global music business, India less so.

In talking about the construction of a global music market, it should be said that I am making a clear distinction between the dominant balladic and western originated forms that do sell successfully around the world, and that loose genre of world music which is about traffic the other way – Damon Albarn's promotion of music from Mali.

Debates on the effects of this global market continue to split between pessimistic views of the effects on local music, musicianship and even music industries; and optimistic views of the creative exchange, with evidence that many local artists continue to succeed in spite of the multi-nationals.

5.3 Production

The production background to the popular music industry, like that of the other media industries, is tied up with an inclination to vertical integration and with a consequent desire to control distribution and what is sold in the retail outlets. 'The aim is to make intellectual property, package it and maximise revenues by selling it as many times as is feasible to the widest possible audience at the highest possible price' (Doyle, 2002).

Production of recorded sound is also tied up with technology, format and costs. Live performance is also a kind of production. But – without ignoring the value of live broadcasting – recording is the device through which PM is turned into a commodity.

Most broadcast music originates in a recorded format. Even TV uses CD-ROM or tape formats. So it is hardly an exaggeration to say that recording created the music industries. Recording has developed through a number of formats, from the original hard vinyl 78s, to the soft vinyl 78s, 45s and LPs of the late 1950s, to tape cassette format from the 1970s, and then the CD in the 1990s, followed by MP3 (not forgetting music video cassettes along the way). The drive has been to make the technology cheap, portable, available and with good sound quality. There has been a struggle between industry attempts to retain control of recording and copying, and audience attempts to use versions of technology to make their own copies for free (not forgetting the important question of mass pirating on an industrial scale). Technology has developed in ways that facilitate that struggle.

On the one hand, the music business has controlled the pressing plants and at least some of the expensive recording facilities. On the other hand (and ironically), other related industries have, for example, produced copying devices and relatively cheap multi-tracking devices which audiences and musicians have used to avoid paying for recordings and to make their own recordings cheaply. One could say that capitalism eats itself. Still, the control of mass production and of material property (CDs) is central to the music business.

Where music majors do not control the production source, then their control of distribution networks and access to retailers means that they still retain economic power, and the ability to make money from the music which is on the CDs that they are shifting.

Production should be seen to start with the musicians. The people who play do indeed produce the music, sometimes in a live context, with immediate access to their audiences. But in the realities of media production, it is the companies who record, and indeed creatively rearrange, the sound of the music.

This last comment raises the point about creativity, origins and credit for production. A & R people and the studio technicians play a significant part in producing the music that appeals to the consumer. We also have a recent phenomenon of the DJ as music producer. From Grandmaster Flash to Fatboy Slim, the DJ as mixer and controller of the sound coming from various sources has become a musician in front of the crowd and the producer of best-selling CDs. In terms of stardom and the marketing of PM, these music makers have become as significant as those who actually sing or play musical instruments.

Historically, the production of popular music has moved on from an early twentieth-century model in which musicians play live to 'the people', and in which the music may be shared with musicians (not least in the audience) via the selling of sheet music. It has moved through a mid-twentieth-century model in which the main experience of popular music was through recorded sound, but that sound was more or less what the musicians would produce at live events. Now we are in a current model in which popular music is the sound of recording studio construction, and in which live performance is also mediated and constructed through technologies. Even amateur groups now use monitor speakers and a sound-mixing desk with effects.

Marketing

Points about the construction of a categorized marketplace and sets of audience through genres are made below. Another feature that is now taken for granted in media marketing is the promotion of the star or the cult of personality. Especially for youth audiences, the point of contact is as much the musician or DJ as it is the music or the song. This reinforces a point that music may be about a complex cultural experience, about practising social interactions, about identity formation. While it is true that PM has always had a share of well-known and admired performers, the songs and the music have also been dominant, even in respect of the performer's public image. It is now true that the performer's image and the performance experience for the audience is sold as hard as the music. The business activity looks for personalities to promote. It has manufactured groups, from the Monkees, to Milli Vanilli, to the Spice Girls. The songs are written for 'the group as product to be sold'. Nobody is arguing that one can successfully market any old music. There are still many songs that become hits on the grounds of their own appeal. But now the music industry is selling more than lyrics and melodies.

6 Genres and styles

'Genre: the way in which musical categories and systems of classification shape the music that we might listen to, mediating both the experience of the music and its formal organisation by an entertainment industry' (Negus, 1999). Music, like other media industries is infused with genres, which offer the dual attractions of giving pleasure to the audience and providing profits for the industries. Genre categories become a kind of 'making sense of music' for both consumer and producer. They are not simply imposed on the audience. Musicians also define themselves in terms of their musical genre/style. Musical borrowing creates a great range of what might be called sub-genres. Rock spawned Heavy Metal, Thrash and the like. Garage gave rise to Speed Garage and interacted with other genres.

In terms of music making, Negus (1996) produces an interesting three-part definition of approaches to genre:

- genericists – those who work entirely within the conventions of a particular style;
- pastichists – those who imitate a style, but only as part of a more varied repertoire;
- synthesists – those who mix and extend the conventions of a style to extend a genre, or even produce a new form.

However, lengthy discussions of the precise features of a particular genre and its variations can lead to unproductive quibbling. What is significant is how genre is associated with lifestyle, ideology and other kinds of media consumption. The significance is both commercial and cultural. Music genres in the media are about social practices and forms of consumption, not just about the style of music.

Negus talks about evidence from the marketing side of the industry, which is absolutely clear that dress codes are key to the visual identity of the music. They are what people think of when they are asked about a particular style of music.

'Record companies initially position acts sartorially in relation to other artists and genres of music, and signify the adoption of an implicit lifestyle and set of values denoted by these visual codes' (Negus, 1992).

Shuker also comments on popular music genres as being about more than the music. He refers to

1 musical characteristics (as in kinds of instrumentation or dominant sounds);

2 image and visual style (as seen in the performers or on CD covers);

3 the primary audience for particular styles.

'The relationship between fans and their genre preferences is a form of transaction, mediated by forms of delivery, creating specific cultural forms with sets of expectations' (Shuker, 2001).

One needs to recognize that PM is integral to other genres and spin-offs in other media. There are rockumentaries in film and on television, documenting the lives, tours, performances of stars and groups. Some explore the history of a given genre. Others are bio-pics of a given star. There are TV showcase programmes which present current hits or aspiring groups. There is MTV channel available world-wide, with well over 100 million households subscribing. There are rock musicals in the theatre and in cinema. There are dramas constructed around song, the music industry and dance performance. There is the sound track from the film. There is the music video. These might all be regarded as genres in their own right. They all represent ways in which PM is heard, promoted and familiarized, other than through radio, CD and the Net. They stand for the integration of media and the intertextuality of its genres. They represent a stage in the development and dissemination of popular music which is a long way from a hundred or so years ago, when one might reasonably talk about popular music as being the stuff of the music hall and of folk culture, as being something that was performed.

The significant issue underlying genre-ness is how far categories of music are used as convenient labels within marketing strategies, and how far they stand for a category of musicality and experience which is validated by the audience. The labelling within music stores is, I suggest, a convenience but only a starting point, for both the industry and the audience. It is arguable that in musical terms the genres keep on changing because of experimentation, interaction, cultural influences and technology. 'What is really striking about the recent development of popular music is its progressive shift away from conventional tonality and structured conformity' (Goodwin, 1992).

Toynbee (2000) argues that audiences are as much constructed as found, that they are constructed for commercial reasons, that they are exploited through a desire to achieve and express identities. 'Musical communities . . . provide the basis for genre markets', 'the music industry has helped to construct musical communities by commercially exploiting the desire to find a common identity in music.' So he tries to extend a definition of genre from identifying style or product or audience preferences, to something described as 'genre cultures' in which identity, lifestyle and values give the genre life. This moves the weight of genre definition from institution to audience. Unfortunately it does not look so convincing in practice when he talks about categories such as 'race music' or 'cross-over'. It is more convincing when explored through a discussion of 'dance music'. It is more useful when discussed in terms of genres which seem specific to a time and a style, and those which appear to transcend time and place.

Negus (1999) also talks about genre cultures as 'an unstable intersection of music industry and media, fans and audience cultures, musician networks and broader social collectivities informed by distinct features of solidarity and social identity'. So he too is arguing that genre is about more than musical style – 'genres are more than musical labels: they are social categories'.

Brackett (2002) refers to the fluidity of genre characteristics and sees them as being more specific than transcendent. They 'exist as a group of stylistic tendencies, codes, conventions, and expectations that become meaningful in relation to one another at a particular moment in time'. He also elaborates the industry – audience relationship – 'genres may be understood as mediating the discursive web (spun between the media, consumers and industry personnel) in which musical meaning circulates'. But he argues that genre is about more than style – genres are defined by 'performance rituals, visual appearance, the types of social and ideological connotations associated with them, and their relationships to the material conditions of production'.

Toynbee (2000) discusses the idea of 'mainstream' both as a genre category and as something to which other genres stand in relation. He argues against mainstream as being the antithesis of subculture and as being ideologically normative. He talks in terms of affiliations. 'A mainstream is a formation that brings together large numbers of people from diverse social groups and across large geographical areas in common affiliation to a musical style.' His view is that the PM mainstream is informed by three 'currents':

- hegemony – in which there is alliance and negotiation with subordinate groups;
- 'a popular urge to find an aesthetic of the centre, or stylistic middle ground';
- economics – the industry trying to 'map a Market' on to audience tastes.

Further, he argues that there have been three recognizable mainstreams in PM – TinPan Alley/Hollywood, rock and rap/reggae.

In the case of rap, Negus (1999) argues that the industry is still trying to contain the style and label in genre terms, whereas so far as the audience is concerned it crosses 'numerous borders of class, neighbourhood, gender, ethnic label and "national" belonging'.

Toynbee (2000) points out that genres are distinctive through their difference from other musical styles (as much as through a coherent body of characteristics). In marketing terms the industry has gone for either the mainstream (with high-volume production and rapidly increasing returns on start-up costs) – or for segmented markets, in which categories may be marked by their difference from the mainstream (with lower volume but good audience targeting that produces good returns). Negus (1999) refers to the inflexibility of genre categories as used by the music industry to determine its finance and marketing strategies. In at least some cases, 'artists, audiences and industry personnel remain within genre boxes'. Certainly the music conglomerates base many of their divisions on genres and allocate resources accordingly.

So genre-ness may positively create bonds and affiliations between the music and the audience, but it may negatively confine creative interactions between musicians and limit opportunities for audiences to hear (or want to hear) different genre material.

These bonds depend on knowledge and enjoyment of the conventions which make a genre distinctive. In terms of understanding audiences and the meanings they may generate from the experience of music, Frith (1993) argues that one essential question is

'How do words and voices work differently for different types of pop and audience?' One cannot talk about text, audience, meaning in general terms. Genre makes a difference.

7 Audiences and consumption

Popular music may be a solitary experience – heard privately at home or within the personal technology of the Walkman (even in public places). But generally speaking, PM is something that is shared. That sharing may be part of a large cultural experience (festivals) or it may be more intense and confined to listening and discussion with friends at home.

The process of consumption can have many features, apart from listening and participating in public music events. For some it is about collecting and cataloguing, about the pleasures of searching and purchasing. For others it is about exploring one genre of music. For others it is about accruing group credibility and personal identity – in the ownership, in the discussion about what one owns. For others it is about the personalities and background of the singer/group. It may be about enhancing moods. It may be about diversion from other experiences. It may have the retrospective effect of becoming a key to unlock a life experience, a period of living. It may be about various combinations of these experiences. Clearly consumption is not just about a bare commodity transaction – cash for goods. It is about a cultural transaction in which the listener/purchaser may buy pleasure, status and a sense of place within the cultural flow.

Figure Carrying Ipod
Audiences for popular music are as much individual as collective. Individuals may take their own music with them.
In what ways might it be argued that technology has put the audience in control of the experience of popular music?
(Corbis)

A popular song, an album, is not something that is simply used up through consumption. For the listener, it is a reusable commodity. It runs through the memory. It unlocks emotions. Consumption may be an intentional act, but also an unintentional experience – the ubiquitous ambient music of public places. It is interesting how the music of artists such as Moby moves between this foreground and background in style and in use. His tracks have been used for many adverts on television. The music, like much of that produced by Brian Eno, does not demand attention through lyrics or assert its location in one popular genre. The notion of consumption by stealth has even spawned a mini industry of mood music, pinned thematically on for example, the Celtic harp, or the sounds of the sea. Compilations are sold on television as being 'cool music' or 'music to relax to' or 'romantic music'. The possibility of silence and solitude is being lost as we are sold music *for* silence and solitude. This kind of PM may be seen as simply a backdrop – or perhaps as a distraction from the inner spaces of self.

7.1 Defining audiences

In media marketing terms, audiences are out there waiting to buy. In media critical terms, audiences are a concept waiting to happen, to be given life through the acts of buying, listening, going to musical events. For the media and the cultural analyst the important thing about the audiences is what they do with the music. The audience becomes defined by interacting with the music, but in all sorts of ways.

In saying this I am not arguing that the notion of audience as genre creature is entirely invalid. There are audiences for types of music. They do have very general characteristics of age, gender, lifestyle, dress. But those characteristics are to an extent the result of genre commodity selling – people are given an image to buy into, however much that image may once have originated 'on the street'.

The same people may be parts of the different audiences for different types of music. They may behave differently in response to the same type of music according to where and how they experience that music. In terms of a post-modern, cultural approach, it is possible to argue audiences out of existence – the collective audience vanishes as one approaches it, to the point where there is only an individual interacting with one piece of music at one time in one place. I suggest that it is not so hard to take on both a media analysis notion of audience as interacting with a text and having some collective features, and a rather more culturally oriented view that it is more important to make an account of the interaction than it is to conceptualize the audience.

7.2 Reception

I have already talked about the context of reception and the uses to which music may be put by an audience.

Middleton (1990) talks about values which both accrue to the music, but more importantly to its meaning and its use for the audience.

- Communicative values – does the track say anything affective or relevant to the listener? This could be about how tonality links to emotional state or how lyrics relate to some life experience.

- Ritual value – does the music perform a 'culturally prescribed task'? This could be about emphasizing bonds with a social, group or about 'taking the mind off problems'.
- Technical values – within its own terms of reference, how skilfully made is the music? This could be about admiration for musical virtuosity or the mixing of some effect.
- Erotic values – does the music generate an emotional/physiological response? This could be about the pleasure of dancing or forms of arousal related to excitement and energy.
- Political values – does the track (and indeed associated visual elements) refer to interests and positions that the listener identifies with? This could be exemplified thorough reggae's reference to Rastafarianism.

So music may be valued for different things in different contexts by different people. At least it is clear that its reception is not a passive experience (pace Adorno). It is actively used and engaged with. Indeed that very activeness causes periodic moral panics and bouts of vilification in the mainstream media and politics – from the outrage around torn-up cinema seats and the film *Rock Around the Clock* in the 1950s, to the changing of the law to trap revellers on acid in rave culture of the 1990s.

Activity, then, is not just about cerebral appreciation or emotional charge for the individual (though it may be). It is as likely to be about participation in a multi-faceted experience, in which the music itself is transformed by interaction, lighting and the technology of sound equipment in clubs. The idea of reception is not just about listening – it is more fluid than that. It is not just about the music. It is about the variety of places, situations and social relationships which may come to bear on reception. It is about the variety of media through which music is received. It is about the variety of cultural experiences and commodities with which music is associated.

Fandom

Another dimension of reception and a way of describing audience is recognized in the concept of *fandom*. We are talking about that kind of audience member who is obsessed with things like specific performers, certain genres. The obsession may be in terms of collecting information and relevant artefacts. It may also be seen in terms of getting locked into a certain kind of musical experience. Fans and fan clubs (core fans) operate both as a cultural entity, celebrating repeatedly the object of their fandom. They also operate in a material sense (general fans) purchasing and promoting that which they admire. But one may also argue that the state of being a fan is not entirely admirable. An obsessional view of particular music and performers is by definition unlikely to be open to cross-overs, co-relations, global influences. It may be said that fans both support and confine musical forms and presentations. They represent a particular kind of listening and reception. It would be unfair to represent fandom as deviancy, but it is a kind of excess – of consumption.

Fandom is not just about singers, groups and genres. Nor is it just about youth – for example, popular media images of young females at concerts or gathering at an airport to see their favourite group arrive. It also has a media dimension. There are fans of film musicals. There are fans of radio DJs. The delivery of some day-time radio shows is clearly aimed at a less than youthful female audience. The material has facets of romance, domesticity, emotional experience, recollection of relationships. This is a kind of talk radio in which the music is at times just an excuse to conduct the conversations, the quizzes, the letter readings which are the devices designed to give life and meaning to the pseudo-relationship being set up between the DJ and the individual listener, and sometimes between the listeners themselves.

What we need to remind ourselves of here, is that reception and consumption is not merely passive. For instance, styles of dance music keep mutating rapidly, fuelled by the role of the DJ as producer, experimenting, mixing and responding to the audience in live situations. The companies have to work hard to keep up with what is happening out there, to be able to produce saleable compilations of new styles before they become out of date. This is why the DJs are wooed by the companies for the knowledge of what is happening at the point of reception, and for their skills in a new form of musical production.

7.3 Subcultures and identities – resistance

PM is much talked about in terms of youth culture and kinds of resistance. This is both valid and yet misleading. Not all subcultures are about youth – ethnic groups, gay groups, regional groups. And 'youth' itself is a notion that contains great diversity. It is a label that appeals to marketeers and sociologists, but which still conceals a range of ages and of cultural behaviours. So consumers of Irish folk music or of Indian film music or of reggae may feel their identities are being reinforced, and may feel that they are asserting that identity against dominant cultural forms – but they are not necessarily young, and they are not resisting with a kind of loud public display which makes the tabloids. Brackett (2002) talks about the dangers of interpreting music only through youth culture and of a 'naïve romanticised celebration of youth rebellion'. Demographic realities mean that youth audiences have grown old, yet have not simply abandoned the popular music of their younger days for some form of easy listening. Rock music is still part of the identity of a now middle-aged generation. Where they stand in relation to kinds of resistance and to counter culture, has not been adequately explored.

Of course it also valid to recognize the relationship of youth to forms such as punk or bhangra or drum 'n' bass. Punk has been famously analysed by Dick Hebdige, and clearly shows kinds of anger about and resistance to the status quo of the 1970s. The pared-down energy was a reaction against the elaborate pomposities of some stadium rock music. There was anger about the effects of an economic downturn. There was contempt for a self-serving establishment, famously encapsulated in the furore over the Sex Pistols' ironic version of *God Save the Queen*. And it can be seen that punk as a style was colonized by other countries and cultures as an expression of protest. But it also needs to be recognized that punk was as much to do with a middle-class art college movement as it was about working-class protest. It had as much to do with film and theatre and display as to do with music. And people like Malcolm McLaren and Derek Jarman, while young, were not exactly teenagers.

In the same way, reggae, from which punk borrowed elements of its musical style, was about youth and yet was not. It was about a new generation of Afro-Caribbeans in Britain celebrating black identity, and not being prepared to be as accommodating as their parents. But it was also about a fair age range of rude boys and Rastas, about Black culture as much as age, about social conditions in Britain but also about social divisions back in Jamaica. So there is a danger in presenting PM and even particular forms of this as simply belonging to the young, let alone as being a ritual form of resistance against the current status quo, or their parents' generation.

One may not argue with the kind of comment made by Lull (1992): 'historically, much subcultural music has come from oppressed groups'. But one may argue with the notion that all examples have come from youth and are for youth. Preferable are comments made by Toynbee (2000): 'popular music publics may . . . be articulated with social formations of class, race, gender and sexuality'. And (of Britain in the 1990s) – 'class subordination intersects with regional and ethnic identity to produce musical genre-cultures' – thinking for example of Manchester and the Oasis version of Britpop, or of South London and Jungle. Again, he refers to ethnicity and class as much as youth when commenting that 'music-making can represent social formations in struggle'. He invokes ideas from Bourdieu to justify a view of the active role of music and musicians in expressing and working through social relations (not merely reflecting them).

Hebdige (1979) expresses the idea that style (including music) becomes a form of resistance. He is still in effect arguing (vis-à-vis punks) that there are class elements. But style covers fashion and fashion objects, as well as social behaviours and physical locations. Resistance and subculture become synonymous. Longhurst (1995) includes chronological diagrams (pp. 212–13) which try to map subcultures, change, music, class and resistance to socio-economic circumstances. Certainly it would be hard not to see some media texts as products of their times, with something to say. What they may actually do about such conditions is another matter.

To an extent one might argue that the association of PM with 'resistance' has to do with views of the musician in society. The musician is seen as a free and creative spirit, having little to do with 9 to 5. In this view, music making is intrinsically resisting the system, and involves work temporally out of step with most of the population. Sara Cohen (1991) has explored this in a study of the Liverpool music scene. She found that music making was seen as both exotic and pragmatic – the youth labour market was sufficiently inadequate and the music scene sufficiently strong, that a 'career' in music did not seem unrealistic.

A now traditional post-modern take on the idea of resistance is exemplified by Potter (1998) in which he talks about kids from the South Bronx reclaiming 'the consumed' through 'aural recycling of previously existing sounds', using technology where previous music cultures had used wood and catgut. This is the manufacture of hiphop 'on the streets'. This is 'resistance that literally takes control of the means of production, that produces out of the consumed'. This is musical practice which fits back against the commodification of the musical experience.

Andrew Goodwin (1992) is in the same territory when he argues that 'pop production and consumption should be interpreted as building resistance to corporate control and rationalisation'. One would not argue about some examples of music, lyrics, audience behaviours challenging social norms and even political attitudes. But still there is a lot of popular music which is ideologically conformist.

Maxwell (2002) warns us against getting caught in 'the Birmingham oppositionality paradigm when talking about music and audience – "insider versus outsider; authentic versus mass market" (referring to a tradition within the Birmingham Centre for

Cultural Studies). It is indeed fair not to assume that all music from the streets is culturally, let alone politically oppositional. It is fair not to label youth movements (and musical developments) as working class and oppositional, simply because some of those involved happen to be working class. Because people belong to a certain class, does not mean to say that their media consumption will be either oppositional or passive. PM is an experience. It is woven into everyday routines. It is not necessarily a tool of resistance.

We also need to ask whether oppositionality and the consumption of music feeding resistant attitudes belongs only to youth. Somewhere in this debate one has to factor in examples like Bono of U2 touring Africa with a senior American politician (2002), opposed to economic imperialism, and seeking material support for crisis situations in Africa. This is a long way from Johnny Rotten spitting on the audience in 1979. And from Rock Against Racism opposing neo-Nazi movements in the 1980s. One has to accommodate various takes on resistance – opposing or subverting dominant cultural forms of music – opposing dominant social attitudes and prejudices – possibly as political activism.

7.4 Gender

Both in performance and in reception, the music media show various kinds of gender affiliations. These are, not surprisingly, most apparent in relation to young audiences, in their identity-forming years. So it is easy to point out the masculine and narcissistic posturings of what has been called 'cock rock'. Similarly, there is the idolization or idealization offered by young female audiences to certain groups, both as screaming live audiences (what used to be called 'teenyboppers'), and as followers through articles in girls' magazines.

In terms of young fandom, one might reasonably talk about gender bonding. The male groups bond around the sometimes aggressive sounds, lyrics and stage postures of rock 'n' roll forms – the guitar as 'axe' as phallic symbol. Female groups bond around the look of performers, discussion of their lives, the lyrics of balladic forms.

This argument about musical style and gender affiliations may be extended into other genres – the rhythmic and technical masculinities of drum 'n' bass, the balladic femininities of R 'n' B. It is interesting that female audiences have allegiances to female as well as male stars. Whereas, considering hiphop for example, male audiences only latch on to female performers when they are marketed sexually and with their own kinds of explicit lyrics – Lil' Kim.

Of course all these observations are ultimately generalizations. Performers and audiences don't fit rigid moulds. Groups and purchasing patterns throw up ambivalent examples – Pulp, for instance. Middleton (1990) argues that one should attend to a 'variety of gender-specific subject positions constructed within musical discourse, and their relationship to other discourses, rather than insisting on music's representation of pre-existing social stereotypes'. This is fine, so long as not insisting also means not denying.

Negus (1996) in a useful section on gender, music and identity, also argues that there have been dangerous assumptions about gender difference in popular music. He points out that in terms of the youth subculture approach, part of the 'problem' has been that male youth has been much more visible in the public arena than female youth.

He talks up cultural variety and change over a period of time. For example, he discusses a disjunction between gay culture and jazz music, as well as the support k.d. laing gained from female fans in support of her lesbian orientation and after the problems she had in trying to break in to the country music scene.

Longhurst (1995) discusses writing on female fans and audiences. He points out that such evidence as there is suggests that they enjoy the bonding and the tie-in materials, as much as the music or the group. It appears that girls may make sense of male performers as pseudo-friends: where boys may seem the same performer as a kind of sexual hero. To this extent the audience appears to impose meanings on the music/ musician. The evidence also indicates that the emotional quality of the experience is important, as is the question of what is done for the individual's sense of self.

There are indeed a number of gender inflected strands to reflect on in popular music. There is the tradition of the female singer-songwriter and their female audiences – from Joni Mitchell to Alanis Morissette. There is music for, and appropriated by, gay sub-culture, from Dusty Springfield, through Jimmy Somerville and the Pet Shop Boys, as well as Queen and Freddy Mercury. There is the placing of a line of 'rock chicks', from Susie Quattro through Chrissie Hynde. One might evaluate the attraction of the male audience to the female singers such as Shania Twain. There are questions about the nature of the audience and audience attraction in relation to performers presenting ambivalent sexuality – Morrissey, Boy George, Brett Anderson. There is the successful marketing of a singer like Britney Spears to both females and males. And as audiences grow older there is the question of how far the notion of gendered genres or gendered audiences really holds up. Country and western would be an example of this. The older audience for C & W has moved beyond a stage of same-sex bonding, and into stages and experiences of one-to-one relationships, loss and ageing.

Shuker (2001) raises acute questions about where our understanding of gender in PM comes from:

66 99 Dance pop is generally seen as 'a girls' genre', while hard rock and heavy metal are regarded as primarily male-oriented genres. Women performers predominate in a cappella and gospel music, and are prominent in folk and country, and among singer-songwriters. Male DJs are the norm in the contemporary dance music scene. How 'natural' are such associations, and what ways are they social constructs?

He refers to the male-dominated music industry and to evidence that women are actively excluded from the band experience. Instruments are seen as masculine or feminine – and the guitar (and the music shops which sell guitars) is seen as male territory. He refers to Bayton's work in evidencing gender socialization as a major factor in producing a gender divide in popular music. The strength of this divide is evident when one tries to consider counter examples, and has to see them as exceptions to a 'rule' – Hazel O'Connor and Punk, or Riot Grrrl and Hardcore.

It would be surprising if PM was not a site of struggle, of alternatives, of norm affirmation, of challenge to norms – given that it is part of the cultures which embrace and express different and contradictory positions on gender, all at the same time. But there is a danger of missing the variety of those positions. And, apart from issues of gender, PM is appropriated by culturally diverse groups both to celebrate their character and to be enjoyed for its own sake. As much as being associated with public disturbances and drug use, PM is a unifying force across age groups and geographies.

8 Discussion extract

Sub-cultures express a response to a set of conditions and the different aspects of the sub-culture are tied together into structured relatively coherent wholes . . . Hebdige read sub-cultural styles using the tools of the structural and semiotic approaches . . . he focused on the different dimensions of the style of sub-cultural groups . . . he argued that the styles expressed by different sub-cultures are a response to social conditions and experiences. Furthermore, according to Hebdige, such styles often encode an opposition to the dominant or hegemonic forms of culture associated with dominant groups. Such challenges are often indirect and can involve the utilisation and transformation of forms of culture which were previously the property of dominant groups. In engaging in such practices, sub-cultural members act as bricoleurs engaging in a process of bricolage, responding to the world around them by improvising in a structured fashion, creating meanings that are different from those of the dominant culture or dominant groups . . .

Hebdige argues that sub-cultures often resist the dominant social order, though indirectly and in symbolic ways. However, he also argues that forms of sub-cultural expression are often incorporated into that dominant social order through two main routes. First, there is the commodity form which involves 'the conversion of sub-cultural signs (dress, music, etc.) into mass-produced objects'. Second, is the 'labelling' and re-definition of deviant behaviour by dominant groups – the police, the media, the judiciary.

Brian Longhurst (1995) referring to Hebdige, D. (1979)

1 What material is there in this chapter which argues for or against Hebdige's position?

2 How applicable are Hebdige's ideas to contemporary subcultures and what they do with music?

3 In what ways do the media and their technologies now contain popular music within an industrial model – or alternatively allow it to develop?

9 Further reading

Bennett, A. (2001) *Cultures of Popular Music.* Buckingham: Open University Press.
Hesmondhalgh, D. and Negus, K. (eds) (2002) *Popular Music Studies.* London: Arnold.
Longhurst, B. (1995) *Popular Music and Society.* Cambridge: Polity Press.
Negus, K. (1999) *Music Genres and Corporate Cultures.* London: Routledge.
Shuker, R. (2001) *Understanding Popular Music* (2nd edn). London: Routledge.
Toynbee, J. (2000) *Making Popular Music.* London: Arnold.

CHAPTER SEVEN

APPROACHES TO FILM

The missing British film industry: audiences, gazing and meanings

"cinema-going remains an incredibly popular pastime, but the challenge is to ensure that people across the country (Britain) have access to a wide range of films."

John Woodward, chief executive of UK Film Council, in the *Guardian*, 4 March 2004

1 Introduction

It is true that many people still go to the cinema in Britain. But what they see is predominantly the product of a foreign culture –that of the USA. One may question whether the British audiences care about this, or indeed whether they realize that when they go to see a 'British' film, in most cases the product is really not British at all. And yet, from the point of view of understanding audiences as interpreters of text and producers of meanings, one could say that the provenance of the material does not matter.

In this chapter I want to yoke together approaches towards making sense of two key areas of media study –institutions and audience. The very contrast between a factually inflected study of what passses for a film industry, and a semiotically and psychologically inflected examination of looking at film images, brings out the range of the discipline. It underlines the idea of the media as having both a material dimension (companies and products), and a more notional dimension (meanings and social practices). The text, as an object of production and a subject of consumption, becomes the ground on which the material and the notional meet.

Firstly I want to take a look at the condition of the British film industry, which in a sense does not exist. There is a background to this condition which, it may be argued, relates to the fact that the Hollywood film industry was into globalization and cultural imperialism in the 1920s. Even then, the USA was flooding Europe with a product that had already recouped its production costs in the US market, which could therefore be distributed relatively cheaply to the rest of the world, and which had already cornered a mass market with a seductive mix of romantic, dramatic and action material. In 1926 92 per cent of films shown in Britain were from the USA (Petrie, 1991). This kind of economic history and its impact on national film cultures is not so peculiar to Britain. Many other countries in Europe and elsewhere (Canada, for example) have seen their national film media sapped by the same forces.

But having accepted that film production in Britain today is to a fair extent at the mercy of international exchange rates and government tinkering with the climates of financial support and tax breaks, not to mention the US majors, still one can ask if it really matters that we do not have a film industry in the conventional sense.

Secondly, I want to look briefly at spectatorship, at ideas about how the film audience may see and understand the film text. There is an interesting hiatus between that kind of criticism which privileges the text and refers to textual features as controlling the eye and the understanding of the viewer –and criticism which considers the act of looking and understanding, which refers to the nature of the engagement with the text as constructing meaning. I use the word 'hiatus' because not all critical texts refer to questions about 'looking' and 'gazing' –viewing is taken for granted. But other works, especially some in the area of feminist theory, do examine the nature of gaze and its implications.

2 Major questions

1 How may one define terms such as 'British film' and a 'film industry'?

2 What economic and political factors explain why the British film industry is frequently described as being in a state of crisis?

3 How has it reached a state of crisis?

4 What is the relationship of the US majors to British film, both historically and presently?

5 In what ways can it be argued that looking upon the film screen is governed by the film text?

6 How is looking and gazing concerned with the production of meaning?

7 In what ways are notions of the gaze involved with notions of the self that does the looking?

8 How has psychoanalysis contributed to understanding the above questions, especially with relation to gender?

3 Political economy and the British film industry

This section is concerned with the economic factors which have shaped production, distribution and exhibition of film in Britain. It will also refer to the role that government has taken, or failed to take, in producing an industry which is not so much a coherent whole, as a collection of related businesses. For convenience, I am framing this exposition within a historical survey of the past 50 years. But I also want to show through a PE perspective, that something called a British film industry has never stood a chance, because of market forces, and because of the nature of and failure of government intervention.

Where 'British film' is dealt with in critical terms, it is interesting how often it is discussed in terms of national identity or the past success of a studio such as Ealing, or of certain film texts. In this last case, one may be talking about examples such as social realism, from the 1950s/1960s 'working class' films through to the work of Ken Loach in the 1990s, or about successes such as *Chariots of Fire* (1982) or *Trainspotting* (1996), which temporarily produce more investment and speculation about the 'revival of the British film industry'.

Yet one could say bluntly that those British people working with film in Britain are as much bothered about having a job in film, as they are about whether the films they make and show are about British society. In financial terms, it is as important to talk about whether the profits from a film made in Britain get back into the British economy. This is another way of talking about Britishness, as much as the cultural resonances of the material. Of course, one might like to have it both ways. But still, a film such as *Notting Hill* (1999) may be critiqued not just in terms of its ability to evoke the Britishness of a certain place or of certain characters, but also in terms of its economic Britishness. It did well for British personnel, but, typically, it did badly for the general economy of British films, in that swathes of the profits went back to the USA and American backers.

3.1 Historical considerations

In so far as there is and has been a British industry which manufactures films, this has always been caught between the pressures of the marketplace and the disinclination of any government to intervene in a financially supportive manner. These two factors have operated in the context of an aggressive and successful American film industry. These pressures and this context have been very evident in the past 50 years.

As Britain came out of the Second World War it seemed that cinema was healthy, with admission peaking at around 30 million a week in 1949. But, typically, the money was not going into a British film industry. British films occupied only about 20 per cent of screen time. Hollywood had the product everyone wanted to see. Even though for a while there was a British duopoly with vertical integration of production, distribution and exhibition, it still could not provide the product and serious funding needed to sustain a British film industry. In this case we are talking about Rank Films and ABC (Associated British Pictures). Rank, for example, owned two of the three major cinema circuits – Gaumont-British and Odeon. It owned production companies – Gaumont British, Gains- borough and GFD. It had a stake in Pinewood and Denham studios. As regards the US majors, it had links with Twentieth Century Fox and an interest in Universal Pictures. ABC had for a while a 25 per cent stake in Warner Brothers (see Petrie, 1991).

Still, the British government set up a film quota system to try and protect British product – though they quickly had to back-pedal on a 75 per cent duty 'tax' because the Americans simply refused to send any films. Nevertheless, from 1949 until 1980 there was a 30 per cent quota for the showing of British films – latterly more honoured in the breach than in its observance. The National Film Finance Corporation (NFFC) was set up (1949), with £6 million of government money, to encourage the production of British film. At the same time, the so-called Eady levy was established, taking a proportion of box-office receipts, and returning these to the NFFC and to producers. But again this was not very helpful because the Eady definition of a British film – concentrating on person- nel – allowed the money to go to American backers and distributors. Indeed, the sliding scale of money skimmed off box-office returns meant that the better the film did finan- cially, the more money went to the USA. The British duopoly simply could not compete with the popularity and production values of American product. In commercial terms, they wasted away over a period of time. ABC was taken over by EMI in 1969; Rank stayed stronger for longer, but still was in no position to seriously compete with the American majors. Its production facilities might be used by American-backed films. It remained strong in distribution for many years, but again only because of monopolistic affiliations with American majors. It continued in exhibition (the Odeon circuit), though again this was all about access to American product. In 1970 American distributors dealt with 75 per cent of films shown in Britain, even though 60 per cent of these films were de- fined (dubiously) as being British. Ninety per cent of these British films were made with American money (see Dickinson, 1983).

The financing, distribution and screening of films in Britain has continued to be dominated by the USA for the past 50 years, because the forces of the political economy have prevailed. Up to 1946 when there 635 million cinema admissions in Britain, it was still possible for a British film to recoup its investment in the domestic market. After this, in spite of a recovery from the 1984 low of 58.4 million admissions, this has never been realistically possible. Hill (1996) also refers to the fundamental problem of the 'divorce of production from distribution and exhibition interests' – the failure to have and to control access to a stream of British films.

Government has intervened in terms of censorship – regulation of text. It has never intervened significantly in terms of the market, to privilege the production of British financed films in British studios, and about British subject matter. The economic forces of the market – mainly the strength of the dollar – have determined whether anything that could be defined as a British film would get made and shown. To this extent the financial success and Britishness of film making in Britain has see-sawed according to the strength or weakness of the dollar. Cultural or creative value has had some part to play. But in terms of film as a commodity in the marketplace this has also been about the question of whether or not British material sells. So, there was a wave of British film production in the 1960s: *Tom Jones* (1963), *A Kind of Loving* (1962) etc., because it was cheap to makes films in Britain and because British culture was temporarily trendy and successful (the decade of the Beatles). But then this was followed by the trough of a recession by the end of the decade, when exchange rates shifted and a new wave of American directors became popular (*Easy Rider* (1967) and the like).

Problems during the 1970s were compounded by further pressures against American investment in British film – pressures consequent on new audio-visual technologies such as satellite and cable spreading the attractions of television in the USA, and on financial troubles, as US majors continued to adjust to a post-studio era and to becoming part of the leisure arms of large corporations.

The rollercoaster effect continued. Companies like EMI and British Lion invested in films for the US market, partly encouraged by British production expertise and perhaps by the successful move to Hollywood of some British directors. But while they were behind successes such as *The Deer Hunter* (1978), they also suffered losses on films such as *Honky Tonk Freeway* (1981). They pulled back from production. Similarly, Lew Grade's then Associated Communications Company (including the very successful ATV channel) made a terminal loss on the mega-production of *Raise the Titanic* in 1981, and also gave up on a brief foray into film production. Not that their films were, in a cultural sense, British films. Street (1997) quotes from a report of the government's Political and Economic Planning Unit in 1952: 'The crisis in British film-making . . . started long ago . . . Of a stable production industry there has been no sign.'

And so it went on, and has continued. For example, *Chariots of Fire* (1982) and the film-making commitments of a new TV Channel 4 seemed to promise a resurgence of British production. Oscars were won. Yet by 1986 Thorn/EMI, Virgin and Goldcrest had all pulled out of film production, having made expensive misjudgements. But this was mainly because they simply did not have the cash resources to fund the risks of film production and take the losses. A Hollywood studio could have coped with the losses incurred through the failure of *Revolution* (1986), starring Al Pacino – but not Goldcrest.

Political intervention in the 1980s, driven by a mistaken belief in the power of the marketplace to make everything all right, had made things worse. The Thatcher government's Film Bill (1984) abolished

● the remains of a quota system protecting the screening of even 25 per cent of British films;

● the Eady levy;

● a 25 per cent tax break for those investing in film production;

● the NFFC.

In its place it put British Screen Finance Ltd, to which it gave £1.5 million a year – far less than the cost of one Hollywood film, even at that time. This was the financial undertow that was going to cause yet another trough in the story of British film production, even at the time when British films seemed to be doing well at the box office and in the USA.

Pre-production phase
• constructing a package
  [star, property, director, treatment]
• making a deal
  [for financial backing, distribution,
  marketing rights]
• making a schedule
  [for shooting and completion]
• making a budget
• contracting stars and principals
• booking crew, equipment, studio space,
  locations
• drafting the publicity campaign
• drafting a shooting script
• obtaining completion insurance

Production phase
• shooting film
• recording live sound
• keeping to schedule and budget
• checking rushes
• developing marketing campaign
• shooting special effects

Post-production phase
• recording [dubbing] dialogue
• recording music and effects
• mixing sound
• adding special effects
  [optical or digital]
• editing film
• making trailers
• striking prints
• running advertising campaign
• marketing the film and its star

Film: Main production functions
Getting a film into a cinema or out on DVD involves a great deal more than directing actors and cameras. The summary chart above barely alludes to the hundreds of workers, millions of dollars and months of labour needed to produce a text which may alternatively be described as a work of art or a product/commodity.

Nor does it do justice to the work on set, involving principals such as the director of photography; the art director, set design and construction, hair, costume and make-up – let alone the work of the producer on administration and finance.
(*Graeme Burton*, 2004)

Relatively big players such as Goldcrest (see above), with the resources of the Pearson media group behind it, gave up. Producers scrabbled around for money – mainly from television – to finance one-off projects. This was not the Hollywood-style portfolio of films, from which one might hope for a couple of hits. Money might come partly from TV sources such as ZDF in Germany or Le Sept in France. In the 1980s in Britain 342 production companies were set up, 250 of them supporting only one film (Hill, 1996).

The 1980s consolidated a tendency to rely on television presales to finance the production of films in Britain (not always about Britain). In the late 1980s the four major sources of finance were British Screen (linked to the National Film Development Fund), Handmade Films (raising cash partly through TV deals), Zenith (a spin-off of Central TV) and Channel 4. It might have seemed that television was saving British film as much as killing the industry. But it has been argued that television, and video (which took off in the 1980s, and was a competitor in terms of film viewing) did not really pay enough for the benefits they were getting. Petrie (1991) asserts that 'there is enough revenue being earned in the various media which depend on film product to support a healthy production programme in this country'. British film production was not getting that revenue – nor does it today.

As I have indicated, British Screen, as a political intervention in the marketplace, was not backed by sufficient cash or regulation of the market in favour of British product (unlike many European countries). Anyway, in a typically British political fudge, the organization was required to run on a successful commercial basis, yet was not free to operate as a purely commercial enterprise, because of requirements to support what were defined as British films (in terms of subject matter and personnel). The question raised here – and referred to in the next section – is what do we mean by a British film industry? A commercial industry of British production, with money coming back into that industry, has to be set up to compete with Hollywood, and has to acquire appropriate funds to match US production values. A cultural industry dominated by British material has to be protected and resourced with privileged finance.

The figures for television investment in film do look impressive. For example, between 1982 and 1994, Channel 4 invested £90 million in 264 films, from Greenaway's *The Draughtsman's Contract* (1982) to Kureishi's *My Beautiful Laundrette* (1985) to Loach's *Riff Raff* (1990). Other television organizations invested on a lesser scale, though this was still significant in terms of keeping British workers producing films with British qualities – for example, the BBC's investment in *Truly, Madly, Deeply*. There were some financial/tax advantages in making films through television – for instance, the crewing levels and payments are less for television than for film. On the other hand, a financial disadvantage is that the unions involved will not agree to TV contract films having cinema release without receiving additional payment. And, Hill (1996) is sceptical about the commercial viability of TV funded film enterprises. He points out that Channel 4 did not have to show a direct profit on its film production ventures, in that its real income is from advertising, and film support is only part of its activities. He goes on to assert that 'the relatively high percentage of the channel's overall budget (6–7 per cent) devoted to feature film investment has not been matched by the number of programme hours or audience ratings which the resulting films have provided'.

It is also the case that in this period of the late 1980s and early 1990s other economic changes affected British film production adversely. Although it did not have an immediately damaging effect, changes to Channel 4 caused it to rein in film investment after 1993. This was when the channel ceased to receive compulsory support from the big commercial TV companies – designed to get it off the ground – and had to survive on its own advertising. In 1988 the collection of the ITV levy changed – in effect a special tax on TV profits. It became a tax on advertising income, which in effect meant that ITV lost a tax loophole through which it could write off 30 per cent of film production costs.

3.2 Present factors

Things have not changed much, from the 1990s to the present day in terms of

- cycles of British film success, followed by US investment, followed by withdrawal;
- film's interdependence on television;
- the contradictory and unhelpful interventions of governments that do not want to spend money on supporting a distinctively British film industry;
- the stranglehold of US distributors on sources of finance and on a global marketing machine;
- unresolved attitudes towards supporting British workers in film and wanting a distinctively British film product.

Economic verities working within a market economy continue to dominate the performance of whatever passes for a British film industry. Films are in effect sold to distributors through a pattern of financing which is dominated by pre-sales and equity investments. Distributors are interested in box-office appeal. A film has to earn two and half times its production costs at the box office before any profits are seen (Petrie, 1991). Barring practices work against independent cinemas being able to screen films while they are still 'hot'. The major exhibitor circuits practise centralized booking, and are inflexible about taking on 'alternative' film (which may well, in practice, refer to low-budget British material). In any case, exhibitors take about two-thirds of receipts. This means that once the distributor has taken a big bite of the remaining third, there is very little to go back to the actual film makers. The major distributors and exhibitors do not much care, because they are part of the same US multi-nationals. On top of this, British film work has, like that of television, been largely casualized. These facts, among others, work against the existence and financial viability of a coherent national film industry.

Some might argue that in a global economy this is an unrealistic aspiration, that co-productions and international links should be the order of the day. In 1991 the government established a British Film Commission which taps into a European Co-production fund via British Screen, and which contributes to the Eurimages project, which itself supports production and distribution for independent film. The European Media 92 initiative – generally intended to develop AV industries in Europe – consolidated European support for film, not least to resist American dominance. Specifically, it made provision for free loans towards the distribution costs of low-budget films. It was European money which helped to establish the Glasgow Film Fund (GFF) in 1992. The GFF, together with the Scottish Film Production Fund helped finance what became a very successful cult thriller, *Shallow Grave* (1994), and, certainly, it was agreed that the film had a successful but economical marketing campaign. Yet it could also be argued that the above account exemplifies a system in which financing for distinctively British or regional films is hopelessly labyrinthine. It is wastefully time-consuming, and makes no difference to a general production and screening situation which continues to be dominated by US money. Anyway, alliances with Europe continue to be undercut by the issue of language difference – which is not a problem for American product. In any case, the production of a film is no guarantee that it will be seen. Murphy (2000) points out that in 1996 of 85 films that were made only 34 achieved distribution.

Films made in Britain continue to be in thrall to American distributors and exhibitors. Working Title has been and is a very successful British production company, but it was bought firstly by the entertainment arm of the Dutch company, Polygram. Then Polygram Film Entertainment was itself bought out by Seagram/Universal of the USA in 1999. Polygram raised £16 million to make the film *Bean* in 1997 – a British film pitched at a global market. The film made $198 million world-wide, most of which once more ended up with American backers. Before the Seagram buyout, Working Title (Polygram) had put £50 million into 14 productions – work for British film personnel, even if these were not all exactly British films.

Government has intervened with minor tax break schemes, to encourage British film production (The Enterprise Investment Scheme). But films such as *Sliding Doors* (1998) or *Notting Hill* (1999) successful as they were, still needed American stars and a certain transatlantic inflection to attract the American money to get them made.

One should not, to be fair, underestimate the tremendous success of Working Title at the box office. *Notting Hill* made $350 million (but most of this went outside the UK). *Billy Elliott* (2000), about a very British working-class boy succeeding as a ballet dancer, did well in the USA, and made $100 million world-wide. It was made for less than $5 million, when the average Hollywood movie costs $56 million. But then the arguments about American backers and their recouping most of the profits still remain. And there is a well argued critical view that very successful films like *Love Actually* (2003) nevertheless represent an American mythology about British culture (and romance), rather than anything truly home-grown.

Television continues to play some significant part in the production of British films. The BBC spends about £5 million a year on production, as well as contributing indirectly through the purchase of TV rights. Channel 4 had been spending rather more than that, but in 2002 announced that it was winding up its Film Four operation and most of its production commitment. It is true that in 1998 Channel 4 films accounted for only 1 per cent of UK box office take (Miller, 2000). As an aside, it is also worth observing that many European television systems put more money into film, partly because of the cultural status of film in countries like France and Germany, but also because the details of economic legislation have required this.

Generally speaking, dominant sources of funding have been British Screen, the European Co-production fund, the BFI, Channel 4, ITV and the BBC. For example, these were significant in helping *The Crying Game* to be made in 1992. But the film's success came too late to save Palace Pictures, the ailing young British company behind it and other successes. Behind British Screen (most importantly) has been money from the National Lottery from the late 1990s onwards.

The picture of cinema in Britain might seem positive in some ways – for example, an increase in admissions from 97.37 million in 1990 to 135.5 million in 1998 – or an

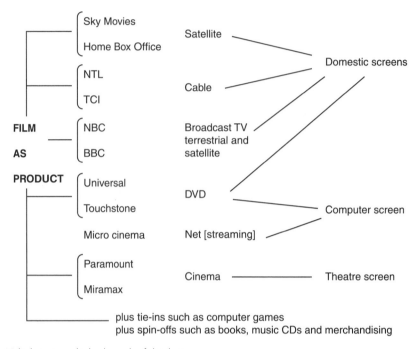

Film: Multiple texts, multiple channels of distribution
(*Graeme Burton*, 2004)

increase in investment in films from £169 million in 1992 to £560 million in 1996. But in the same period Rank distributors were sold to Carlton television, and went out of business. Palace Pictures – a success story of the 1980s – went out of production business in 1993. (Though Working Title has survived from the 1980s, and is doing well for its American backers.) The general story is one of a pattern of false dawns for a British film industry. American multiplexes have come to dominate exhibition – 'cathedrals of consumption', as Branston (2000) calls them, offering 'kiddie-adult food'. In 1997 films defined as British had only 10 per cent of the British film market. The BFI has pulled out of funding even very low budget feature films. As Miller says, the Tory government of the early 1990s was indifferent to the British cinema industry: 'The trend is very clearly towards horizontal connections to other media and a break-up of public–private distinctions in ownership, control and programming philosophy.'

In terms of something called British cinema, a struggle goes on between a desire for a viable film sector that provides employment, and for a representative and even regional British cinema.

In 1997 a tax credit system (15 per cent tax relief) did provide a shot in the arm for film production – it doubled. And indeed this rate will increase to 20 per cent from 2004 to 2005. However, the 1998 government report on the industry, *A Bigger Picture*, describes British film production as a cottage industry. The same report points out that British films (*sic*) have only 23 per cent of the British audience, whereas US films have 73 per cent of the home audience. To be fair, as Murphy (2000) points out, film investment is high risk. In 1998, British screen and other backers put £6.4 million into the film *Wilde*, which sank without much trace. In the same year, *Mrs Brown* cost only £1 million, and was a minor hit at the box office. The Lottery Fund was part of this backing, and assigned £90 million to three production groups – The Film Consortium, Pathe Pictures and DNA. But the money was spread thinly across a number of productions and went into a fragmented British film production base which suffers from a lack of continuity, of throughput, and of sufficient investment. In general, investors in the British economy are less inclined to produce venture capital for risk investment than, say, the USA. Our economy is more dominated by the relative size of pensions funds, and the caution of their managers.

So in spite of European funds and television money, the economic climate for British film still is dominated by temperature changes in the US economy and film industry. In spite of government reports and the goodwill of the ministry for culture, politicians still believe in the global market economy and its forces. In that case, it is no surprise that British film making is subject to what Sarah Street (1997) described as 'the punishing fluctuations of the market economy'.

The British do like going to the movies. In 2002, cinema admissions reached 167.3 million, though they dropped by 5 per cent in 2003. But then, only three British films made it to the top twenty (and top ten) in terms of box office take – *Love Actually, Calendar Girls* and *Johnny English*. And on television, over the past eight years, of 1,125 films shown on the main channels, only 33 were British (*Guardian*, 4 March 2004). It seems that nothing changes. Comment in the *Independent on Sunday* (24 November 2002) from a media and film lawyer, states that the film industry is in trouble and is 'reeling from a 40 per cent drop in production activity'.

At the moment, if 20 per cent of a film's staff and facilities are from the UK and UK producers contribute at least 20 per cent to the budget, then investors can defer tax payments over 15 years. The government has proposed changing the ruling to a figure of 40 per cent. In February 2004, new tax avoidance rules 'have left film companies reeling. Industry figures are warning that changes will force some companies to the wall and lead to hundreds of job losses' (*Guardian*, 12 February 2004). There has been at least temporary chaos in respect of film financing and of location work in Britain.

In the following sections I want to take on themes incorporated within the above, without needing to repeat information and arguments relating to US economic dominance and the problems of defining what is British about British film.

3.3 The problem of British film and industry

66 99 Most national film industries are highly capitalised, corporately constituted, commercial enterprises which tend to structure their products within sets of rather narrow guidelines.
Petrie (1991)

This, of course, is not the case for British film, nor is it ever likely to be. But in any case, phrases such as British film industry need to be examined in light of the separation between those who are talking about employment in a film business, and those talking about a cultural product that represents Britishness.

Some would argue that, either way, it is hardly meaningful to talk about a British film industry any more: 'Production in Britain is no longer the same as British-originated films; nor does either necessarily have anything to do with British culture for British consumption' (Nowell-Smith, 1985).

In industrial terms, and as far as British Screen is concerned, to be British, 75 per cent of a film has to be created in the UK, regardless of where the backing comes from. But in fact, a coherent, integrated industrial base just does not exist. Todd (in Murphy, 2000) quotes Eric Fellner of Working Title Pictures as saying baldly: 'there is no clear-cut British film industry'. Fragmentation means that directors/producers spend a lot of time raising money and promoting their films, relative to actually making them. The catalogue of backers for Loach's *Land and Freedom* (1995), costing £3 million to make, is depressingly long, and largely not British: Eurimages Fund, European Co-production Fund, British Screen, BBC films, FNW (Germany), Canal Plus (Spain), Television Espanola. Yet it is worth recognizing that this is an 'alternative' film (about the Spanish civil war of the 1930s, and British participants), with a political commitment, made by an esteemed British director, which was critically praised. It did get made, and it was seen by a reasonably large audience.

The Full Monty (1997) is apparently a typically 'British' film. It is set in Sheffield, and concerns a group of unemployed working-class men looking for a way out of their economic hardship. The actors, writer and director are British. But then it may be argued that class and location are only a backdrop to a feel-good comedy success story, which could have been set anywhere. And certainly most of its profits went back to Fox and NewsCorp – doing nothing for the future of British film.

In terms of 'film and industry', one also has to take account of the cross-over between media. 'When it comes to personnel, ideas, genres, funds, companies and the State, the lines (between cinema and TV) are very blurred indeed' (Brown, 2000). We are looking at a situation where video rental and sales earn more money than is taken at the box office. Also, the biggest audience for films, including films which can be described as British in their subject matter, views these films via television. Technology, globalization and the market have, to a fair extent, integrated what were separate media. So there is a material problem in talking meaningfully about a distinct film industry.

In cultural terms, one may also raise problems about defining Britishness. At the very least, the term has to be inclusive of a wide range of experiences. Meera Syal's *Anita and Me* (2002) is indeed a British-funded film about growing up in a multi-cultural but not very inclusive British society. Hers is an Asian experience. What about the Afro-Caribbean experience? Or films from the regions? One has to ask how well films from or about marginalized Britons will sell to mainstream English viewers in English urban conurbations. Certainly we know that European and US views of what is 'British' do not match the complex reality of British society today.

If one is looking for 'films' which address such variety and consequent social issues, then it is arguable that television does the job, and renders calls for an enhanced British cinema irrelevant. 'The principle strength of made for TV films lies in their ability to address specifically domestic issues, as against home-produced theatrical films which need to keep one eye on the overseas market' (Auty and Roddick, 1985).

So is concern about a lack of British culturally oriented cinema misplaced and irrelevant? John Hill (1991) points out that national cinema does not have to be nation-alist, or have to support mythologies of Britishness. Indeed, he suggests that British film could be critical of the nation and of its terms of national identity. *My Beautiful Laundrette* (1985) would be an example of one such film.

Somewhere in the debate about the nature of Britishness on film, and the definition of British film in general, one also needs to take account of the non-commercial sector – art school productions, BFI-supported alternative and experimental film, and the like.

In terms of the identity of this problematic entity called a British film, I offer Petrie's (1991) definition of major British genres, with examples and without comment, as follows

Eccentric comedy	*My Beautiful Laundrette*
Thrillers	*Mona Lisa*
Biopics	*Prick Up Your Ears*
Liberal epic	*Passage to India*
Novel adaptation	*Room with a View*

The problems with talking about the British film industry remain, and may be expressed as a series of questions.

- What does one mean by British in a multi-cultural society?
- What does one mean by British film, when production is dominated by American money, and when many films have to respond in casting and treatment to the demands of these backers?
- What does one mean by film when the audio-visual industries are so intertwined, and when the cinema audience is less than that for video and television?
- What does one mean by industry when there is no integrated British film industry as such, and no continuity of production?
- What does one mean by film industry when film workers and film texts are so dependent on the television industry for their survival?

3.4 The USA, globalization and economic imperialism

66 99 Hollywood has dominated the British market since the days of silent films, due to its size, commercial strength, the quality of its product and the publicity and glamour generated by its star system.

Petrie (1991)

I have already said enough above to indicate that in many ways it is economic imperialism that we should be concerned about, rather than cultural imperialism. British film making of any scope depends too much on finance from the American majors and on expensive marketing by US distributors. A limited release pattern for a film in Britain can easily cost £500,000, and a saturation release of 400 prints would cost twice as much. With prints costing over £1,000 a time to strike, and given the huge costs of film production, it is no surprise that distribution is dominated by the Hollywood majors, who account for 80 per cent of the box-office take. A film in Britain has to go into a multiplex to find a large audience. These dominate the 2,500 screens in the country, and are mostly American owned. Anyway, most of the total box-office take (around 90 per cent), goes to a few American high concept movies. American movies also dominate film TV screenings, and film as video/DVD rental and purchase. Indeed, these two outlets make more money than cinema screenings. Equally, if a British made film wants to make a decent profit, then it has to sell in the US market – once again controlled by the majors.

It would be dangerous to make Hollywood the whipping boy for failures by British governments to intervene protectively in the economy of film making in this country. It would be unreasonable to assert that British product is either superior to American work per se, or that British audiences have some kind of obligation to pay to see that British product. It would be unfair to ignore the fact that American money has kept a lot of people in work. It would be culturally chauvinistic to suggest that British audiences are not allowed to find American products attractive or to make choices with their wallets.

Multiplex Exterior
Cinema-going is about consumption (including front-of-house purchases) and about a social experience (visiting in groups). It offers a choice of movies, not a dedicated text. It offers a variety of associated merchandising.
   Does the fact that films can be viewed on different kinds of screen, in different places, with or without other people, change the meaning of 'film' or 'cinema', in your opinion?
(*Corbis*)

But as Shane Meadows says, 'budgets to promote American films here are routinely higher than what we get to make a film'. As an independent low-budget film maker, Meadows was pleased to get £3 million to make *Once Upon a Time in the Midlands* (2003). 'People complain that's all they get from British films (character driven stories) – but we are forced to work around intensive performances' (*Observer*, 2 August 2002).

It would also be naive to ignore the effect on the British of having watched decades of US film product. It would be stupid to ignore the workings of the market economy, which is selfish and ruthless in its pursuit of profit. This economy is not concerned with the cultural value (and pleasures) to be gained from texts circulating within a culture and reflecting the concerns and values of a given society.

I am suggesting that the British film production is not necessarily in a bad state just because it does not have a vertically integrated film industry. This may not be possible or desirable within a global economy. It may ignore the benefits and products of an integrated media economy, and of what television in particular has achieved. But I would suggest that the guaranteed throughput of British film as a culturally distinctive text is in a shaky state. This is essentially because it has no secure financial base. Having said this, one should not then have global aspirations for British film, but should for the most part accept low budgets and limited audiences precisely because that which speaks to a specific cultural base cannot necessarily expect to have pan-cultural appeal.

Processes of globalization are not just about the size of companies or the economic muscle which they can deploy. They are also about audiences and cultural attitudes. Hollywood has produced the blockbuster, the action film, the comic-strip movie. These forms have universal appeal, and are easy to market. They are culturally unselective in some respects, though ideologically and mythologically committed to a Western/US view of how things should be. In terms of how things are, and of the difficulty in preserving a distinctively British film industry, Brown (2000) comments that 'a populist, big-budget, apolitical model is preferred to an artisanal "poor" cinema articulated around social issues'. The world prefers *Terminator 3* (2003) (and an industry which is able to produce such a film) to the latest offering from Ken Loach.

This is acceptable so long as people like Loach (and, not least, newcomers) have a fair chance of raising money and getting to an audience. It might be argued that the US majors are not paying enough for their access to and dominance of that British market which includes cinema, video/DVD and television. It might be argued that they should not have such a degree of control over access to screens in Britain. This argument refers to the mantra of consumer choice, which is protected through legislation in other industries. It also has a certain irony when one remembers that it was the invocation of anti-trust laws in 1948 which in the USA led to the Hollywood majors being forced to sell off theatre chains and their dominance of exhibition.

I now want to turn from a historical analysis and questioning of the nature of the British film industry in particular, to an account of some critical views on the process of looking at films in general.

4 Looking and gazing – spectator, image, meaning

This section has to do with how we look upon and understand the screen image. In critical terms, dimensions of the film spectator's look upon the screen cover

- the nature of screen material and its effect upon the look;
- the process of looking and attending to elements of the image;
- the nature of perception and its effects on understanding of screen material;
- processes of cognition, of manufacturing meanings about that material;
- the physical and conceptual context around looking – in which the place of viewing, ideological frameworks and cultural experience also contribute to making sense of film.

4.1 Just looking – mise en scène and the image

At one level, looking on film is seen as being relatively unproblematic – everyone sees the image, and the image drives meaning. Looking is transparent. This apparent transparency seems to come from a perceptual correspondence between screen viewing and life viewing. Prince (1996) observes that 'a wide range of evidence indicates that film spectatorship builds on correspondences between selected features of the cinematic display and a viewer's real-world visual and social experience'.

Prince goes on, indeed, to criticize psychoanalytic theorists for constructing 'theoretical spectators' and ignoring communication research which shows that, for example, viewers seem to use the same perceptual apparatus for assessing motive in film characters as they do in real life.

Mise en scène

Of course the film image is a constructed thing and so (apart from being two-dimensional) its correspondence with life is an illusion. Mise en scène is a notion which draws attention to elements of the film shot. It refers to the framing of the shot, plus composition and movement within the frame. It goes on to embrace elements such as background, lighting, colour, focus and costume. As a critical tool for explaining why we may infer some meanings rather than others from the film, it was used by the French critics of Cahiers du Cinema in the 1950s. They were interested in a theory of authorship which validated the quality of work produced by popular Hollywood directors such as John Ford or Nicholas Ray. The expression of mise en scène could itself be used to prove consistencies of style and theme across the work of a director; to prove a creative skill and deliberation in the construction of the film. In many ways it was a paradigm of literary authorial criticism, in which style is praised and authorial consistency gains critical approval.

Kolker (1998) comments that 'a focus on mise en scène permitted an emphasis upon the elements of film that made it distinct from other narrative forms and was used to explain how images . . . generate narrative even and guide our perception through a film'. But as Williams (2000) says, there are limitations to this approach, in respect of its emphasis on the role of the text in governing the act of looking, in shaping the way in which the spectator makes meanings: 'the spectator takes part in making the meaning of the film, but only within the framework of what the film itself . . . tells him or her to do: the spectator must co-operate in fulfilling the film's form'.

Fuery (2000) talks about mise en scène as a cinematic practice 'based on constructing realism to have an effect on the viewer'. Whereas, if one wishes to 'theorise the gaze' one then has to 'engage in the interplay between cinematic textual systems (diegesis, montage, mise en scène, intertextuality, etc.) and the act of viewing'.

Elsaesser and Buckland (2002) refer to a useful essay by Adrian Martin in which he elaborates definitions of mise en scène into three categories:

- classic mise en scène is that in which style is unobtrusive, in which form and theme come together. It is the stuff of what we have come to understand as conventional, straightforward story-telling – a coherent fictional world;

- expressionist mise en scène is a version in which there is coherence, but style may be used to bring out particular meanings. The work of the Coen Brothers would fit here, in which elements of pastiche and parody in a film like *Fargo* (1996) are created by a deliberately self-conscious use of the elements of mise en scène.

- mannerist mise en scène is a version in which style dominates, coherence and realism do not rule. Style does not serve subject matter. The approach is at least post-classical, if not also post-modernist. The viewer will become conscious of the constructive work that is film making. Realism would not be equated with naturalism, with the invisibility of the narrative. Films such as Resnais' *Last Year in Marienbad* (1961), or *Being John Malkovich* (2000) would fit the notion of mannerism (with some expressionism).

But, however Martin could be said to be rescuing mise en scène analysis from the trap of equivalence with the classic realist text, he cannot help it to escape from its textual location. It is arguable that the mannerist version allows for spectator consciousness: the viewer might be more actively engaged with the film and possible meanings. Yet the underlying assumption is that the text initiates a relationship with the viewer. The look is understood to be more directed than free-ranging, let alone driven by terms of reference which exist within the mind of the viewer and their cultural environment.

Indeed, it may be argued in this case that film viewing is a reflexive process in which the spectator identifies not only with elements such as characters within the film, but also with the process of looking that the film carries out through the camera. The classic realist text exploits a cultural history of living with the camera, and a biological history which privileges vision. There is what is called 'subjectivity', in which the spectator appears to be the subject of the film's discourse, in which we inhabit the cinematic world – talking of both realism and narrative – as if by magic. We identify with the screen image and the screen world, although it is an illusion, a construction, is socially produced, and is a manifestation of ideology. 'One of the pre-eminent pleasures of cinema is this illusion of mastery over a perceptual field that seems to be without a source, that positions the spectator as its own subject' (Sconce, 1993).

4.2 Gazing reflectively – notes on psychoanalysis

Psychoanalytic approaches to understanding how the viewer may gaze upon and make sense of the film image are not necessarily tied to gender, though they have a lot to say about this. They are also part of a larger critical project which tries to explore the act of spectating as well as the relationship that is created between the spectator and the film through the act of viewing. In terms of understanding the production of meaning, they shift emphasis from the text to the audience and to the act of engagement with the text, in a context. As Fuery (2000) says: 'for psycho-analysis, when we analyse the gaze we are also examining the structures, functions, and operations of ourselves as subjects'.

The remarks which follow are intended only as signposts towards longer, but still summary discussions in sources such as *The Cinema Book* (Cook and Bernink, 1999), as well as to more sustained discussions such as that of *Silence of the Lambs* (1991) in Elsaesser and Buckland (2002).

It is probably the ideas of Freud which have found their way most explicitly into cinema texts, and which have been most used to interpret the nature of the gaze. So, for example, *The Forbidden Planet* (1956) is not only a revamp of *The Tempest* story, but it also talks explicitly about the monster from the Id, that manifestation of the Ego that is about unrestrained Passions, and which has to be controlled by the Superego. The viewer of this film understands in general terms that they are watching a symbolic statement about the dark forces that are buried within us – symbolized by the out-of-control intelligent computer. Films are in some ways constructed versions of our dreams, which so absorbed Freud in his efforts to understand the workings of the unconscious. As spectators involved in the process of constructing meaning, we are allowed to dream, in wakefulness. Our gaze is turned outwards upon the film image, and inwards upon the operations of the mind (as critics theorize them). Freud talks about fetishism – the substitution of a specific object for the object of our desire. He talks about sublimated pleasure, about male fears of castration, of the female body.

The film *Peeping Tom* (1960) is a film about a psychopath making films of women as he murders them. As we gaze upon the film and are directed by a subjective camera, we understand that he kills what he fears rather than being able to face it. And of course the issue of gender figures large in this spectatorship. The female viewer can only deal in the projected male gaze by proxy (see also the next section). But her gaze can also be understood as identifying with the female victims, and symbolically with a fear of sexual penetration (made explicit by the use of a camera tripod as a phallic murder weapon). Fear in horror films in general is not necessarily a gendered thing. In Freudian terms the spectator is often faced with monsters from their own Id, they gaze and reflect upon their own compulsions and their alter egos.

Fuery asserts that an important aspect of Freud's theories lies in what he says about the interplay between opposing forces, not least in relation to the 'scopic drive'. As we gaze, we may take pleasure in the idea of looking or being looked at, of being active or passive. We move between those positions, between masculinities and femininities. To this extent he is arguing against the idea of a polarized, gendered gaze.

Sconce (1993) offers an excellent discussion of spectator positioning and identification in the horror film. He examines the reality-position shifts within the *Nightmare on Elm Street* cycle of films (in and out of dream and media worlds), together with their appeal to the viewer's privileged knowledge of the genre. He argues that we identify with the monster itself, the Freddy character, who then allows us to 'play' with the nightmares. He asserts that as with all films we must 'make this identification and assume a certain subject position for the images to be "meaningful" '.

For Lacan (1993), the key to gazing would lie in the notion of *the mirror self*, and that stage of development in which – through literally looking in a mirror – a child can conceive of itself as an individual. Ever after, the child can call itself to mind – that mirror image. It can conceive its own identity. But of course the mirror self – like the film image – is an illusion, a representation. There is excitement and pleasure in looking upon the image, whether in a mirror or on a film screen. There is also a puzzling separation, in that the image in the mirror is of the self, and yet is not truly the self. In the case of film, this separation (but wish to understand the image as if it is real) sets up contradictory positions within the viewer. This viewer gazes upon the image as if it is real, yet knows it is not. The viewer is actively involved with the experience of the image, yet is passive in being unable to control the flow of images upon the screen. The viewer feels in control of the production of meaning and of an inner world, and yet has no power over the world on screen. Lacan's style and arguments are difficult. But the main ideas make gazing a dual experience, in which we both look upon the screen world out there, and take the screen world into our heads and make it part of our knowledge about ourselves and the world. Fuery talks of 'the subject viewing the image in terms of the self, and the self viewing the self in terms of the image'. This is about how the image is understood in terms of who we think we are, but also how who we think we are is understood with reference to the image. In this circular relationship and cross-referential world it becomes difficult to talk of 'the real'! Lacan's ideas suggest that our gaze upon the film image is active, makes meanings in terms of our sense of our identity, and simultaneously reassesses that identity in terms of what is understood from the film image.

Film criticism has often used the implications of Lacan's ideas about identity and gazing, to understand difference and gender identity. Lacan himself was concerned to explain sexuality and sexual difference. In gender terms, there is difference and division felt when the female – and the mother in particular – is understood in terms of lacking a penis. But the self is also divided in ways regardless of gender, as I have indicated: 'there is always division between the self which speaks and the self of which one speaks' (Jancovich, 1995). We attempt to bring these two kinds of self together, by reference to that ideal self which we understood in the mirror phase of development. Lacan uses the metaphor of surgery to explain this bringing together: 'Suture is the process by which the subject tries to repair the divisions within the self' (Jancovich, 1995). And so it has been argued by film critics (for example Heath, 1981), that looking on film and making sense of it involves a process of suture, as one makes a coherent meaning out of different shots, bringing them together in one's mind.

A third and dominant framework of psychoanalysis for thinking about the gaze and about the relationship between the spectator and the screen was drawn from the work of Christian Metz. In this case, the two main strands of Metz's theories relate to identification with seeing and with narrating. He suggests that we conflate the idea of our eyes as looking with the idea of the camera as looking. So we are inclined to accept the work that the camera does in making meaning. 'Metz argues persuasively that we "identify" with the mechanisms of the cinema because they become, as it were, extensions of ourselves' (Turner, 1993).

The idea behind narrative identification is an extension of this. The characters are the point of entry. We project ourselves into them, into their world, into their story, by the same process of sympathetic analogy. In this view, making sense is involved with being in control. It should be said that this is easier to accept as a critical position when one is dealing with that kind of third-person, objective camera position. It is arguable that when the camera is subjective then it would seem that the camera is directing understanding, as much as the intelligence of the viewer: the viewer must become aware that they are not necessarily a 'controlling force'.

Metz suggests that there are three psychic processes at work as the spectator produces meaning through viewing – identification, voyeurism and fetishism. I have referred to the first process. The second is one which is part of the context of viewing in cinema. Neither the screen character nor the audience in the dark can look at you, so you are in a privileged position of being able to look at the screen and its people in private – a voyeur. The fetishistic process is explained by analogy with sexual fetishism – making parts of the female body assume erotic significance, and distracting attention from what is not seen (including in Freudian terms the missing penis). The film image, the film shot, charges the imagination, and stands for things which actually are not there, because it is all an illusion. There is for example, no 'person on the screen'. 'The cinematic signifier is itself imaginary. Hence cinema uniquely involves its audience in a play of absence and presence', and, 'The spectator is the camera at once actively training its gaze upon objects and passively receiving the imprint of its perceptions' (Lapsley and Westlake, 1988).

What this last quotation does is to raise a debate about the extent to which the gaze either distances or involves the spectator. How far is one passive and positioned at some psychological distance from a screen world: and how far is one part of that screen world, rightfully taking pleasure as it mingles with our consciousness?

The philosopher Gilles Deleuze would emphasize this mingling, the continuity of the spectator's world and the film world: 'the cinema experience for Deleuze is an unmediated and enveloping reality, at once actual and virtual, at once mental, somatic, physiological' (Elsaesser and Buckland, 2002). These writers draw attention to Deleuze's conception of cinema as being all about movement (not a succession of still images). Cinema is about matter fused with consciousness, about material which is real in its own right. In this view there is no issue of the separation of spectator gaze from screen gaze, of the discontinuity of the reality of the spectator from the reality that is the film. At this point, one is moving away from comment on psychoanalysis as such. But the writers take these ideas further through a study of *Silence of the Lambs* (chapter 9), in which Deleuze's work is referenced. Similarly, a previous chapter is to be commended for its study of Oedipal narratives (referring to Freud and Lacan) via *Back to the Future*.

4.3 The gendered gaze

Tessa Perkins (2000) argues that pychoanalysis entered the critical field in the 1970s and 1980s because Marxism failed to take on issues of gender. It was also at a time when structuralism and Marxism had moved apart as critical enterprises. She refers to 'the ways feminist research suggested that patriarchy was as significant in explaining women's oppression as capitalism'. As she says, this was generally a period when new terms recognizing unresolved 'problems' appeared on the critical agenda – racism, homophobia, orientalism.

For film, gender becomes an issue in respect of the male-dominated Hollywood institution, its textual representation of gender difference and sexuality, its assumptions about gendered viewing positions and of ways in which gender is given meaning by the spectator – a gendered and gendering gaze. A great deal of theorizing about the gaze points out that it is often a male-gendered gaze which is naturalized as the dominant way of looking. In psychoanalytic terms, this male gaze is also often located in notions of Oedipal desire – the male desires the woman – the woman is modelled on the mother, the first female on whom the male gazes. It may be said that there are three kinds of male gaze in cinema:

- There are characters on screen who may be seen looking at women with desire.
- There is the gaze of the camera looking upon the women, sometimes subjectively as a character within the film.
- There is the gaze of the spectator in the cinema, looking via the camera upon the character.

In an essay on horror films, Cynthia Freeland (1996) refers to a now conventional connection made between gazing, aggression and masculinity. She also refers to Mulvey's well-known essay which discusses how mainstream cinema uses women and serves men – serving the male gaze and male pleasures. Male viewers identify with male protagonists. Freeland refers to the tension in a horror film between the desire to look upon the female victim and the horror of what may be looked upon – female damaged, female sacrificed to monster, even female as monster. But she goes on to point out that the looking in horror films (and some others) is more complicated than Mulvey's view entirely allows for. Within such films, the woman also often gazes upon the monster, as do male protagonists or privileged male viewers. And both females and monsters at least sometimes seem to stand outside the male order of things – the Dracula story, in which the fascinating and deadly male vampire seduces female characters away from a patriarchal order. And all this has to be understood in terms of the female spectator. Women are as much horror genre fans as men are.

There is a question of what the female gaze is meant to make of gendered looks on screen. Some commentators would emphasize that it seems the female gaze within the film is punished for looking or has to be redeemed by an expert male (again the Dracula story) – which preserves a male dominance. On the other hand, others would point out that the women do resist the male gaze. *Halloween* (1978) has a female protagonist (Jamie Lee Curtis) who conquers her fear of the male monster, does her own gazing and wins out in the end. It is true that there is the expert male psychiatrist in the background. But that does not diminish her achievement, any more than it does that of Agent Starling gazing upon the male monster Lector (*Silence of the Lambs*, 1991), or Buffy slaying the male vampires in the TV series.

Clover's (1992) take on this is that more recent horror films invite a more bisexual gaze, in which the actively successful female protagonist becomes masculinized.

However, I would argue that it is simply a redefining of what it is to be female: that a certain contradictoriness between female 'winners' who are also at times objects of male desire (Ripley in *Alien*) is simply a sign of contradictory times.

Mulvey (1989) draws on Metz and Freud in proposing the term **scopophilia**, and drawing attention to the pleasure of looking. It suggests that the female in the film is both the object of desire and a passive object within the action. The gaze of the male spectator identifies with the desire of the male protagonist in the film and with that protagonist's part in driving the film narrative. The gaze of the female spectator identifies with the woman as object within the film – a passive gaze for a passive role. This is also a process of objectification, or the turning of the woman into an object of desire, and away from being a person of free will, of her own desires, away from being able to say 'no'. So the woman's pleasure becomes the male's pleasure. And the female spectator is to enjoy adopting the male point of view.

But critical views over the past 25 years have shifted and embroidered (if not suppressed) the Mulvey position. In particular, audience studies try to engage with a 'real' female spectator, within a shifting ideological climate. This is opposed to the rather theorized female spectator of Mulvey's essay, who was forced to adopt the male gaze. For a start, one has to explain all those male bodies displayed in films, not least in the classic period of Hollywood. Of course, there is the homo-erotic theorizing of Dyer and others. But readings of fan magazines and discussion with female fans makes it clear that there is a female gaze of desire. *The Full Monty* (1997) coyly exploits a given social practice of women looking at male strippers. Certainly there has been a shift in gender behaviour, and/or making female desire more explicit. It is no accident that this coexists with a change in the economic and social status of women. In many ways, film is the most conservative of media. Mulvey argued that it was special in building the way the women were to be looked at into the spectacle of cinema itself. But I would suggest that one cannot understand cinema viewing in isolation, or ignore that learning about gazing which comes from broader cultural experience. And so one may refer to the male bodies on display in magazines for teenage girls, as well as in ads for Armani and the like. Men are being objectified for the female gaze. It has to be recognized that the nature of the gaze (for the female spectator in particular) is more complex than can be recognized by post-Freudian theories and notions of patriarchy. It is not just about a (white) male – (heterosexual) female polarity or binary opposition. The gaze also has dimensions of the lesbian, of ethnicity, of social positioning. [For some discussion of this, see Judith Mayne, *Paradoxes of Spectatorship*, in Turner (2002) and Kaplan (1992)].

Others have pointed out that there has been, for a long time, a kind of ambivalence or contradictoriness about a cinema industry which has courted a female audience, yet tried to maintain a dominant male discourse. It is not necessarily enough to say that the female gaze has been placed passively within that discourse. Jackie Stacey (2000) discusses the evidence of fandom and the female pleasures of cinema-going in the 1940s and 1950s. Using Dyer, she points out that cinema-going as escapism is also a kind of wish fulfilment which is resisting the masculine status quo. She is not trying to ignore the ideological (and patriarchal) realities of the period, but is indicating that the act of spectating takes place in a lived context.

The notion of **masquerade** has been proposed in relation to the female spectator looking upon the image of the women on screen. In principle the female viewer cannot achieve the voyeuristic distancing of the male spectator/gaze because she is the subject, the one to be looked at. But within masquerade. it is suggested that the trappings of femininity (the more the better) are conceived of as a mask, something that conceals. It is as if the male is gazing upon a surface of femininity not knowing it is a mask – but the female spectator knows, and can stand back from being sucked into being a creature of the male gaze: 'By opening up a distance from the female image the masquerade allows it to become controllable, readable, producible by the woman' (Lapsley and Westlake, 1988). These writers provide a useful discussion of positions taken by Mary Ann Doane (1982) on masquerade and on femininity itself. Doane sees this notion as being part of discursive practices, a place to which women are assigned. One might also go on to argue that this masquerade in the film text constructs femininity for the female gaze, which in turn absorbs its meaning, naturalized as it is. In this negative view, a process of disempowerment continues.

'One of the functions of narrative . . . is to "seduce" women into femininity with or without their consent. The female subject is made to desire femininity' (Cook and Bernink, 1999).

Theories of gaze are, then, very much influenced by ideas developed from psycho-analysis. Many of these ideas support the notion that the gaze is gendered and male, and positions the female spectators as the subject of that gaze. Indeed many critiques are in effect saying that the very narrative is framed within a masculine world, is manufactured for the pleasure of the male viewer. However, there have been attempts to recognize the validity of the cinema-going experience in female terms, to explain ways in which the male gaze is resisted, to recognize female pleasures in female subject matter within what is loosely called 'the women's film' and 'melodrama'.

'Looking' is, then, about the idea of 'making sense of the object of the gaze. Making sense of an image clearly has a range of dimensions, not least those to do with identity (including gender and sexuality). These dimensions reach into the whole range of topics covered in this book, including the construction of narratives and the endorsement of ideological positions, for example. 'Making sense of' is also part of a process of consumption which, from one point of view, complements the process of material production by media institutions. It relates to that model which sees the encoding of meanings being the obverse (but not the equal and opposite) of the decoding of meaning.

5 Discussion extracts

66 99 One of the many reasons why it is so difficult to raise production finance for a British film is that once monies have been found and the film actually made (both fraught enough processes in themselves) there are yet more problems to be faced, this time in the inter-connected sections of distribution and exhibition. Difficulties in finding a distributor (let alone one who will handle a film sympathetically), costly delays waiting for vacant screens, the vagaries (to put it politely) of West End exhibition practices, an uncommitted critical climate – all these factors, and more, are enough to make any potential investor wonder whether it is really worth the risk of investing in a production in the first place.

Petley (1992)

1 What are the sources of the difficulties described in this piece?

2 How far might the subject matter/preoccupations of 'British' films contribute to these difficulties? Refer to specific examples.

3 Research how film industries in countries such as France and Sweden respond to the problems of funding a national cinema, in respect of production, distribution and exhibition.

> One of the most significant directions in spectatorship studies has investigated the gap opened up between the ways in which the text constructs viewers, and how those texts may be read or used in ways that depart from what the institution valorises.
>
> Judith Mayne (2002) Paradoxes of spectatorship, in G. Turner (ed.) *The Film Cultures Reader*. London: Routledge.

1 How can the text 'construct viewers'?

2 How can film spectators read the movie as text in ways that 'depart from what the institution valorises' – and what does it valorize?

6 Further reading

Branston, G. (2000) *Cinema and Cultural Modernity*. Buckingham: Open University Press.

Collins, J., Radner, H. and Collins A.P. (eds) (1993) *Film Theory Goes to the Movies*. London: Routledge.

Cook, P. and Bernink, M. (eds) (1999) *The Cinema Book*, (2nd edn). London: BFI.

Elsaesser, T. and Buckland, W. (2002) *Studying Contemporary American Film, a guide to movie analysis*. London: Arnold.

Hill, J. and Gibson, P.C. (1998) *The Oxford Guide to Film Studies*. Oxford: Oxford University Press.

Kaplan, E.A. (ed.) (1990) *Psychoanalysis and Cinema*. London: Routledge.

Mulvey, L. (1989) *Visual and other Pleasures*. London: Macmillan.

Murphy, R. (ed.) (2000) *British Cinema of the Nineties*. London: BFI.

Petrie, D.J. (ed.) (1992) *New Questions of British Cinema*. London: BFI.

Turner, G. (ed.) (2002) *The Film Cultures Reader*. London: Routledge.

Williams, C. (2000) After the classic, the classical and ideology: the differences of realism, in C. Gledhill and C. Williams, *Reinventing Film Studies*. London: Arnold.

CHAPTER EIGHT

THE MEDIA AND NEW TECHNOLOGY

The effects and implications of technologies for the media and their consumption

"[Technology] is always historically informed not only by its materiality but also by its political, economic and social context, and thus always both co-constitutes and expresses cultural values."

Vivian Sobchak (2000) The scene of the screen: envisioning cinematic and electronic presence, in J.T. Caldwell (ed.) *Theories of the New Media – A Historical Perspective*. London: Athlone Press.

1 Introduction

All media use a range of technologies to manufacture representations. In whatever way media make a connection between their productions and their audiences, this connection is dependent on technology. All technologies are new in their time. There is an assumption behind this chapter that we are talking mainly about computer-based technologies from the 1980s onwards. But just as one wonders what comes after post-modernism, so also one wonders when new technology starts to seem old. Even hot-metal type was new to the printing industry something over a hundred years ago. Now it has gone. But in its time it made possible the mass production and mass circulation of daily newspapers from the late nineteenth century to the late twentieth century. The cassette tape video recorder is on its way out, after about 25 years of being part of domestic culture.

1.1 When is technology new?

New technologies are not always that new, but depend on developments of earlier technologies and their applications. Truly new technologies are usually not the creation of the media themselves. It is often the technological pressure-cooker of military innovation which provides the opportunity for later civil applications, and for the media. Satellites were at first developed and launched (1960s) for their military applications – surveillance and communications. The Internet was originally created for its military convenience – to find a robust form of communication that could not be knocked out by a couple of Russian inter-continental ballistic missiles (ICBMs).

Cornford and Robins (1999) talk about 'an accommodation between old and new' and point out that 'new media are often heavily reliant on repackaged older media content'. Even interactivity is not new in itself (radio phone-ins): rather it may be the speed and embeddedness of interactivity on the back of technology, which is new. And this interactivity is not all about benefit to the audience. 'New technologies . . . enable producers of new media products and services to monitor, segment and target audiences in new ways' (Cornford and Robbins, 1999).

1.2 When is the future present?

There is also a run-in time to technologies, so that one may forget how long it takes for a technology to become really embedded in cultural usage. For instance, the public in the West was well aware of the media potential of satellites through early but laborious broadcast links. However, it was not until the 1980s that the launch and proliferation of communication satellites had become so common that the period of technological novelty had worn off, and audiences began to take for granted the idea that they should expect to see images from more or less anywhere on the planet. Vested interests in media businesses may be keen to tell their consumers that the future is here now. But experience tells us that the real, lived-in future takes a little longer to arrive. This is what Paschal Preston (2001) refers to as 'a long history of undelivered promises'.

One should also be cautious about making assumptions about what constitutes new media/new technology, and about how these are being taken up. For example, the clock-work Freeplay radio is a recent invention, using old technology, and with great benefits for Africans who can neither afford nor get access to electric technologies. By contrast, a city like Tallin in Estonia is one of the most wired-up communities in the world, in that it has jumped straight to the latest wireless technology that links every mobile in the city, and gives users access to other technologies. It is Preston again, taking a cautious and even sceptical view of the advance of technologies of new media, who identifies three kinds of error perpetrated by pundits and the industries.

1 an over-emphasis on technology which misses other factors which influence innovation and acceptance;

2 a tendency to talk about products (gizmos), related to a failure to attend to process innovation (how products will be used by the average consumer);

3 an inclination to ignore political or economic brakes on matters of demand and consumption.

Lister *et al.* (2003) warn against overemphasis on technological features when trying to make sense of new media. They point out that, for example, virtuality and cyberspace are about senses of self and of identities as much as technological ingenuities. They also warn against assumptions as to how technology will be used, and as to what future media will look like. There is no inevitable line of development towards some predictable kind of media world, based on technological reductionism – 'when we get enough computing power'. What they do lay out is what they see as being six characteristics of what is happening with new media.

- the creation of new textual experiences;
- the arrival of new ways of representing the world;
- the development of new relationships between subject (both users and consumers) and media technologies;
- the creation of new experiences of the relationship between embodiment, identity and community;
- new conceptions of the biological body's relationship to technology and media;
- the development of new patterns of organization and production.

Their work most usefully develops areas outside the remit of this chapter – realisms and the history of representation, virtual realities and the transformation of the sense of self through media technologies.

Andrew Brown (*Independent on Sunday*, 19 September 1999) makes the interesting point that new technology will only really have arrived in the domestic sphere when one no longer recognizes its presence, nor where information comes from. Technology becomes invisible and unremarkable – like the television set.

2 Major questions

1 Does technology shape the development of media?

2 Is the development of technology itself shaped by commercial forces and social pressures?

3 How has technology affected the work of media businesses, and their outputs?

4 How has technology affected the relationship between media and society?

5 Is the significance of technology as much about information as about entertainment?

6 How may one describe the nature of the change in media practices and media experience for the audience, brought about by new technology?

7 Has technology affected the 'balance of power' between media institutions and society (audiences)?

8 What is the place of the Net, in particular, within all these questions?

9 Has the arrival of new media, and changes to old media, produced any kinds of benefit for society?

3 Determinism or opportunism? Technology and media developments

The essence of the debate here is about how far one may see technology as determining the nature of media developments and output, and how far one sees the media or even media users as grabbing technological opportunities when they come along.

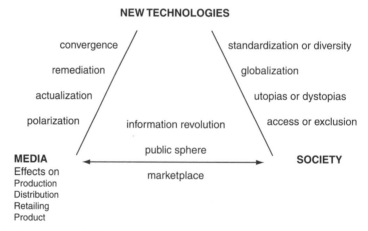

Media Technology: Terms and debates
The co-relationship between technology, media and society is most obviously characterized by kinds of change to production and text/product, as well as by issues then raised concerning that relationship. What is ambiguous is how far technologies and media drive changes, and how far society and audiences induce them.
(*Graeme Burton*, 2004)

The notion of **technological determinism** represents an argument that technology of itself shapes society and can be a cause of social change. However, I would argue that while any technology may have kinds of potential, it does not of itself have intentionality. It has to be used and developed, and media industries determine that development. It may simultaneously be true, that once a given technology has reached a certain level of development and availability, then the exact nature of its continuing use, especially by consumers, it is not so easy to control. Opportunities are not so easy to envisage. And whether technology works for social benefit or social damage is neither certain nor consistent.

Classic and largely opposing positions on technology and media appeared in the 1960s and 1970s in the writings of Marshall McLuhan (McLuhan, 1994; McLuhan and Fiore, 1967) and Raymond Williams (1974). McLuhan advanced ideas about the power of technology within a new electric culture – powers to create a new age of complex relationships. He had a facility for the arresting phrase – 'global village' is one of his. He spoke up for television at a time when it received a lot of bad press, critically speaking. He saw television as a medium which engages the senses, and opposed it to the sensory alienation of what he describes as the Gutenberg culture of print media. He was interested in effects as much as in causes. He saw the media as extensions of the senses. He was interested in characteristics of media, and saw media as being more than mere carriers of content – the medium itself was the message, for McCluhan. For him, technology was a determining factor in media development and use, though he would also have seen new developments like the World Wide Web as providing opportunities for users.

Williams, on the other hand, argued that media development is more about the economic and social structures that shape this (not the technologies). He is interested in things like cause, agency, context. He does not see the technology of any given media as determining its use. He would see opportunities as accruing to media institutions, driven by economic determinants. He would not have interpreted the Web within an optimistic framework.

As Bolter and Grusin say (2000), 'The idea that new electronic technologies of communication will determine our social organisation is clearly not threatening to corporations that produce and market those technologies.' The market does not see new media as being out of their control.

The debates around the Napster case (2001–2) saw the coexistence of equally valid views. Shawn Fanning, who set up the Napster website, had taken an opportunity to use Internet technology to provide a community of music users and copiers – file sharing and downloading without paying. Music providers, both corporations and many groups, saw the technology as being used to deny their copyright and to deprive them of rightful income. They sued Fanning and Napster on this basis, and forced closure of the website.

The consequences or implications of the uses of technology are, in this sense, complex and fluid. Bertelsmann has bought a controlling interest in Napster, and is now trying to make money out of the site through legitimated selling of music files. AppleMac is making millions out of I-Tunes' website because it has created the iPod, a very successful digital, portable MP3 music store/play device. It is paying for the rights to offer tracks for downloading (for a fee, of course). It is now estimated that I-Tunes has 70 per cent of the online music market (the *Independent*, 10 June 2004). One thing leads to another in unpredictable ways. Determining factors or conditions are malleable.

John Street (1999) refers to this, with a political rather than a commercial inflection.

66 99 At one level, the technology is the embodiment of certain interests and possibilities, but at another it is the bearer of effects: it changes what we can imagine and what we can want, it alters our politics. Though we can identify the interests and choices around a technology, they do not automatically become the authors of that technology. The technology is not something [that] exists as a simple object for our use. It acts to structure our choices and preferences, but not in a wholly determinist way. The relationship is in constant flux: political processes shape technology; and then it shapes politics.

Similarly, media cannot control audience use of technologies. And once technologies are in the public domain then they, and the ways that they are used, shape the media, just as the media once shaped the technologies. For example, concern has been expressed over the relationship between children and their mobile phones. In a *Guardian* article (10 May 2001), Michael Fitzpatrick refers to the concerns of sociologists (and of research in Japan) that a generation of young people may be developing in ways which

1 make them unable to form and maintain relationships without the help of mobiles;

2 make them dependent on the act of contact via the mobile, rather than being able to conduct a sustained and face-to-face relationship.

Again, Bolter and Grusin (2000) emphasize the interaction between media, especially the reworking of old media by new and the appropriation of new technologies by old media. 'We cannot even recognise the representational power of a medium except with reference to other media.'

So it is that they discuss the remediation of medieval manuscripts by Gutenberg's printing technology, or the remediation of classic works of art by digital artists. Their view is that 'new' media successively mediate that which has already been mediated – hence the notion of remediation. Remediation is also about an inseparability between processes of mediation and constructions of reality (see actualization). In the case of current new technologies, this would be about that continuing cultural project which seeks to make the process of remediation (and representation) a transparent one, in which the medium apparently opens up access to that chimera, 'reality'.

Both the reworking of material through different media and the appropriation and manipulation of texts in digital form, raises interesting questions as to what the text is, and who is the author of which text. Ownership (copyright) and authorship are deeply embedded values within a capitalist system. This is exemplified by a public row over the validity of information released by the British government in relation to the run-up to the US-led invasion of Iraq. Much had been made of the fact that one foundation for this information was an old PhD thesis which was not credited to its author (found by trawling the Internet): the issue was about plagiarism as much as about accuracy. And yet, every day, both undergraduates and advertisers are 'plagiarizing' material to produce new texts. Technology has created ideological conflict. New media forms are generating cultural stress fractures.

Media production and distribution is not run by technologies: it is made possible by them. Technologies are developed which it is believed the media will want to take up. So one can just as well argue that it is the media that drive technologies. In any case, the applications of and success of technologically based change in the media is something which cannot be predicted with certainty. One can indeed argue that there is a kind of inertia, related to investment costs and costs to the consumer, which actually works against the introduction of new technologies.

It is understood that we 'should' be moving to high definition TV and to digital TV broadcasting in Britain. But the technology is not driving this change simply because it is there. Consumers are slowing down the change because they are not prepared to spend the money – and so government dates for switching off analogue transmitters have been put back progressively.

At the time of writing there is every evidence that huge investment in G3 mobile phone technology is not paying off. The operators have tried to develop and sell the technology in order to make money. The producer has determined the technology, but the consumer determines take-up and profit. And the consumer is not that interested in the cost of the technological opportunity. Equally, the explosion of text messaging via mobiles a few years ago was not determined by either producers or technology, in the sense of being intentionally targeted on the consumer, but was a facility of which the users took the opportunity. With hindsight one can see the attractions of this low cost function to the millions of young users, as well as the email-like advantages of not having to make voice contact in real time. It is estimated that text and image messaging will be worth £2.4 billion in the European Union, by 2006 (*Independent on Sunday*, 1 July 2001).

4 The impact of technology on the media: production, distribution, exhibition/retailing, consumption

Firstly, I want to clarify the fact that the applications and implications of technology for the media needs to be understood within the functional areas of media business. Media technology is not just about the drama of, say, a live night-time videophone link with a correspondent in a war zone being shown on evening TV news.

Technology is embedded in every area of a business. So I make but passing reference to digitized research material, computer graphics in publicity divisions, spreadsheet predictions in accounts, email communication, client databases – all the applications of technologies that have changed the nature of work and of how businesses operate. They have transformed general company functions such as accounting, administration and PR.

Outside the media, one may look at our everyday experiences of department stores and supermarkets. Technology enables these businesses to monitor stock purchase, sales and reordering very tightly. But what is going on here is not just about the purchasing experience for the customer – choice and availability. Indirectly, the technologies involved affect, for instance, farming practices or factory work, around the world.

Media studies has traditionally understood media organizations in terms of institutions which manufacture product, which get these products directly to audiences, or to outlets where audiences may purchase them. In this way consumption takes place. A magazine is composed and printed, distributed by road and rail, and is sold in shops. A television programme is also made, distributed via cable/broadcast/satellite, and shown on screen.

However, before commenting on the impact of technology within this framework, there needs to be a further caveat about describing the media landscape. The institutions/functions model works for general categories of media – radio or the Press. But it does not properly recognize the huge number of specialist media industries, and their complex relations with categories of media in general. For example, Reuters provides material for the 'trade', not directly to audiences. It is fundamentally a distributor of news material (although it is possible to argue that it produces a kind of product and has news operations as its audiences). Music may well be manufactured in an independently owned studio, even if it is distributed by EMI. The entire advertizing industry is integral to the distribution and promotion of media goods. But it is not one of the media in itself: it uses the media. Then there are the specialist businesses which supply services integral to the production of a film or of a newspaper, but which have nothing to do with processes such as writing or editing. There are the catering services which feed film and TV crews on location. There are the independent printers that produce magazine supplements for newspapers. New technologies affect the work of all these specialists. Indeed, often the basis of their specialist value is a particular expertise and investment in technology – such as the small digital editing businesses that use AvidPro programs.

In this sense I am arguing for simultaneous kinds of understanding of the media – as fitting a vertically integrated general functions model at the macro level, but looking much more like a 'services to core business' model when one looks at them closely. I am arguing for both examination of general industries, and for recognition of interlocking and specific businesses. The BBC is a classic example of a move from in-house control to outsourcing and freelancing, during the 1980s and 1990s. I am arguing for both a simple general model of media industry, which recognizes for example, the cycle of news gathering, composition, production, distribution and retailing for a newspaper, yet also for a complex model, which recognizes the interlocking media businesses that make possible the detail of this cycle for the newspaper industry.

Returning to the general model, within limited space, it is important to identify key features about the impact of technology. The sections which follow – for example, on convergence of technologies – are also relevant, but will examine overarching implications, and the effects of technology on product in particular.

4.1 Production

- *Reduction of cost*: as in electronic animation used by Pixar and others, which is far cheaper than manually drawn cell-type animation production, used for classic Disney films; as in digicam production of TV material for Reality TV shows in particular. However, this is partially offset by factors such as the cost of investment or buying in of technology. Also by factors such as, in the case of movies, the ever-increasing above the line costs of key personnel such as stars and directors.

  Digital production is slowly emerging as a huge cost saver. George Lucas has not shot on 35 mm film since 2001. Digital post-production is becoming commonplace in

New Technology for 'Old' Media
The interior of this newsagents doesn't look so different to what it would have been like 30 years ago. Often the main effects of NT are invisible or un-noticed. They affect production and distribution, as much as product. Consumers quickly become used to new features of media texts, such as the digitally produced colour image in a newspaper.

What else has changed about newspapers and about their production, distribution and retailing?

How may this have affected both our understanding of newspapers and the ways that we consume them?
(*Graeme Burton*, 2004)

film. It is also becoming cheaper – the reason for its prevalence in advertising. And, of course, news and advertising photography is now entirely digital.

● *Reduction of labour* is a major component of any organization's wages bill (last section). All media industries have seen a reduction in the numbers of people it takes to make their product (except possibly film), not only because of general 'efficiency' pressures, but also because, for example, promotional material can be made, edited and printed by one person. The move from mechanical to electronic technologies has greatly reduced the numbers of people needed to put together a newspaper.

- *Ease of use*: without denying a continued need for creative expertise in the use of technologies, it is the case that many examples have made the practicalities of production easier. Time-based editing machines transformed television/video in the 1970s and 1980s, meaning that one no longer needed costly, technically expert operatives. In music production, multi-channel mixing, electronic sampling and sound production, digital editing, have made production in one sense less technically skilled though in other senses more creatively complex. But again, 'domestic' versions of industrial technologies have also brought easy-to-use music production literally into the home and sometimes out into the marketplace (for example, some DJ mixes of dance music).

- *Access to information*: as in the use of the Internet as a research source for the press. A scandal involving a *New York Times* reporter (2003) who wrote pieces on people and places that he had never met or been to, is a nice example of how access to data (and indeed to images) has been hugely enhanced by technologies.

- *Speed of production*: it is faster as well as easier to compose magazine copy electronically. It is possible to acquire news material for TV via satellite from the other side of the world and edit it, all within minutes.

- *Enhancement of production values*: most obviously to audiences, the material that they read, see and hear has qualities dependent on various applications of technology. One example is the arrival of colour images in newspapers since the 1980s, now sourced from digital cameras and printed on digital presses. Movie theatres have digital surround sound. Film action sequences may incorporate electronic effects to make the impossible appear plausible, using electronic matting and inserts. CD music is 'clean' and has a tonal range not generally heard in the home even fifteen years ago.

In general, both new forms of media and new developments in old media have created, so far as the audience is concerned, a much more 'image-rich' media landscape, as well as a more completely 'real' set of media representations. In other words, we have more pictures in more places, from more sources, than our grandparents did. And within the bounds of representational conventions, technology has made film and television in particular seem more real.

4.2 Distribution

An electronic divide has opened up between those media which can be distributed in a material form and those which can be transformed into digitized electronic data. This divide in some cases has a further separation in terms of distribution for production, as opposed to distribution for consumption. So, television reaches its audiences via electronic carriers, but newspapers remain as objects to be thrown on the front lawn, or bought from a shop.

The complication of this divide is that some media may distribute their texts in electronic form within the production industry. It will be interesting to see if the film industries can move to digital distribution successfully. In Britain, money is now being pumped into a project to create digital distribution to about a hundred specialist cinemas. The idea is to make minority film more accessible to audiences and at the same time to get round the huge costs of striking prints in conventional form (up to £1,500 a time) and carrying them around the country. In Britain, the total cost of this was estimated as being £100 million in 2002, plus £30 million in freight charges (*Guardian*, 20 March 2003).

In the music industry traditionally, like magazines, an object (a CD) has to be carried to a point of sale. Internet downloading is now moving from a pirate stage to one where the music majors are setting up their own websites for selling their product direct into the home computer, which then produces the CD. These kinds of division of distribution reflect on the context of use (domestic–public), on the nature of use (individual–collective), on economics (high cost of shifting objects as opposed to data), on copyright (it is relatively easier to pirate media texts as objects).

Global reach is a consequence of the arrival of satellite communications and enhanced cable links, in the second half of the twentieth century. Distribution of media goods, as well as of the information which goes into the manufacture of those goods, is something which now happens world-wide. Television is the obvious example of a new era of distribution which offers multiple channels to trans-national audiences. Newspapers and magazines are available in a global range of major cities, partly on the back of electronic distribution to regional printing, but mainly because of the explosion of global air travel.

Radio has been transformed by the arrival of VHF and the allocation of many channels, which has turned it most successfully into a regionalized and genre specific medium. Technology has made it possible to run a radio station with very few staff – like *Klassik Rock* in Europe. There is much excitement about digital audio broadcasting (DAB), but so far the cost of receivers, and the output available has confined DAB to a small audience. What is just as interesting is distribution via the Internet. Barnard (2000) enthuses about this – it 'automatically redefines radio's notion of "territory" and, with it, changes the very concept of a listening community from the parochial and domestic into something more powerful and challenging'.

Elsewhere he is more realistic about what is actually available on the Internet, balancing the possibility of a local station having a world-wide audience against the fact that this has not actually happened. What is happening more is the availability of radio via satellite – all BBC networks for example.

Alternative channels are about new forms of media and their distribution. Examples are embedded in the paragraphs above. In the film industry, distribution can be about the transportation of DVDs to retailers, as much as about moving large cans of 35 mm film to movie theatres. It can be about PayTV and films accessed via cable, as much as via satellite movie channels. It is now possible to transmit movies directly from their production house to exhibition, via satellite. Different formats require different forms of distribution. And different forms of distribution may influence different kinds of production – micro movies on the Internet.

4.3 Exhibition and sales

Domestic consumption has increased as a result of technologies making possible new media formats and new kinds of distribution. Of course all this goes along with increases in disposable income and in leisure time. One is looking at a proliferation of examples in the past 20 years, from mini hi-fi sytems, to interactive TV, to the Internet, to digital image making, to domestic minicams, to multiple-function CD players.

What is noticeable here is the proliferation of technology in the home not merely for reproducing images and sound, but also for constructing materials (for example, editing home produced music and burning it onto a CD). Domestic screens have increased greatly in number because not only are they dedicated to functions such as computer display, but they also serve multiple TV channels, teletext, email, electronic games, DVD viewing and so on. 'Home television is being redesigned to concentrate recreation and cultural consumption within the home, thus lodging within private space the means to manipulate public opinion and taste for a corporate sector with increasing need to sell images and information!' (Johnson, 1996).

Preston (2001), on the other hand, argues for caution in making claims, even for the private sphere and domestic consumption. He has produced tables of data drawn from a range of sources which demonstrate that old media like telephone systems are well embedded, and that the take-up of new media is not as great as many claim. He asserts that its (new media) rate of diffusion among households is much less than was the case for previous new technologies; that the Internet is relatively expensive and technically unreliable.

Similarly, there is a tension between the sides of a debate which on the one hand applaud the Internet as a convenient point of sale offering consumer choice, and those who point out that goods still have to be delivered reliably, and that security breaches on the Internet frighten away customers.

5 The information revolution

It has become fashionable to use this phrase as if it is clearly understood that such a revolution is taking place and is to the general public benefit. This is not so. Questions need to be asked about 'what information?', 'to whose benefit?'

Technology has for example made it easy to produce colour, image-rich junk mail/ advertising which pours through the letterboxes of the data-identified, 'wealthy enough to spend money' citizens. Data on ourselves as citizen/consumers is held electronically by credit agencies and market researchers (not to mention the police, banks and government agencies). Any telephone contact with an organization offering goods and services produces an identity check in which it is clear that one is being matched against a name/ place of residence database. Exactly what kind of gain to the citizen there is in such examples of information storage or distribution is rather questionable.

What *is* clear is that 'the revolution' has benefited institutions of government and the media. The ability of media organizations to acquire, exchange and manipulate information has made it easier for them to function economically, to compete with each other and to target their consumers/users. There are industry-serving businesses such as DataMonitor whose work is the processing and provision of information. The revolution has given media access to information about us: the ability to target households on grounds of lifestyle. There is not much traffic the other way.

This does not denigrate the value of information sources on the World Wide Web. Genuinely, there is a speed, scope, volume and precision of information out there which is wholly dramatic compared with research facilities a generation ago. But it is patchy and specialized, and only as good as the search engine being used. Websites for media organizations tell us what they want to reveal, not always what we want to know. And those citizens who cannot afford computer access at home, those who cannot afford or cannot get to (for technical reasons) broadband, are actually disenfranchised from the information revolution.

Preston (2001) is especially sceptical. He acknowledges the capacity of the Internet to bring together technologies in a new way, but also asserts that it 'falls far short of meeting the promise of a seamless, fully integrated and interconnecting communication system offering "instant access" to diverse forms of information'.

Our government can spend millions cabling information highways alongside British motorways (apparently to facilitate display of information and use of cameras), but it does not spend similar amounts on the provision of Internet access at public information points such as libraries and advice centres. From a negative point of view this reinforces interpretations of the information revolution as supporting existing mechanisms of power and control. This invokes Foucault and ideas about state surveillance of its citizens. One is talking about benefits to media institutions and to capitalism in general – preserving the status quo of power.

Underlying issues here are about the effects of technology and new media, about the rate of their take-up, about social and cultural change. Underlying positions vary from the conservative to the enthusiastically proselytizing. In terms of information revolutions, it is worth asking who has what access to what sources of information, as well as asking what power they may have to act on that information. It is worth remembering that so-called old media are still vital sources of information, especially television. All the evidence assembled and referred to in this chapter points to the fact that new media may be part of a process of transformation, but in fact they are not the dominant source of information for most people about the world, even in the USA. And finally, we need to remember that the very word 'information' is not just about data, nor even that questionable term, 'facts'. The information that comes via any technology is importantly also about how we understand social relations, how we form social practices, how we understand terms such as community and society.

6 The nature of change

6.1 Interactivity

This is much talked about with relation to new media and digital technology. Computer games are interactive, within terms of reference determined by the provider. Some would argue for the value of the choices and problems that games users have to make and to solve. Others would look more cynically at the value of the games market (over £800 million a year in the UK), and at the spin-off of clearly passive media texts such as TV programmes and magazines about games. Again, one could say that audiences can email newspaper editors and programme producers – and so they do, in their hundreds. But this is not real-time interaction and guarantees no response from the institutions.

In this regard, of course, one must acknowledge the real-time interaction that

Texting
The development and social uses of new technology are not necessarily predictable.
(*Corbis*)

happens in Web chat rooms. However, in general, much interaction on the Web is about completing questionnaires, moving to shopping baskets, responding to menus.

There is much talk about power accruing to the user/consumer/audience. But generally speaking, this only happens within a commercial framework, and has been much hyped up. There is some interactivity in examples of video on demand (PayTV to watch the movie of your choice when you choose via your TV set). Shopping channels are obviously interactive. Famously, the UK docu-gameshow programme, *Big Brother*, was available on the Internet in 2000. It picked up audiences of 750,000, and allowed these Internet viewers to choose camera views and to watch at will. Voting on game shows, or grabbing links to programme connected websites is becoming more common. But all this begs questions about what interactivity really means, or should mean. Not only do audiences have an experiential history of assuming passivity in viewing and listening, but also one has to consider what active role an audience could actually play, especially within a commercial framework.

6.2 Convergence

Technology has brought about a convergence in the electronic codes which carry the material of media texts. There has also been some convergence of the formats that carry this encoding. Predominantly, this is about our ability to encode all visuals, sound and print in binary digital terms, and about the CD/DVD disk. One can store, copy, edit and transmit media content in this binary code. The disks can carry print, movies, photos, music. All media functions which use computers at some stage are also using digital.

THE MEDIA AND NEW TECHNOLOGY 211

British television will probably become totally digital in 15 years' time. Movie theatre screening is starting to move that way. Home entertainment – music, film, games – is largely digitized. Cassette tapes are no longer available in major stores. Hard-disc formats for recording off-air TV are becoming ever more common. Digitized domestic photography is well established. Mobile phones can take and transmit digital pictures – they allow connection with the Internet. Digital compression means a greater use of bandwidth, whether broadcast or carried by cable. The Internet is the most complete example of such convergence. In principle, it is a means of distribution of all media content. But commercial providers have to find ways of making money from sending such content. And moving images, for example, require a degree of compression which has yet to be achieved in order for standard length movies to be transmitted in anything like an acceptable time. Castells (2002) observes that there is limited convergence between the Internet and multimedia because of a lack of bandwidth. This cannot cope easily with the demands of video, and is susceptible to excesses of local use and therefore over-loading in any given area. In other words, the technology is not here, now. What has happened in general is that previously separate industries of telecommunications, broadcasting and computing (information technology) are merging, both commercially and technologically. These mergers are therefore also about globalization, about larger corporations with a larger reach across the planet.

Who will benefit from this convergence is debatable. It is convenient for media producers if their material is in digital form because it can most easily be edited and manipulated. For example, computer-based film rerecording studios can move and 'stretch' voices to achieve perfect synch and to change emphasis, rather than have to go for endless retakes. Digital distribution is cheaper than moving objects around.

What is not evident is a reduction in cost of the domestic technology which stores or records this digital text (at least, not after the initial and expensive period of establishing a new format). Benefits of cost and availability to the consumer only seem to come when the multi-nationals lose control of product and copyright – music on the Internet, pirate DVD copies, cheap copies of equipment from the developing world.

Convergence does not simply generate new media. It opens up new possibilities for 'old media'. Barnard (2000) neatly sums up the situation for radio, exemplifying these possibilities

> Convergence offers the radio industry flexibility of operation, new means of delivery, raised production values and improved sound quality. The trade-off is the integration of radio into multimedia as a whole and the loss of control and distinctiveness that this implies, together with the opening up of radio to competition from new forms of broadcasting such as 'webcasting'.

This convergence and exchange between media is about more than the underpinning technologies of distribution and their codes, important as these are. Convergence is visible to the consumer through the simultaneous release of books, computer games and music CDs with the high concept movie. Convergence is visible in what Bolter and Grusin refer to as 'the CNN look' in which the TV news screen has been reconfigured to include updates and inserts around the newscaster, so that it looks as much like a website or multimedia application as a 'traditional' news image. Convergence of screen aesthetics merely redefines what is 'normal', and what we expect to see. Convergence of technologies leads to mergers of companies on the basis of economies of scale and convergence of interests.

6.3 Diversification and diversity

Technology has created some diversity of media formats and channels of communication. It appears to have generated more consumer choice – but it is a commonplace that 'more' is often about 'the same'. A diversity of cable and satellite channels conceals the fact that on the whole this just means more sport, more recycled movies, more of the same genres. Similarly, diversification into new formats such as DVD does not produce new movies (though it does offer supplementary material that would not otherwise be seen). What this diversification through new technologies does do for media companies is to produce new sets of profits through sales of new (or even recycled) products. One must also recognize the positive in respect of new work for new companies making more television for these new channels.

The Internet typifies these progressive and retrogressive forces. It is a new medium in which the user controls access, and has that access to services and information sources that were previously far less available. On the other hand, it does not give direct access to that many media leisure products. And media company websites are – not surprisingly – cast within a traditional model of enticement and publicity, but do not give anything away. The Internet is used socially for cultural exchange – chat rooms, but it is also used commercially for profit, for example, eBay. Amazon is probably the most successful online retailer. E-commerce has now passed 1 per cent of total sales in the USA. When one looks back to cross-media ownership, then the question of who benefits from diversification of technologies becomes rather sharp. AOL/Time-Warner owns dozens of successful media companies, and has a turnover greater than the GDP of many developing nations. It has interests in television, publishing, film, cable, satellite, the Internet and music. It owns HBO, CNN, DC comics, New Line Cinema, Time Magazine, Warner Records, Netscape, Warner Picture, Warner Television, Turner Broadcasting – to pick a few of the better known names. What is clear is that the 'old' media are doing very nicely, and are exploiting new technology where it suits them. In spite of specific changes like a significant fall in CD sales over the years 2001–3, in general, media consumption is holding up.

Issues around diversification have to address apparent contradictions about a measurable increase in media channels, media products and media consumption – set against a lack of actual diversity. In a commercial sense one can talk about media companies diversifying into related businesses. One may talk about the media in general as offering product diversity, where diversity is defined as 'numbers of'. But one may not be able to talk about diversity in terms of choice. The argument here relates back to more general debates about the nature, and validity, of pluralistic interpretations of the media.

6.4 Actualization

What is referred to here is the use of technologies to enhance a sense of that which is visually immediate and present and 'real'. This actualization of representations has a history going back into the nineteenth century, at least. The camera gave the illusion of capturing an immediate scene and experience. Victorian painting went through a movement which tried to reproduce the texture and surface of reality, the actuality of experience, the immediacy of a scene or a portrait. It is of course, all about the illusions of representations and the tricks that we play on our own sense of the real, because we accept and are seduced by conventions of the media. But actualization in various forms has continued to fascinate the media, even though there are also plenty of examples of media forms in which material actuality is deliberately ignored and challenged. So the placing of minicams in cricket stumps or birds' nests to capture the immediacy of the game or of the wildlife is, I would argue, part of this tradition in which we are complicit with the media. In various ways, new technologies contribute to a sense of 'being there', of the material experience.

Lister *et al.* (2003) make an excellent discussion of new media and visual culture in which they explore ideas about how technology is affecting:

- image making and images as texts;
- an emphasis on effects and sensual experience above the manufacture of narrative and meaning;
- new experiences of being immersed within images.

They would see actualization as being part of western discourses of the truth and of the real – and opposed, for example, to Islamic ideas in which seeing is no guarantee of the truth or of reality. 'Different realisms are not mere aesthetic choices, but each correlates with a particular ideology of what constitutes the "real world" in the first place' (Lister *et al.* 2003). They would point out that technology has proliferated images in our culture well beyond a conventional media frame. Different kinds of judgement and visual literacy are required to make sense of, for example, CAT scans, computer games or holograms.

They point out that a sense of actuality is not just about technology used to reproduce the world out there, but is also about the manufacture of that which seems actual by virtue of being believable. This is true of cinema in particular, in relation to which they quote Allen (1998): 'The intention of all technical systems developed since the beginning of the 1950s (in cinema), has been towards reducing the spectators' sense of their "real" world, and replacing it with a fully believable artificial one.'

6.5 Polarization

Technologies have enabled a polarization of audiences and markets by simultaneously reaching out to mass markets and focusing on very specific audiences. Set-top hard disc recording devices can read preference patterns into our viewing, and offer a selective recording of TV that is meant to represent our interests. Cable channels can serve very local audiences with very specific material that is of no interest on a national level. New technology enables relatively cheap yet quality production of texts such as specialist magazines for niche markets – something that Emap specializes in. The Internet can be used to search for specific books or CDs in an individualized way, that runs counter to the generalized global marketing areas and genres of the music business. Emap has its own web-based magazine (FHM.co.uk), which is typical in that it enables individuals to make specific purchases from specific features in the magazine (this makes more money than the advertising around the site). There is nothing so new in this stretch between large and small audiences. But technology is sharpening different kinds of media provision and use. This may be challenging the argument that mass media produce homogenization. Some media may indeed offer mass appeal products, or products of the 'lowest common denominator'. But there are small media producers out there. Individuals can become producers and distributors on a limited scale. There are the indies and the alternatives. In this sense, polarization may be nothing but a good thing if it is about genuine alternatives to 'mass'. It suggests that media critiques which only focus on major media players, popular products and mass audiences are missing some of the point. Political economy pessimism is not inconsistent with post-modern cultural optimism.

6.6 Confirmation

From one point of view, however, technology may appear to be about innovation but, actually, it is used to confirm our experience of and views of the world. In commercial terms it works to confirm the hegemony of certain genres. In industrial terms it confirms the existing powers of media ownership.

For example, technologies employed for television news gathering offer live on-the-spot reporting from around the planet. They provide on-air interviews across continents. But – news values being as they are – what those technologies actually do is to confirm a world in which the footballer David Beckham gets more coverage than Aung San Su Chi, the elected but imprisoned ruler of Burma; in which stories about rulers predominate over stories from the ruled; in which some parts of the planet merit many news stories and others apparently deserve none. In other words, it is what the technology is used for which is more interesting than the 'wonders' of the technology itself. It would be perfectly possible to use the same global reach of technology to provide stories from other news organizations – from another point of view. It would be possible to offer a digital choice of news stories within a news programme – stories at the press of a button. But what the technology is used for is to enhance the long-existing conventions of news genre, to enhance the predominance of certain kinds of stories, and to confirm our picture of how the world works.

In a similar way one can see technology used to produce more of the same entertainment genres. Cinema has always had special effects and action movies – a love of spectacle. Technology has enhanced the commercial possibilities of these over the past 30 years in particular. The high concept series of Bond films or of *Star Wars* films has amalgamated post-production optical effects with on-screen graphics and such technology as robotics, to make the impossible appear possible, to make that which does not exist seem to exist. So technology confirms the power of given genres, but also constructs 'the real' – and in doing so confirms that cultural project which is to make our material and imaginative worlds equally real. And in the case of all media, the financial investment needed to deploy and develop technologies to produce all kinds of product is such that the market dominance of a diminishing range of companies is confirmed.

All this is not to deny the impact of new technologies on the operation of media institutions, on production processes, on what is produced, and so of course on the audiences. But it is to argue a view that technologies have in general not been revolutionary in their long-term effects, so much as evolutionary. There has been less of a big bang than a slow burn.

6.7 Naturalization

I am referring here to a naturalization of the consumption of technologies of the media. We are talking about an assimilation of the uses and effects of new technologies into the pattern of everyday life. This naturalization is not just about some quick decay of the impact of novelty in the minds of the audience. It is also to do with the uses of technology by the media. The BBC may have made publicity capital out of the effects used in their technologically ground-breaking series *Walking With Dinosaurs* (2001), but in fact the relatively low-budget combination of models and computer animation was used within a familiar wildlife documentary format. The voice-of-God narrator placed us on location. The editor constructed mini-dramas to hold our attentions. We were conscious of being educated, but pleasurably, within a familiar model (see previous comments about genres).

A central value of computer games has to do with the continued development of authenticity. Memory and programming, for genres such as car-race games in particular, is devoted to providing natural looking backgrounds and smooth movement, as much as interactive options. 'Realism' of representation contributes to the cultural naturalization of the experience of computer games playing (see previous comments about actualization). We become used to certain kinds of media experience in which the use of technology becomes invisible. Even where the textual experience is changed – personal sound systems, or morphing in advertisements – the audience rapidly becomes used to that which is 'impossible' in an image, or to people wearing earphones in public places.

The cross-over and intertextuality between texts, especially in the medium of television, also contributes to this naturalization of what is in fact a technically adroit experience. In TV thrillers, the creation of false CCTV footage or the use of night vision cameras has a lot to do with their use on reality TV shows, just as the use of reconstructive drama sequences in *Crime Watch* owes a lot to fiction examples. That which is familiar becomes natural by virtue of its repetition within everyday experience.

7 The Internet, the World Wide Web

> The Internet is a communication medium which allows, for the first time, the communication of many to many, in chosen time, on a global scale.
>
> The Internet is, above all else, a cultural creation.
>
> **Castells (2002)**

7.1 Dominance and use

Here, you should cross-refer to previous comments on the Internet, especially as they relate to a debate about the potential for the Internet to remain 'a users' paradise', or to become colonized by the major media institutions. Again, one needs to preserve a sense of caution and realism when talking about the impact of new technology. Ofcom research (2004) indicates that only 59 per cent of homes have Internet access, and a mere 12 per cent have some form of broadband access. This is far from the vision of a wired-up, interactive society, tapped into a global Web (ofcom.org.uk). Certainly the Internet is exceptional as a medium of distribution because it is not (and cannot be) owned by any commercial media conglomerate. It is not a business but a medium of exchange, a carrier. It is not set up as a broadcast medium – though it does carry radio broadcasts. It is not set up as a medium for selling 'hard' texts, but it is used to sell books, for example.

The issue becomes one of dominance rather than of outright control: dominance of content. It is the same issue which dogs cable providers. It is one thing having a means of distribution, but without attractive product there is no audience or consumer. Williams (2003) refers to the Warner/AOL merger as an example of how 'in a market-driven system control of new technology will be dominated by large media conglomerates'.

Preston (2001) disagrees that a product or content based revolution has happened or succeeded, except in the case of computer games (though I would say that these are generally very derivative of old media products). He would argue that distribution is everything, and argues that 'the mature media are the real masters of multi-media markets'. In the case of the Internet, dominance can be specifically about the portal providers or ISPs – the companies that give you access to the Net – AOL is the biggest. It is not just a question of profit from this service; it is about the advertising on screen. It is about the other companies to which you are linked when you make some generic enquiry. They own the biggest doors to the Web, and direct users to sites of their choice. This control of access is technologically represented through objects such as the set-top boxes which Sky is offering at knock-down prices in order to get us to access their digital satellite TV in Britain. The boxes are being more or less given away, because once we have them, 'they' own our attention to their content, their promotional material. If the system becomes market driven then it may be argued that the Web becomes just another means of consumption, rather than (possibly) some kind of global forum for the free exchange of knowledge and ideas.

One should also understand that the user is complicit in this process. It may be argued that we are well-practised at being seduced, but one cannot throw the free-will position out of the window. It may be that Web users are choosing to become consumers, to use technology to buy goods, book tickets and so on. Taking the audience/consumer perspective may also invoke a pessimistic take on new technologies, in that one cannot assume that the way forward is a moral, interactive and politically aware high road. Indeed there is every evidence that there will be at least as much taking from and using of the Internet as there is contributing and exchanging. People will be free to choose sites at which they are (as with much of the rest of media use) simply entertained. Users can choose their own cultural capital, whether this is represented by the Amnesty International site or by those purporting to offer webcam views of the goings-on in college dorms.

The very accessibility of the Internet has raised interesting questions about freedom, consumption and regulation. If the Internet is about private use of a media resource, then who is to argue about users accessing S & M 'rooms', for example? However, British

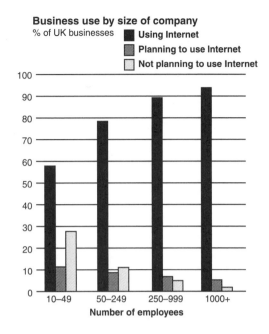

Business use by size of company
% of UK businesses

■ Using Internet
■ Planning to use Internet
□ Not planning to use Internet

Number of employees

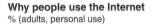

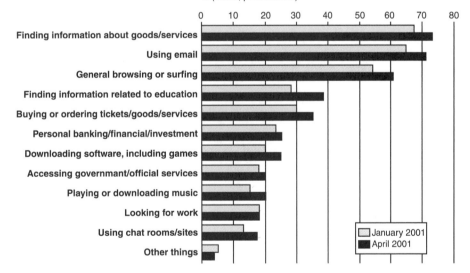

Why people use the Internet
% (adults, personal use)

- Finding information about goods/services
- Using email
- General browsing or surfing
- Finding information related to education
- Buying or ordering tickets/goods/services
- Personal banking/financial/investment
- Downloading software, including games
- Accessing governmant/official services
- Playing or downloading music
- Looking for work
- Using chat rooms/sites
- Other things

□ January 2001
■ April 2001

Internet Use in the UK
Although it may be argued that such use is changing year on year, still the chart draws attention to the fact that
e-commerce is not as important to users as email.
(*Office for National Statistics*)

authorities have been prosecuting people for accessing paedophile websites set up in the
USA and in the public domain. The US authorities moved to close down a website of an
anti-abortion group which included a hit list of pro-abortion names, one of whom was
murdered. There are a range of control programs available to parents which deny
children access to certain sites.

Those who talk up the freedoms and the virtual communities created by the Net tend to forget the downsides – surveillance, for example. A company named Ewatch asserts that it can trace the identity of any name on a screen – for a fee of US$ 5,000.

Television and new technology

Curran (2002) argues that the supposed dominance of new media and new technologies is largely a myth. He points out that in 2000 for example, 89 per cent of British prime-time TV was viewed across only four (largely broadcast) channels. He asserts that PSB is far from collapsing, that audiences have not fragmented, and that this is generally the case, being one of the myths of globalization. In particular he argues against the position of Elihu Katz (1996), which he summarizes as suggesting that

1 because audiences are being dispersed by consumption of new media, nations are no longer united by a shared experience of mass television viewing;

2 people are less informed because of the decline of public service broadcasting, under 'the constraints of new media technology' and 'the seductions of multinational corporations';

3 liberal democracy within the nation state is being weakened because new media and globalization have weakened a sense of national identity.

But Curran argues that

- 'British television continues to be a national medium';
- 'the life-support system supposedly supporting national democracy is not about to be switched off';
- because of regulation many broadcasters across Europe are in fact PSB broadcasters (like Channel 4);
- there is plenty of information material in prime time (whatever is happening in the USA);
- even globally, while economics and technology may have brought about some changes, they have not torn apart the national channel;
- in Britain, at least, forecasts of the take-up of the new technologies of satellite and cable have proved to be manifestly and expensively wrong (for the companies concerned).

7.2 Utopias/dystopias

Much critical comment on new media and on the Internet in particular tends to fall into either utopian camps which propose attractive visions such as new communities in cyberspace, or dystopian futures in which a pessimistic political economist's nightmare of a totally commodified world comes true.

Schiller (1996) would see technology as being driven by the economy and dominated by US capitalism. Stevenson (2002) interprets Schiller's position as seeing that: 'Economic forces are the main structures behind technological developments such as the super information highway and the Internet, and they also help determine the superficiality of mainstream mass culture.'

Of course, the optimist would argue that mass culture is being fragmented by these same technologies, which are putting more power in the hands of the consumer/audience. The pessimist would argue that technologies are extending the power of the market, giving it a new realm in cyberspace. Interactivity may be seen as working for greater market access – log on, sign up and pay up. Malls in cyberspace can be reached at the flick of a finger. The notion of the American imperium, currently materialized through its dominance as a world military power, extends to the economy, is backed by technological imperialism, and revivifies theories of cultural imperialism.

On the other hand, one can well argue that, in spite of increased consumption by and through technologies, our social realities are more diverse and less determined than pessimistic models suggest. People are still mobile, community action still happens on a grand scale, technology is used for political resistance and by alternative media, the media majors do not control everything, least of all the Internet. Castells has argued for positive outcomes from media and technology. He refers to various social movements and political groups as making use of technology and the media to get their views on to national and global agendas, to resist dominance. He gives the example of the Zapatista guerrilla movement in Mexico, in particular, using the Internet – email and online discussion – and video coverage. Castell's (1997) measured views on the coexistence of opposing trends and possibilities are summarized by Stevenson (2002): 'New media technologies therefore simultaneously reinforce relations of cultural capital, hierarchy and distinction while enabling social movements to publicise campaigns and connect with distant publics.' Castells rejects the idea that new media can be simply read in terms of domination or emancipation.

Elsewhere, commentators refer to alternative practices and the opportunities afforded by new media of communication. Atton (2002) makes the point that 'alternative' does not always have to been radical or politically resistant. He cites the example of one Jody LaFerriere's website (bigdumptruck) in which the owner is by any definition an ordinary citizen doing her own thing – pretty alternative to mainstream practices. But the material on the site is framed within dominant ideology, is about personal enthusiasms, and for example endorses that very materialist enterprise, Amazon.com. Again the point is that technologies are malleable and can be used for a variety of purposes.

7.3 New democracy, new marketplace

So in the first place, there is an issue as to whether the Internet offers us a new democracy or a new marketplace. Its uses, qualities and potential as a medium, are only as good as its users, its websites, its search engines and portal providers. One could say that, seen as a technology, it is of itself value free – yet it certainly is not in respect of its operation. Sites supporting minorities or ecological causes, coexist with sites offering pornography or with those encouraging a range of eccentric beliefs. It seems to offer a new democracy of a free exchange of ideas, but that democracy includes some pretty tacky ideas and no means of achieving political change. It offers the chance to satirize and criticize the media themselves, but it also provides media institutions with a point of sale for their products and with an extension to their publicity machines. If the media provide the most attractive sites (and use new technologies to develop accessible streaming of moving images) then, de facto, the Internet could become an extension of the media. If governments baulk at the democratic free-for-all and introduce legal sanctions against those who set up sites they do not like (as they are now doing against pornography), then they can close down politically dissident sites. This happened with a Chinese political/spiritual movement named Falun Gong, whose leader was based in New York, and which had thousands of supporters on the Net. When it came to street protests these were severely suppressed in China, where the authorities also sought the means to close down access to the Internet. If the Internet becomes a propaganda tool for any position on given political issues, then it becomes a tool of both the Right and the Left. It becomes more confusing as a source of information. It has in effect moved out of a radical phase. As technology makes it more accessible to more people with more materials, so it becomes a mainstream medium, albeit one with special qualities.

Accessibility and take-up are also issues at stake. Stephen Lax (2000) raises questions about just how much use is made of the Internet, just how many people are connected to it – in Britain, at least. He refers to the fact that where there are examples of community or area Web communities with social and political concerns, the evidence seems to be that involvement drops away after an initial surge of interest, and that core elites within the community come to dominate its agenda. Not much democracy there, then. Lax also refers to research which indicated that two out of three people neither had, nor intended to get, access to the Internet. Further, the profile of those least interested in these technologies is dominated by females in the C/D/E socio-economic classes. So politics and democracy may not be well served through new media, and women in particular may be 'disenfranchised'. Such evidence suggests that great caution is needed before proclaiming new technology as the bearer of new democracy.

7.4 A public sphere (see also Chapter 10)

By the same token, the idea that the Internet becomes a redefined public sphere is not impossible, but not a done deal. Its technology has potentially created a new public forum for social and political debate. The relationship of that debate to the political process is still in formation. For example, Oxfam campaigns on specific causes worldwide and does invite lobbying action by its email recipients. But it is not a complete public sphere if sections of society do not possess and cannot afford the relevant technology to access it. Neither is it a *global* public sphere, for the same reason – access to the Internet is partial. And in some countries – China for example – governments are using various strategies to control access to the Internet, just as former East Germany tried to stop its citizens watching TV from the West.

Even within national boundaries, one is talking about technological inequalities. We may well be creating a new definition of 'underclass' – those without access to new technologies and their political and material opportunities. Globally, there is a similar division between developed and developing worlds. Williams (2003) quotes Thussu (2000) when he refers to the fact that only 12 per cent of Internet usage is in the global South where two-thirds of the world's population lives.

Similarly, Eoin Devereux (2003) refers to Cullen (2001) when stating that South-east Asia has 19 per cent of the world's population, but only 1 per cent of Internet connections.

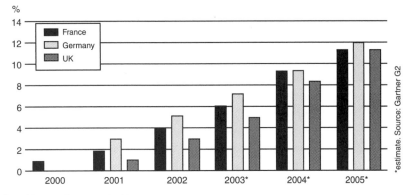

Broadband Internet Access in the Home
Broadband is central to realizing a vision of an electronically interactive society. This chart makes it clear
that, at the moment, few British homes are going to have that access.
(*Independent on Sunday*, 17 April 2002)

Castells (2002) points out that in 2000, 266 million of 378 million global users
were in North America and Europe. Even within designated areas of study there are
huge differences of take-up. In Europe, for instance, Scandinavia has by far the greatest
of national populations online. He talks about a digital divide in the USA, in which
teenagers had twice as much access to the Internet as those over 50 years old; in which
50 per cent of white and Asian Americans had access, but only 29 per cent of African
Americans and 23 per cent of Hispanic Americans.

Somewhat contradictorally, he also talks up the importance of the Internet to
various social movements and protests such as those against the World Trade Organization meeting in Seattle in December 1999. He argues that the Internet is indispensable
because

1 it permits mobilization around values shared electronically;
2 it replaces 'the shells' of vertically integrated organizations such as political parties,
   which, he argues, have become agencies of information dissemination, but are no
   longer about real, value-laden debates;
3 it has a global reach which matches that of other power structures (multi-nationals),
   and by-passes the limitations of the nation state.

These points may be true, but I would draw attention to the fact that they are of
advantage to fascism, as much as to democrats or environmentalists. And they give the
advantage those who are already technologically equipped and articulate – as opposed to
those who are socially and financially disadvantaged. In any case, the point that may be
missed here is that, like other examples, the Internet may be a generic description for a
given medium built on the back of given technologies. But, in fact, all media are fragmented in their use. So the Internet is not so much one giant forum for political debate as
it is a collection of discussion rooms. And this public sphere does not have to be an
overtly politicized space, least of all one that especially benefits a democratic model. Its
coexistent spaces are inhabited by paedophiles, Friends Re-united, dating rooms,
memorial sites for the dead, sites for ethnic groups, religious groups, and so on. In fact,
technology has allowed an Internet that is more like a cyber society which can be just as

fragmented as the real-space society from which it emanates. 'The public', rather like 'the audience', becomes less cohesive and collective the more one interrogates its features. Indeed, in many ways this is but a notion that the media themselves have played a great part in manufacturing. News people and politicians are fond of referring to 'members of the public' as if the phrase meant something definable.

Who is *not* a member of the public? But being a 'member of the public' does not necessarily put one in a public sphere. And neither is the nature of the public sphere something to be taken for granted.

There is an issue of how far one has a genuine free flow and interchange of information and rational public debate. The media in general have already failed, we might say, as a forum for open public access and discussion. And certain media uses – especially the political lobbying around elections – point to a corruption of an ideal. Whether the Internet in particular opens up a genuine freedom, or itself is now polluted by power interests and hobbled by lack of whole public access, is part of an ongoing debate.

8 Discussion extract

66 99 [M]ost of the writing on the Internet has either pointed to ways that new technological forms are linked into the accumulation of capital, commodification and the disappearance of public space, or has optimistically pointed to the communicative possibilities that are suggested by horizontally rather than vertically organised information structures. Within these arguments lies a deeper debate as to whether we are witnessing a transformation away from an industrial society to an information or network society. This argument, first proposed by the sociologist Daniel Bell (1973), argues that knowledge and information are becoming the key factors in economic and social development. The central argument here is that productive and distributive processes within the economy are increasingly driven by knowledge-based inputs. In this way, the development of new media technology needs to be linked into the transformation of the economy, and related changes within politics and culture. Many writers prefer the term network society to information society. Van Dijk (1999) has argued that the most important structural change impacting upon media is the convergence of telecommunications, data communications and new and old media. Within these circuits of information we are witnessing the digitilisation of communications accompanied by the convergence of television, telephone systems and the Internet. The second related change has been the shift towards interactive forms of media that allow two-way forms of communication. These twin changes move contemporary society from the age of industrialism and mass culture into an era governed by networks and interactivity. Their coordinates point in a different direction to the debates as to whether or not we should become technological optimists or pessimists. The idea of a network society offers a different model of the capitalist economy, a rethinking of the link between communications and politics, and consideration of the changes taking place within our cultural life.

Stevenson (2002); Bell (1973); van Dijk (1999)

1 What changes is the writer arguing for, with relation to media and communications?

2 How may the media be contributing to these changes?

3 How may such changes be seen in our social and cultural lives?

9 Further reading

Atton, C. (2002) *Alternative Media*. London: Sage.

Gauntlett, D. and Horsley, R. (eds) (2004) *Web Studies* (2nd edn). London: Arnold.

Lister, M., Dovey, J., Giddings, S., Grant, I. and Kelly, K. (2003) *New Media – A Critical Introduction*. London: Routledge.

Preston, P. (2001) *Reshaping Communications*. London: Sage.

Mackay, H. and O'Sullivan, T. (1999) *The Media Reader – Continuity and Transformation*. London and Buckingham: Sage/ Open University Press.

Turkle, S. (1995) *Life on the Screen – Identity in the Age of the Internet*. New York: Touchstone.

Street, J. (1999) Remote control? Politics, technology and 'electronic democracy', in H. Mackay and T. O'Sullivan, *The Media Reader – Continuity and Transformation*. London and Buckingham: Sage/ Open University Press.

Winston, B. (1998) *Media Technology and Society*. London: Routledge.

CHAPTER NINE

ADVERTISING

Its relationship with the media audience: the consequences for society and culture

66 Advertising manipulates consumers and instils false values, it extols a materialistic and consumerist ethic, it deals in emotions and irrationality, it leads people to buy unnecessary or overvalued items. 99

Fowles, J. (1996) *Advertising and Popular Culture*. London: Sage.

1 Introduction

The conduct of the advertising industries, and the materials that they produce, has sometimes given rise to fierce differences of opinion over the functions and effects of advertising in society. Some might see certain television adverts as little creative master-pieces. Others might damn advertising as condescending in its representation of social groups, trite in its view of human behaviour, and even as pernicious in being a creature of capitalism and its ideology.

In this chapter I want to examine advertising mainly in relation to key concepts and debates already outlined in this book, not least in relation to ideas about media influence. The intention is not to describe the functions and working of the advertising industry – that has been sufficiently covered by books such as *The Advertising Handbook* by Sean Brierley (1995), as well as being supported by resources such as the website for the Advertising Standards Authority. My purpose is, rather

- to engage with critiques of advertising;
- to relate advertising to key terms central to this book; and
- to comment on the relationship of advertising to the media in general.

The lead quotation above identifies a classic critique of advertising which nevertheless does not represent all perspectives, let alone all concerns about the role and effects of advertising. Schudson (1993), for example, argues that the process of influence through advertising media is not so much about the advertising as such, as it is about culture and social context.

2 Major questions

1 What is the nature and place of advertising in society, and in relation to media?
2 How may one relate advertising to critiques of the relationship between media and society, between institutions and consumers, between texts and audiences?
3 How do adverts relate to consumers, especially in terms of persuasion?
4 How does advertising relate to ideas about commodification?
5 In what ways does advertising promote mythologies through its representations and its invocation of discourses?
6 How may advertising be understood in the special case of the child/consumer?

3 The nature of advertising

It needs to be clear that what follows is inextricably connected with marketing and promotion, as much as being about advertising alone –paid-for intentional persuasive communication. Publicity usually works alongside advertising, and is about activities which draw attention to, and create a favourable attitude towards, the product or service being sold. Publicity is not paid for, as in a TV slot or a magazine page. But it still costs – for example, to run a promotion party or to create a press pack.

Marketing and promotion are more suitable terms to describe persuasive activities which work across media, which use more than just media, which operate on national and even global scales, and which resonate off one another. By this last comment I mean, for instance, that a TV interview with a film star may in the first place be set up to market a given movie. But then it also promotes the star as a business, and the idea of stardom in general, and film as a medium, and the attractions of television. Marketing as an activity is utterly pervasive within the media, but also within our cultural and social experiences. 'Each promotional message refers us to a commodity which is itself the site of another promotion' (Wernick, 1991).

Goods themselves become a kind of advertisement. Like an advert they are referential and intertextual. Advertising, marketing, promotion, publicity, commodities, are all stitched together. The so-called developed world and its cultures are a dominant part of this stitchwork. They are extending their reach globally. The advertising world is one of multi-national corporations, regional markets such as South-east Asia, and trading blocs. It operates on the back of international money markets, internationalized labour practices and information technologies.

Advertising in itself is such a vast economic activity and is so explicitly devoted to promoting partial views of products and services that it merits critical attention. This is true even if there are questions about the extent of its effectiveness, as well as about the nature of its 'collateral damage' in ideological terms.

In May 2001 Coca-Cola spent approximately $400 million worldwide on its brands. In the same year, it spent £30 million in the UK on promotion.

Jamieson and Campbell (2001) report that in the USA in 1990, 13,300 new products were introduced, 75 per cent of which were foodstuffs. In 1998, $200 billion was spent on advertising in the USA, an increase of 7.5 per cent on the previous year. It cost $2 million to place a 30-second ad around TV screenings of the Superbowl series.

Doyle (2002) refers to the level of global expenditure on advertising in 2000, estimated at $330 billion. The advertising industry operates like its hosts, the media, in respect of the global dominance of three agencies – Interpublic, Omnicom and WPP. Advertising expenditure is itself dominated by the media of the press and television.

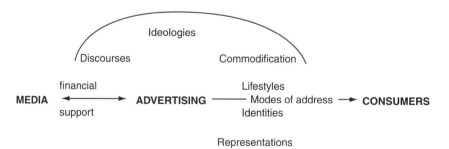

Advertising: Key words
There is a relationship of mutual benefit between advertisers and media.
 It is less easy to see mutuality in the relationship between advertisers and consumers, where it is not in the interests of the former to empower the latter.
(*Graeme Burton*, 2004)

In Britain, 85 per cent of expenditure is on these two media, and twice as much is spent on the press as on television.

At least some of this advertising has had the effect of creating new sales, increasing market shares, maintaining sales and generating profits on a gigantic scale. Some advertising does work some of the time. What is more interesting to the context of this book are its effects on social attitudes, social practices, cultural values, identities and people's understanding of the kind of world that they believe they live in.

We tend to take advertising for granted, as a cultural experience. It has been around for so long that we take it as a 'given' in everyday life. Kline (1993) refers to the fact that by 1900 the pages of some daily newspapers were literally half full of adverts. Even 50 years earlier, laws were passed to stop the proliferation of advertising carts choking up city streets. But it does not have to exist in the form that it does. Indeed, Falk (1996) points out that an interesting shift took place roughly from the early nineteenth to the early twentieth century, to produce the kind of promotional environment that now seems normal to us. There was a shift from product-centred adverts to those that were about a product–user relationship, about the experiential aspect of the product concerned. There was a shift from adverts whose copy provided arguments about and for the product, to those that represented satisfaction from using the product. There was a general shift from adverts dominated by verbal and literary modes, to those dominated by visual modes of communication. This has led to a kind of advertising in which the advert is detached from the product as such. It has led to a situation in which the consumption of experience and the experience of consumption are interlinked.

Advertising came to fill that space that opened up between production and consumption, when people no longer lived next to, or were themselves the source of production. Broadly, this is also about the shift from rural economies to predominantly urban populations in the West (by 1920, 52 per cent of Americans lived in towns and cities (Fowles, 1996)). Mass production, with all its advantages of economies of scale, also meant that a throughput of goods needed to be maintained in order to justify investment and to keep those production lines in business. Advertising to maintain consumption helped keep that throughput going. 'Advertising offered itself as a way of efficiently creating consumers and as a way of homogeneously controlling the consumption of a product' (Ewen, 1977).

Kline (1993) refers to Ewen's work when he says that a crucial point was reached in the development of advertising when industrial producers recognized 'that all goods were cultural artefacts and that selling them was mostly a matter of communication'.

Fowles (1996) provides some interesting ideas about oppositions and tensions which are part of the nature of adverts and of the advertising process. These ideas question that surface of inevitability that ads present to us. They suggest that the production of such texts and their meanings is problematic. They are now set out, with some paraphrasing and interpretation.

The needs of the client v. the needs of the agency
(that conflict between the needs of the agency to be creative and to gain the approval of their peers within the industry, and the direct need of the client for promotion through whatever works)

Research information v. creative execution
(the disjunction between what researchers may tell the agency and what their creative instincts may tell them about the market and promotional methods – e.g. the famous and surrealist run of Benson & Hedges cigarette ads would never have seen the light of day if the agency had listened to what research was saying)

Product v. appeal
(devices to appeal must not lose sight of the product: this is a conflict between actuality and the ideal – that problem where people remember the ad but not the product)

Words v. images
(negotiating the symbolic order of spoken/written language, as opposed to the direct iconic impact of images)

The frame as container v. bursting the frame
(alternative strategies in which the ad is either contained and ordered, or those in which images and text may appear to be bursting out of frame, or bled to the margins of the sheet)

Text v. text
(that sense of intertextual strain where, in their subconscious, consumers are setting one product against another: ads, their genres, their categories of product cannot live in a conceptual vacuum – the problem is to make the comparisons favourable without seeming to recognize the opposition)

Advert v. consumer
(the problem that advertisers have, especially nowadays, to combat consumer resistance and scepticism towards a communication process which is seen to be manipulative)

The one v. the many
(negotiating that stretch within the ad and the campaign in which the appeal has to address the individual and yet also reach a mass market)

4 Advertising and media – a relationship

Marketing and promotion are integral to the workings of a capitalist economy, in which goods (including their cultural dimensions) have to be sold to consumers within a marketplace (whether literal or virtual). The media are integral to the workings of advertising. Advertising is integral to the finances of the media. In Britain, as globally (with the exception of the BBC and its licence fee income), virtually all media depend on selling advertising to stay in business. There is also income from devices such as sponsorship and product placement to be taken into account.

This relationship has predictably produced opposing critiques which talk up the dependency of the one element upon the other, and vice versa. Those who defend the marketplace economy would argue that advertising provides a kind of subsidy to the economy (and possibly the media), whereby its activity boosts and maintains sales (and in so doing also covers the cost of advertising). The other view is that advertising inevitably pressures the media that depend upon it into assuming certain ideological positions, which of course are favourable to the work of advertising. This view would also draw attention to the dominance of the few in all markets, and to the consequent lack of real consumer choice.

It is clear that both media and advertisers are interested in reaching audiences. There is a view that media 'locate' audiences for advertisers and therefore operate in the interests of advertisers as much as those of media audiences. One may also argue that the way media have developed has quite a lot to do with the history of their relationship with advertising. Broadcasting could have been more of a regional or local medium early on. But in the USA, and in Britain from the 1950s, the mass market characteristics of television may be at least partly to do with commercial interest in its ability to reach into millions of homes at one time. It offered the kind of visuality and immediacy which the press did not have. Equally, the development of magazines into niche markets and their characteristic of running features which in effect promote their subject (computers or cars or fashion) may also be said to be a result of the interests of advertisers – whose interests are in turn those of their paymasters, the companies who commission them.

Andersen (1995) provides many examples of self-interest at work. He comments on the 'banned list' which many US companies have, with relation to TV programmes with which they will not be associated. For example, Mars will not advertise M & Ms in or around a list of 50 programmes. Andersen refers to that practice of agencies and their clients which routinely provides 'complimentary copy' for inclusion in magazines. He refers to Gloria Steinem writing about her own experience in the magazine industry when he says that ' "advertisers" control over the editorial content of women's magazines had become "so institutionalised that it is written into insertion orders or dictated to ad salespeople as official policy" '.

'Advertorials' have been a major element of such magazines since the 1990s, using devices such as the celebrity interview, and involving for example, tie-ins with a travel company. In many magazines the page headed quietly, 'advertising feature', is hardly to be distinguished from the general features. What is not said may also be about the power of the advertiser in their relationship with the media. The magazines *Cosmopolitan*, *Nova* and *Marie-Claire* refused in 2001 to run an RSPCA ad against the use of animals in testing for cosmetic products. The proposed ad showed a rabbit having its eyes sprayed. Such magazines do, of course, obtain a significant income from ads about cosmetic products. Promotional activities may extend to apparently neutral and factual TV programmes, which one might think fall outside even the practice of product placement. Andersen refers to 'the escalating unity of entertainment, news and advertising on television'. He describes how in 1990 three successive nightly editions of NBC news featured an item drawing attention to a new machine for detecting breast cancer. He points out that this item did not appear on other networks; that the machine was made by General Electric, who own RCA, who own NBC.

Of course, one has to recognize the moderating influence of political regulation of the advertising industry, when arguing for the debilitating effects of advertising on the media. These effects are to do with the dependency of media on advertising and the shaping of media development by advertising. But again, the effectiveness of regulation within individual nation states is very much open to question.

In Britain, media industries are largely self-regulated. The Advertising Standards Authority covers magazines, the press and cinema. It was set up by the Advertising Association. The Broadcast Advertising Clearance Centre was set up by broadcasters. Until December 2003 this worked closely with the Independent Television Commission and the Radio Authority. Now this relationship is with the new broadcast regulator,

Ofcom, a quasi-independent body set up by government, but given autonomy in that it is not run by any government department. But clearly the hand of government is upon it, just as government may also affect advertising indirectly through the legal system. For example, the Obscene Publications Act (1959) would ensure that nothing too extreme could be 'published' by advertisers. Yet it may not be straightforward obscenity that needs regulating. In 2002 an advert for Opium perfume caused public protests. The objections were not so much about the apparent nudity of a reclining female model, with orgasmic signification, but were about the renewal of the objectification of women in a public display.

There are practices and possible effects wider even than those where advertisers interfer with the free choice of content in media texts. For instance, intertextuality is an established commercial strategy, most obviously in cases where personalities and stars lend their persona to a product. Angela Lansbury (of the much rerun series *Murder, She Wrote*) has been used to promote aspirin on US TV. Music tracks and old film clips are frequently used in adverts. One might argue that such devices falsely attach values to products which have nothing legitimate to do with such referents. It might be said that such intertextual appropriation is a form of cultural terrorism.

In terms of the relationship between the media and advertising, it is assumed that the debate is mainly with relation to television. But more cash is spent on press advertising. It is true that TV remains the only really mass medium. But still, its income from adverts is diminishing. The audience share of the US networks is down to around 40 per cent (Doyle, 2002). The ITV share in Britain is less than a quarter of the audience, with the BBC having nearer to a 30 per cent share. In 2002, ITV advertising revenues were down by 17 per cent from the 2000 figure, when it grossed £2 billion. Satellite and cable is competing for its share of advertising. So is the Internet, where advertising is actually more expensive than on TV, on the grounds that this medium offers a better match with individual audience targets.

5 Advertising and society – critiques

Critical positions on advertising in relation to society reflect a range of views.

- *Pluralist positions* argue for the benefits of consumption and choice for the consumer and for the economy.
- *Neo-Marxist positions* argue against the debilitating effects of monopoly markets and the corrupting effects of representations in advertisements.
- *Cultural critiques* would emphasize the insidious effects of commodification.

Sinclair (1987) sees the critiques in terms of an opposition between optimistic and pessimistic views, between those who see advertising as a tool whose function is to make the economy work, and those who see the working of the economy as destructive of social and cultural values. 'For the functionalists, advertising in society operates towards the utilitarian end of creating "the greatest happiness for the greatest number", while for the Marxists, advertising maintains the illusions by which an exploitative and irrational system is perpetuated.' Pluralists might object to a conflation of functionalism and pluralism, but in Sinclair's terms there is little distinction to be made between the two.

However one understands the functions and effects of advertising, what is clear is that it is bound up with a complex relationship between society and economy and culture and politics. Critiques of advertising are a paradigm for critiques of those media that provide advertising with a means of approaching audiences. Transparent views of advertising see it being synonymous with democracy and consumption and choice of goods. Opaque views would draw attention to what advertising conceals. 'Advertisements obscure and avoid the real issues of society', 'they create systems of social differentiation', 'basic issues . . . are sublimated into "meanings", "images", "lifestyles", to be bought with products, not money' (Williamson, 1978).

Differentiation, it might be said, has to do with advertising constructing us as audiences, creating social categories, generating what become naturalized truths. These differences are as false as differences between commodities, which advertising also constructs. Commodities may appear to be different from one another, defined by their patents if nothing else. But it may be said that such differences are insignificant until advertising makes them appear so. Differences are validated in terms of the discourse of individualism. To be different or individual in these terms is a 'good thing'. The illusion is fostered that one becomes different by choosing a brand. But of course this is nonsense. The inherent contradiction is that thousands of others are also buying your brand of jeans or car. This is guaranteeing sameness at the point at which you are being told that you have guaranteed individuality. You are what you buy or consume. But you are not who you think you are.

One may also contrast critical views in terms of those which are more holistic and those which are more selective. Neo-Marxist views are concerned with the 'big picture', the part played by advertising in the overall relationship between media and society. In this view, advertising flatters to deceive. It subverts use value into exchange value. Its representations incorporate the meanings of the dominant ideology. Its naturalized place in social experience would place it at the heart of hegemony. It helps engineer acceptance of difference and of inequality. All adverts, in varying degrees, are trying to sell capitalism.

A cultural approach, on the other hand, would tend to concentrate on texts and audiences, just as a political economy perspective would tend to emphasize institution, production and regulation. The former would look at the part played by advertising and advertisements in respect of meaning and consumption. The latter would look at the influence of advertising on the workings of media institutions, and at the influence of regulators on both producers and the text.

Nava *et al.* (1996) is unsympathetic towards what she describes as totalizing, Fordist views. She argues that the advertising industry itself is unsure or sceptical about the effects of its own work. She suggests that investigation of the industry's own analysis of advertising (and not its confident pronouncements to its clients) demonstrates 'demoralization, fragmentation and suspension of belief'. In this view, holistic models which include unqualified assumptions about persuasive effects and especially assertions of a Marxist nature about mass media and mass culture, simply do not work.

By way of contrast, Robert Goldman (1992) works out of an essentially Althusseran Marxist position when he sees advertising as 'a key social and economic institution in producing and reproducing the material and ideological supremacy of commodity rela-tions'. In this case, one is looking at ways in which a system of production reproduces itself. This reproduction of a system and of ideology has a lot to do with advertising, and how deeply it is embedded within our social and cultural lives. It is seen rather as a force of nature, than as a tool of corporations. Advertising helps manifest those imaginary relations of the individual to the real relations in which they live: the imaginary conceals the real.

Capitalist pluralism sees advertising as benign, and tends to regard it optimistically, as an information provider, drawing attention to the merits of goods and services. This was much more true in the Victorian period. Though this is a position still argued for by many in the industry, it really has not been valid for decades. Ever since Pears soap began to construct mythologies around cleanliness and childhood, advertisements have become increasingly about culture, not raw goods; about values, not facts; about mythic worlds, not social reality. Sinclair (1987) takes a PE (political economy) perspective when he describes the idea that advertising is merely a source of information as disingenuous – 'truth in advertising is what the law says it is'.

Both a political economy and a market perspective on advertising would see media funding as an important part of the place of advertising in society. The latter would see advertising as a kind of engine of the market, maintaining the circulation of goods and wealth and providing employment.

A political economist, on the other hand, would regard advertising (and its income) as underwriting the power of media institutions. This economic power is only checked by the regulatory power of political institutions, acting through law. And advertising does not just underwrite media businesses financially, by providing much of their income. It also underwrites them culturally by constructing a view of the world which legitimizes what they produce, how they produce it, and the very operation of advertising itself. Advertising has become a naturalized component of the media economy. Naturalization legitimizes its work, its products, its effects. It is a product of ideological positions on freedom of speech and the idea of a free market. But in another social context one might argue that these freedoms are relative, and tend to benefit those with the power to exercise such freedoms. The freedoms in turn become a source of power. From this follows an argument that there should be no advertising, or that it should be heavily regulated.

Doyle (2002) points out that there is a strong correlation between advertising expenditure and economic wealth in any given country, however that wealth is meas-ured. But even if one agrees that advertising contributes to economic growth, this does not mean that it contributes to social well-being. Indeed, by helping a few corporations become globally successful, it actually helps create a situation of commercial oligopoly in which the few dominate the many. Again, it is Doyle who points out that 'advertising is a feature of oligopoly market structures'. In this sense one needs to deconstruct not only advertisements, but also the very process of advertising. For example the notion of 'the market' is itself a construction which is convenient to the promotion industries. 'Con-trary to marketing ideology, markets do not already exist "out there" in social reality but are "constructed" ' (Sinclair, 1987).

This links with a wider point about media audiences – they are not ready formed, out there, waiting for their programme to come along. They come into being for the programme, and only for as long as the life of the programme. Similarly, a consumer market only exists while consumption takes place. The consumer and the market are only ideas that are waiting to happen – to be given life through purchase and use.

Cronin (2000) also develops ideas about the imagined world that advertisers manufacture. She argues that audiences and their relationships are indeed imagined, not discovered. The very work of marketers – through focus groups for instance – is a way of confirming as real what is in fact only imagined. It is a way of validating the work of agencies to their industry clients. Imagined markets are incorporated within the textual address of an advertisement – their existence is assumed. As readers/consumers we are invited to share that assumption.

While acknowledging that there are cultural consequences to the way advertising operates, still a PE perspective would emphasize the economic significance of advertising and promotion. Within a Marxist framework, examining how dominant classes deploy cultural power, this position would be interested in the economic sources of that power.

It may be said that positions drawn out of Marx are interested in the production of consumption, while more post-modern and culturalist critiques of advertising would concentrate on modes of consumption.

Matterlart (1991) is critical of advertising in terms of how it dominates 'public space': 'It forms a social network which enervates media economies, cultures, political and civil society, international relations.' It takes over public space, especially that created through media, for its own ends, and pushes aside genuine public interaction. It privileges form and image above content and the interchange of ideas – 'the new public space will be more and more driven by "images" '.

Kenway and Bullen (2001) make a similar point about public spaces being dominated by advertising and by practices of consumption. Jameson (1991) or Baudrillard (1988) might, on the other hand, critique advertising and a market culture in a more post-modern way. This approach would draw attention to a world of simulation, to a kind of hyperreality. Advertising is full of simulated experiences. Even shopping in the vast new mall complexes becomes a kind of alternative reality, even an 'out of body' experience. There is a lack of distinction between the real and the imaginary. Identities become fluid, as people become detached from a real social world by advertising and by its capacity to cause us to continually redefine ourselves. We live in a world of commodity experiences, manifested through advertising.

6 Advertising and audiences (see also Chapter 3)

The demographic approach to explaining 'audiences' places them in objectifiable categories such as age, gender, occupation, place of domicile (see BARB, Broadcasters' Audience Research Board, or Nielsen in the USA). Audiences are constructed, through marketing, for advertisers, by those in the business of promotion, out of social groups that may or may not interact in everyday life, that may or may not share cultural experiences. The notion of 'consumer' has so far become naturalized – we are so far accustomed to the idea that adverts speak to bodies of people called 'housewives' or 'car drivers' – that it is difficult for people to detach themselves from the unreality of such identities. Words such as 'consumer' stand for a certain state of cultural and political affairs – like 'the public' or 'the viewer'. Their coinage, and the kind of reality they stand for, works in the interests of institutions rather than of any social group. We talk about the 'advertiser' but not the 'advertisee' because the process of marketing does not involve an equal relationship. The 'consumer' has a subordinated function, just as the 'audience' is supposed to have a passive function. In both cases, there are arguments that the consumer/audience may be more active and constructive than appears to be the case. But one can hardly argue that advertising actually intends to empower the consumer with choice, with unbiased information, with the tools of resistance.

The urge of the advertiser to objectify and classify is exemplified by the approach of the company, Experion, and their marketing tool, Financial Mosaic. This produces ten general classifications of consumer, based on postcodes and information about debts, loans, investments etc. Categories range from 'discerning investors' to 'burdened borrowers'. The audience is defined in the material terms of a commodity culture, which have nothing to do with social values (*Independent on Sunday*, 5 September 1999).

Equally, one should balance such an instrumental example with reference to the use of ethnographic research by advertisers. In this case, the researchers may be out on the high street, or in clubs, talking to people, and observing shifts in fashion or in patterns of consumption. The ethnographer gets into life as it is lived, and completes a feedback loop to the producers. The chip-maker Intel commissioned ethnographic research into children's social behaviours and preferences, as part of the development of computer games consoles (*IOS*, 15 July 2001)

The arrival of 'viral marketing' in 2002 was also interesting in that it engaged the audience directly through an elaborated 'word-of-mouth' principle. For example, Dulux paints emailed 10,000 women, inviting them to play a 'belly fluff' game on a specially created website. Some 13,000 responded. Respondents get interested. Some make purchases; more tell their friends. Other devices in this area might include the use of street

Boycott Esso Advert
Advertising may be used by non-commercial clients, presuming they have enough financial backing, and that they can obtain the necessary media placement.
(*Stop Esso Campaign*)

flyers, lamppost labels, backed up by regular posters and websites. Mobile phones have been stencilled on pavements. The Cerne Abbas Giant (a huge primitive fertility figure cut into the hill chalk of Dorset) has been 'dressed' in a pair of jeans.

There are multiple audiences for advertising. Many are part of 'the public', but some are trade audiences. And these audiences are sought for a variety of reasons, not just to persuade consumers to buy. Other reasons for advertising are to

- hold on to one's share of a given market in the face of competition;
- get a bigger share of the market;
- create awareness of a given product or service;
- reassure existing customers that what they have been buying is still good;
- reassure the trade and one's sales force that the product is good and that advertising is working.

In the context of advertising, the audience itself becomes a product, another commodity. The circulation and marketing managers of any magazine will talk about being able to deliver a certain kind of reader with a certain kind of profile to the advertiser – the one who really pays the bills. As Robin Andersen (1995) puts it, the audience has 'market value' – and, television seeks to package its viewers 'into more desirable commodities'. Sut Jhally (1990) picks up the same theme when talking about how goods acquire value through their exchange. Advertisers use the media to sell goods to consumers. In this process of exchange, goods might acquire value of social status or of sexuality – one is never just buying a sweatshirt or a lipstick. The consumer gives cash as their part of the exchange. But, Jhally says, businesses and media organizations are also engaged in a process of exchange – audiences as a commodity in exchange for cash or some other kind of reward.

Advertising plays on ideas about individualism, it invokes this discourse. It often appears to address the individual consumer. Of course, the contradiction is that it does not, and cannot. The market is committed to packaging and delivering consumers in the plural. It is equally committed to packaging the goods that it sells to consumers. Volume production and economies of scale would be impossible otherwise. So the market sees the audience in one way, but the advertisements produced by the market pretend to see the audience in another way. 'Consumer ads usually invite viewers into fantasies of individualism, though the promise of individuality is likely to be premised on conformity of consumption preferences' (Goldman and Papson, 1998).

Lifestyles

It has become a commonplace that audiences are conceived of in terms of their lifestyles. Once more, it would be ingenuous to argue that as members of society we simply have lifestyles which the market identifies and slots into. The market (as all our cultural assumptions about consumption) has been around for so long that we are born into lifestyles which it has already shaped. We grow up into a set of assumptions about what living is, what shopping is. And the market continues to work on the idea of lifestyle through an apparently everlasting succession of campaigns. It is constructing and reconstructing lifestyles all the time. The main thing that lifestyle is about is the consumers' conception of their place in society, their social relations, their persona – it is nothing to do with material needs as such. The possession of SUVs or 4×4 vehicles is about how the owners wish to be seen by others. Few of these owners could support an argument that the vehicle was necessary to their work or the well-being of their family.

Lifestyle advertising involves what is called psychographic research, in which the intention is to profile work and leisure time, interests, attitudes and opinions. People are categorized by sets of characteristics and defined in such terms as 'those who are achievement oriented', or 'those who are driven by the need to belong'. Gough-Yates (2003) refers to a significant change in the way that the advertisement addressed the consumer from the 1970s onwards. These new forms of research attempted to stay 'close' to the customer, to address the individual.

What these lifestyles all have in common is consumption. Audiences already believe in consumption as a way of life. Advertising seeks to fit the nature of the consumption to the particular lifestyle preferences of the consumer group. 'Consumption is now recognised as a defining characteristic of the life-style of the Western world' (Kenway and Bullen, 2001). But, in line with the alternatives of the passive–active audience debate, Kenway and Bullen also recognize that consumers do things with goods. So, in terms of a kind of passivity and arguments about what the media do to people, they assert that:

> It is through advertising and marketing that commodities acquire certain cultural meanings or "sign value" and it is thus that advertising participates in the social construction of our needs.

We are taught to need things. We learn to be an audience for ads. But then they also argue that people may use ads in unexpected ways – 'people use consumption to create identities, social bonds or distinctions'. Ruddock (2001) refers to the 'communicative function' of goods which are 'purchased not only for their function, but for what they say about the user'.

Kenway and Bullen go on to suggest that ads are changing and that the ad–audience relationship is also shifting. They say that there is a 'broader cultural shift to a concentration on style, form and image and away from use-value, substance or direct address'. Who dominates this relationship is another matter, and still a matter for argument.

7 Advertising and persuasion

Advertising is a bit like a gun in the hands of a drunkard on a firing range – sometimes it hits the target, sometimes it does not – as in the famous case of the 1985 Coke fiasco, when market research misled Coca-Cola into marketing a new-tasting Coke, and then had to write off millions of dollars when it all went wrong, and the consumers made it clear they were not going to buy the taste. Equally, although arguments about oppositional reading and the power of readers to appropriate cultural goods and use them in their own interests (for example, Fiske, 1989), have some validity, this does not contradict the presence and effects of persuasive devices within advertising. The form of words and images is constructed to resonate with the psychology of the consumer. Promotion locks into our attitudes and values. Advertising, above all textual forms, does have preferred readings. 'Advertising's first-order function as promotion leads it to engage with values, norms, goals and dreams of those to whom it is addressed' (Wernick, 1991). And of course those values and norms have an ideological dimension because ideology is already in our heads, as much as in advertisements. We may be the more easily persuaded if, as it were, we are ready to be persuaded. We already believe in the 'rightness' of possessing things, of taking pleasure in leisure time, of doing things 'for love', of cleanliness and personal hygiene. It may be that, historically, advertising has been one of the sources of such beliefs. It may be that presently, advertising and the media reinforce those beliefs.

Up to a point one may argue that the point of origin of an ideological position is not as important as the fact of its existence. So adverts for slimming products (always for women) may be linked to myths and ideologies about body shape, which themselves may have some historical location in Victorian advertisements for corsets. There may also be a classic ideological contradiction at the heart of both products in both eras. That is to say, beliefs in health are also invoked: but corsets and the over-use of slimming products (and diets) are in fact injurious to health. They are certainly injurious to clear thinking about one's identity as a woman. The quality of the person has nothing to do with a wasp waist, body weight or body shape. We only think it does. And because the consumer thinks it does, so the conditions for persuasion by the advert have already been set up. Adverts are persuasive because they are based in premises which we are disinclined to question.

Devices of persuasion always have beliefs and values at their heart. Classically, ads are about rewards or punishments – it is good to purchase; it is bad not to purchase – based on core values about love of family, the importance of self image, and so on. It is common to see adverts invoking needs or anxieties which can only be assuaged by purchase. Reading the advert creates an internal dissonance between what one believes and what one is not doing (consuming). So the anxiety or **cognitive dissonance** is relieved by purchase of, say, the baby goods or the medicine, which makes one a good mother or a caring wife.

Jamieson and Campbell (2001) suggest that most adverts are based on principles of identification, differentiation and association. That is – what person or lifestyle do we identify with? What makes us feel different from others? What do we associate favourably with the world of the advert? They point out that salient life experiences such as birth, marriage and death are often invoked. They too comment on how adverts trade on values, and they refer to environmentalism, status, nationalism and love as examples. They also recognize the punishment model, and discuss adverts which invoke guilt. They identify the device of participation in which the consumer is made a kind of accomplice within the world of the advert, through mode of address. They talk about how admired models and even mythic characters are used. In the case of the former, the use of endorsement by sports stars is a common example. They refer to ways in which 'good names' are exploited – the name and image of Lincoln would be a classic example.

There are common devices of cause and effect – where the consumer has, for instance, the pseudo-medical causes of pain explained graphically, and is then promised the effect of pain relief after using the medication in question. There is the common device of juxtaposition, often practised graphically: placing a 4 × 4 vehicle in some beautiful country background juxtaposes two visual elements, but more importantly juxtaposes ideas about leisure and the splendour of nature with possession of the vehicle. They refer to the device of the 'unspecified other'. In this case, one needs to think of adverts which use the comparative argument – that the product or service is 'better than' that of someone else – but that 'someone' is not specified (unless one is thinking of particular and unusual examples of 'knocking copy', where the competitor is actually named in some price comparison).

One thing they do refer to is the use of children in adverts in some persuasive capacity. Of course, children are the specified audience of a certain range of adverts – toys and snack foods, for example. But Jamieson and Campbell point out that children are also targeted in respect of goods for apparently adult consumers because it has been recognized over the past 20 years that children have become increasingly important in influencing adult decisions about certain kinds of sales – most obviously domestic goods bought in the supermarket run.

Schudson (1993) constructs an argument against the persuasive power of advertising: 'Advertising is propaganda and everyone knows it.' As part of arguing this case, he suggests that market domination by a few companies means that people are deprived of alternative sources of information about products, so it is not surprising that advertising appears to work. He argues that received beliefs about the extent of the power of advertising are not borne out by the facts. He suggests that there are few instances where one may identify advertising as the dominant factor in decisions made about purchases. He addresses a range of conditioning factors. So, there is clear evidence that factors such as distribution and packaging are as important as advertising to sales. He points out that retailers prefer to stock well-advertised goods, so it is no surprise that those goods sell well. He refers to the effect of big marketing budgets on the morale of sales staff, suggesting that it is they who actually make the sales happen. Big public advertising campaigns create a high profile for any company, as well as for their goods. So that company sees itself and is seen as a success. He points to the illogicality of setting next year's advertising budget as a percentage of last year's sales – a fairly common practice. And he cites an example of a period in the 1980s when coffee consumption fell at the same time as expenditure on advertising coffee was going up. It seems that people had decided that they just did not want to drink as much coffee as before. He draws attention to the fact that advertising is often a defensive strategy in the marketplace, trying to hold on to the market share rather than actually to boost sales. The Hershey company in USA used no media advertising until 1970, when it finally decided it had to use ads to fight off rivals such as Mars. Concerning the limitations of advertising and misplaced claims for its persuasive effects, as he sees them, Schudson states that 'the capacity of advertising to persuade is contingent on the social and informational location of the consumer'.

8 Commodification

I do not want to rehearse previous explanations of the essential ideas behind commodification and the fetishization of goods, but it is worth underlining various points, such as the fact that advertising refers to cultural as well as material commodities. It refers to the turning of material goods into cultural commodities. As Kenway and Bullen put it, advertisements 're-make the meaning of goods in order to sell them'.

There is indeed a wonderful contradiction behind commodification and the capitalist enterprise of marketing. That is, implicitly commodification needs leisure time in which goods can be consumed – but it also needs work time to produce the cash to pay for the goods (as well as to produce the goods themselves). The use of technology and the exploitation of cheap labour from the developing world makes perfect sense if it minimizes earning time and maximizes consumption/purchase time in the West. But where this leaves that labourer is another matter.

Jhally talks of different kinds of value generated through advertising. In Marxist terms he is talking about the transformation of the practical, material value of goods into something else: 'In market societies, the exchange-value of commodities dominates their use-value.' But he also points out that the notion of objects having a symbolic value beyond their usefulness has been around in societies for a very long time – certainly before advertising was developed. Societies which are not obviously materialistic nevertheless have fetish objects that are valued in terms beyond what they are made of, or what one can do with them. In our market societies it is advertising which has given such a range of goods their symbolic dimensions. Jhally sees advertising as having a social role.

large table and chairs set **£699**

Lifestyles and Consumption
Adverts construct ideas about how we should live our lives: they reinforce ideologies of consumption; and they give life to discourses about home-making.
   What different kinds of lifestyle can you find represented in advertising?
   What may such differences say about advertising, the media and their effects on social relations?
(*NEXT Home Collection Summer*, 2004)

He argues that it creates connections between – person and object; use and symbol; symbolism and power; communication and satisfaction. 'Through advertising, goods are knitted into the fabric of social life and cultural significance.'

Similarly, Kline suggests that: 'goods also locate daily acts of consumption within the continuities of personal and family history, group and national styles, the cross-cutting tensions of work and leisure.' Goods are 'social symbols that can articulate social aspirations'. I would say that it is advertising which encourages that 'location', which generates the symbolism.

Of course, advertising does not just promote material goods. It is about services, corporate images and many more subjects. Nor are 'commodities' just about objects. Lee (1993) for example, identifies 'experiential commodities' which are exemplifed by sport as a spectacle, or by theme parks. These are, of course, promoted through advertising. They are also very much part of lived-in experience.

Commodification becomes as one with living. It is difficult to separate one part of experience from another. However, I would argue that not only can one spot the joins, but also that one is entitled, for example, to criticize the commodification of sport without denying the pleasure of the experience.

Ewen (1977) is cutting in his contempt for what commodification has done in terms of misappropriating values and subverting ideals: 'The linking of the market-place to utopian ideals, to political and social freedom, to material well-being, and to the realisation of fantasy, represents the spectacle of liberation emerging from the bowels of domination and denial.'

9 Discourse, ideology, myths and representations

It is a truism to say that adverts are about discourses. As vehicles for ideologies, they must be. They often invoke dominant discourses of gender and age. Their representations are constructed through the language of these discourses. Car adverts talk through discourses of technology, sexuality, fashion, urban and rural environments and individualism, among many others. The language of advertising depends on the language of discourses because it depends on invocation of and identification with the value meanings generated through the discourses.

And just as there is an interrelationship between discourse, ideology and representation, so also one must place mythologies within this model. One may see myths as false ideas of the false consciousness of ideology. One may see them as the meanings generated by the language of any discourse. One may see them as embodied by the representations which also depend on discourses. The myth of everlasting youth is embodied within visual representations of 'active'; and 'beautiful' young men and women – especially in those ads for age-defying beauty products. The language of such ads actually talks out of its discourses about youthfulness and 'not age' when it uses words like 'rejuvenating'. The myth becomes ideological when it intimates that the young are empowered, socially and culturally, and by implication the old are disempowered. The release of the movie *Terminator 3* (2003), starring the now ageing Arnold Schwarzenegger, condemned to be ever superman, young and fit (with the help of technology), encapsulates such myth-making.

Celebrities and Reality TV
The media enter real lives in order to transform them and re-package them for sale. When people become celebrities and commodities through media appearances, what is it about them (what ideas) that is being sold to us?
(*ITV*)

What is not said in texts is as important as what is said. Fowles (1996) remarks of adverts that 'missing is most of human life work, duty, routines, small kindnesses as well as unpleasantness'. Reality is reconstructed. There is a disjunction between the world of adverts and the lives we live. The work of advertising is to conceal this difference, to construct representations which so permeate our consciousness that they affect our perception of what is really going on. Schudson refers to research that he carried out, looking into images of couples depicted within magazine ads. He identified a frequency of behaviour shown in which these couples were 'invariably attentive to each other'. As Schudson points out drily, this level of attention and mutuality is simply not sustained by real-life couples.

Of course, many adverts do not pretend to be about life, to be real, to act as a social document. But what they all aspire to do is to get inside our heads, to frame our consciousness in a way that is favourable to their clients. As Ewen says when surveying the development of advertising in the USA: 'In the broader context of a burgeoning commercial culture, the foremost political imperative was what to dream.' So, we are faced with a further argument – that advertising and the development of the market, with its representations and discourses, has also been a political and social project. The political vision is that what is good for the market is good for the people, and is good for a happy and stable society. The political problem is that this correlation manifestly does not hold good.

In terms of the reconstruction of social experience and the construction of representations, Kline draws attention to the way in which media, especially television, 'privilege fiction as a cultural form and the fantasy mode of consciousness and expression'. He is referring to texts for children in particular. But what he says could easily be applied to entertainment for older consumers. All modes of realism involve construction and representation. Fiction and fantasy have a particular licence. The success of the *Lord of the Rings* trilogy in cinema (2001–3), or the creation of docusoaps on television, both exemplify this inclination.

Fantasy may not be just about, say, cartoon forms, in advertising and other texts. It is also about idealization and myth-making. Cartoon promotions for a cereal (such as Rice Krispies), involving invented characters, are a kind of fantasy. But then so was the Gold Blend series of coffee adverts on TV, in the early 1990s – this was fantasy romance. Family life in the television programme *The Fresh Prince of Bel Air* is another kind of fantasy and myth-making. I am not saying that there is no difference between adverts and other kinds of texts. But I am trying to draw attention to their similarities, their connections, and to a critical line of continuity which links them.

One might ask if there is any real difference between the self-absorption of women in, say, the Gaultier perfume adverts of 2000 (witty as these are, showing, for example, the woman as goddess worshipped by young animal men), or the qualities and fantasies manifested in the character of *Ally McBeal* on TV (who experiences her dream moments played out as life).

O'Barr (1994) examines the representation and discourse of race in US advertising, both through historical and contemporary examples. He examines how notions of tourism (as opposed to travel) emerged and were appropriated by advertising. He provides many examples of photographic colonialism and of the representation of racial groups not only as stereotypes, but also as 'others'. Such implicit oppositionality is common in discourses. O'Barr also notes for example, that where non-western groups are shown (in airline adverts for instance), there are subtle oppositions set up between a west which has a history and other cultures which have (only) traditions. The essential opposition is between power or lack of power, as he notes in an examination of adverts using Afro-Americans: 'at the core of this discourse are lessons about dominance and hierarchy, subordination and inequality'.

Goldman and Papson (1998) discuss examples of female representation in the context of Nike adverts. In general terms they argue that, while female representations (in sport in particular) may have largely got away from sexist bodies and the male gaze, still the ads invite self-absorption as much as self-celebration. Even when they cite Nike campaigns such as 'If You Let Me Play', as addressing gender discrimination in childhood with regard to sport, still they are uneasy about the corporate self-interest residing behind the series. There are interesting questions here about the validity of adverts that refer to the empowerment of women, while belonging to an industry which in many manifestations celebrates the disempowerment of women.

In any case, I would suggest that the objectifying and mythologizing of women in adverts has by no means been left behind in the twenty-first century. Substantial critiques offered by Williamson (1978) and Goldman (1992), still apply.

Mistry discusses the 'use' of gender ambivalence in adverts on the basis that 'advertising has become a central socialising agent for cultural values connected with gender'. But she is clear that both images of 'new woman' and ambivalent representations are nothing but a front to confirm the validity of heterosexual differentiation.

' "New" images of men and women merely update bi-polar definitions of gender.' Even where there are apparently transgressive images used in chic advertising, we are not, Mistry argues, looking at a genuinely political challenge. We are actually meant to experience heterosexual transgressive pleasures which, apart from the frisson, merely confirm the heterosexual position from which the gaze is meant to come (http://www.theory.org.uk/mistry).

'Research into the portrayal and use of the sexes in advertising has revealed widespread stereotyping in terms of gender roles and gender traits', asserts Gunter (1995b). 'Stereotyping in television advertising is typified by the way the sexes appear to be allocated disproportionately to different types of product and in the degree of authority attached to each sex in commercials.' From the late 1980s onwards, 'more advertising emerged featuring women in central, independent roles . . . As yet this new pattern in gender role portrayal has been visible in advertisments aimed at adults, while recent research has indicated that adverts aimed at children have remained as gender-stereotyped as ever.' However, elsewhere, Gunter points out that there is no evidence of television's part in constructing children's attitudes towards gender roles. Indeed he says that one has to look at other and social sources of attitude formation.

Johnson and Young (2002) nevertheless argue that gendered representation in advertising is especially important when children are the target audience. 'One main type of image based influence targets gender identity, and uses it to link products to their consumers.' They argue that one can see gendered characters, gendered behaviours and gendered language used in commercials. Toy names may be used as example: – 'Big Time Action Hero' or 'California Roller Girl'. They refer to the gender of voiceovers, to the kinds of voice, to the choice of action verbs and to the invocation of discourses, not least that of power. They argue that gender differentiation enhances market targeting. 'From a marketing perspective, it is also more profitable for producers of children's toys to create separate toys for boys and girls as a way of placing more items in the market-place.'

10 A special case: advertising and children

Children have always been seen as a special interest group in terms of advertising, because of their assumed vulnerability to its persuasive devices. The Ofcom code of practice and the guidelines of the Advertising Standards Association both give an insight into how our culture understands children and the concept of childhood. There are implicit beliefs about the innocence of children, and assumptions about their (in)ability to distinguish fact from fantasy at certain ages. In the case of the assumptions, these are, of course, based on some research. But, in fact, the full range of research suggests that children are much more capable than the advertising regulators give them credit for. Gauntlett (1995), for example, summarizes evidence that children as young as 3 are quite able to distinguish fact from fiction.

So far as childhood is concerned, this really is a social construct. The notion of the innocent child and of a sacrosanct period called childhood, did not exist much before the Victorian period. Earlier on, children were treated like the potential adults that they are, and were inducted into the world of work at an early age. It was also convictions about

Indirect Selling: Of ideas
This box image from a quiz game for children as well as adults actually prioritizes the idea of adult and male. Could this be because of the nature of the game?
     Images on the packaging of games and toys for children quite often represent a certain conceptualization of childhood for adults, of what a child's world is supposed to be for children, and notions of gender difference
     In what other ways do media promote or reject ideas about difference within child-centred material?
(*Gibsons Games*)

education and child employment that created the notion of childhood which we now own. Even playthings were mostly a Victorian creation, especially the manufacture of specific objects called toys. The notion of a child's world built around these toys was also a cultural creation.

     Even then children were not targeted by advertising, though they might be invoked within images as a selling device, especially for domestic products aimed at the wife/ manager of the household. This invocation of the child really took off in the later part of the twentieth century when the influence of children on parental purchases became appreciated – the 'pester power' of very commodity-wise, developing consumers. But the targeting of children, in various age bands, as consumers themselves, only took off when affluence put cash in the hands of young people. Gunter and Furnham (1998) report that in 1997 the 28 million American teenagers spent $57 billion of their own money. A survey of children aged 8–11 years revealed that they received $9 billion from their families, and that they had some influence on $130 billion of parental purchases. This is serious money.

     Kline (1993) notes the change that occurred between the 1950s and the later

1960s, when children's TV programmes were initially underfunded simply because they did not represent a viable market for advertisers. But by 1987 US toymakers were spending $350 million a year on TV adverts alone, aimed at children.

Children had not only become a target for advertisers, having money to spend, but also they had learned how to spend. As Kenway and Bullen say, a child who is shopping with adults from a young age 'learns to be a particular sort of child'. They are being inducted into a culture of consumption. Shopping as an experience becomes a dimension of socialization. Even the fact that parents may use the giving or withholding of material goods as forms of reward and punishment, contributes to this consumer socialization.

Toys for the child market can represent not only cultural positions on childhood and adulthood, but also changes in the psychology of marketing. Until the 1950s many toys not only stood for the gender divide – a miniature cookery set for her and some variety of building set for him – but they also represented a pragmatic connection between childhood and adulthood – some emphasis on role playing. But as the market identified consumers, and the adverts had to be targeted, so at least some toys became more completely assimilated into 'a child's world'. The Mattel Corporation's Barbie appeared in 1959 on the back of market research which led to the toy being constructed as personality, not just a doll; and which led to the marketing of a relationship with the toy. Toys, as Kline comments, became concepts that were ever more heavily realized through TV commercials. My Little Pony, now coming round for the second time, was originally created as the expression of those imaginings which little girls had before they went to sleep (according to the research done by Hasbro).

Advertising and marketing aimed at children has followed many of the patterns of marketing in general. For example, the notion of marketing a suite of related entertainment goods across a range of media goes back to the 1970s and to cinema in particular – merchandizing and tie-ins. Similarly, children's toys might be sold on the basis of creating a 'world', of inducing children to buy the inhabitants and infrastructure of this world – GI Joe, Transformers, The Cabbage Patch Dolls.

Kenway and Bullen refer to a process in which entertainment for children and advertising to children have converged. TV programmes become like commercials. Commercials are mini-narratives. Product placement suffuses child and adult programmes, especially in the USA. Indeed, they go further, to argue for a convergence between the child and the adult. There is a simultaneous exaggeration and collapsing of adult/child differences. There is a creation of adult-like children (clothing for children), and of childlike adults (the computer gaming Playstation is for adults as much as for children).

In terms of the persuasive powers and influence of advertising directed at children, there are unresolved differences of opinion about the degrees of understanding of the audience and about the deviousness of the advertiser. Kline asserts that: 'Research has shown that by five years of age about fifty per cent of children understand the persuasive purposes of advertising. By eight, almost all know that advertising is intended to make them buy things.' So does this awareness of children allow them to resist advertising? Advertisers would argue that persuasion works – but then, they would, wouldn't they? Kline again it is who reproduces a trade advert which outlines persuasive devices which, it is said, work on children. Among these are the following (paraphrased)

- Children like stories which involve fantasy or conflict or mystery.
- Children respond to emotional stimuli, perhaps through humour or action or music.
- children like to see themselves.

Gunter and Furnham (1998), on the other hand, are very sceptical about claims to persuade. They argue that research tends to concentrate on the process of influence, and takes insufficient account of variables such as demographics or parent–child interactions. They suggest that research into exposure to commercials is unreliable in its methodology, saying little about, for example, talk and play during the commercial or about 'zapping' while commercials are on. It appears that below the age of 9, children may well confuse adverts with general programming. But then, by 10, most children seem to understand the message of the advert and how this message is being delivered. Equally, one cannot generalize about child development, least of all in relation to advertising. Gunter and Furnham would seem to be right when they talk about inconclusive and contradictory evidence.

So it is that they conclude that 'the influence of television advertisements on children's consumption behaviour is not greater than that of other factors', and that 'the precise influence of an advert on a child will vary from child to child and from advertisement to advertisement. It has been shown, however, that younger children from lower social classes are more susceptible to the influence of television advertisements than other children.' So it is one thing for Kline to assert that the marketing context has become naturalized as a cultural experience for children, it is another to assert what that naturalization may have led to. Young (1990) talks about the effects of TV advertising to children on

- their knowledge, attitudes and values;
- their choice of consumption behaviour;
- other people (especially parents).

But still it is difficult to make links between advertising and purchasing without, for example, taking into account the influence of the peer group. At one point, Buzz Lightyear from the animated film *Toy Story* (2000) was a must-have Christmas present. But there was little actual advertising. Word of mouth, new media reports and the effect of the original movie, combined to generate a need.

One might conclude that rather than be concerned about the direct marketing of toys in particular to children, one might have greater concern for more diffuse and long-term effects. Among these effects is culturalization into the marketplace. One might empathize with the concern of Kenway and Bullen about, for example, the corporate invasion of schools and of the education process. American high schools have contracts with Coca-Cola: British secondary schools allow specific banks to sponsor financial information and advice, even to offer 'free' merchandising. The concern is about how children learn to think, rather than about what they buy. It is about how they learn to live, as much as what they play with. It is also about how what is bought (by them or others) to play with may shape how they think, how they choose to live.

In fact, we may say that these last concerns for children are equally applicable to worries about the functions and effects of advertising on society in general. There are anxieties about how the weaving of advertising into the fabric of everyday life, not just the stuff of the media, subverts our ability to form objective views of the value of both goods on offer and the social relations which are promoted in tandem with those goods.

11 Discussion extract

6699 It could be argued that advertising is the most influential institution of socialisation in modern society: it structures mass media content; it seems to play a key role in the construction of gender identity; it impacts upon the relation of children and parents in terms of the mediation and creation of needs; it dominates strategy in political campaigns; recently it has emerged as a powerful voice in the arena of public policy issues concerning energy and regulation; it controls some of our most important cultural institutions such as sports and popular music; and it has itself in recent years become a favourite topic of everyday conversation. However, we should not let its enormous presence in a wide variety of realms obscure what it is *really* about. At the material, concrete and historical level advertising is part of a specific concern with the marketing of goods. It rose to prominence in modern society as a *discourse through and about objects*. It is from this perspective that an analysis of advertising has to unfold. More particularly, this discourse concerns a specific, seemingly universal relationship: that between people and objects.

Jhally (1990)

1 How may one sustain the assertion that advertising 'controls some of our most important cultural institutions'?

2 What arguments could you use against the idea that advertising is a highly influential institution of socialization?

3 In what ways does advertising and its discourse intervene in the relationship between people and objects?

12 Further reading

Brierley, S. (1995) *The Advertising Handbook*. London: Routledge.

Ewen, S. (1977) *Captains of Consciousness*. New York: McGraw-Hill.

Goldman, R. (1992) *Reading Ads Socially*. London: Routledge.

Gunter, B. (1995) *Television and Gender Representation*. London: John Libbey.

Jamieson, K. and Campbell, K. (2001) *The Interplay of Influence – News, Advertising, Politics and the Mass Media* (5th edn). Belmont, CA: Wadsworth/Thompson Learning.

Jhally, S. (1990) *The Codes of Advertising – Fetishism and the Political Economy of Meaning in the Consumer Society*. London: Routledge.

Williamson, J. (1978) *Decoding Advertisements*. London: Marion Boyars.

CHAPTER TEN

TELEVISION SOAPS

The question of the gendered audience: the nature of soap operas: the effects of soaps on TV drama

66 Television serials together constitute one of the most popular and resilient forms of storytelling ever devised. 99

Allen, R.C. (ed.) (1995) *To be Continued, Soap Operas Around the World*. London: Routledge.

1 Introduction

In this chapter I want to engage with some textual features of soaps, in terms of their female gendered nature (female protagonists and narrative concerns), and in terms of how these features have 'bled' into much other drama programming on British television. This then raises questions about how far the soap is a distinctive genre and how far it blends with other genres. This chapter will also open up questions about the female reader and empowerment. Arguments were advanced in the 1980s and later, which not only sought to refute the popular view of soaps as worthless trash culture, but which also validated the soap text in feminist terms.

The persistence, indeed the expansion of the soap opera form is some kind of tribute to its attractions and cultural validity. If soaps seduce us with myths, then it will also be useful to examine some of those myths, not least in relation to discourse and ideology.

Soaps were an intentional creation of US radio in the 1930s, seeking to promote cleaning products (and inevitably promoting the mythologies surrounding cleanliness in western culture). Of course the radio (and then the television) networks had a pretty good idea that these domestic dramas would be popular, given the proven success of magazines for women based on key elements such as gossip and problem solving. Just how globally successful the form was to become, could not have been foreseen. The broadcasting institutions needed to sell advertising time. They wanted to sell to women on the basis of women's control of the domestic spend, as much as (in the first place), their personal income.

For the US audience, the idea of soaps is linked with afternoon weekly programmes aime at a female audience at home. For the British audience, the term equally includes early evening shows, some aimed at young people, and all now taking into account, in varying degrees, a male audience. Further, I want to argue that the qualities of the soap opera have spread more widely through mainstream British television drama.

In Britain, BBC television's *The Grove Family*, in the 1950s, was about an ordinary but middle-class family, whereas ITV's *Coronation Street* in the 1960s went directly for the working-class North (however much both were idealized). BBC radio also produced a rural soap, *The Archers*, which is still running.

The 'success' of soaps cannot be in doubt. One programme, *Guiding Light*, in the USA, made the transition to TV and has been running since 1937. During 1987–8 the Hindu religious-based serial *Ramayan* was watched by 80–100 million viewers in India. One particular episode of a Televisa serial was watched in Mexico in 1991 by 70 per cent of the TV viewing population. The productions of Brazil's TV-Globo corporation have been watched in over 100 countries (Allen, 1995).

In critical terms, and with relation to their production, content, structure and consumption, soaps have raised a number of issues (of which more below). For example, there is the matter of their relationship to the lived experience of a largely female audience. There is the squaring of their traditionally low cultural status with their high cultural profile, and with the evident pleasures that women from all backgrounds gain from soap viewing. 'Soaps are the absolute bottom of the television hierarchy, lumped with game shows and professional wrestling in terms of their perceived moral worth' (Harrington and Bielby, 1995).

There are issues surrounding hegemony and ideology, and ways in which soaps may be seen as either subversive or as a gendered ghetto. 'My own struggle (is) to reconcile my pleasure in the genre with my recognition of the form's tendencies to reproduce the repressive ideology of the capitalist patriarchy' (Mumford, 1995).

Soaps may also be critiqued for degrees of stereotypicality in their representations – the buxom barmaid, the moody teenager, the cheekie chappie and so on. But Hobson (2003) argues that soaps' characters are more than just types. She suggests that there is a distinction between being a type and typical ways of behaving. She points out that the degree of screen exposure for the characters, and the succession of episodes, means that they have to be developed and so cannot remain stereotypes.

2 The nature of soaps

As a background to what follows, I would like to propose the following.

1 What soaps are and what they mean depends as much on what the audience chooses to make of them, as on textual qualities. Different audiences, different soaps, different times, all contribute to a range of varying experiences. But to be provisional is not to argue that soaps are without influence or have no ideological significance. Whatever a soap is, whatever its meanings are, exist in 'a dynamic relationship between texts and interpretative communities' (Allen, 1989).

2 Soaps and their readings are full of contradictions or dualities – of which I offer some examples.

 ● Real life, but not real: Soaps invoke a reality experience through elements such as naturalistic sets, probable situations and the authentic appearance of characters. Yet the coincidences of characters meeting or not meeting, the relative absence of

Soap Operas: Key areas
The narrative and generic qualities of soaps have become more common in TV drama. Whether or not this represents some kind of emotional liberation or feminine empowerment is arguable.
(*Graeme Burton*, 2004)

work time on screen, or the thin plot excuses for a character's absence when the actor needs a break, all exemplify ways in which this is not real life.

- Real experience, but still the stuff of melodrama: Soaps contrive to be authentic and extraordinary at the same time. For example, the experience of death and associated grief is for real, and realistically portrayed in such scenes as those with characters waiting outside a ward or an operating theatre. At the same time, soaps will produce melodrama through over-extended shots of the sick person, or perhaps through the emotive juxtaposition of cross-cutting with other story elements (a point of view which of course we can never experience in reality).

- Valuable and disposable: By which I mean the cultural positioning and the consumption of soaps; the way in which they must have value for the millions of viewers who watch every day, and yet will be talked of as being disposable and forgettable not only by some critics but also by many of those same viewers.

- Pleasure and guilt: This relates to the last point, not least in respect of some feminist criticism, which has tried to accommodate feelings of guilt about taking pleasure in a genre that has been branded as cultural dross. I will refer below to positions around the idea that the consumption of soaps is empowering for the female viewer. What I would say now is that there is another duality here – it is possible to argue that soap consumption is both empowering and yet disempowering for the female viewer.

- The contradictory nature of this position may be further exemplified through the yoking of emotional strength with economic weakness. This refers, though only generally, to the female characters within soaps. They often show emotional strength in adversity and in support of others. Yet in a material sense they may be not very well off, without the economic leverage and status that would make them able to match financial to emotional support.

Whatever the moral status of soaps in a television programme hierarchy, there is no doubt about their commercial status. In the early evening slot they anchor scheduling for the evening. As soap-infused drama (for example, *Charles II – The Power and the Passion*, BBC1, 2003) they have become central to audience pulling power in prime time. They are more expensive than some TV programming. *EastEnders*, for example, costs about £130,000 an episode. *Casualty* costs approximately £450,000 per hour episode. But then major drama can cost more than twice this again for an hour-long episode. And for commercial television the crucial factor is that the pulling power makes the advertisers happy.

Soaps and telenovellas are both hugely successful exports. Telenovellas from the Mexican Televisa state corporation have topped television rating in countries as diverse as Russia, South Korea and Turkey. O'Donnell (1999) also refers to the global example of soaps from Grundy Worldwide, makers of *Neighbours* and now owned by Pearsons. This company had four soaps (1998) running in Germany, as well as one each in Italy, The Netherlands, Sweden and Britain.

Soaps, it has been argued by Brown (1990), are special in the way that they are linked to an oral tradition, within a medium that itself favours talk. The genre is about various kinds of talk and gossip, about relations which are maintained through conversation rather than action. Soaps are also distinguished by their strong fan base, by the awareness of and responsiveness to this fan base on the part of producers. Telephone calls, emails, letters on air, in magazines and to the broadcasters, keep another kind of dialogue going about how characters and issues are developed. The very process of writing soaps is an oral one, in that there are teams of writers who talk through ideas before writing.

Although this chapter goes on to discuss soaps in gendered terms, it needs to be said that there are increasing challenges to the assumption that the genre is the 'property' of women (even though it does have features and attractions that are still identified as female). Gauntlett and Hill (1999) ask whether we should still classify soap operas as women's programmes. 'In our experience, students in the 1990s reject these gender-divided approaches completely, finding them bewildering and laughable.' They do refer to figures which show that 'women are three times more likely than men to rate Soap Operas as "very interesting" '. But then they go on to use their own research interviews to argue that there is a large male audience, especially among the young. They say that it is questionable how far gender differences are significant in terms of understanding audiences and their responses to soaps.

'It is felt that identifying women with Soaps is a strangely conservative approach which creates parodic images of both "women" and "soap operas", trapped in worlds of "emotion" and romanticism, and does no service to our understanding of either.'

One might be more cautious about dismissing gender factors out of hand, given the accumulated literature on the subject. Equally it is fairly clear that there has been a shift over the past 20 years, in which, for example, the producers of *EastEnders* clearly made a pitch for a younger audience, including males. They introduced male characters and constructed storylines around them. This shift has been paralleled by the arrival and popularity of the 'Teen Soaps', coming from Australia, the USA, and some home grown (such as *Byker Grove*, BBC, set in the north-east and placed in the younger viewers' slot).

3 Major questions

1 How may one define the distinctiveness of soaps, especially in terms of narration?

2 To what extent may one define soaps as gendered texts?

3 In what ways has the soap form infused other drama on television?

4 What are the arguments for soaps having achieved a kind of social realism?

5 Does the soap empower women in any ways, or does it provide another means of ideological containment?

6 What are the pleasures of soaps?

7 How may these be undercut by a process of myth-making?

4 Defining soaps – the quality of soap opera

66 99 The essence of soaps is the reflection on personal problems, and the emphasis is on talk not action, on slow development rather than the immediate response, on delayed retribution rather than immediate effect.

Geraghty (1996b)

In the first place, and in the global way of things, one needs to make some distinction between the soap opera, with its so-called endless narrative, and the telenovella, emanating from Latin American countries. These latter are distinctive for having a narrative closure or resolution, even if it does take 200 episodes to reach this. O'Donnell (1999) distinguishes between one type of telenovella coming from Brazil, which tends to deal with issues of the day, and another type coming from Mexico or Venezuela, which tends to deal mainly in the currents of emotion within relationships. He suggests that the telenovella is characterized by being one ongoing 'story', whereas soaps are a series of stories. In either case, the form embraces large casts, lead female characters and multiple storylines.

It may be argued that the similarities between soaps and telenovellas are more frequent and significant than are the differences. Issues raised about female viewing and pleasures are held in common. Narrative distinctions between these overlapping forms seem insignificant when one is into the hundred and something episode of a telenovella. The telenovella runs for five or six days a week over some six months before achieving its closure. In any case, there are arguments for saying that soaps do not actually lack closure, even if they are clearly not the kind of packaged and closed text exemplified by the average Hollywood feature film.

Characteristics of soap opera

Drawing on a number of sources, including Brown (1994) and Allen (1995), one may summarize the characteristics of soaps as follows:

- stories dominated by female characters, some of them strong woman types such as 'the matriarch' or 'the bitch';
- male characters who are 'sensitive men' or who are weak, and/or who are lacking in social skills and articulacy;
- a large cast of characters, polarized round a few core families;
- stories located in places which allow for social interaction and which include occupations which positively require conversation, e.g. homes, pubs, launderettes, cafes;
- a construction of screen time which more closely matches real time than other genres, partly by referring to real life cultural occasions such as Christmas. Soaps are all about the present;
- multiple storylines rapidly cross-cut through parallel editing – often abruptly and on the assumption that the viewer knows enough to keep up with what is going on. This is also described as segmentation;

Family Mythologies
Soaps are ideologically conservative in their promotion of the extended family, which nevertheless is often dysfunctional and riven by conflict.
   What are the key features of family life and family interactions represented through soaps?
   How do these match evidence of the nature of families as evidenced through research and through surveys such as Social Trends?
(BBC)

- in Britain, stories which implicitly recognize a class system, and which are often located within working-class culture (or rather a mythologized view of what working-class culture is);

- a serial form in which the narrative resists closure: indeed encourages continuity and viewer anticipation from episode to episode and week to week;

- the capacity for reversing events. This is far more common in US soaps than in British examples. It refers most obviously to instances where dead characters have been brought back to life through some (improbable) plot device;

- an emphasis on relationships, problems and dialogue, rather than action – especially these within family or of a romantic nature;

- a lack of reference to real life and specific events which might draw characters into ideological positions. (So it is one thing to debate issues around abortion or homosexuality, for example: another to open up discussion about British support for American foreign policy, or even reference to a train disaster);

- a long and complex history (after a few years) which demands much commitment to the soaps on the part of the audience/fan if they are to keep up with all the nuances and implications of the ongoing story.

I now want to deal with at least some issues and consequences stemming from the list above.

5 Soaps and narrative

Open and closed

Much has been made of the open-ended nature of soap narrative. It is the 'never-ending story' which matches the never-ending flow of television material. It is all about the serial as opposed to the series. The supposed lack of closure implies that problems are not solved, that resolutions are not reached in terms of issues raised. This is not true. Marriages and deaths take place. Relationships end. Deceits are uncovered and the consequences worked through. What is true is that the closure of one narrative strand leaves other strands open. The culmination of a relationship in a definite act of marriage closes one phase of that relationship, but opens up another. Characters leave the soap, but others continue and new ones arrive.

The notion of closure and the absolute end to a story is in fact quite a strange notion. Some would say that it is a masculine conceit that life is about events and actions as much as people, and that actions may be final. Even in the case of closed narratives – the villain is caught and punished – one may argue that one can conceive of the story going on. Closure is a piece of representational trickery. Even in the case of action adventure plots, there are interlocking characters with lives that might be teased out if the producer or the audience so chose. So one can say that the soap genre actively exploits the continuity that is implicit within all narratives. On the one hand, one may agree that the mere existence of multiple episodes of the story, week on week, and multiple strands within these episodes, makes soaps special within the sphere of story-telling. But one may equally disagree with the view that nothing is ever settled or finished within the soap form.

The debate raises questions about what one means by closure, anyway. So, for instance, a romantic relationship between two characters in a soap may be 'resolved' by their marriage. But the larger story about these two will go on. The device of closure may be in part occasioned by texts which have a last page and a last minute. Soaps do not have this pressure. I am suggesting that they do have kinds of closure to given story strands, but never an absolute end to the 'whole story'. Indeed, there is a nice tension between the pleasure of achieving some kind of resolution and the pleasure of having a continuing story.

Mumford and others would argue that non-closure is a feminine trait and is subversive. Nochimson (1992) suggests that linear syntax is masculine, and is opposed to feminine discontinuous and elliptical syntax. Soaps do not have main plots and sub-plots, only multi-plots, any of which may predominate for a time. Allen (1989) interprets Modleski (1982) when he describes a gendered narrative: 'a feminine form of narrative structure, which inscribes its reader as ideal mother, values dialogue over action, disperses the viewer's attention over large extended families of characters, and forever retards ultimate resolution'.

Mumford also argues that what closures there are, assert moral and ideological imperatives. In other words, they endorse the primacy of beliefs in romantic love or family, for example, 'Closure helps to manage women's discontent.' So she might say that hegemony is at work. Certainly this view about dominant ideology and closure would support an argument that soaps only appear to be subversive, but do not actually operate in the interests of women at all.

Scales of narrative

O'Donnell (1999) takes a formalist and structured approach to describing *different* scales of narrative in the soap, summarized as follows:

1 micro-narrative: which deals with relationships between characters;

2 meta-narrative: which most frequently deals with issues such as race and drugs; which less frequently deals with AIDS and lesbianism, for instance; and which is least likely to deal with poverty and unemployment;

3 macro-narrative: which embraces the notion of the kind of 'mini society' being created – i.e. it may be characterized as being working class;

4 trans-narrative: the scale of which is the sum of all soap stories seen at one time;

5 hyper-narrative: refers to a similar scale of collective stories, but to those seen over a period of time.

Clearly here we have related points about implicit value judgements regarding social deviancy thrown up through the meta-narrative; about intertextuality and genre spinning off the notion of the hyper-narrative.

Other

Tulloch (2000) refers to the way that the soap viewer knows a lot about narrative, yet is not in control. The fan will be familiar with the genre, and will know the history of a given soap. They can draw on this knowledge to predict the narrative. And yet, whatever power this seems to give them is checked by the fact that, in the end, they cannot change the narrative.

Gripsrud (2002) would prefer to emphasize within narrative the primacy of dramatic structure over plot order. He refers to the 'emotional kicks' enjoyed by the audience, to the shaping of the dramatic structure to fit programme breaks and the end of episodes. Such is this emphasis on drama over event that he calls it 'a sign of the dissolution of narrative'. Certainly this would fit a notion of the post-modern text, in which plotting is less important than form and effect.

6 Soaps and social realism

The continuous production commitment to the soap raises another point about realism and time. By being broadcast two or three or more times week, soaps are given the capacity to mimic the continuity of life, to appear real. This is what Geraghty (1996c) refers to as 'the notion of realism as a plausible picture of everyday experience'. She also quotes Julia Smith, original producer of *EastEnders*, as saying, 'we don't make life, we reflect it', and Phil Redmond, producer of *Brookside*, as saying, we want to make 'programmes that tell the truth and show society as it really is'. Clearly, there is a production commitment to social realism.

This reality is enhanced by an investment in authentic sets – the famous Granada *Coronation Street* set – and sometimes by location work – *EastEnders* goes to Spain for two weeks. It may be said that all this is part of the realist urge in the history and culture of British television. It has nurtured documentary, created docudrama, developed outside broadcasts.

On the other hand, while it is true that the bedrock element of conversations in soaps is largely shot and cut to follow real time, equally, one half-hour episode is having to compress the events of perhaps a whole day. One episode is rapidly repositioning the viewer in relation to six or more narrative strands. Events and even conversations may be referred to and not actually shown.

So realism is still a process of illusions, however much viewing is woven into the leisure patterns of viewers' lives, and however much the lives of characters enter the lives

Naturalism, Location, Context
Naturalistic locations underpin the illusion of social realism in soaps.
  How, may it be argued, do such features of soaps promote mythologies about community and class?
  In what ways may this be in the interests of institutions or of audiences?
(*ITV*)

of viewers as they are discussed and relived among fans and friends. Harrington and Bielby (1995) go so far as to say: 'Soaps' appeal can be explained in part by their virtual reproduction of the substance, form, and rhythm of everyday life.'

Yet, apart from the fact that media representations do not, by definition, reproduce actuality – this idea is questionable in that it generalizes about the notion of 'everyday life', not least for the female subject. Soaps produce a seductive version of everyday life. They trade on a manufactured mythology about the 'realism' of 'working class' experience. In this sense, the British soap, with its emphasis on working-class worlds, is fairly distinctive. Geraghty (1996c) talks about the way that British soaps place a value on 'the representation of working-class life and an exploration of the problems caused by social change'.

These working-class characters, having ordinary jobs and usually seen in ordinary places, come out of the so-called 'kitchen sink' drama and novels of the 1950s. British culture has constructed a rather strange, even anti-snobbish view that somehow the lives of those in modest jobs (and especially if they come from the North) are more real than the lives of those who are better off, who hold managerial posts, who evidently live in some comfort. It was noticeable that the teen soap *Hollyoaks*, which started out as a relatively middle-class affair located in the comfortable city of Chester, was repositioned as something more 'downmarket' and with the inclusion of more working-class characters and locations. Even the actuality of Brookside Close, built for the eponymous series, rather falls apart when one reflects on the fact that one never sees Liverpool, just down the road.

All this in itself raises interesting questions about the relationship of the audience to the text, in respect of this culturalized realism. One view might have it that the more affluent viewers are engaged in a kind of class colonialism, gawping at the goings-on within the exotic working class. More plausible is that perspective which sees soaps as a site of struggle over the identity of the family, and as a focus for aspirations to retrieve the myth of the strong and united family – a quality ascribed to 'ordinary folk'. In fact this view would be just as applicable to older US soaps such as *Dynasty*. They were partly about aspirations to, and myth-making about, a certain kind of material lifestyle. But they were also about family loyalties and coherence, as well as about schisms. The archetypal piece of mythology and nostalgia about the family was of course *The Waltons*, on US TV – about down-home folk who always pulled together to heal threats to and breaches in the family.

At the same time, one may recognize that while ideological realisms about the central place of the family may cross cultures, still, different cultures may produce different notions of realism. One may compare examples of the telenovella with the 1980s US soap, *Dallas*, or with the more contemporary *Friends* – which itself raises questions about the line between soaps and sitcoms. Peter Salmon, a BBC scheduler (in Hobson, 2003), asserts that 'It's not just a Soap, it's a way of taking a health check on society and its issues as well.' This a bold claim indeed.

Allen (1995) recognizes a kind of realism in the 'potentially controversial and contentious social issues' which soaps can raise. But he then admits that they do not have to 'make any ideological commitment to them'. In any case, it is one thing raising issues which may have a general currency in social exchange, but it is another to work with contemporary political events. The selective realism of soaps improbably avoids such events, perhaps because it would be difficult for them not to make some ideological commitment. Their world becomes a parallel universe in which one even has no idea what government is in power. It is a tangential reality in which melodrama rather than actuality is the key to finding a mode of realism through which to understand soaps.

Geraghty (1995) argues that some soaps are more realist than others, and argues that *Brookside* (in 1982) and *EastEnders* (in 1985) started a serious approach to dealing with social issues, as well as trying to appeal to a young male audience. They attempted 'to deal realistically with difference and conflict'. She suggests they try to challenge cliché notions of family entertainment (as with the murder of Trevor Jordache in *Brookside*). She suggests that they try not to idealize, even when depicting family life. However, Ang and Stratton (1995) are far more robust in questioning the realism of soaps when they describe it as the realism of bourgeois ideology. For them the nuclear family, seen in soaps, is the cornerstone of this kind of realism. It is 'the ultimate legitimacy and authority of the prevailing moral order'.

It is a problem that realism can be pulled in so many directions. Female viewers may identify in some respects with the realism of the experience of characters on screen – a kind of emotional realism, perhaps. But then this does not square with realism as probability – consider the frequency with which soaps' characters hold back information or fail to ask the most simple questions that would lead to revelation and the end of false dramatic tension. Ideological realism raises yet another set of problems with soaps, in which believing in the plausibility of a situation or the authenticity of a character is one thing, but accepting the ideological truth of the narrative is another thing. A structurally open narrative may still be ideologically closed.

Hobson (2003) argues that soaps are true enough for their audience. They may be representations, but they bring out truths even if they don't reproduce life. 'It is an affirming genre, and the audience responds to the productions by recognising that affirmation and completing the circuit of production by accepting the version of their lives which the Soap Opera presents.'

7 The 'soaping' of TV drama

British television programming has long been anchored in the early evening (7.00 p.m. to 8.00 p.m. start) by the audience-pulling soap operas. *Coronation Street* (ITV, urban North), *Emmerdale* (ITV, country heartland) and *EastEnders* (BBC1, set in London) often top the ratings in a given week, pulling in about 15 million viewers. ITV also resuscitated the motel based soap, *Crossroads*, in 2000 (5.00 p.m. screening), which is being revamped in a camp, melodrama format in 2003 – an interesting reflection on the nature of the genre and on its parodic potential. Most interesting in audience terms is that Channel 4 axed its declining realist northern set soap, *Brookside*, at the end of 2003, having already moved it into a late evening graveyard slot. The channel now relies on its 6.30 p.m. screening of the teen-soap *Hollyoaks*, three times a week. And Channel 5 blocks out its entire weekday schedule at 6.00 p.m. and 6.30 p.m. with the youth-oriented *Home and Away* and *Family Affairs*.

In the context of ITV's declining audience share and concern over its advertising

The 'Soaping' of Prime Time Drama
Qualities of melodrama and priorities of emotional action are now common in mainstream TV. Characteristics of the soap genre – not open-ended narrative though – have bled across into drama, talk shows and actuality material.
　　　Do you think this process has happened in any ways with other media?
(Shed Productions/ITV)

rates, these changes in the positioning of the staple soaps says something about a changing market. I suggest it also has something to do with the soaping of TV drama.

By this, I mean that over the past ten years there has been a noticeable infusion of soap qualities into prime-time television. One might say that this has made the qualities and the position of the early evening soaps a little less distinctive and strong. This soaping of TV drama has also been evident in US television, where it cuts across genres. *Hill Street Blues, Frazier, The West Wing*, like soaps, have all been pivoted on a particular location, have involved a core but wide cast of players, have addressed relationships and emotions as much as events and actions, and have a degree of open-endedness, of continuity from week to week.

The same thing can be seen in British television. If one looks at the nature of the drama in many series, their casting, their themes, then often one sees what have been described as female preoccupations for female audiences. One also has to remember that there are considerable male minorities viewing these dramas and the mainstream soaps – 30 per cent is common. Be that as it may, there is a wide range of programmes that one may cite as picking up the soap banner. *Heartbeat* (ITV) is ostensibly a nostalgic police series, set in archetypal English countryside in the 1960s. *Footballers' Wives* (ITV) is gossip drama about infidelities and a certain lifestyle – a short jump from the tabloids to the screen. It centres around certain couples, certain houses, a certain aspirational lifestyle, in which the players are ordinary by virtue of being bourgeois and well-off.

It cross-cuts subplots. It uses the subject matter as an excuse for providing soft porno shots for a female audience, often in the showers. *Playing the Field* is also for a (heterosexual) female audience, but is referenced to a female football team, so there are few shower shots. But a lot of it is about talk, about an emotional landscape, about relationships. These are not ' "open" serials' which 'trade narrative closure for paradigmatic complexity' (Allen, 1995). They are episodic to a degree, but some story lines and characters provide a degree of seriality from week to week.

Two Thousand Acres of Sky (BBC1) was a soap drama (third series, 2003) which was driven by the seriality of a story line in which the audience knows that the two main protagonists should be in a relationship – but everything, including their own uncertainties, conspires to get in the way. Meanwhile, each episode also had closure, as some other problem involving other relationships was resolved. All this contradicts the idea that an entirely open-ended narrative is a key marker of soap. In this case it is, rather, about the generic elements of location (a small community on a Scottish island, a farmhouse, a cottage, the bar of the only hotel); of permutations of relationship between a set cast of characters (the incomers, the hotel owner, the crofters, the fishermen, the ferryman); of conversation as much as action; of emotional/social issues (the bringing up of children on the island). Characters die or get married, as in all soaps. Some appear and disappear. It is relevant to note that the female protagonist who is 'trying to get away from it all' is played by the actress Michelle Collins, who in 1999/2000 starred in a holiday reps drama/soap called *Sunshine*, and who was in *EastEnders* until 1998.

Hospital dramas

Hospital dramas have long provided another take on the soap form, from *Dr Kildare* in the 1960s, onwards. Hobson (2003) asserts that dramas such as *Casualty* are series rather than a serial, and cannot be considered as soaps. But I would argue that programmes such as *ER* or *Holby City* or *Casualty* do have generic qualities of seriality, continuity of characters and actions, plus several story strands per episode and an ensemble cast. They foreground romantic relationships and melodramatic life-threatening problems, as well as the realist representation of medical procedures. One of the more interesting issues they throw up is about the role of males in the drama. There is a high proportion of expert males with status, who are the object of romantic attraction for women. On the other hand, any of the males may be shown as needing 'lessons' in emotional intelligence from a female character, regardless of status. In other words, female social life skills are shown to be as important as male material medical skills. Melodrama provides a heightened emotional impact. Women are empowered through their possession of life skills.

Docusoaps

Another example of soap infusion is the docusoap. *Airport* has been running for a number of series (ITV1). Ostensibly part of reality TV, the cast are real airport workers, the location a real airport, the events involve real passengers and real problems. But the shooting and editing concentrates on interactions. It turns the workers into a familiar ensemble of players. It focuses episodes on conflict and human problems. It prioritizes entertainment over social comment and information about the real background and related issues. It is all about character and personality, and, indeed, turns the workers into celebrities.

The form has its origins in specific fly-on-the-wall documentaries such as Paul Watson's *The Family* (1974) and *Sylvania Waters* (1993), set in Australia. It relates to developments in technology – cheap digital cameras and sound equipment that makes this kind of actuality footage possible. It has also been used for secret filming in investigative documentaries such as *Macintyre Undercover* (2001). The commercial attraction is that docusoaps can achieve relatively large audiences. *The Cruise* (1997) or *Vet School* (1998) sometimes pulled in 10 million viewers an episode. What these programmes also offered a female audience was the dramatized vision of Jane McDonald and Trudi Mostue as (respectively) entertainer and vet having their lives transformed. As with a straight soap, the interface between life and TV representation was made permeable. And women were shown as succeeding in their own right.

Examples such as *Loverats* (ITV, 2003) show how the 'women's talk' of chat shows can be fused with such talk in docusoaps. There are arguments here for seeing a feminizing of mainstream television. But this does need to be understood in the context of a broadening of channels and of choice – which includes distinctly unfeminized channels devoted to sport. One has to be equally careful about generalizations concerning a female audience, when even soaps have a substantial minority male audience. Brown (1994) reports on a survey made in 1988 into daytime soaps in the USA, which showed that they had a 30 per cent male audience, 45 per cent of whom were aged 18 to 34. Forty-four per cent of the female viewers worked either full time or part time (for further comment on docusoaps see also Burton, 2000, pp. 156–9).

Soaps for the young

It is interesting to see that, even while soaps have a broad appeal across age groups, still there are some which are targeted at the younger viewer – a phenomenon of the 1990s onwards. *Hollyoaks* (Channel 4), with its young cast, is an obvious example, though *Grange Hill* (BBC) has been running since the 1980s. Although initally seen as children's programming, set in a comprehensive school, it is in effect a soap, with all the genre characteristics in place. Indeed, some of the original protagonists, as they grew up, ended up in the adult soap, *EastEnders. Home and Away*, from Australia, (Channel 5) is another 'young soap'. So is *The Fresh Prince of Bel Air* (BBC2), from the USA, and still being repeated.

And when one looks at soaped drama, here too there are examples like *Buffy the Vampire Slayer*. This is a hybrid with the horror genre. It can be related to the Point Horror books, which have a considerable female readership. *Buffy*, like those books, is about the occult, mystery, female identity, female relationships, and a positive female protagonist. Although it is a series, and not continuous, there is an underlying seriality as we see the characters get older and move on to college. The house, the town, the school/college are typical of soap locations. They allow for a lot of talk. And while some of this is about planning for bouts of action, some is about feelings and motivations. There is an ensemble cast including the characters Willow and Xander who are Buffy's friends, and the 'sensitive male' watcher, Giles. There is at least some narration from a young female point of view. And certainly the female protagonist (as well as some other females from time to time) is a metaphor for female empowerment. She is a young, active female who fights evil, and gets an education. She cares for her appearance, but also cares for others.

8 Soaps as gendered genre

'Soaps are described as being centrally about personal relationships and emotional dramas' (Geraghty, 1996a). Literature on the soap opera makes much of the fact that it is a genre which appears to be dominantly about women and for women. 'Soap Opera is about women and desire', it 'dramatises an innate gender distinction' asserts Nochimson (1992). She says that 'the desire for intimacy propels the storyline onwards'. Soaps are about trust, about emotional proximities, about developing and securing relationships.

Allen (1995) identifies three kinds of relationship: those of kinship, of romance and those which depend on social bonds. He speaks in ideological terms when he describes white heterosexual characters as being able to move freely through these categories – where blacks and homosexuals cannot. He says indeed that they are 'invisible'. This is less true for British soaps, where all of them have included at some time ethnic minorities and gay characters. (However, inclusion says nothing about how such characters have been represented.) And as Hobson (2003) points out: 'No characters from ethnic backgrounds have remained as long-standing characters.'

Soaps share the preoccupations of girls' magazines, or romantic novels, of melo-drama in movies – which, among other things, are about feelings, about the state of relationships, about security and insecurity, about nuances of social behaviour, about personalities, about the uses and effects of talk. The emphasis on relationships is mani-fested through an emphasis on talk and on non-verbal behaviour. This itself matched by the use of the close-up, which allows the viewer to read the face in detail. Apart from the domestic concerns of some story lines, to which the female reader can relate, the talk about feelings is also part of self-disclosure. Women are more likely to disclose than men are. They feel more positively about doing this – in other words, it is not necessarily a sign of weakness. And disclosure is a factor which produces trust and bonding in relation-ships. So there is unarguably a gendered depiction of interpersonal skills in soaps, espe-cially as many of the males (but not the 'sensitive male' characters) are shown to lack these skills.

Mumford argues that soaps are addressed to a female audience in the sense that they require 'a set of knowledges and skills normally associated with women in patri-archal culture' (although there are further assumptions here implied by the author about the cultural position of the female audience).

The world of soaps is significantly a social world in which female social skills are seen to be of advantage. It encourages reflection on those skills, in that it raises questions about relationships and motivation, interrupts their narrative exposition and does not provide answers before even more questions are raised. I have heard discussion about these taking place in my local shop. This is the same phenomenon of audience participa-tion and discussion which Hobson (1982) writes about, with relation to female office workers in Birmingham. 'Soaps at once rely upon women's socialised skills in attending to the needs and desires of others and further develop those skills' (Kaplan, 1992).

Reception studies

Reception studies of women reading soaps place some emphasis on the idea of the shared experience. In one instance, Seiter *et al.* (1989) report women as watching a soap

Strong Women
The matriarch is a powerful icon of soaps, offering models of emotional intelligence, social power and control of domestic space.

In what ways do such female representations challenge or confirm the positions of a dominant ideology? (ITV/BBC)

together 'over the phone', talking through the viewing experience as it happens. Modleski (1984) and others suggest that the soaps matches domestic experience: the interruptions to dramatic development that characterize soaps parallel the interruptions of their domestic experience. Archer (1992) argues both for the importance of female values and for relevance to the domestic experience when she says: 'If Soap Operas celebrate affiliation rather than the individual, they celebrate not only a feminist priority but also the realistic terms of many women's lives.'

Hobson (2003) says that, 'The concept of a strong woman who copes with problems, brings up her family, supports and enjoys life with her friends, survives when men betray her and sometimes lives happily with a male partner, has become a major tenet of the Soap Opera since its inception.'

In terms of audience identification, Geraghty (1996c) refers to the centrality of mothers as characters, as a prop for others in the face of emotional or practical crises. These characters often have close female friends who also act as props to them in times of crises, not least problems which involve 'weak men'. But one can still be critical and argue that these demonstrations of emotional strength are often of a sacrificial nature. At best the mother may not be protecting herself and nurturing herself. At worst, propping becomes an act of rescue, where in reality the rescued should be shown how to manage their own crisis. One can be talking here about a mythologizing of motherhood, which is not helpful to female autonomy, and in specific instances reflects on a kind of male exploitation.

In this sense, the exploration and celebration of family is also ideological by being a gender dimension of soaps. Story lines depend on splits within families, conflict between families, the extension of families through birth and marriage – the affirmation of the cultural and ideological primacy of the concept of family through occasions such as birthdays and funerals, in which women play a central role. Even though many stories show the family in kinds of crisis, the ideal remains – heterosexual, white, nuclear (but perhaps extensive) families. Contented single parent families do not figure. Characters and behaviours which disrupt the ideal are branded as deviant. Gay people may appear – their gayness becomes a social issue which is explored. But their sexuality is never simply accommodated, naturalized, treated as undeserving of comment. Geraghty (1995) talks of a 'model of an imperfect family working towards a harmonious ideal'. But, of course, the discourse through which the 'working' is explained, the ideal which is implied, is a particular and ideologically infected model. This is not to say that it is necessarily a good model or a bad model – but it is never a neutral one.

Identity

Soaps are about community, romance, sexuality, family and, in various ways, women's identity. 'Intimacy goes along with identity, as the female comes to know herself through her relations with others' (Gilligan, 1982).

These kinds of topic are surely supportive for those female viewers closed within a domestic sphere in particular. As Tulloch (2000) put it, fans draw on a 'competence in the discourses of domesticity'. But then, so many of those viewers now in fact have jobs and external responsibilities that one cannot simply argue for the appeal and pleasures of soaps to be explained through a process of straight identification with a domestic situation. I would suggest that the feminization of the narrative lies not so much in a 'female situation' as in a 'female way of understanding' (and dealing with) given situations.

One could look at domesticity and identity in a more cynical way when commenting on the never-ending story of a female role within family life. The woman's work is never done, the final meal is never cooked, the floor never stays clean. If there is a pleasure of identification for the female viewer, then from this point of view it is one that is ideologically naturalized. It is no part of women's genetic inheritance to become cleaners and cooks. So one might say critically that if soaps offer identification with a domestic role, then they also require an uncritical acceptance of the status quo. If such gendered roles are part of the social realism of soaps, then this realism is also an expression of ideology.

Melodrama

Soaps may also be described in gendered terms because of their qualities of melodrama. Although I would argue that melodrama is a mode of realism, it is also described as a genre, and a genre with a strong female following. Deeming (1990) argues firmly for the value of melodrama, especially in a feminized form.

> Melodrama's emphasis on affiliation, as opposed to individualism (its preference for moral order over the glorification of the individual hero), not to mention its fascination with the ordinary, point to the form's attraction to feminine conceptions of morality [. . .] men tend to see moral problems as a result of conflicting rights, women tend to see moral problems as arising from conflicting responsibilities.

It is interesting, with relation to these remarks, to reflect on an episode of *EastEnders* (13 January 2003), in which it is actually a senior male character who lectures a younger male on his responsibilities both to his wife and to his unborn child by another woman. But the situation is not presented in terms of which woman has the greater or lesser rights in the matter.

Private issues

Geraghty (1991) refers to the ability of soaps 'to open up for public discussion emotional and domestic issues which are normally deemed to be private'. Apart from the 'standard' material of affairs, deceits and infidelities, soaps have engaged with issues such as the lesbian daughter, the HIV-positive son, the husband who has committed a crime, mastectomy and senility in a loved one. A female position vis-à-vis these issues is assumed – it is the female viewer's daughter or son or husband who is 'spoken of'. It reminds us that part of the 'femaleness' of soaps is simply to do with the range of female characters, the screen time given to them and the amount of narrative that is constructed from their perspectives. Females are identified as, for example, the older woman as matriarch, the rebellious daughter, the overworked young mum, the trusted friend, and so on.

Seiter *et al.* (1989) report research in which respondents described their emotional involvement with soaps, and the drawing of parallels with their own lives. The soap opera 'has considerable potential for reaching out into the real world of viewers'.

Hobson (2003) gives a concrete example of this when she points out that after an episode of *EastEnders* (2002) in which a character speaks of childhood abuse, the tie-in Helpline received 5,000 calls.

Also, the understanding reached about the soap is collective rather than individual. 'What we found in our interviews over and over again was that soap opera texts are the product not of individual and isolated readings but of collective constructions – collaborative readings, as it were, of small social groups such as family, friends, and neighbours, or people sharing an apartment' (Borchers, 1989).

The media themselves encourage such response and an illusion of participation by providing various materials. There are chat rooms on websites where one can 'meet' the stars. There are dedicated soap magazines, and innumerable articles in other magazines which breathe 'life' into the pseudo world of the soap. One hears references and speculations from the mouths of talk-radio hosts. Audience participation is an illusion in one sense – viewers have no direct control over narrative outcomes and changes. But then the illusion becomes real in so far as it is part of the lived social world of some fans.

In another kind of study, Baym (2000) has examined online communities of soap fans. She argues for the particular importance of audience communities, many of whom are female. She emphasizes interpersonal relations between audience members, as much as any relationship with the text, in trying to understand the gendered significance of soaps. She proposes that 'the Internet makes audience communities more common, more visible, and more accessible'. She argues that for women viewers of soaps, these 'create a social space, enhancing women's bonds to one another'. They also create 'a community in which traditionally female concerns and values are honoured'.

Harrington and Bielby (1995) emphasize the notion of privacy when they talk about the depiction and use of private areas out of the workplace to deal with private issues.

On the other hand, Mumford (1995) talks about ways in which public spaces are gendered for the working out of private matters. Arguments about a relationship may take place in an office. The revelation of infidelity may happen in the pub. Relationships may be developed in the street. In other words, gender issues and interests so far predominate that social conventions regarding the use and function of public space become distorted from those of our life experiences. People have jobs which require talk. Locations are used which allow talk. The emotional landscape becomes more important than the social landscape. Female interests take over the narrative and its use of background. 'In the Soap Opera world, everything is *everyone's* business' (Mumford, 1995).

Confessions

This gendering of public space and of strategies to deal with situations has much to do with the idea of a 'confessional mode of discourse'. Characters are 'required' to confess, and sometimes need to confess. The drama of confessions is most effectively experienced as private revelations in a public sphere. It is interesting to note once more how this gendered feature of soaps may appear in other drama programming. For example, the series of *Judge John Deeds* (BBC1, 2001–4) exploits this in the context of the courtroom. It also demonstrates other soap features in the drama outside the courtroom, which always involves the judge personally. In this drama, it is the judge who 'grandstands', rather than the prosecution or defence counsels.

The confessional mode assumes that the right to privacy is rightfully denied, in this female-gendered world. Female characters in a female discourse work on the principle of controlling information. They obtain it through questioning or through kinds of spying.

They withhold it or release it selectively. They use it to exercise power. They are represented by the power of the discourse as showing concern and care, when in fact they are simply interfering in the lives of others. This is an exercise of power through the use (or misuse) of talk. Its importance as a female 'tool' is underlined by many situations in which male characters (though not always male), are confronted with their secrets, with unpalatable information. They may be seen as being inadequate in the face of a female exposition, or are simply inarticulate by comparison with the woman. Whether confession becomes a kind of proper expiation, or is actually an improper humiliation is another matter. Either way it confirms an 'understanding' of the expertise of the female in identifying concealment and deceit, and in controlling conversation so as to achieve the outcomes that they want. How far that undertstanding is valid, in what terms it is judged to be valid and whether its outcomes are always desirable is a matter for debate.

Paternity

One especially interesting discussion that Mumford has is about the place of paternity in soap stories. Maternity cannot be questioned – it is manifest in pregnancy, and (at least if legitimate) has something of 'a state of grace'. But paternity, whether as insemination or as responsibility, is certainly questioned through soap plots. At one level it creates plot itself – the mystery of 'who done it'. At another level it creates storylines about identity, about the nature of relationships, about the capacity of men to be adequate fathers. Mumford sees it as being patriarchal when storylines involve questions of status, property, rights or inheritance. She argues that too often pregnancy is depicted as a passive activity in which women are carrying a baby 'for the man'. She says that lies about paternity are shown never to lead to 'true love'. But legitimized paternity is bound up with a vision for the female viewer of a world in which 'women like themselves are in control of the central fact of family life'.

However, I would wish to make links with the section on mythologies at this point. The argument would be that to an extent, the soap mythologizes the status of motherhood and the position of women to represent the ideal of a sense of control at a time when the woman is necessarily feeling vulnerable. Conservatively speaking, one would say that soaps foreground paternity in order to reaffirm its importance in patriarchal terms. But one might also argue that single paternity is made a storyline in order to deflect attention from the fact that (in social reality) women are more promiscuous than in the world of soaps. Paternal biological parentage is less certain in the real world than it is in the world of soaps.

9 Empowerment, resistance, ideology and pleasure

In the first place, notions of audience power go back to the 1980s, and in the case of soaps in particular, to seminal work by Dorothy Hobson (1982) and Ien Ang (1985). Ethnographic approaches to audience studies worked against absolutist notions of textual power and examined how audiences may equally negotiate meanings as they decode material. These studies also identified kinds of pleasure in viewing, as well as the fact that the female audience was not homogeneous. They would argue against simple effects readings, pointing out that there are a variety of 'subject positions' which the viewer may take up, through which to experience and understand the soap text. Viewers may be aware of the 'unreal' nature of soaps, but still respond to them in certain ways.

As an experience for the female viewer, it is suggested by commentators such as Ien Ang (1985), that soaps are about pleasures in the narrative experience, in identification with storylines, in escape, in celebrating a female situation, even a subordinated one. Drawing on Raymond Williams's ideas about 'structures of feeling', she argues that soaps work validly on an emotional level, even if they do not work in terms of realism. The latter becomes irrelevant to the truth of what is expressed through the genre, with all its conventions and rituals. Further, the audience may take pleasure in constructing meanings that are subversive. This is an idea that other critics such as Fiske take up when they talk about audiences 'playing' with texts.

Allen (1995) talks up the pleasure of audience participation. He argues that soaps invite response and involvement because they raise 'unanswered questions' and because they incorporate 'interruptions' to the unfolding narrative – the unexpected guest at the wedding would be an example.

Hobson (1982) in a study of audience discussion of soaps in the workplace, talks about the pleasure of sharing: 'the pleasure which is derived from exchanging views and opinions with friends and colleagues'. Her respondents made active comparisons with their own experiences. Whereas Gripsrud (2002) proposes evidence from his research that shows some women offering an ironic response in taking pleasure in watching soaps. This links with melodramatic qualities and improbability in soaps, as well as their low cultural status. He sees this response as 'a way of legitimating and thus "saving" the pleasures'. This then becomes a kind of distancing, through which the female viewer makes it 'all right' to enjoy the soap.

Harrington and Bielby refer to the pleasures of

- identification and imagining characters as real people;

- entertainment and escape;

- intense emotional experience.

One may dream of true romance. One may feel empowered, at least within the family. But it is, as they say, another kind of **scopophilia**. There is an issue here about whether fantasizing is a temporary pleasure, tempered in the longer run by a greater realism. Or does it becomes disempowering because the soap (and material like it) becomes a device of deferment, because subordination and inequality is never really dealt with? Tulloch also asks whether immersion in pleasure brings the danger of denying a vital 'critical distance' from the text. In another sense, everyday life is myth-ologized. It is invested with a significance and an emotional charge that is a device of concealment. Subordination and inequality is covered up. The dream becomes dis-empowering when it endorse mythologies. These mythologies are themselves idealiza-tions of ideological positions, which work against the interests of women. For instance, one notices that when female characters produce money, perhaps to help sons, lovers or husbands, the amount provided is often implausibly great in relation to the woman's circumstances and earning capacity. The myth of the female provider and rescuer prevails over material reality.

There are opposing arguments about the degree to which soaps may empower women through recognizing the validity of their experiences, or disempower them by recuperating those experiences within the dominant ideology. These arguments also assume on the one hand that there are (questionably) distinctly gendered understandings of the world, and on the other that there is an identifiable (and probably patriarchal) dominant ideology. Rather than be too dogmatic, I suggest that it is reasonable to talk about dispositions of power. It is true that soaps can show women for instance as exerting moral power over errant offspring, as exerting empathic powers in the exploration of relationships. They may exert powers within the domestic sphere, especially the matriarch or the feisty young female. But it is also true that, looking generally at soaps, women's spheres of action and influence are limited. There is a kind of containment about where they live, where they are seen on the social stage, what jobs they do. As Mumford (1995) says, 'women characters almost never achieve money, success, or political power through their own exertions'. There may be something of an argument here about a difference between American and British soaps. The latter have shown women as managers, or as owners of businesses. But still, for the majority it seems that it is an emotional and relationship landscape which dominates. In this sense there is an issue for the female viewer about the relative importance of material empowerment or emotional empowerment. But a feminist view might say that it is very convenient for men that women should learn to value their emotional powers, while being denied other kinds of power. Why – as it were – does one have to choose?

Brown (1994) speaks up in the first place, for the resistive power of the soap form. She describes soaps as an 'irritant to dominant culture', as being subversive of the dominant classic narrative form with masculine closure. Part of her argument is for the 'tertiary text' – that version which is women's heads as they decode the soap and make sense of it in the own, resistive terms. However, her arguments are not entirely convincing when she can also say: 'While the discourse of the powerful seeks to construct reality for women in ways that suit the dominant, feminine discourse constructs reality for women in terms of their perception of the social order in which she is subordinate.' It is not made clear how far this 'perception' reveals the mechanisms of subordination. It is true that recognizing the reality of a situation is one step towards dealing with it. But it is not the same as dealing with it. And one could take issue with the idea that soaps offer empowering revelations, anyway. It could be said that to be really empowered, female characters would have to leave the soap opera space and be someone else, do something else, live a different life in a different way.

Her argument is that hegemony is 'leaky', and that soaps are a place where leakage happens. She proposes that the community of the female audience is the real place where resistance happens. She sees the talk of the fans she interviewed as questioning rather than accepting or confirming their status in the order of things. The debate remains about how far this constitutes meaningful resistance. One could see soaps as a gendered ghetto as much as a space of empowerment. It is often true that the strengths of the female characters are exercised within the confines of the home, the shop, the café, the pub.

Harrington and Bielby (1995) point to kinds of empowerment which have less to do with economic achievement or scope of action. At one level they argue that even the act of watching a soap can be an act of resistance, if the female viewer is choosing this as opposed to, say, domestic labour. More interesting is the discussion of a female discourse and the validation of 'gossip'. To participate vicariously in this kind of talk is to take a kind of pleasure. It is to say that talking about people, emotions, lives, personalities is indeed valid. This is empowering. As Brown (1994) put it: 'discourse networks, or gossip networks, are important for women's resistive pleasure'.

Fiske (1987) also talks about the relationship between pleasure and resistance when he says: 'The pleasure of these viewers in playing with the relationship between the representation and the real questions the power of the programme to control the representation and illusion, and is a way of exercising control over their own viewing practices.'

Others may argue that empowerment can be just about validation. It is OK to watch soaps. It is valid because, however imperfectly, they do say something about the experiences and views of women. 'It offers women a validation and celebration of those interests and concerns which are seen as properly theirs within the social world that they inhabit' (Dyer *et al.*, 1981). Yet again, Van Zoonen (1994) sees these views as being problematic. She points out that if one talks up the positive dimensions of soaps in providing female pleasures, then it becomes harder to go on complaining about and arguing validly against the negative construction of gender identities which are represented.

Altogether, there are questions to be raised about how far one may validate soaps in terms of female empowerment, as well as questions about the nature of their distinctiveness as gendered genre. I would argue that the gendered distinctions are there, but that the separation of soap genre programmes from other programmes has become blurred.

10 Discussion extract

❝❞ Some writers have seen in the relationship created between soap operas and their female audiences the potential for women to defy dominant understandings of femininity and the appropriate position of women. . . . Women's recognition of and identification with the world represented by soaps combines with the discussion and gossip that marks soap opera viewing to create space in which women might express the inexpressible. In this space, it is argued, what Mary Ellen Brown calls a 'feminine discourse' can be established, in which relationships can be discussed in terms of power, and the subordinated position of women in their social roles can be acknowledged by women viewers. In this analysis, the viewer is not merely active in the process of understanding media products . . . but also resistant. . . . Soap operas can be understood not so much as a mass media product imposing a particular kind of representation on women from above, but as a product of popular culture, claimed from below because it can support women's resistance to male domination. . . . The emphasis has been on how meaning is established within the context of domestic viewing and often in talk between women viewers.

Geraghty (2000)

1 What do you understand to be 'the inexpressible' that is referred to?

2 Do you agree that the two ideas of representations imposing meanings, and of audiences claiming meanings, are mutually exclusive?

3 What evidence have you found for the argument that soap operas construct a subordinated position for women?

11 Further reading

Allen, R.C. (ed.) (1995) *To be Continued, Soap Operas Around the World.* London: Routledge.

Brown, M.E. (1994) *Soap Opera and Women's Talk – The Pleasure of Resistance.* London: Sage.

Geraghty, C. (1991) *Women and Soap Opera – A Study of Prime Time Soaps.* Cambridge: Polity Press.

Hobson, D. (2003) *Soap Operas.* Cambridge: Polity Press.

Nochimson, M. (1992) *No End to Her – Soap Opera and the Female Subject.* Oxford: University of California Press.

O'Donnell, H. (1999) *Good Times, Bad Times – Soap Operas and Society in Western Europe.* London: Leicester University Press.

Seiter, E., Borchers, H., Kreutzner, G. and Warth, E. (1989) *Remote Control – Television, Audiences and Cultural Power.* London: Routledge.

Van Zoonen, L. (1994) *Feminist Media Studies.* London: Sage.

CHAPTER ELEVEN

NEWS

Different kinds of news: constructing the world

66 Terrestrial television news is about our relationship to political and democratic processes, our sense of identity, our feelings of safety, our understanding and tolerance of other members of our society. 99

Harrison, J. (2000) *Terrestrial TV News in Britain, The Culture of Production.* Manchester: Manchester University Press.

1 Introduction

In this chapter I want to attend to the unusual position which news has achieved within media output. This will involve revisiting key concepts and laying out critical positions on news, not least as it is meant to represent an interface between the public and ideas about 'the truth out there'. The unusual position of news rests on its mass of contradictions and its special place in social and political consciousness. There are contradictions between

- news as it appears to be an open conduit to a world of events, and news as it actually is – controlled, and constructed through a 'closed' factory system of production;

- news as an apparently agreed general truth about what matters and what must be told, and the fact that across a range of newspapers and channels, across nations, there is actually no agreement about what is important out there in the world. There is certainly no agreement about how events are to be interpreted.

- news as it is at least loosely understood to be about important matters of the day and important people, and news as it actually is – about providing entertainment, about providing gossip, as much as politics;

- news as an apparently objectified account of source events, and news as it in fact is – an ideologically inflected selection and account of such events;

- news as an apparently neutral and expert report, and yet also being a global business enterprise – with all the partiality that must follow from that.

So what follows is something of a critique of the pretence of news. We should not be surprised that news is like it is, given the circumstances of its production. It is not surprising that in various ways it reflects the interests of commercial cultures, of the market, of national preferences, of cultural values. And one might suggest that audiences collude in news being like it is, as much as news operations making it like it is. There is an extent to which people hear what they want to hear, and get the news operations that they deserve. Yet, given the unique position of news media in providing us with information about all aspects of our lives, and of a world that we do not experience directly – and in shaping that information – it is not enough to give a critical shrug of resignation. That would be to collude in an imperfect process. In many ways news is at the political cutting edge of the making and maintenance of societies. So newsmaking should be understood, deconstructed and at least implicitly be offered an agenda for reform.

2 Major questions

1 What may one understand about the constructed nature of news and about the consequences of this?

2 How does news represent the world?

3 What values and practices inform newswork, and with what effects?

4 What is the significance of the fact that one may critique news as, entertainment, as genre, and as being defined and manufactured in different ways for different audiences?

5 How meaningful are the concepts of objectivity and impartiality when one looks at how news is made?

6 How do concepts such as discourse, representation and ideology help one understand news institutions, news texts and news audiences?

7 How meaningful is the notion of global news?

8 Does news material and news presentation contribute to a viable and active public sphere?

3 Defining news

There may be an assumption that the term 'news', as it refers to certain media material, is generally understood and agreed. If something is 'in the news' then it is assumed to be the subject matter of main daily papers and broadcast news programmes. But in spite of the dominance of TV news as a source of 'news', there is no universal pattern of news material or of news consumption by audiences. If a million people read the *Daily Mail* every day, that leaves a lot who do not. Even if 9 million on average watch BBC1 *10 O'Clock News*, still there are millions of others who do not; and not all of these people are consistent readers and watchers. So even if there is a dominant agenda of news items across news media in a given week still this does not mean that all people have the same news experience. It is not hard to demonstrate that across the eight leading daily newspapers in England there is fair variation in definitions of what news is, especially if one looks beyond the lead articles and the first few pages. Even leads will vary, and there is pretty clear division between the hard news of the broadsheets and the soft news of the tabloids. Television (and radio) is not allowed to editorialize in the partial way that newspapers may. Yet even here there are huge variations in what is shown and heard. Radio 1 news bulletins are headlining, populist and tabloid, where Radio 4 and the *Today* programme in particular are much more mainstream hard news – political events and social issues. Channel 5 TV news is populist in its selection of news items, and relaxed in its presentation and linguistic style, where Channel 4 is much more formal and indeed investigative. Both channels are commercial ones. So while one can articulate some general truths when talking about definitions of news, the differences and variations in news are almost more interesting.

Deregulation of broadcasting has brought in a multiplicity of channels, brought to life a variety of audiences and so manufactured a variety of 'news'. 'The news' is not a coherent object of attention. Neither is it as varied as it could (and perhaps should) be. If we believe that we do have an understanding of a coherent thing called news, then that is a false notion. On the one hand, people may well assume that what they read and view and understand as individuals is 'the news'. But that cannot be so because there is this variation – more than one news, in terms of both content and treatment. Our understanding of what news is, what it should be and how it should be presented, assumes a view of politics, an ideological inflection. On the other hand, just because there is a

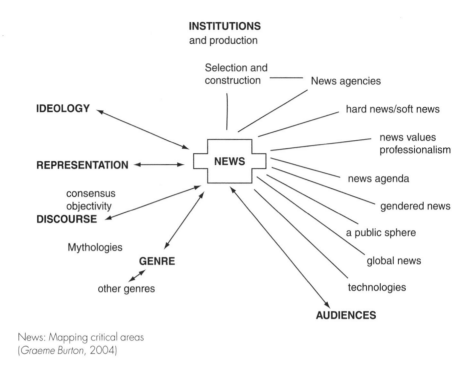

INSTITUTIONS
and production

Selection and
construction — News agencies

IDEOLOGY

hard news/soft news

news values
professionalism

REPRESENTATION ← → NEWS

news agenda

consensus
objectivity

DISCOURSE

gendered news

Mythologies

GENRE

a public sphere

global news

other genres

technologies

AUDIENCES

News: Mapping critical areas
(*Graeme Burton*, 2004)

variety of news content and news presentation styles, this does not mean that news is truly plural. Versions of news can be different and yet at the same time similar in some respects. There are consistent discourses and ideological threads that run through different versions of news. For instance, deaths as a consequence of acts of terrorism are usually magnified in news reports – certainly by comparison with the greater number of people who are killed on the roads every year. Terrorism, which threatens the state, is higher up the ideological agenda.

The substance of news has been characterized in various ways by commentators. One example is that which describes news values – the well-known catalogue that is offered by Galtung and Ruge (1970), for example. In this case it would be said that news is defined as being about events and people, characterized by factors such as

- consonance with audience beliefs
- continuity with what is already in the news
- cultural proximity
- elites
- negativity
- personification of what has happened
- size of the event
- unexpectedness

Or there is the work of Herbert Gans (1980), in which he identifies news as being defined in its composition by

- 'actors' who are likely to be known already;
- predictable 'activities' such as crime, protests and government decisions;
- either divisions or examples of unity in the nation and society;
- domestic themes which relate to foreign news (the relationship between America and Israel would be relevant here).

'News is a constructed version of its source material. It is a kind of narrative. It is a media representation. It is a selective version of original events, utterances and behaviours. 'News, like all public documents, is a constructed reality possessing it own internal validity' (Tuchman, 1976).

If news is a 'constructed reality' then it may be argued that it is also bound up with that slippery notion of 'social reality' – that which seems real and true for the society and which shares a certain set of views. Stuart Allan (1997) says that 'news is a form of social knowledge'. One might say that it is shared information and shared understandings about how the world is. But again, one problem is that knowledge which is shared and so included, must presume information which is excluded – other knowledge. And knowledge is not a matter of fact or even of truth, so much as a matter of 'understandings', which comprise ways in which that knowledge is valued and used within social practices. News about football presumes understanding of the place of football within our society. But knowledge of football, or understanding of that place, may not be shared by other societies. Or the very notion of 'football' may be different for different societies, as in, say, England, Brazil or the USA.

We also need to understand that 'news' is something which we gather from a range of sources, not least within the media. Any given newspaper includes elements such as reports, features, interviews and editorials. Any given news topic within any newspaper is likely to be supported (in the mind of the reader) by material on the same topic acquired from other sources. Documentary programmes such as *Horizon* on BBC1 expand on news topics and debates. There are kinds of spin-off programmes and reality shows – *Crimestoppers* on ITV – which cause the news genre to bleed into other programming. But then a street conversation may also contribute to that same topic. Commonplace phrases such as 'on/in the news' promote illusions not only about the coherence of some notion of 'core news', but also about the dominance of the national press or of 'flagship' broadcast news programmes.

Such dominance of certain news providers in the public consciousness, combined with the undoubted control exerted by specific news (and media) producers, conspires to deny a substantial place for 'other kinds of news'. Yet these exist. There are local and regional newspapers. Globally, there are regional news agencies. There are various alternative news providers, from the British *Undercurrents* organization, putting out news videos with ideologically challenging items, to a range of Web-based providers. Manning (2001) is critical of the lack of profile of and lack of access to such sources. 'The obstacles faced by subordinate news sources in the struggle to supply a wider range of sharper (critical) tools are rather more perplexing than is good for the health of democracy.' It is also Manning who criticizes the adverse effects of the reliance of newspapers and many news broadasters on advertising revenue. He points out that the circulation of news, indeed the nature of news, is affected by this. It advantages 'certain kinds of newspaper and particular broadcasting formats to the disadvantage of others'.

It may be argued that the nature of news also makes it inherently ideological. McNair (1998) asserts this both on the larger principle that it is a work of human agency and that, 'as an authored narrative, (it) is at the same time an ideological force, communicating not just "the facts" but also a way of understanding and making sense of the facts'.

He goes on to invoke notions of hegemony and the public sphere when he says, 'journalism is thus an arena between competing ways of sense-making'. It is difficult to argue that news may be defined as anything other than ideological work. It patently brings us version(s) of the world; it brings certain kinds of understanding of the world, and indeed of what we refer to as the truth and as reality. Its material is in part explicitly about politics and the state, and in part implicitly about social politics, about power relations between social groups.

In the same vein, The Goldsmith's Media Group (1999), taking a political economy approach, argue that the news media, 'although a site of social conflict, relays the "dominant ideas" of the ruling classes'. Their view is that economic concerns prevail, given that: news production is expensive, business is the main financier of news and news is a commodity.

4 Hard news, soft news

I have already referred to the fact that often 'proper' news is assumed to be about weighty political and social matters – hard news. It is also assumed that gossip, celebrity news, even the human interest angle on disasters, is just soft news. But from its broadsheet beginning in the seventeenth century, news has always covered this range – from the times of tides to accounts of murder. Soft news sells – as popular newspapers like *The Enquirer* have found out – even if it includes a degree of dramatic licence, or downright invention. As broadcasting proliferates channels, so news for niche markets appears. This is often soft news, concerned with domestic events, with celebrity-dom, with tales of the unexpected. It gets ratings. Even the mainstream providers of evening hard-news programmes, soften the news for breakfast and lunchtime viewers. One might say that in these respects news is simply going further down the road of entertainment. It has always sought to amuse its audience, notwithstanding perceptions of hard news as defining the genre. Victorian newpapers, like those of today, were full of crime stories and lurid engravings. Stories about pop stars, dramatic news footage such as that of the helicopter chase across America in the O.J. Simpson story (1994), celebrity newscasters – these are all about an ongoing tendency in news to want to entertain, to dramatize, to attract readers and audiences.

The supposed shift towards an emphasis on entertainment values (tabloidization) has indeed been deplored, even by newsmakers. The *British Journalism Review* (1989) talks of a downward spiral in standards of journalism: 'the trivialisation of material, vulgarisation, invasion of privacy, squalid behaviour by certain groups of publishers and journalists' (in Bromley and O'Malley, 1997). But one needs to be clear that such a debate about the 'dumbing down' of journalism – and whether this has really happened – should not be confused with discussion about the nature and 'validity' of soft news. Human interest stories do not have to be expressed in simplistic terms, nor are they unworthy in themselves.

It is true that the debate about a coarsening of press journalistic standards in particular, and what is assumed to be a deplorable softening of news in general, does go on. In terms of standards, there are in Britain periodic calls for legal regulation of the

Soft News Headlines
Soft news stories also fit news values. They represent a social world, and celebrity-dom.
    But are they any the less valid for not being about major events, or about political and economic power?
(*Graeme Burton*, 2004)

press with respect to invasion of privacy. Doorstepping of victims of tragedy, chequebook journalism to induce sources to talk about intimate details of the lives of the famous – both are pretty difficult to defend. But again, here the danger is that criticism confuses arguments about the morality of the way that news is gathered with those about the worth of the subject of news.

Critics such as Langer (1998) are robust in defending the validity of soft news. He points out that 'populist, emotional journalism is well established'. He argues that so-called trivial news may in fact be very political. So one could argue that paparazzi journalism is a kind of challenge to the false status and privileges of celebrity, a questioning of the nature of celebrity. The problem here is that the very inclusion of any person – but especially established public figures – in the news, serves to confirm the idea that they are newsworthy and therefore do have a kind of status. This is how news values are confirmed in the ideological consciousness of the audience.

With broadcasting especially, it may be the newscasters and reporters who themselves become celebrities. The BBC's Rageh Omah opted to go freelance (2003) after himself becoming the object of media (and female audience) attention while reporting news from Iraq. He was cashing in on his celebrity status. Macdonald (2003) points out that there has been a shift in news reporting. This shift is about the reporter emphasizing his or her experience of an event and a location, perhaps on an emotional level, to make the piece feel more immediate for the audience. But this then draws attention to the reporter. It creates that danger that the reporter becomes the news rather than what they are reporting on.

Even broadcast news is expanding the soft end of its spectrum – and not only populist channels such as Channel 5 (that has changed its news provider from ITV News to Sky News (2004)). In 2001 ITV1 made a conscious decision to run with more human interest and sports stories, losing its traditional reference to ITN and then re-badging as ITV News. And Langer points out that our notion of 'news' is itself an ideological construct. He says that most critiques of news assume a liberal democratic approach in which 'proper news' provides a reliable source of information for the good citizen. Populist TV news is commonly damned for being a commodity enterprise, for becoming mere entertainment, for providing gratuitous spectacle, for offering too much image and too little information, for indulging triviality and emotionalism, for descending into exploitation of its subjects. But, Langer would argue, soft news secures hegemonic consent as much as does hard news. Disaster stories are designed to restore faith in the idea of a harmonious world, with emphasis on reassertion of control, on rescue, on coming to terms with disaster. He argues that the 'other news' on television is about four main story types:

- the especially remarkable; victims;
- communities at risk;
- ritual;
- tradition and the past.

Contradictions are played out, for example between a world in which the state is supposed to be in control of crime, and yet assaults do take place. We 'learn' to react resignedly to events 'beyond our control'. Soft news endorses the idea of elites. So, one may argue that soft news is no more or less valid as news than is hard news. It performs kinds of social and mythic functions in providing topics of social exchange. It does the same ideological work as hard news. It may be said that the reporting of domestic and private matters concerning Prime Minister Blair or a star footballer, is equally about celebrity-dom and an endorsement of masculine power.

It is also interesting to argue where one draws the line between hard news and soft news (if indeed this matters); where one draws the line between prurient poking around in people's lives, and genuine investigative journalism. It has been commonplace to talk about the tabloidization of news. One could say that one sign of this has been the number of articles about the private lives of the royal family – a journalistic soap opera of celebrity-dom. And yet it could also be argued that this newswork has in fact exposed, to the benefit of society, the various failings of a group of people who hold a unique position of cultural status and privilege. Similarly, although other investigations involved human interest stories which looked at details of private life – the *Guardian*'s investigations (1994–7) of Tory MPs over cash for questions in Parliament and of the acceptance of free hotel accommodation (Neil Hamilton and Jonathan Aitken) – it may fairly be said that these were to the public benefit. Indeed some might argue, given that the Tories lost the general election in 1997, that the news media were exercising power and fulfilling a kind of political function (see the idea of the **Fourth Estate**). This kind of news was about both hard politics and soft gossip stories.

If news has been reframed, not least in its presentation, to make it more accessible to a female audience, then this raises an interesting debate about motives and effects. Is the motive behind 'softened' news a selfish economic one, driven by market interests – soft news sells. Or is it driven by a genuine urge to democratize news reporting? One might say, to take it outside a masculinized, politicized ghetto? And if it achieves that end of greater accessibility, then do the motives matter?

It is argued that soft news is gendered news: human interest stories appeal to a female audience. It is also said that such news is gendered in production because its stories – about celebrities, motherhood, caring – are assigned to female journalists. This is less true than it was fifty years ago. But again, successful war reporters such as Kate Adie have given accounts of having problems in being taken seriously, not least by male colleagues. She has commented on her success being put down by others to use of her sexuality (Skidmore, 1998).

However, if there is an increase in soft news, a softening of hard news – a change in news which feminizes it, in terms of reporters, reporting, presentation, audiences – then this will work to the benefit of women working within news. Van Zoonen (1998) asserts that ' "human interest" has become an integral part of the news'. She argues that a shift towards soft news is market driven. This kind of journalism is, she says, dominated by audience needs, emotional investment and sensationalism, as well as by human interest. And it is this kind of journalism which, it appears to be assumed by journalists, women are especially good at producing. Economic arguments support the expansion of soft news and the validation of female newsworkers.

5 News values

News material is selected from sources and constructed into a text. Sources are dominated by news agencies such as Reuters. Wealthy news operations carry their own teams of reporters and can dispatch these people to events if they do not already have a correspondent geographically near. But many news operations rely on agency sources. All news makers can use stringers, or local sources who are paid by the item. Press releases and news conferences are also a major source of information. But of course, as with agencies, the material has already been selected and processed. Institutions such as government departments or local councils, which have information that news makers want, do therefore exercise indirect control and power over the production of news.

But for all this variety of sources, news remains a made thing. So one may ask the questions:

- Why are certain events selected in and others left out?
- Why are news items treated in the ways that they are?
- Why is it that, within the qualification of remarks made above, news makers may select identical stories on a given day, and often treat the subject matter in a similar manner?

One concludes that certain values inform selection and construction. That which is valued is included. Certain ways of telling stories are valued. Such values may be peculiar to news operations, to the news discourse. They may also be part of more general social values and ideological positions that are shared by other institutions or indeed by society at large. This 'sharing' of values makes it difficult to determine where they are located, where the impetus for news practices really comes from. Because, generally speaking, the public shares a sense of news values with news producers. News agencies are producers as much as, say, CNN. And institutions (and their PR departments) will also understand those values. News values would select in a story about a multiple pile-up on a motorway. But then is this an imposition on the audience? Do they get their sense of values from newspapers? Or should one argue that readers have an interest in such disasters anyway? Is it in a sense audience pressure which induces the papers to put the story in? And certainly the emergency services would expect to have to release information to the press because, sharing the same area of values, they would see this pile-up as an important event in their working lives, and something which needed to be told.

What one is saying is that news makers, like the media in general, are both of society and yet different in certain ways. One is renewing those earlier questions about the relationship between media and society, about how concepts such as hegemony may explain that relationship, about where power really lies, about how far our understanding of the world is a shared construction or an imposition. Certainly it is hard to think outside the ideological framework. But at least understanding what these values are, how they are expressed, where they may come from, enables one to see that there is a framework. Seeing the framework denaturalizes the apparent truths of news and exposes its constructedness.

News values are selective and cultural and ideological when they lead to reporting of deaths in Iraq (in 2003) as

- the result of terrorist attacks, assuming that the word 'terrorist' accurately describes the motives and social location of those who are prepared to kill themselves in order to kill others;
- resulting in the deaths of X numbers of American troops, or embassy staff or of UN officials, assuming that it is normal not to report the numbers of Iraqis killed (or indeed anything about them).

Allan (1999) argues that, while news values are not set in concrete, from time to time or from provider to provider, still they are significantly consistent. 'While news values are always changing over time and are inflected differently from one news organisation to the next, it is still possible to point to these and related news values as being relatively consistent criteria informing these assignments of significance.'

Von Ginneken (1998) offers an interesting five-part categorization of core values in news which is not so much about types of story as thinking about the world within broad areas –

Economic: free enterprise and the free market;

Social: individualism and social mobility;

Political: pragmatism and moderation;

Lifestyle: materialism and autonomy;

Ideological: we have no ideology.

In other words, events will be chosen that allow a story be constructed around these sets of beliefs, the last of which links with the news myth of objectivity. The news story comes out of these beliefs and values, and feeds back into them, reinforcing their apparent validity.

5.1 Professionalism as a value

The illusion of being non-ideological is something which like other journalistic values, is bound up with the production of news and with notions of professionalism. 'The journalist is a professional communicator whose work is structured and shaped by a variety of practices, conventions and ethical norms' (McNair, 1998).

The invocation of the term 'professionalism' conjures up a discourse in which ideas about expertise, codified behaviour, status and reliability are also invoked. These are reasons why people like to call themselves professionals. News produced by 'professionals' is therefore truthful and reliable. Journalists share a culture in which they operate out of standard practices. 'A journalistic culture is produced by and produces a set of consistent formulas, practices, normatives judgements and explicit values' (Harrison, 2000).

Langer (1998) says something similar, but is more explicit about the ideological work of news: 'Through processes of selection, classification and repetition, the practices of journalism produced sense, meanings and interpretations of events which naturalised ways of looking at the world that were implicated in validating and reproducing the existing authoritative and distributive order.'

Allan (1997) also refers to the development of journalistic practices and to a certain kind of journalistic language that came out of the beginnings of Associated Press in 1848. In this case, 'dry language' and 'routinised newswork practices' helped 'secure the codification of objectivity as a normative standard'. Soloski (1997) sees professionalism as an instrument of control used by those behind the journalists. 'Professionalism is an efficient and economical method by which news organisations control the behaviour of reporters and editors.' In effect it incorporates values and working practices which are in the interests of news owners and which are assimilated by news workers. This assimilation is itself helped by an industry-controlled training system and by the press card system, through which journalists ratify the right of others to practise journalism.

This is not to argue that any codified training or invocation of professional values is entirely suspect. But it does constitute a kind of regulation which leads to values and practices that are not easily challenged. Other factors in news work contribute to this. For example, the British Lobby system, by which the Whips of political parties accredit certain journalists, and give them (and not others) access to information, is clearly undesirable. It echoes the British class system in respect of turning selected political correspondents into a club. Its very informality as a social practice makes it difficult to challenge. Similarly, the habit of journalists of covering stories in groups and feeding off one another, is clearly not conducive to critical, independent journalism. But, given that news organizations encourage competition, then pack journalism becomes a way of keeping an eye on the competitor. It is also the case that other working conditions encourage this group behaviour and group-think. Journalists are in a group at press conferences and briefings. The military corral journalists into given locations when they are covering wars – and can keep 'undesirable' journalists out of the privileged pack if they wish.

Of course, one should not imagine that professionalism is uniform, or that formal and informal strategies for regulating news always work in the interests of the powerful. In 1999, the British government could not prevent the names of 117 MI6 agents being published on the Internet.

6 The news agenda

The idea of the news agenda is that news operations tend to consistently prioritize certain categories of news material. Here, there is natural progression from discussion of news values, since the construction of a certain kind of agenda itself implies a value system. It is a commonplace that news values and prioritizes stories that have pictures. The notion of categorization also links agendas to genres. It is difficult to separate matters of content and treatment, when talking about agenda setting. So it may be argued that stories about crime are consistently on the news agenda, especially negative ones. The public is induced to see the idea of crime and issues around crime (for example, the use of guns in crime) as being important. This might be contrasted for example with a lack of a firm place on the agenda for stories about social inclusion – that is positive news about ways in which social minorities (such as migrant workers) are brought into a more equal relationship with the mainstream of society. The presence or absence of such stories implies value-laden decisions. So does the positive or negative treatment of the subject. Indeed negativity as a news value (see Galtung and Ruge, 1970), infuses the content of the news agenda, as much as the content of that agenda commonly includes stories about powerful politicians, for example. And in a sense politicians (and others) are defined as being powerful simply by being the stuff of news. The 'not powerful' are defined by their absence.

The negative agenda is ideological because

- it defines what is meant to be unacceptable behaviour;
- it defines which are to be seen as unacceptable (or deviant, unimportant and not valuable) social groups;
- it defines beliefs that are unacceptable to the dominant ideology.

Asylum seekers are described as being 'on the run' when they leave holding centres without permission: a phrase associated with criminal escapees. But these people are not known to have committed a crime.

In terms of categories of news, Hartley (1982) summarized the news agenda as being about – politics, the economy, foreign affairs, domestic stories, one-off items and sport. This is still a fair account. But the agenda also has particular features. For instance, one will get particular stories at particular times, or in particular eras. So, the reunification of East and West Germany (and related problems) often resurfaces on the news agenda in relation to stories about the German economy or about German politics. The Israeli–Palestinian conflict remains on the agenda at this point in history, not least

Newspaper Front Pages
Different headlines on the same day remind us that there are different versions of news, contradicting the idea of one truth labelled 'the news'.
    Do these differences add up to enough to argue for a real pluralism of news texts, in terms of diversity and choice?
(*Mirrorpix* and *The Independent*)

because it continually generates newsworthy events involving global politics and loss of life.

The idea of the news agenda is important because it helps manifest a structure of thinking about the world. It suggests to news consumers ways in which the world should be understood. News values and the news agenda give form and direction to practices of news gathering and news making. In a sense they legitimize their illegitim-ate normative power. It feels acceptable to see certain kinds of story because that is what one expects to see. It denies alternative views, and in that sense denies real pluralism.

Chomsky argues that this agenda is dominated by the interests of the state. And one needs to remember that the state not only exerts degrees of regulatory power over news, but also is an essential source of news material. The debate over the relationship between news media and state (as between news media and advertisers) is one in which it is possible to argue in both directions, that one is the client of the other, that one is subordinate to the other. 'The mainstream media not only allow the mainstream agendas of news to be bent in accordance with state demands and criteria of utility, they also accept the presuppositions of the state without question' (Chomsky, 1989).

In the setting of the agenda there is a co-relationship between news media and news agencies. The media set the agency agenda in the sense that items they ask for and then choose will tend to be ones that agencies prioritize. Equally the agencies set the media agenda through their choice of topics. Behind all this is the influence of technology – what it enables the news producers to obtain – how investment in it puts pressure on news makers to justify such costs by using the technology.

7 News as genre

News clearly has repetitive elements of content and treatment which the producers may trade on and the audience may expect. What is in the news in any given week is therefore to an extent predictable – contradicting the idea of news as new. Repetitions range from the 'stand up to camera reporter piece' to the editorial/opinion section of any newspaper. As with other genres, production routines can operate, predicated on these expectations. Sources are regularly trawled. TV news has a daily schedule of meetings and news exchanges with other providers around the world. News conferences and story exchanges involving Eurovision and Asiavision happen six times a day, as the broadcast news organizations buy from and sell to one another. Indeed, significant analogies may be drawn with fiction genres. The production base for TV news is little different in principle from that of a soap opera, with a continuous production of familiar storylines to satisfy the anticipation of an established audience. News broadcasts have their long-running mythologized heroes and villains (David Beckham or Saddam Hussein) like any fiction genre. They have stock characters like the 'expert' or the dedicated correspondent. They have repetitive storylines: 'police have recovered drugs worth X on the street', 'plucky mother of four averts disaster when she raises the alarm'. The fact that a news article may be referred to as a news *story* alludes to the blurring of lines between fact and fiction. Although, in terms of trying to preserve the integrity and distinctiveness of the news genre, we should recognize that reputable journalists do base their stories on verifiable facts.

One example of news operations working to routines – the repetitive character of genres – is given by Tuchman (1995). In this case, she is talking about a 'news net' and assumptions made about the interests of the audience. This net works through notions of geography, organization and topic, and is about the rationale behind the assigning of reporters. Geographically, the world is divided into areas that may be systematically trawled for news events. Organizationally, one is talking about the systematic assigning of reporters to those organizations that are known to provide news (e.g. local government). In terms of topic, one is talking about specialization, news departments, the categorization of news.

Genres evolve, and one may recognize this in news, not least broadcast news. Even the heavyweight, flagship evening television news programmes have moved in the direction of entertainment. Compared with twenty years ago, they offer a greater range of human interest stories and personalization of news content and news presentation. One has star presenters who have become celebrities. Many stories are about celebrities. Presentation is faster. Studio sets are 'warmer'. More dramatic content is offered, not least as it is shown on camera. Stories are often shorter, so that there are more of them within the programme. The programmes look for happy endings. These tendencies are more marked when one looks at newer channels and the provision of something more like soft news in broadcasting.

The fact that news may be seen as a genre only matters in the context of what news purports to be. It pretends to be different from other print and broadcast material, not least because it *is* different in respect of its ability to bring us information about the world in all its forms – political, social, economic, geographical, cultural. It assumes a truthfulness and an authority – especially mainstream broadcast news – which is actually dissipated if one realizes that it is just another genre. This diminishing of its status will be endorsed by critical points made in other sections, not least that which questions the objectivity of news.

Consideration of the institutional side of news as genre may alter the perspective taken on the value attached to news within media operations. News also has to pull in audiences and has to pay. It is a commodity with a market value. Routines help keep down production costs. It may be seen as a standardized product with a standard set of values. It has to meet competition in the marketplace. So one can hardly talk about getting at the truth at all costs. News can hardly be all about 'breaking events' and what is 'up-to-date' if it is predictable, and if it depends on factors such as a news editor deciding to allocate resources to a story before there is much of a story. Many events stories are put together after the event, i.e. the news people were not actually there when something happened. Much of a so-called live news broadcast is in fact prepared before it happens.

Gitlin (1980) and others refer to the idea of 'frames' which structure the understanding of journalists and their news material. In some respects one may say that these frames refer back to news values, to the idea of what is newsworthy. 'Frames enable journalists to process large amounts of information quickly and routinely.'

It is production routines allied to routine ways of thinking about news which link to genre, which produces versions of the news that are characterized by similarities, under the appearance of difference. These frames are inclusive, and do ideological work in the sense that they may incorporate some views that dissent from the dominant ideology. Under the guise of objectivity, they manage to contain contradictory views. An example of a frame specific to Britain is that which contains inconsistent views about the National Health Service. Views are inconsistent in respect of simultaneously talking about the need for private and selective funding for health services, and yet also talking about a public and comprehensive service. The frame contains contradictions within a spurious assertion that everyone believes in this service, that indeed Britain actually has a genuinely national health service (however imperfect).

It should be understood that these and other criticisms of news in this chapter, should not lead to conclusions that newspapers and news broadcasts have no importance. To recognize news as a genre is to put it into a context. To describe news as partial if it employs degrees of dramatization like other genres, should be to generate reservations about what we are being told, not necessarily to lead to straightforward rejection of it as a useful source of information.

8 Global news (see also Chapter 12)

It may be believed that global news is with us and is happening now. It is true that technologies allow a worldwide reach of information exchange. There are at least some relatively international 'global newspapers' – the *International Herald Tribune*, the *Guardian*, the *China Daily*. There are 24-hour satellite based news services, dominated by CNN, but including BBC World, NBC, Asia Business News, EuroNews, Fox 24 and others. News stories about different places, events and personalities around the planet can appear on national news, just as CNN has its *World Report*, with contributions from national journalists around the world. Yet it is also true that one may argue that a global news service only exists in part and only serves sections of the population of this planet. One has to ask questions about who is able to view *World Report*, and about what kind of world it speaks of anyway.

One needs to make a distinction between the one definition of global news as that which is generated by a global producer for a global audience; and that which is actually news about 'the world', but for a national audience. Most global news is actually the latter – at best for a regional audience. There is no global social or cultural coherence which would make possible global news, in the full meaning of the term. This point has, of course, consequences for the idea of a global public sphere.

Globalization as a notion is nothing new – news has been brought back from far places for hundreds of years. It just took a lot longer to arrive, and might not have been so accurate. Anyway, globalization is a problematic concept: it is not about some inevitable line of development or process of **homogenization**. Globalization has a lot to do with global financial networks. In this case, it is no accident that from the beginning of modern news services, one thing that (commercial) organizations were prepared to pay for was news about trade and about finance. ' "News" represented the re-formulation of "information" as a commodity gathered and distributed for the three purposes of political communication, trade and pleasure and was directed in its generic form by technology . . . scientism . . . and the development of mass media markets' (Boyd-Barrett and Rantanen, 1998).

Reuters became a global news agency on the back of its ability to control and distribute such information. Globalization also has a lot to do with what we call 'the West', and not so much to do with the rest of the planet. The dominant global news agencies, like most of the dominant global money markets, are located in the West. Reuters is based in Britain; AP in the USA; AFP in France. Reuters has 'commercial understandings' with Murdoch's Newscorp in particular. Reuters has over 260 client broadcasters in 85 countries. TV material is dominated by Visnews (part of Reuters) and WTN. WTN has commercial links with AP, ABC and CNN. ABC network is owned by the Disney Corporation. CNN (ex Turner Broadcasting) is part of TimeWarner/AOL. The global web of ownership and alliances is as powerful in respect of news as it is for the rest of media.

The greatest volume of news flow is in and about the West. News is about what is happening in London, Paris, Brussels, Washington. A disproportionate number of correspondents are based in the USA and in Europe. And only the biggest news organizations can afford them anyway – hence the power of the agencies. So one has to dispute the idea that news flow and access to news material is global in the proper meaning of the term. 'The perspectives of the great mass of the world population are under-represented in global news, while those of relatively small elites are over-represented' (Von Ginneken, 1998).

The western dominance of news operations also once more raises questions about imperialism and power, about the hegemony of the West. The answers are not cut and dried. Paterson (1998) asserts that 'the cultural product of the international television news agencies serves to perpetuate a western hegemony hostile to developing nations'. But globalization such as it is, has been accompanied by counter forces of regionalism and resurgences of national and intra-national identities. So too, the creation of global news agencies and news makers, alongside other trans-national media institutions, has been accompanied by the appearance of regional news centres and specialist agencies which feed into the multi-nationals.

One example that has risen to prominence in recent years is the Arab station/ agency, Al-Jazeera, based in the Gulf state of Qatar. Its very status is of interest. Certainly it broadcasts news: 'Approximately seventy percent of Arabs who own a satellite dish rely primarily on Al-Jazeera for news, documentaries and political information' (El-Nawawy and Iskandar, 2002).

But it is also in a sense a news source, because of the material which it creates and supplies to other broadcasters, most famously video recordings sent to the station by the western styled terrorist leader, Osama bin Laden. It has a huge influence in its region of the Middle East. As a news source it rivals the global provider, CNN. It has a liberal editorial policy, one that has caused waves among Arab nations, not least when, for instance, it has broadcast a range of views on Muslim polygamy. It is diplomatic in avoiding criticism of its host state, whose ruler is its protector. As a successful and influential regional station it runs counter to notions of globalization of news. 'Al-Jazeera has revolutionised the Arabic Middle East, challenging censorship imposed by the government-controlled media, addressing any relevant issue, including weak democratic institutions, fundamentalism, state corruption, political inequality, and human rights violations' (El-Nawawy and Iskandar, 2002).

The authors' most telling remarks are those about global news being part of global information wars. They see news institutions as being used in these wars, which dispute views of how the world should be, and compete for the acceptance and beliefs of audiences round the planet. This would be a nice example in action of Gramsci's notion of the struggle for the hegemony of ideas. Certainly this is how Boyd-Barrett and Rantanen (1998) see it:

> a process of dialectic, not least between the local, national, regional and global, a process of conflict and struggle both among the agencies of globalisation and the alleged subjects of globalisation.

If news is perceived as being generally truthful (whether or not it is), then it is attractive for governments (and other interests) with positions to promote in global politics, to get on the news agenda, to get their positions heard. News has always been a target of propaganda. Propaganda has been part of state news services in various places at various times. News programmes have been simulated in propaganda wars.

Von Ginneken (1998) points out, drawing from a *New York Times* article of 27 December 1977, that 'the CIA has at various times owned or subsidised more than 50 newspapers, news services, radio stations, periodicals'. And that was written over twenty-five years ago.

In terms of propaganda and influence on public opinion, Flournoy and Stewart (1997) suggest that world news providers have become unavoidably involved in the conduct of diplomacy. Technology can bring events, comments and diplomatic statements into the home as things happen. News is driven by valuation of immediacy, of the 'scoop', of drama, of bringing us an unfolding narrative in which it might be said, things have to happen. But diplomacy needs time for negotiation and reflection, for things not to happen immediately.

McGregor (1997) exemplifies the start of this time, and scoop-obsessed, technologically supported revolution in global news through the early reporting of CNN. On 28 June 1986 the fledgling world news channel took unique video footage of the shuttle *Challenger* explosion, as much by luck as judgement. In 15 minutes pictures were on ITN news in Britain.

In terms of the partiality and ideology of western news businesses, one may argue that news about the rest of the world is very selective. Some places, events and personalities appear on the news briefly and then disappear again. 'The viewer gets a dispersed mosaic of events' (Horvat, 2001). He points out cultural bias in terms of production and reception. For example, a British newspaper might well favour a story about a train crash in Pakistan, given the historical links between the two countries. Equally, viewers in the USA or in Britain, viewing images of a demonstration in a given eastern country, may be missing cultural nuances. They may read the demonstrators as a strangely dressed rabble, even assume a position of superiority to the scene and its people.

In other respects, where there is more continuity of attention, it may still be largely negative. One could argue that chunks of the south and east of the planet (relative to the West, of course!) are seen mainly in terms of crises. Disasters often make a 'good' news story for the West. But so-called 'natural' disasters may be nothing of the kind when, for example, deforestation is the major cause of flooding off hillsides. It is not fair to say that no newspapers have investigated causes of such stories – including perhaps the responsibility of western business interests for the cutting down of forests. But the popular tabloids and much of TV are interested in picture impact and scale. They do not give time or space to background, especially if it is uncomfortable in political terms.

The development of global news, like other facets of globalization, depends on technology – this has been referred to already, for example, in terms of news gathering. The Internet, supporting the World Wide Web, is a whole new technology and provider. Newspapers have online versions; so do some radio channels, including news. With all the qualifications made elsewhere, the potential audiences are huge. Star satellite in Asia has 220 million viewers in 12 countries. In 1999 18 per cent of the British population (10.6 million) was online. In the USA the figure was 27 per cent (in Herbert, 2000).

Of course, having access to the Internet does not reveal what people are actually doing with it. And we know that over 90 per cent of western populations still say that they get their main news information from television. Yet the satellite news audience is growing every year. And news on the Web is important for its diversity and alternative character (see Pavlik, 2001, for an account of various world websites offering alternative accounts of events). CNN.com will post information on the Web from CNN broadcasts that certain governments will not allow on air. It is always difficult to evaluate the potential and effects of new technologies as they are being innovated. Some will turn out to be passing experiments. For instance, Pavlik accepts that online news is unlikely to be profitable for some time because of a lack of public ownership of the necessary technology, and because of a lack of access.

Of course, technology is not just about specifically global applications. The arrival of kinds of digital technology affects national as well as international news reporting. Pavlik (2001) refers, for instance, to the advantages of digitized newsrooms:

- increased efficiency;
- greater productivity;
- enhanced creativity;
- greater accuracy and range of cover;
- fully searchable digital archives /news libraries.

On the other hand, Burton (2002) points to the deleterious effects of bringing in computer controlled news studios – less staff, more reliance on syndicated news, less reflection and analysis because this requires time and labour.

At the same time, such resources and facilities place greater pressures on newsworkers, in terms of requiring greater speed of response to events, of meeting ever shorter deadlines, of coping with ever sharper competition. Television news is 'a competitive, technologically intensive industry where great value is placed on being one step ahead of the competition' (McGregor, 1997).

There was a furore in 2003 over the BBC's reporting by Andrew Gilligan of what an expert adviser is supposed to have said about the reliability of intelligence information, leading to a decision to go to war in Iraq. This episode owed a lot to news technologies, the importance to government of news as political communication, and to competitive practices, all putting pressure on government and reporter to 'talk up' the news.

Pavlik (2001) refers to this talking up, and to other issues around changes in news ownership and provision, when he says that there are 'enormous threats to privacy, increasing concentration of ownership, a shrinking diversity of voices, an ever-escalating race to report the news more rapidly, an inequitable access to information technology and digital journalism'.

He argues that technology is changing the nature of journalism, on global and other levels. 'There is emerging a new form of journalism whose distinguishing qualities include ubiquitous news, global information access, instantaneous reporting, interactivity, multimedia content, and extreme content customisation.'

Certainly immediacy through technology was a characteristic of the war in Kosovo in 1999. Evening news would show video taken from attacking aircraft of missile strikes made that day. Burton points out that not only has one's sense of immediacy and reality been changed, 'but also the very definition of war and news of war has shifted', bringing us

- war from the front – now

- war as spectacle (the computer game syndrome)

- war as techno-combat

- clean war

- war as refugees (Burton, 2002)

All this raises questions.

- How far is news technology used for its own sake, because of a love of gadgetry, because it connotes professionalism, because of the millions invested in it?

- Or is it used because of the professional imperatives of news, the value of immediacy, of getting the news first?

- Or is technology, as elsewhere in the media, used because it is part of an ongoing reality trip in which the illusion of reality is constructed in the cause of creating actuality?

And of course news operations value the notion of 'being there' because that contributes to the sense of the truth of news.

9 News discourse, news mythologies

One needs to understand that inevitably news texts draw upon and recirculate discourses. They use discourses to make sense, within an ideological framework, of that about which they speak. Some discourses, such as those of gender, are dominant – they are frequently inscribed in news material and the assumptions that this makes about how the world is. To use a discourse is to use codes in such a way that certain meanings about the discourse subject are privileged. So news will talk in certain ways through the language of pictures, through the language of the newscaster or reporter, about any of its subjects – from Parliament to poverty, from a given nation to a given social group. It may be said that news, as with all forms of communication and especially the media, talks about and visualizes the world in ways which privilege and make dominant some cultures and some ways of understanding that world. For example, there is much talk in news about 'democracy'. It is represented in approving ways as if one inevitably agrees with the concept. Even a definition of democracy is assumed. But, for instance, if just one way of understanding democracy involves the practice of 'one person, one vote' then how does democracy really shape up when, as in some elections, more people don't vote than those who do? And why should the West assume that any model of democracy (as endorsed through news) is beneficial to a nation torn apart by tribal disagreements (and there are many such examples in the world)? News discourse becomes a prism through which certain meanings are refracted. Other meanings may never escape the prism.

News also has its own discourse or way of speaking about itself. It speaks of its own authority and credibility. It speaks of these things through its presentation. Studio sets, newscasters' body language, actuality footage are all part of the language of this news discourse. As discourses do, it also speaks through a pattern of oppositions, talking up that which is approved, and diminishing or simply ignoring that which is disapproved of. In terms of the previous point about democracy, news always speaks in favour of **consensus**. In political or industrial disputes we hear that 'no agreement has yet been reached', as if it is inevitable that it must. Indeed, it speaks about disputes in terms of opposing views, as if there is some middle ground to be found along an axis which joins two sides. It hardly ever talks about three or more differing views, let alone about how the notion of 'middle ground' is going to be realized in such a case.

The mythologies, or false understandings, which news promotes, may be understood in the same way as discourses are. Indeed, it is perfectly arguable that the subjects of a given discourse and the meanings which they generate are one and the same as these mythologies. The same core meanings are approached through different critical terms, and methods of analysis. Von Ginneken (1998) comments that 'news discourse refers to the common-place views of certain issues, shared by (most members of) a society or culture'. One instance might be the (western) idea that having rapid population growth stunts economic growth. This has not been the case in China or India or Brazil. Bird and Dardenne (1997) say much the same thing when they argue that one has to look at the totality of news stories in order to see the large framework within which news stories fit.

Through doing this one understands that news is a myth-making process in which people are told about themselves, about others, and about the world. An example, they say, would be stories about social behaviour and the way in which deviant behaviour is defined and boundaries are set. So, for instance, there is an emphasis on murder in news reporting, but not on the far more frequent occurrence of car theft.

Consensus

One could also take the example of 'consensus', which I have described as being part of news discourse and its meanings. One could as well say that the idea of consensus is a myth promoted through news language. It is part of a way of understanding the world and of talking about news events which helps simplify explanations of news. It is simultaneously very ideological and convenient to the hegemony of a dominant ideology. What I mean by this is that consensus invokes the ideas of agreement and compromise. Its discourse also defines it as a 'reasonable position'. Therefore any person or group who is not for consensus is against compromise and against reason. This is very convenient if the consensual position on an issue either actually works in favour of the powerful or in practice undercuts the views and actions of those lacking power. Therein lies the myth that consensus is always the reasonable solution to any problem. Consensus is indeed an ideological notion.

To take an example of one news story (2003), Diego Garcian islanders went to court in order to try and get back to their homes on an Indian Ocean island from which they were evicted thirty-odd years ago by the British government, so that the USA could build a base there. The story is not to be explained in terms of a consensus to be sought – between the needs of the islanders and the needs of the USA, or even of some world security policy. The nub of the story is that either the islanders get back to their homes or they do not (they didn't). Consensus is a mythology that becomes a cloak to conceal the naked exercise of power.

Reese (1997) asserts baldly that 'the news media play an essential role in maintaining the authority of the political system'. He also points out that consensus starts with how news is gathered, and is linked with its hegemony because agreement about what should be gathered is itself naturalized. It is defined as being normal. So is the notion of consensus when it is about making sense of news stories themselves. 'The consensual nature of news gathering supports the notion of a guiding news paradigm', 'the self-policing nature of the news paradigm is essential for its hegemonic effectiveness' (Reese, 1997).

Objectivity

Similarly, one may argue that other ways in which news makers operate and make sense of news are also mythologies, are also part of news discourse, as well as possibly being seen as subordinate discourses in themselves. For example, 'objectivity' is a notion integral to news. It is an abstract, even an idealized notion. It is an aspiration. But to say that news is or ever can become truly objective is nonsense – it is a myth. Larsen (1997) calls it 'the myth ritual of objectivity' when arguing that it is bound up with the concept of professionalism in journalism. This means that it is also bound up with the training and induction of journalists.

A version of the classic industry position is expressed in Herbert (2000): 'Although absolute objectivity is impossible, the quest for factual accuracy, balance and fairness remains the goal of every professional reporter.' The desire is to create an aura around news, to attach meanings of 'authority' and 'truth' to news productions. The idea is to validate newswork, to create a certain kind of relationship with the news audience: 'the claim of journalistic objectivity is essentially an appeal for trust' (McNair, 1998).

News values are patently cultural and partial – they are subjective. News stories are plainly constructed with an angle – often the 'human interest' angle. The whole selection and decision-making process of news is one in which degrees of subjectivity must appear. Omissions will occur. Normative judgements will be made. This does not mean that news is a pack of lies. Neither does it mean that one cannot argue for degrees of objectivity and subjectivity. One may still talk of at least some facts behind a news story. But again, hardly any stories are simply a recital of bare facts. Any act of communication carries some inflection and interpretation, coming from the experience and world view of the communicator. So one may say at least that the way the news aspires to and asserts objectivity is part of its own mythologizing about itself.

Von Ginneken (1998), remarks that 'the notion of objectivity . . . is always implicitly related to the notion of (an agreement between) relevant audiences'. The idea of what is objective depends on news audiences seeing things the same way, the same way, indeed, as the news makers. He also points out that objectivity can be seen as merely a set of rhetorical devices which do not necessarily express 'the truth'. For example, news items commonly incorporate facts about date, time, place, person, happening; but a collection of facts do not express the truth of an event. Anonymity – of source, of newspaper journalist, of TV camera operator – also is a device that contributes to the illusion of objectivity.

Exnomination

Anonymity may be identified with Fiske's concept of exnomination (Fiske 1987). In this case he argues that sources such as companies and government departments which are spoken of as institutions rather than represented through specific names or faces, acquire a certain authority. There is respect implied in the distancing, respect for the status and truthfulness of the source. It has been interesting to see the dissolution of this authority in reporting of the Hutton Inquiry (2003–4) in Britain. This inquiry examined the death of a weapons adviser and conflicting statements made by the British government and by a BBC reporter, in relation to the lead-in to the US/UK war on Iraq. In this case there was a reversal of a common news process, which emphasized the personal involvement of one named journalist (Andrew Gilligan), and even of a member of the secret services (John Scarlett). This naming, continued through the personal involvement of the Prime Minister (Tony Blair) and his Director of Communications (Alastair Campbell), served in reverse to show how the anonymity of the exnominating process does blow out a kind of smokescreen of false objectivity.

Impartiality

Much the same may be said of notions like balance, impartiality and (lack of) bias. Balance implies a mid-point between two views – criticized above. Impartiality suggests a capacity to be objective – just criticized. And lack of bias suggests a capacity to avoid being subjective – also criticized.

Whatever they are, these key words invoked by news makers and news regulators to manage and defend the status of news operations, do not stand up in an absolute sense. Internal guidelines within the BBC and ITN, or external reports, do not so much talk about objectivity as such. But they do invoke that discourse, through words such as 'fairness' and 'dispassionate'. They are creating a cradle supporting news conventions, news values and journalistic practices. Any sensible discussion of the meaning of news texts has to work around the degree of, the nature of, the possible consequences of, the kind of partiality and imbalance that must be present.

10 News representations (see also Chapter 4)

If one understands that news – in any medium – is a text, then it will by its nature be full of representations. Texts must be representations of the world, of groups, of institutions – and so of ideas that are the dominant views of the society which produces those texts. Understanding of representations also needs to take account of the nature of the news institutions that construct them, as well as of the audiences that assimilate and interpret them.

It may be said that the representation within the text is carried out through the operation of discourses. The way the subject is talked about is how it is represented. For instance, news tends to talk about certain social groups as problems. Young people are 'making trouble on the street'. They are 'truanting from school'. Currently (2004) we are hearing about young (male) footballers who are 'getting out of control' and involved with sexual escapades (not old or female footballers!). This is an updated version of the ongoing representation of 'youth as trouble'. I am not suggesting that the news reports are based on fabrication. On the contrary, there are real and serious issues around certain kinds of behaviour. But I am saying that the nature of how the subject (the young) is being spoken of does tend to generalization and to exaggeration, in the popular press in particular.

The very fact of news makers operating as a kind of pack also tends to make this distortion worse. News makers compete for headlines, check each other for stories being broken, and so one ends up at one time with the same stories being told through many news outlets, as the agenda principle cuts in. This collation of the same stories, and indeed similar approaches, tends to profile the subject, to emphasize the kind of representation.

The 'other' and 'difference' in news

One may also revisit the notion of 'othering' through news. Just as certain kinds of social behaviour are branded as 'deviant', so certain groups are implicitly represented as 'other' from 'the rest of us', not least on grounds of ethnicity. To label someone as an 'asylum seeker' is to define them as being distinct from the rest who are not asylum seekers. To identify them as Kurdish is to imply that they are therefore 'not British' – and to imply that this matters. The same emphasis on 'difference' and on western values as a benchmark by which a news story is assumed to be properly judged was seen in 1997. An American schoolboy was caned by a Singaporean court for an act of vandalism. For all their usual tendency to talk tough on crime, the western press was in this case rather more vocal about these 'others' who dared to commit a kind of violence on one of 'our' children.

The 'othering' principle in news representations is of a piece with the oppositions within discourses. In the case of asylum seekers (who have been in many British news stories over the past few years), what news is doing is to make all sorts of assertions about British identity and British territory. It takes ideological positions on immigration – in other words, that it is not a very good thing, and 'we' don't really want all these people here. Lest this interpretation of the news representation of so-called asylum seekers seems too unkind, then consider other possible kinds of representation and treatment that would be reasonable, but are never seen in the following terms.

'Among the latest group of asylum seekers to enter Britain are three qualified doctors. The Chief Medical Officer welcomed them into a conversion course which will enable them to work in and support our National Health Service.'

'Interviews with refugees who flew into Britain four days ago (i.e. who were not put in a holding centre for many weeks) have established evidence of torture in X country. The Foreign Office is making strong representations to X regarding this evidence.'

Macdonald discusses the othering of Islam and of Arab peoples. She refers to a range of media strategies in which the words and images contained within a discourse produce this effect. Emphasis on the wearing of the burkha by women, as news photos select this dress to make an iconic image, is an example of this process (not to mention the mingling of discourses).

The 'difference' of Islam has been repeatedly emphasised, serving both to alienate Islamic practices from modernity and from civilisation, and to shore up the West's own sense of self-worth, and its liberal and fair-minded credentials. Signifiers of difference can be apparently modest, but insistent in their reiteration. British radio news items making reference to Islam almost without exception feature the 'sound effect' of the Muslim call to prayer.

Macdonald (2003)

Of course, such examples make the point that the ideological othering of groups is something which news does not invent of itself. It is something which extends into various sections of society, and into government. Equally, if one is making a critique of news, then to say that the ideological positions emerging from representations are socially pervasive does not mean that one should excuse news. News makers are aware of the power of their position, and not entirely unaware of the choices that they are making in representing the world. Some have, for example, castigated politicians for ways in which they deal with refugees (see Robert Fisk in the *Independent*).

Nevertheless, one could argue that, in general, news services support the status quo and naturalization of dominant ideas, rather than challenging these. They will support the interests of a political and economically powerful social establishment. It has to be repeated that this is likely to happen not least because of contextual pressures from proprietors, shareholders, advertisers and powerful news sources. It is interesting to see how (September, 2003) news reports critical of the British army and the notorious Bloody Sunday shooting incident in 1979 have emerged. One paratrooper is reported as admitting shooting and killing unarmed demonstrators. At the time of the original events, almost all news reports represented the incident in ways supportive of the institutions of the army and of the state.

10.1 Misrepresentation and moral panics

News media have a well-established tendency to represent certain events in such a selective and emphatic way that they both engender and represent what have been called moral panics (see Cohen, 1973; Cohen and Young, 1973). Their seminal studies of the representation of youth gangs, or those by Hall *et al.* (1978) of 'black muggers', recognized a pattern of news reporting in which public anxiety and moral issues were hyped up. This hyping often takes place over a certain period of time and is tied to one or two emblematic incidents. Moral panics may be revived if a suitable incident of sufficient impact occurs. In 1996 the so-called Dunblane massacre in Scotland, of a school teacher and several children by a deranged person, provoked a media debate about gun crime, and contributed indirectly to the legal ban on handguns, made law later in the year. The killing of a little girl in 2003 in what appeared to be a gang hit led to a revival of the debate about gun control. Kinds of criminality are often the subject of the exaggerated and selective reporting that characterizes a moral panic. Misrepresentation by the popular press in particular is common in such periods of panic. One has bouts of fear about personal assault, concentrating on female and elderly victims. Statistically, young single males are nearly twice as likely to be attacked as are females.

Certain social groups may be demonized by the news media, as part of a moral panic. Reference has already been made to engendering fear of asylum seekers. In 2001 there was a moral panic around the issue of paedophilia. In this case, the *News of the World* led a campaign to 'out' paedophiles by identifying them and revealing where they lived. One consequence was an outbreak of mob vigilante violence on the Paulsgrove estate in Portsmouth. Another was the hounding of a few individuals who had simply been wrongly identified.

10.2 Gendered news

One may consider issues around gendered news as relating to representation. As an aside it might be said that one could also, therefore, validate particular studies of, say, 'age-ized news' or 'ethnicized news'. In the case of gender, and within a brief space, it has to be understood that one needs to take account of the gendering of news operations as much as of news texts.

So it is that Van Zoonen (1994, 1998) describes how women are culturalized into the news business, into an occupation in which the majority of senior positions are still taken by males. Skidmore (1998) describes research by Dougary (1994) in which she established that across 12 tabloid newspapers, top editorial jobs were held by 64 men and 11 women. The ratio was worse in the case of the broadsheets.

Jamieson and Campbell (2001) report an analysis conducted by the *New York Times* in 1993 which found that 82 per cent of senior newspaper editors were men (and that women were the subject of only 13 per cent of all newspaper stories).

Van Zoonen (1998) reports on research into news media in which it was found that in 1995, for the USA, 34 per cent of press employees were women and 25 per cent of TV journalists were women. For Britain, the figures were 23 per cent and 25 per cent respectively. Although there is a majority of females in journalism training, they do not end up in the mainstream press, but rather in associated areas such as public relations and magazines. (It is interesting that the circulation of magazines is rising as that of newspapers falls steadily.) There is evidence that it is nearly impossible for women to combine a mainstream journalistic career with bringing up a family. It is tough to attempt investigative journalism with its unsocial hours if you have a family to care about, and easier to take on the more flexibly-timed news called 'features' – which abounds in magazines.

'Most newsrooms appear to be characterised by a gendered division between "hard" news (such as economics, politics, government and crime) reporters, who tend to be men, and "features" reporters, who are most likely, at least in relative terms, to be women' (Allan, 1999). The culturalization of females into newswork raises interesting questions about gendered work and gendered discourses. Is newswork in fact just about masculine work patterns, which keep women out? Are the news values which drive news working really gender specific? And if there is a feminine discourse which links for example to the human interest story, is this in fact just a construct of the masculine discourse, rather than a genuinely female discourse in its own right?

There is a gender imbalance in terms of who produces news. There is a gender bias in terms of who gets to cover what kind of story. How this relates to representations of gender within any news text may be more complicated than assertions about men grabbing big factual stories about power, and women being given (and producing) softer stories about emotion and relationships.

At any rate, the gender bias of women's representation in the news media is unquestionable. Women are described and judged through news stories, in terms of their appearance in a way that hardly happens for men. News photographs often reproduce 'difference', showing for example women as fashion objects with articles on health and diet, and men as politicians or scientists influencing world affairs. Women are often talked about in relation to a man – husband or boyfriend. Women more than men are identified as being a wife, a mistress or a girlfriend. The tabloids, far more than the broadsheets, sexualize women, whether it is through pin-up poses or through stories which talk about women dominantly in terms of their behaviour and their looks (stories about sex and footballers in 2003). Sometimes stories are actually about gender bias – for example, when the female judge appointed to the Appeals Court (November, 2003) talks about sexism in the legal profession. Ironically, in that this story made all the papers, it also endorses that kind of gendered representation that actually remarks on the fact that the subject is female (whereas a male judge would not be remarkable).

This kind of meaning has to be sought out in the face of a journalistic ethic of objectivity which would claim that truly objective reporting cannot by its nature be sexist!

Women Represented Through the Popular Press
Newspapers are gendered texts, in which the effects of representation are reinforced through generic repetition of images and verbal features.
Describe kinds of reporting or image construction which might challenge this kind of representation in the popular press – in terms of achievements by women, the appearance of women, and the social roles of women? (In other words, try creating an alternative news, bearing in mind what is *not* said.)
(*Graeme Burton*, 2004)

Holland (1998) talks about the 'reassertion of the female body as spectacle' and points out the political implications of stories which obsess about women and sex (not to mention, which assumes that stories about women should naturally be placed in domestic or caring contexts). Sexualization closes off democratic discourse. To represent women as sex objects, or even only as mothers and wives, is a way of trivializing them at worst, and at best of denying them access to equal exercise of power in the political and economic spheres. One might also say that all this is symptomatic of a Gramscian ideological struggle for hegemony, in which conservative forces are trying to put women back in a box, as women do indeed slowly achieve commercial and political power.

On the other hand, Allan (1999) does bring out arguments in at least some favour of the tabloid press and the values which it endorses for women. 'The tabloids attribute a positive value to many aspects of daily life, particularly nurturing and personal relationships, typically devalued elsewhere in the news media due to their identification as being "feminine".'

Where politics is the subject of news reporting, the way it is 'told' also represents a gender and a class divide, according to Macdonald (2003). She describes the talk in the House of Commons as 'a public school, masculinised tradition of confrontational rhetoric', and as 'potentially alien to the majority of non-white, female and working-class citizens'. The implication is that hard news reporting which reproduces this talk is itself gendered.

Brookes and Holbrook (1998) provide a case-study example of gendered representation through discussion of the news and the BSE crisis (1996) in which links were being established between brain disease in cattle and in humans. They describe how public concern was often depicted as female hysteria. Authoritative male actors in the news version told us how there was nothing to worry about. But the Shadow Health Secretary at the time (Harriet Harman) was represented as panicking and causing panic. The *Daily Star* misrepresented a male Tory MP as calling her a 'mad cow' (though his original wording was also abusive). Women who were 'approved of' were represented as housewives and mothers, who only wanted to feed their men good British beef. The difference between the treatment of women in public and private roles is interesting – something of a subtext of 'know your place'! The authors talk about a 'discourse demarcating different gender roles across the public and private spheres'.

Silverstone (1999) points out that even as news viewers, audiences are gendered. It is men who prefer to watch the mainstream news programmes. It is men who like to wield the remote control! Men do not see news watching as a social function, whereas women are more likely to talk about news items as they come up.

11 News audiences

Like media audiences in general, the audiences for news output have, in varying degrees, polarized and fragmented. Polarization is seen through the increasing division of the Britsh press, from the mid-twentieth century onwards, between populist, soft-news tabloids, and the hard-news broadsheets. The takeover of the *Sun* in 1967 by what is now Newscorp, and its transformation from a short-lived attempt at a soft left-of-political-centre broadsheet into a right-of-centre tabloid with the first bared female chests, is symptomatic of this division of readers. The middle ground between two kinds of news has been slipping away. The *Daily Mail* has attempted to hold on to this, in tabloid format, with some success. But the *Daily Express* has not so succeeded. It has, significantly, vacillated between inclinations to the right and the left in recent years. There are signs that this phenomenon of polarization is being repeated through broadcasting, as channels multiply. The nature of regulation limits extremes of polarization. All the same, the audiences for BBC2 television news, now targeting the over 35s, are different from those for Channel 5, targeting a younger age group. The kind of news and kind of audience for a big commercial radio station like Capital Radio is very different from the news presentation and audience for an upmarket kind of channel like BBC Radio 3.

Such an example would also serve as an instance of fragmentation, and of the niche markets that have emerged from competition in the newspaper industry, and from the deregulation of broadcasting. Equally, this change does need to be kept in perspective. The audiences for the flagship evening BBC and ITV news programmes are still very big, and run into the several millions a night. They have been eroded since the 1980s by the arrival of SkyNews, of two more terrestrial channels and by a variety of cable/satellite providers. Broadcasting is moving towards the situation of the press, in which different audiences may get differing understandings of what news is, of what is going on in the world. These differences may not particularly undermine a dominant ideology or a dominant news discourse. But it does represent some kind of change.

All this talk about the audience for news needs to be qualified. In terms of the newsworkers, there is evidence from Burns (1977) onwards that journalists are less conscious of the audience out there, than they are of their peers and of their editor as audience. Journalistic induction practices mean that this is likely to be so. Audiences only impact on journalists via circulation or viewing figures, and possibly via direct correspondence with the editor. In this sense, the conceptualization of audience is as much a critical and sociological undertaking, as it is much to do with the news media industries.

One audience that effectively does not exist for news is that of the child viewer. The only television news programme that now exists is *Newsround*, on BBC1. There was for a while *NickNews* on the Nickleodeon digital channel. It even won awards. But it has been pulled because of the low ratings. Conversely, children's programming is stuffed with drama and animation. This small but interesting corner of the media landscape may be connected with

- commodification and market forces: ratings count for more than educational desirability;
- advertising: advertisers pay the piper, and swing commitments to programme expenditure and production;
- regulation: clearly the only force that could counteract this kind of behaviour would be that of the broadcast regulator, Ofcom;
- violence and media: those who include news material in their concerns about the effect of violent material on children, ought to be concerned that there is no alternative interpretation (to main news) of the world, for children. This might be especially relevant in the case of news stories about violence committed on children;

● socialization and media influence: children are not (unsurprisingly) great readers of newspapers or watchers of TV news. Notwithstanding critiques of how news represents the world, one may ask where else will children acquire any factual understanding of the world into which they are growing? The balance of children's programming (with the ads within it), tells them pretty clearly to consume and have fun – that is what living is about!

There is of course a large global audience for news, which has some connection with the arrival of global news makers such as CNN. This also relates to questions about how far one may recognize something called 'global news' or a 'global public sphere'. But in fact this audience is pretty selective in its characteristics. For a start, much of it, as within national boundaries, is based in cities – and the nature of news reflects this. This also relates to the wealth of audiences – again, the highest per capita incomes are concentrated in urban areas. So these are where the greatest range of newspapers appears. These are the audiences to which news stories must appeal, because these are the people who have the money to spend on whatever it is that the newspaper advertisers (and TV channels) are promoting. As Von Ginneken (1998) puts it, 'most global media organisations are primarily geared to the interests and views of audiences in the G7, the largest Western nations'.

McGregor (1997) comments on the competition for audiences: 'In order to reach the largest possible audiences, news has become consensual.' This is the argument about pleasing the greatest number, about taking mainstream ideological positions. It is about endorsing a generality of news values and about approving established ways of telling news. It is one side of the debate about a stretch between mass and niche audiences, and about which direction globalization is moving in.

Jensen (1998) is interested in how news audiences around the world may be affected by news material. He is sceptical about simplistic assumptions regarding the influence of news. He refers to a Unesco report (Sreberny-Mohammadi *et al.*, 1998) which among other things concludes that national news coverage is tied into its region rather than the world as such; that the nature of news is affected by the fact that most

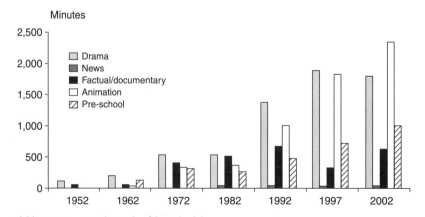

How Children's News Lost the Battle of the Schedules
News for children – serious factual programming – is near invisible on a chart which is dominated by the drama and animation which attracts that audience and pleases the advertisers.
(*Institute for Public Policy Research*, 2002)

journalists around the world are socialized into western practices. So what audiences get is inflected by all sorts of assumptions and background factors. Jensen challenges ideas about audience power. What he does conclude, from a study of TV news, carried out across the world in a given week in 1993, using a mixture of content analysis and interviews, is that

- People have through news a sense of how they are located in relation to the status of the nation and to world affairs.
- News items often relate to a sense of security or of threat to that security, for the viewer.
- People acquire a sense of where power and authority lies, mainly as this relates to their place in a social hierarchy and to the power of the state.
- Within a time frame, people get a sense of what news items signify for where the country is going.
- People get a sense of their identity in relation to others, whether this is others abroad or within the nation state.

These conclusions are distilled out of research in a range of countries, from Mexico to Italy to India. What they do suggest is that people gain a sense of the world from the news, but they do not see themselves as world citizens.

So far as one may talk about the effects of news consumption on the audience, effects are more about ways of thinking than about behavioural changes. News reporting of an election does not so much affect people's voting decisions, as it affects the nature of informational material from which such decisions may be made. As Janos Horvats puts it: 'US journalists inform a domestic public that elects public officials who influence world affairs.'

News promotes agendas in the head. It creates internal visions of geographical and social worlds. Manning (2001) talks about mental maps. 'It is more useful to explore the ways in which intellectual frameworks for thinking issues through are constructed, and the contribution which the news media might make in the development of such "mental maps" among audiences.'

Allan (1999) is very clear that one should not exaggerate either the effects of news material on audiences, nor the participation of newsworkers in the cause of some ideological enterprise

> Just as the claim that journalists are participants, knowingly or not, in some sort of wilful conspiracy to encodify the dictates of a 'dominant ideology' in the newsroom may be safely dismissed, so may the corresponding assertion that news viewers, listeners and readers be regarded as passive, alienated dupes indoctrinated into a state of 'false consciousness'.

Further, Allan points out that audiences are perfectly able to distinguish between different representations of news and to accommodate these. He refers to a study which indicates that the audience may take TV news seriously as a source of information about the world, but acknowledges that tabloid news is just fun.

He points out that the reception of news by audiences has contexts which make glib assertions about influence untenable. For instance, there is the weaving of news consumption into the experience of everyday life. News reading or listening may be a ritual – over breakfast. News viewing may be spasmodic and ongoing, as bulletins are picked up during the evening. The repetition of news, its way of interpreting and containing the world may generate 'a comforting sense of familiarity and predictablity'. He refers to Silverstone (1994) when talking of 'the creation and maintenance of the viewer's sense of well-being and trustful attachment to the world beyond the television screen'. And, Allan argues, one has to recognize the capacity of different sections of the news audience to interpret news in different ways, not least in the context of their own experiences. Such experience might make some news items more salient than others. He talks of: 'the openings for different audience groups or "interpretive communities" to potentially recast the terms by which "truth" is defined in relation to their lived experiences of injustice and inequalities'. Which reminds us that the process of selective attention in news viewing/reading means that not only will some information be either lost or foregrounded, but also the sense and validity of that information will be understood differently by different sets of people. This is not an argument against news having effects on its audience. But it is to say that the audience is part of the making of any effects. And it is to say that one cannot assume a coherence of effects, even while arguing for a generality of influence.

One needs to remember that news makers are not entirely in control of their environment or their sources. The danger of depending on ritualized operations and of using powerful sources in industry and government has already been pointed out. News media are under continual pressures to influence them. For example, Jamieson and Campbell (2001) report on how the Federal Trade Commission launched a successful anti-trust investigation against the Santa Clara County Motor Dealers Association, who pulled out advertising worth $1 million because a reporter on *The San Jose Mercury News* produced an article telling readers how to get a better buy when purchasing a car.

TV news editors are now used to receiving unsolicited video material from many sources, including the environmental lobby (for example, Greenpeace). These videos, like expert press releases, are neatly produced, often to broadcast quality, offering convenient and free footage that fits in with news interests and values. Of course the newsroom retains editorial control. But there is a considerable pressure in some cases to put the story on the news agenda because it fits.

So there are attempts to influence the news from a range of commercial, political and interest group sources. News is produced within a nexus of forces, and in no sense is it something which is simply mined, smelted, cast and the ingots dropped into the laps of the audience.

'The news media are influenced by highly paid news managers and their clients, and by other individuals and groups. The media are also influenced by commercial pressures for ratings and revenues, and by the protests of those offended by news coverage. Finally, they respond to pressure from those in positions of political power' (Jamieson and Campbell, 2001).

12 News and the public sphere

In the first place, one needs to recognize that the very notion of a public sphere is itself ideological because it is bound up with a liberal democratic ideal. It may be linked with social responsibility theories of the press. Without wishing to simply repeat previous points about the media offering some version of Habermas's vision of a public sphere, it is important to remind ourselves of the centrality of news to that vision. If within the term 'news' one includes that material which is about current affairs, or which provides a documentary type back-up to a given news topic, then news media become central to any discussion of this notion.

In these terms, the news agenda becomes an agenda for public debates. Discussion in the media about current issues – who is invited into such discussion – also becomes that public debate, after a fashion. Clearly it is not a debate in which every citizen may join. Its terms of reference are defined by media makers. But one might also say, it is the best we have got. If there is anywhere that social and political events and issues appear to society in general, it is through news. If there is any location in which problems and views are made apparent it is within news. If there is anywhere from which citizens may obtain information and at least witness debate – before exercising their rights to vote – it is from news. Once more it becomes apparent how important news media are within the range of media texts. It underlines the importance of subjecting news operations to criticism, to regulation and to continuing adjustment in the public interest. One might say, to re-mint a familiar statement – news is too important to be left solely in the hands of journalists or indeed their media masters. News has the capacity to be an enabling political and social force in an active public sphere. Or it may become a controlling force, one which closes down open debate through a range of views, one which manufactures a sham of a public sphere.

Some commentators seem to conflate the existence of a public sphere with the existence and survival of public service broadcasting. Granted, if an active public sphere, to which news contributes, is to be more than merely a public domain, then that sphere has to be preserved by regulators, yet supported financially. But in Britain at least, given regulation, one cannot say that issues raised by the (commercial) Channel 4 news are any the less sharp than those raised through the (PSB) channel, BBC1. What one must acknowledge is that, whatever the quality of debate, it is essentially controlled and packaged by the news makers. Harrison (2000) says that, 'For Habermas the public sphere is a space which mediates between civil society and the state, and in which individuals and groups discuss and argue about public matters.'

But neither broadcast or press news, nor most of broadcasting in general, offers public access. Even in the most charitable interpretation, debates are conducted by the select few for the majority who do not participate. And then there are questions to ask. Are the terms of reference of the debate adequate in informing the citizen and voter? Is there a plurality and diversity of debates and views? How does one accommodate the fact of soft news – all that material which is subjective and felt, and not about discussion of social and political issues? In this sense, should we not plump for a model of alternative public spheres – one of which is, for example, where the public hears about and discusses the transgressions of soap stars?

Manning (2001) is highly critical of what he sees as a failure of news and of journalism to create a proper public sphere in which meaningful political debate takes place. 'The interface between private experience and public power is structured through the public sphere' but 'contemporary political news media offer the potential to involve and engage audiences in political debate at a deeper level than ever before, and yet this potential is rarely realised'. He also quotes Protess (1991) in saying 'news journalism has both reflected and encouraged a political apathy among citizens and a retreat from the public to the private domain'.

Through such views it is argued that news media promise much but deliver little, in terms of giving life to a public sphere in which genuine debate takes place. On the one hand one may say that the press provides some kind of forum for discussion about subjects such as the introduction of GM crops or the ethics of stem-cell research. On the other hand, there is the matter of the terms of reference for the debate in a given newspaper, the range of views allowed, and, of course, how far audiences choose to buy certain kinds of newspaper in which certain approaches to such issues are allowed or disallowed.

There is also a notion of the 'public interest', which news makers and politicians invoke, and which one would expect to underpin this public sphere. Regulators work on the principle that such a thing exists. The phrase appears for example in the 1994 White Paper on the future of the BBC. But if there is no coherent audience for a coherent news provision – nor a coherent and working public sphere – then what does public interest actually mean? One might say that it is a rhetorical and ideological device that news makers may invoke to challenge politicians and to extract information, and which politicians may use to resist assaults on their power and control of that information. This would model a public sphere as a battleground between competing ideas and institutions (ideology wars).

Paterson (1998) asserts that 'the globalisation of television new is producing an international public sphere, but one dominated by mainstream Anglo-Saxon ideologies'. But one might dispute the extent of that public sphere, and how it is conceptualized by news consumers, if at all. The Arab viewers of Al-Jazeera might be acquiring an expanded view of a kind of public sphere, not least in cultural and ethical terms. But this does not mean that they share that sphere with viewers in Indonesia.

Jensen (1998) says that 'the general information which is available from media is a decisive resource for the political and cultural action of publics around the world'. But this does not mean that these publics are thinking or talking within the same public sphere. It may be that news has given audiences a larger global dimension as to how they think about the world. But this is not the same as a global public sphere shared by all citizens.

What seems more plausible is that news contributes to a public sphere for an elite – a commercial and political elite, by and large – which works and travels around the world, and therefore thinks in global terms. But given the technological limitations of TV news (let alone the ideological ones) it is simply not possible for citizens to debate or to share knowledge, on a global basis. It may be that supranational agendas are developing – the protestors at the 2003 World Trade Organization summit were clearly thinking global. But then one has to consider their backgrounds, where they came from, and consider the fact that the WTO members themselves could not agree on a global strategy, so leading to the collapse of the conference.

Volkmer (1999) also enthuses about a 'global public sphere, consisting of a world-wide available audiovisual, satellite-transmitted "communication platform", *a global civil society*'. But she does not demonstrate that it actually exists. She talks about the importance of new satellite footprints, as opposed to old political boundaries. But then there is some contradiction in the statement that 'the global distribution of programmes such as those of CNN and MTV has shaped new regional markets which fragment and diversify'.

I am not arguing that the technological reach of news and other aspects of something called globalization have not had some effect on our conception of something called a public sphere (or spheres). But I am suggesting that the world of global TV news is geographically and ideologically selective, as well as limited, in its realization of 'global'. I am suggesting that there is no coherent global public sphere, even if some citizens of some nations are able to access more information about the world than in previous eras.

13 Discussion extract

❝❞ Gramsci's writings on hegemony have proven to be extraordinarily influential for critical researchers examining the operation of news media in modern societies. Three particularly significant (and interrelated) aspects of the cultural dynamics of hegemony are the following. First, *hegemony is a lived process*. Second, *hegemony is a matter of 'common sense'*. Third, *hegemony is always contested*.

This shift to address the cultural dynamics of hegemony displaces a range of different formulations of 'dominant ideology', most of which hold that news discourse be theorised as concealing or masking the true origins of economic antagonisms, that is, their essential basis in the class struggle. At the same time, this emphasis on the hegemonic imperatives of news discourse allows the critical researcher to avoid the suggestion that the 'effects' of news discourse on its audience be understood simply as a matter of 'false consciousness'. An analytical engagement with the cultural dynamics of hegemony provides the researcher with important new insights into how news texts demarcate the limits of 'common sense'.

Many critical researchers argue that news accounts encourage us to accept as *natural, obvious or commonsensical* certain preferred ways of classifying reality, and that these classifications have far-reaching implications for the cultural reproduction of power relations across society.

Text-centred approaches allow for the opening up of what has become a rather empty assertion, namely that news texts are inherently meaningful, so as to unpack the *naturalness* of the ideological codes implicated in their representations of reality. This notion of 'codification' may be used to specify the means by which the meanings attributed to a text are organised in accordance with certain (usually so *obvious* as to be *taken-for-granted*) rules or conventions.

This is to suggest that a newspaper account, far from simply reflecting the reality of a news event, is actually working to construct a codified definition of what should count as the reality of the event. In order to examine these processes of codification, the specific ways in which a newspaper adopts a preferred language to represent 'the world out there' need to be opened up for analysis. That is to say, it is necessary to identify the means by which a particular newspaper projects its characteristic 'mode of address', its customary way of speaking to its audience.

Allan, S. (1999) (edited – italics as original).

1 In what ways, does the piece suggest, can ideas around hegemony affect the concept of 'dominant ideology'?

2 Having an example of a newspaper to hand, what would you say are the characteristics of its mode of address, and what devices does it use to construct this?

3 What ideas and questions do you think that this piece raises about the relationship between news text and audience?

14 Further reading

Allan, S. (1999) *News Culture*. Buckingham: Open University Press.

Harrison, J. (2000) *Terrestrial TV News in Britain, The Culture of Production*. Manchester: Manchester University Press.

Keeble, R. (2001) *The Newspapers Handbook* (3rd edn). London: Routledge.

McNair, B. (1999) *News and Journalism in the UK* (3rd edn). London: Routledge.

Von Ginneken, J. (1998) *Understanding Global News, A Critical Introduction*. London: Sage.

CHAPTER TWELVE

SPORT AND REPRESENTATION

Media making meanings about sport: sport making meanings about ideology, race and gender

"It is the media that not only have created the capacity for sport to reach to a staggering global audience, but also 'service' that audience, that reproduce and transform sports culture through and endless and pervasive process of showing, 'sounding', discussing, depicting – in short, of representing sport in myriad ways."

Rowe, D. (1999) *Sport, Culture and the Media*. Buckingham: Open University Press.

1 Introduction

This chapter deals with ways in which the media frame our understanding of the term 'sport', as well as with the ways in which gender and ethnicity are inflected through their handling in media sports material. Sporting events are dealt with dominantly through broadcast media and the press. But sport, as a cultural phenomenon and as media material, is understood through more than events. It is an essential component of the news genre across the media. It may be the subject of texts as varied as television chat shows, novels and movies. Sport is also a major economic factor in media institutions' finances. It is a staple attraction in newspapers. It fills a lot of air time, sometimes quite cheaply, though not in the case of major national and international events.

Sport has an especially close relationship with television, based on the visual entertainment appeal of contest, the reach of the medium and the consequent income that it can provide. Television has acquired the aura of live-ness and immediacy through its news and sport coverage, in spite of its penchant for replays and recordings. Sport is often quite a malleable material, in that in most cases the length of its performances is known and can be fitted into pre-advertised slots, and in that it can be padded out with discussions and action replays. It can be recycled and repackaged to provide yet more material for the acres of air time to be filled. Sport is a popular activity, made the more popular by television through a process of mutual promotion. Sport provides attractive narratives, stories of success and failure, victory and defeat, on national or global levels. Television brings us such straightforward, rule-clear stories that appeal to a wide audience.

Sport is often represented in terms of individual conflict – going back to examples such as the track race between Mary Decker and Zola Budd in 1985, watched by 11 million TV viewers – or in terms of team conflict, framed in relation to regional or national identities (the Olympics). Sport and sporting figures are the stuff of myth – myths about national achievement, individual endeavour, heroic masculinity – myths which too often preclude heroic femininity. These myths circulate between the texts and the audiences, through representations, confirming a certain view of the world. 'Prominent sporting figures are both reflexive of the character of their public, yet at the same time larger than life. They embody the hopes of their followers . . .' (Tomlinson, 1999).

2 Major questions

1 How have notions of sport changed with the intervention of the media and the market?

2 In what respects is sport bound up with the conceptualization of national identity?

3 In what respects has media representation of sporting events and sports people conserved ideas about masculinity and restrained positive understandings of female gender?

4 How have media representations of sport affected conceptions of 'race'?

3 The representation of sport

We have acquired a web of ideas about sport, predominantly via the media, though partly through other agencies such as education. Some of these are elaborated on below. In any case, sport is more than just a social activity or a cultural practice. It has been colonized by the media. Its meaning is defined through metaphor and discourse (the use of language), through symbols (its stars, for example). The following are dominant ways in which ideas about sport, the definition of 'sport-ness', are represented through the media.

1 As a symbol of national identity – through international competitions, particularly the Olympics.

2 As a world of personalities, stars and myths – through gossip stories about the lifestyles of successful sportspeople.

3 As style – through endorsements of style products made by sports stars, or through the adoption of sports-style clothing by millions of people worldwide spending billions of pounds in the process (in 1995 £2,280 million was spent in Britain on sportswear and sports equipment – see Maguire, 1999).

4 As a cultural activity with status – through the space given to sports people and sports activities, as well as through approving coverage.

5 As a healthy social activity – through items invoking the discourse of fitness and health, from *GQ* magazine to medical dramas.

6 As war – through frequent uses of war metaphor in press coverage of sports events, the discussion of 'tactics' and so on.

7 As scandal – through a range of magazine and news items which have covered everything from marital infidelities, to bad behaviour at nightclubs, to sexual preferences.

8 As commodity – through news coverage of transfer fees, contract fees, media coverage rights and so on.

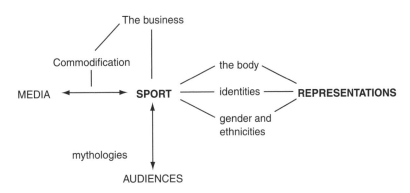

Sport and Representation: Terms for reference
The business of sport and sporting celebrities are represented through the media in ways which tend to conceal the commodified nature of the relationship between sport, sports people and the media. Sporting celebrities are the subjects of myths about nationality, gender and ethnicity. Audiences for sport collude in this myth-making, as it fits in with representations (meanings) in areas apart from sport.
(*Graeme Burton*, 2004)

9 As a spiritual event – through the ritual associated with big national sporting occasions such as the singing involved with Welsh rugby events at the Cardiff Millennium Stadium.

Historically, sport has moved from competitive activities rooted in folk culture to global businesses rooted in commodity capitalism. Sport has moved from being about regulated play, games, to being about work and profit. Some sports like cricket and rugby league had a history of being rooted in class and class difference. The media have assimilated them all into popular culture and the market. At one time, sport was very much about a mixture of patriotism, masculinity and elements such as class and Christianity – the ethos of the 'healthy mind in the healthy body'. Here is the practice for teamwork, leadership and discipline. Sport has been changed by the rise of spectatorship (and the ability to charge for this). It has been transformed by the nurturing of its entertainment value. Only vestiges of the British imperial ethos remain in, for example, the continuing value of the hard and muscular body. Beynon (2002) comments on this, on bodybuilding, on the notion of empowerment (for the man) through the fit body, which continues to be a dimension of sport.

Football became a popular leisure activity in the later part of the nineteenth century, when, along with other sports, it became defined as such, in the modern sense, through the imposition of rules – like the Queensbury rules that created boxing out of bare-knuckle fighting. This regulation of sport sprang out of middle-class impulses, as inspired within the education sphere and gave form to an ethos of 'playing the game'. Rules control performance and outcomes. They provide a shared understanding between players and spectators. They give a form to sports that makes them attractive to spectators, viable as entertainment and amenable to media coverage. At the same time – in the earlier twentieth century – literacy and the expansion of a popular press gave newspapers a new and more working-class audience – for football in particular. Cinema lacked the immediacy and domestic sphere of radio and then television, in the mid-twentieth century, though its newsreels did indeed report on sporting events. But still the genre of sport in news was well established through newspapers, and it is no accident that an early outside broadcast made on British television in 1937 was of the Derby horse race.

The representation and definition of sport has been stretched and redefined through the media, and through the influence of their cash and their technologies. The intensity and sudden death nature of one-day cricket was created to make a more exciting version of the game for TV. The medium has sanctified (and in some cases created) quasi-sports such as wrestling or those competitive action programmes typified by *Gladiators*. These quasi-sports cross the line into being explicitly entertainment vehicles. WWF wrestling is a fiction in which the outcome has been determined (the narrative closure). It is the getting to it that is fun. The extravagant grunts and throws, the illegal moves, the interventions from outside the ring are all part of a ritual and a spectacle. Brookes (2002) provides a useful commentary on WWF wrestling as a soap opera. He points out that most reports on sport define such wrestling as 'not sport' by not reporting it, and do this because it is perceived as parodying sport.

Part of the point of the wrestling bouts is, for example, that they break rules rather than enforcing them. They encourage undisciplined behaviour. But given the ritual surrounding all major sports (not to mention the occasional revelations of outcomes having been fixed), the line between pseudo sports and real ones can be pretty thin. In terms of achieving narrative closure – a kind of reassurance in a world of ambiguities – then, as Ellis (1999) says, 'sport promises that the events it shows will yield a definite ending'. Its representation provides a reassuring version of reality, compared with, say, the often indeterminate outcomes of political stories and events. He also points out the attractions and satisfactions of ways in which the replays and reflections on sporting events allow for a kind of 'working through' of what is going on, for the television audience.

Television's presentation of sport has become more and more dramatic, with commentators hyping elements of nationalism and competition, and with trails building audiences' anticipation of dramatic action (not to mention the now familiar action replay plus views of excited spectators).

The images of sport in the media are often about moments of emotional climax, about success, about implicit domination of an 'other', of the achievement of cultural status. They are of course also about competitiveness, about winning – and about others losing. They are, to a fair extent, about individualism within ideology – even team sports frequently report on the goal scorers, the victorious strikers, the man of the match. These images are about moments of victory, of celebration, of humiliation. 'Images of domination and subordination are central to the reading of the media sports text' (Rowe 1999).

In ideological terms, these image moments yield readings about sporting myths such as heroism, patriotism and the team. These myths are nurtured in school sports, but have their origins in that older version of sport which is about the gentleman and amateur. They come from a time when there was a closer correlation between sports and class, between the ethos of sport and the ethos of social behaviour. It is no accident that Kipling and others referred to the practice of international politics (and of spying) in the late nineteenth century as 'the great game'. In terms of the school analogy, it seems again significant that one will hear managers or captains of teams reflecting on games in terms of, 'the boys' are doing a great job.

It is also ideological (and nostalgic) that a number of films about sport seek to emphasize notions of 'fair play', of (past) 'greatness'. They promote a mythical, even mystical idea of sport nurturing (masculine) virtues and cultural health. One thinks of films like *Chariots of Fire* or *Field of Dreams*.

3.1 Sport, media, commodification

> A large media sports audience is a very precious commodity indeed.
>
> (Rowe 2000)

The media have transformed sport into a global mega-business in which the values of screen time, print space, sports stars, sports teams and their audiences are interrelated and have a serious cash dimension. Brookes (2002) refers to one estimate which says that the global sports industry accounts for 3 per cent of world trade.

The timing and conduct of sports events and contests has been adapted to suit the needs of television in particular, not least because television puts millions of pounds into sport by paying for rights to coverage. The 'real' audience is the audience out there, not the audience in the stadium. The real paymasters are the advertisers and sponsors who buy the slots, buy space on the side of the indie car, supply the kit with their name on, place the advertising in the stadium – predominantly for the camera gaze of television.

In 2002, the sports sponsorship market was valued at £450 million in Britain. In 2003, Vodafone spent approximately £7.45 million to sponsor the football club, Manchester United. In the same year the club had an income of £170 million, the same as the New York Yankees (*IOS*, 7 March 2004).

66 99 Television, more comprehensively than any other medium, has turned sport into an essential component of its organisational infrastructure and textual product, and has succeeded in transforming major sports events (and the remote viewers that they attract) into a pivotal commodity whose value can be realised and exploited in myriad ways.

Rowe (2000)

Where sport used to be a form of organized play, now it is a form of disciplined entertainment, a business, and something which is bought and sold in the marketplace. 'The formation of modern sport could be seen as an attempt both to *discipline* and *commodify* adult play' (Brookes, 2002).

This commodification has gathered pace through developments in technology and through deregulation of ownership in Europe in particular, towards the end of the last century. It could be argued that in Britain, for example, until the 1980s the duopoly of the BBC and the unofficial cartel of the ITV commercial companies meant that while they had an influence on the shape of sport, they also kept something of a lid on market value and costs. The situation in the USA was comparable, until the arrival of Fox Television as a fourth and aggressively competitive network, and then with the growth of specialist channels such as ESPN. Now, the proliferation of satellite and cable channels alongside new technologies has increased competition and the attraction of sport as a reliable and marketable product. The dangers of this expensive relationship between new providers and sports bodies are, however, typified by the collapse of ITV Digital in 2002. The company paid too much for sports rights, mainly to football. The football clubs were asking for more than the market would bear. They operated on the basis of this projected income – not least in terms of buying and selling players. Now they have less money than they thought they would have; and one club (Leicester City) filed for bankruptcy.

In some ways English Football Premier League clubs are like Hollywood product. They have to carry the high cost of stars, who form a collateral industry in their own right. They operate on the basis of preselling rights. The game as core business is sold in different forms (news accounts, replays etc.). They incorporate product placement – the ball, boots etc. They have spin-offs – club magazines or replica kit or video clips for sale. In 2003 David Beckham earned £90,000 a week, and about £11 million in sponsorship deals.

This intensity of the commodification of sport operates in the context of globalization. There are global agencies, such as IMG, that represent and promote stars across sports and across the world. There are global sports bodies managing and dealing on behalf of sports on a worldwide basis. These bodies are themselves big business. Brookes reports that FIFA (the governing body of world soccer) was estimated in 1998 to be worth $250 billion a year. In 2003, a 30-second slot in the nine-game baseball World Series cost approximately $325,000. This may be compared with the £250,000 per 30 seconds which ITV got in 1998 for the World Cup soccer games in France (though it got only £150,000 per 30 seconds in the 2002 World Cup). Trans-national companies negotiate with such bodies for major events that have a worldwide audience – most obviously examples like the Superbowl, the Olympics, Wimbledon. The US TV rights to the 2008 Olympics (in Beijing) have already been sold and are worth $894 million (Brookes, 2002). The right to put logos on sportswear are sold – even sponsorship of the Olympics and the right to use the famous logo is sold.

This should remind us that what we understand sport to be is not contained just within the screening of sports events or within the sports pages of newspapers (though commodity elements are indeed clearly to be seen there). The social status of sport is represented when we see news pictures of sports stars invited to share space with senior politicians. Indeed, one might argue that it is, rather, the status of the politicians that is enhanced by images of such encounters. The cultural value of 'sporting-ness' is endorsed when we walk past stores devoted to these products. The window displays also represent sport. The economic value of sport is represented when transfer fees or prize moneys are reported. The economic power of this material value was recognized when in 1998 the Monopolies and Mergers Commission blocked the agreed takeover of leading Premier Division football club Manchester United by Sky Television. It would have been a logical outcome of mutual self interest. As Tomlinson (2001) says, 'Sport embodies the successful expansion and penetration of the universal market.'

On the surface, sport is still represented as healthy competition, as a struggle between individuals and teams for sporting success and for being recognized as the best in the field. On the surface it is about rankings and places. On the surface it is about winning prizes. Often these are visualized as symbolic – the cup or the plate – while the actual cash prize is not seen and is played down. On the surface sport is about fair play, and a great fuss is made about uses of drugs as cheating. Much is made of the idea that in the arena and on the field everyone is equal. In these respects the representation of sport and of sporting activity accords to a conservative and moralistic set of values, harking back to the nineteenth century.

But the representation of sport as an economic activity and as a marketplace commodity is barely concealed. Cultural capital and financial capital come together in the sports company logo which is seen on the Olympic podium, and which is purchased from the shopping mall in order to be seen.

4 The sporting body

In one sense sport is represented by the body – that body which is so exercised and tested as to excel in a particular activity. It is usually a body in which musculature and other signs connote an exceptional body which is unlike that of the sport spectators and audience. And so the body sets the sportsperson apart.

Some sports – swimming – draw attention to the barely clothed body. We may see a collision of discourses in the case of female competitors in particular – fitness with sexuality. And with all sports the specialized nature of clothing enhances signs of fitness. Lack of fitness undermines the legitimacy of the sport in the case of darts. It may also undermine the legitimacy of the sports person. One might think of the abuse suffered by the golfer, Colin Montgomery, in the year 2000, from course fans who commented insultingly on his being overweight.

Maguire (1999) has defined various types of body that are represented, and which provide a complex understanding of what sport is about. I offer these, with some interpretation of my own.

There is the *bio-medical body* of the world of the trainers, of weightlifters, of cartilage operations on footballer's knees, of calculations of leverage for pole-vaulters.

There is the *disciplined body* of the athlete undergoing dietary and training regimes.

There is the *commodified body* of the major league football player, that is sold for endorsements and sold between teams for vast sums.

There is the *symbolic body* of Venus Williams, that has come to stand for women's tennis, for the success of black women, and which has iconic qualities in the braids and the beads.

These bodies coexist in the media environment and in the minds of audiences. The body has indeed become a controlled and competitive tool in a business called sport, compared with the more casual and amateurish body of the sportsman (usually) of the nineteenth and early twentieth centuries. Professionalism means that this body has an insurance value, a market value, a profit element.

The body is also a sexual and cultural commodity, displayed in media images – discussed further in terms of gender in the sections following. Examples such as Flo Joyner or Sharon Davis or Denise Wilson have been imaged both in the context of sporting competition and as female forms out of context, camera angled and cropped to attend to their sexuality. These female sports stars have also crossed over into the promotion of goods or have become TV celebrities, where once more their sexuality becomes a meaning of their images, as much as their sporting achievements. The image of the American footballer, Brandi Chastain was famously syndicated around the world when she stripped to her Nike sports bra in a shirt-removing victory gesture (1999). In such cases it is, I suggest, important to use analytic tools such as semiotic analysis to be able to demonstrate that it is the text which inflects meaning towards the sexualized body. Alternatively, one has to consider how the spectator's gaze may impose sexual meaning on a sporting image. One may recognize that the still photograph of the sporting body allows it to be examined at leisure, that itself allows for a choice of sexual connotations.

Television has also taken to attracting female audiences through the sexualization of sportsmen. Their bodies have become the subject of magazine articles. Footballers such as David Ginola have advertised coffee, via a film-star glamour pose. As Rowe says: 'Commodity logic and cultural politics have interacted.'

The exercised and toned sporting body becomes exotic and erotic, moving in the disciplined and ritualistic patterns relevant to a given sport.

5 Sport and national identity

❝❞ Sport, especially in the media, becomes deeply incorporated into people's sense of who they are and what other people are like.

Blain and Boyle (1998)

Sports events and sports people have come to represent national identities. These identities are understood in terms of certain sports, certain individuals. Baseball is seen as being quintessentially American, cricket as being very British. Muhammad Ali has been an icon of boxing and of the USA. Kenyans are 'known for' being good long-distance runners. National sports teams are constructed to represent the nation. Their success or failure, their 'uniforms', their use of national flags, their behaviours (see the New Zealand All Blacks pre-rugby match Maori war dance) come to stand for something called national identity. Indeed, it may be said that national identities have been to an extent invented through sport and its symbols. 'The nation constituted around its sporting representatives and communicated internally and externally by means of the media apparatus is the key cultural symbol linking media and sport at deep levels of human emotion' (Rowe, 2000).

There is a sense in which sport is invoked to construct an identity which represents 'the best of' a nation – a display of virtues and a denial of vices which helps the nation feel good about itself. This is what Tomlinson (2001) means when he talks about 'sport as a moral site for the making of a national and sometimes regional identity'.

It could be argued that in so far as the images and the identity include black faces and female faces (see below), it also represents inclusiveness and a moral political correctness. The imaging of this kind of national identity may conflict with the absence of black and female faces in other spheres.

Sport as virtuous behaviour becomes acceptable as a means of competing, of dominating or subordinating. It is not war, even if it is reported in the metaphors and the discourse of war. But then, in the process of competition and seeking pre-eminence, identity coalesces around ideas of difference. The problem then arises that so often 'different' becomes an excuse for the assertion of 'better'. Fans fight on the football terraces because the assertion of club or team identity has become conflated with the need to assert superiority through any means. The outrageously chauvinistic reporting of the 1996 football World Cup encounter between England and Germany in British tabloids, drew on the language of the Second World War ('We have decided to teach the Hun a lesson' – quoted in Ferguson, 1998). It implicitly proposed that a sporting contest was actually a physical conflict. It proposed that identity formation required humiliation of the other.

Beynon (2002) talks about 'Imperial man' as being invoked through international football contests in particular, and as a peculiarly British inheritance from the past which assumes superiority over others: 'It is in sport that the strongest echo of Imperial man survives. His sense of racial superiority and destiny has no place in multicultural, multi-ethnic, postcolonial Britain.'

Ferguson (1998) refers to the ideological work of this kind of representation of national identity. He refers to the notion that something called 'racial purity' is being invoked as part of this identity. This too is a strand drawn from Britain's imperial past –

the construction of identity for Victorian England – an assumption of superiority and difference.

Brookes (2002) sees this invocation of the past as being not about superiority but about a malaise, ennui, a sense of loss and failure. This kind of narration by commentators expects the English cricket team to be beaten by former colonies:

❝❞ The decline of "our" sports teams mirrors the decline of a world order in which Britain was a major imperial power.

National identity may become a kind of commodity, it can be argued, in that for example, one is selling US identity on the back of the distribution and promotion of games of basketball, baseball and American football, on a worldwide basis. This is the cultural imperialism thesis raising itself again. Sport becomes more than a matter of identity formation. It becomes identity marketing. It may be about promotion of ideology as much as the image of a sport or of a nation. For example, ideas about the symbolic importance of physical contact in sport, or of winning at all costs, are exported along with the TV rights and screenings.

The idea that sports stars or star teams come to represent 'the nation' is one which is now undermined by sporting practices. Ideological contradictions are exposed. Ironically, it is the process of commodification which has produced a situation in which star players may move from team to team on a global scale, selling their skills. These are not citizens moved to compete in promotion of a positive national identity, so much as players and entertainers seeking to maximize their worth in the global marketplace. Contradictorily, the marketplace seeks to promote national identities in the cause of manufacturing loyal audiences. Where sport is conducted on a global scale, where the viewing audience is more important economically than the stadium audience, then the market wants there to be an imagined community of the nation 'out there'.

Globalization has also produced some contradictions in audiences, however. Just as players may shift allegiances across national boundaries, so too at least some sections of national audiences may cross these boundaries. For example, in the 2002 football World Cup played in Japan, there was substantial and active Japanese support for the British team.

National identity is partly an account and even a celebration of what the nation is meant to be. It is also an account of what it is not – again, of how it is different from other nations. There is a deal of stereotyping in here as well – that is the staple fare of representations. So sporting commentaries will refer to the methodical organization of the Germans and the passion of the Latin nationalities. Such national characteristics are historical inventions of our cultures – like the English bulldog. But they have always served the interests of groups that wish to move nations in certain directions – such as politicians at times of election, generals in times of war, and media organizations at times of sporting events. Brookes (2002) asserts that 'hegemonic representations define national identities in ways which reproduce dominant class, ethnic, regional, religious or gender interests'.

In this respect one may see the representation of national identity both drawing from and contributing to other representations and senses of identity. Brookes also sees

Rugby and Wilkinson's Winning Boot
Representation can manufacture iconic status for players, as well as construct national identities.
How may this construction take place?
In what ways is it in the interests of the media?
(*Getty Images*)

sport as building some sort of bridge between everyday life as it is lived, and something more abstract – this sense of identity. Sport in the media helps make 'a psychological connection between the everyday life of the individual and the wider abstract category of the nation'.

6 The representation of gender

> By portraying female athletes as feminised and sexualised others, the media trivialise and therefore undermine their athletic achievements. This type of media portrayal results in constructions of female athleticism as less important than male athleticism.
>
> **Kane and Greendorfer (1994)**

I have already questioned the extent to which it is textual producers or textual readers who impose gendered meanings on media texts, and on images in particular. On the other hand, one cannot dispute that sports representation of gender are skewed in various ways. Brookes (2002) refers to the fact that only 36 per cent of the athletes at the 1996 Atlanta Olympics were women. Only 11 of 51 NBC reporters were assigned to cover women's events, and most of the reporters were men anyway. He also comments that 'in general, coverage of women's sports routinely amounts to less than ten percent of the total available'. Kane and Greendorfer (1994) comment that 'women continue to be severely under-represented in the highly prestigious world of sport'. They also comment on research which showed that in 1991 only 5 per cent of US TV air time in sport was given to women's sports.

The sexualization of sportswomen is perhaps not surprising given this kind of stereotypical representation in our culture at large. Tomlinson (2001) refers to the ways

The Female Sportsperson
News photos such as this one can represent a collision of discourses, in which the female body is represented as both athletic and sexual.
   Why is it that sports reporting (in Britain at least) gives more space and imagery to individual female achievement (athletics) than to team sports (rugby or cricket)?
(*Corbis*)

in which participation in sport in public places by women 'renders the body vulnerable to the gaze of others'. If visual representations of women have a long cultural history of assuming the male gaze, then it would not be surprising if at least some sports images are also constructed for that gaze. The reconstruction of sportswear as a fashion commodity by the clothing industries also invites the male gaze and sexually constructed images into the sphere of sport, because these two elements are staples of fashion photography.

Rowe (1999) refers to various analyses of images of sports people which demonstrate that women are represented in more passive poses than men (60 per cent of one sample). He comments on an analysis of an Australian quasi-sporting magazine in which, when the theme was 'naked sports bodies', suddenly two-thirds of the pictures were of women! Again, this fits the dominant model of visual representation of females in other spheres. But Rowe also raises the question of whether it would be equally wrong to represent the sportswoman as rigorously athletic and simply to deny her sexuality. The line between representing a sexual dimension and soft pornographic representations is a difficult one to draw. What he does conclude is that 'sports photographs . . . are neither the innocent nor the "natural" products of value-free sport and sports culture'.

The sportswoman is so often defined by contrast with the man. Margaret Ann Hall refers to work on representations within the America's Cup when she talks about images that 'naturalise the technological and sporting superiority of the man while at the same time marginalising, containing and incorporating visions of women' (Hall, 1996).

Too often, in commentaries and interviews, sportswomen are addressed in terms of appearance, or family relations, or their children or their partners, or even their relationship with their male coach. This is rarely the case for men. There is an assumed contradiction between feminine identity and being a serious athlete, which is not the case for men. Hall discusses the contradictions faced by female bodybuilders when they try to appear muscular and feminine at the same time. She points to examples where to be judged successful women would have to, for example, adopt feminine costumes. One could refer to the notorious example of Florence Griffith Joyner in the USA, who won three Olympic golds, but was reported and photographed more for her nails, hair and running clothes.

It would be unfair not to acknowledge that sportswomen and a female audience have been recognized and valued by the media in some respects. There is an increasing and sympathetic coverage given to sportswomen and female teams. There are more female reporters and writers than ever before in the media industries. For example, Mary Rose has the prime-time evening news sports report slot on BBC television (2004).

And yet the weight of resources, the amount of coverage, the nature of media images still works against women. The very language of sports coverage may be from the discourses of competition, violence and conflict, and favour a masculine, not a female, understanding of what sport is about. Women may be marked as different in taking on what are assumed to be men's sports. No one talks about 'men's football' or 'men's basketball'.

Brookes refers to features of this differentiation:

- *sexualization* – for example the marketing of the Russian Tennis player, Anna Kournokova;

- *infantilization* – the use of the term 'girls' in discussion and commentary;

- *trivialization* – the undervaluing of women's sporting achievements, or their representation as individual (and therefore rather exceptional) efforts: in this case one might think of Tim Henman's notorious endorsement of the inferior rewards for women in the Wimbledon tennis titles;

- *familialization* – the invocation of sportswomen's private lives as a legitimate part of their representation: the assumption that one has a right to enter a more emotional sphere, as opposed to men.

He comments on a tendency for women's sports to be valued for displays of grace or sexuality, on their selective coverage in the media. He refers to the 'ideological role of sport in maintaining unequal power relations between men and women'.

Women who appear to display real physical power make the commentators uneasy. Coverage of female shot putters – especially if they are from Eastern Europe – has made reference to their bulk, to their masculine attributes. Coverage of female tennis players has sometimes seized on lesbianism as a way of explaining their 'unfeminine' strength, as a way of 'othering' them. Amelie Mauresmo, the French tennis player, received this treatment in 1999. Attitudes implied in the reporting of the Williams sisters, dominant in women's world tennis (2004), also allude to the exceptionality of their strength and stamina – as if this is unwomanly. Reporting of them has also revealed another gender framework, which is to talk about women's tennis rather more as if it is a soap opera. The Williams sisters are talked about in terms of conflict between them, or their relationship with their supposedly domineering father. Parents, boyfriends, coaches, emotional episodes (the vulnerable woman) are all the stuff of the reporting of women's tennis – but not of men's tennis.

And 'when it comes to sport playing a role in the construction of the nation it is almost always male sports teams that are seen as most important' (Brookes, 2002).

Active masculine images and hard masculine bodies dominate the pages of newspapers. Games such as cricket, rugby and soccer are seen as 'naturally' masculine. The women's teams get little coverage. There is that underlying cliché that – women form groups for social purposes, but men form groups to compete and to get things done. The coverage of sport on television reinforces a masculine bias and the dominance of male team sport activities. Men keep up with sport and the ongoing narration of how 'their' teams are doing. Indeed, one could argue that sports viewing is part of the 'life narrative' for many males. Gauntlett and Hill (1999) provide much evidence that sports viewing is seen as a male activity, and rejected by many women. So the act of viewing becomes an act of masculinity, just as the images and the style of coverage speaks of masculinity.

Sport with a masculine inflection permeates the press. It appears in lads' magazines such as *GQ* and *Loaded*. It is commonplace on television, not least in panel games such as *They Think It's All Over* and in quiz shows such as *A Question of Sport*. Such shows are dominated by males competing in the factual knowledge stakes, or fooling around.

Male representations in sport are still dominated by the ideal of the body as an 'athletic instrument'. It is a notion that promotes physical achievement and demotes a sexual function. It explains why the image reader is meant to take on those frequent pictures of sportsmen hugging each other in victory or goal scoring, without seeing it as contradicting male social behaviour out of the sports sphere. Indeed, that sphere is like a spiritual bubble that protects the male from criticism. In many ways the male has become a desexualized child. Footballers roll over on the ground when they have scored a goal, like gleeful children. They swagger and posture and square up to one another like competitive lads in rival gangs. Elsewhere, when the sporting male has become eroticized, the meaning is usually ring-fenced by the context – the adverts, the photospread, the pin-up in the magazine for females. It is interesting to read Rowe's account (1999) of the issues surrounding a successful libel case brought by Andrew Ettingshausen, an Australian rugby player. *HQ* magazine published a photograph of him naked in the sports showers in 1993, without his permission. This exposed the penis as a sign of sexuality and it was out of the arena of the sports event. There was no context protecting the concept of sporting masculinity. The body and male-ness was represented as that of a real person carrying out a conventional social activity. The person was not in athletic mode within the sphere of sporting activity.

Brookes discusses the hegemonic nature of masculinity (as opposed to femininity). He argues that there are various kinds of masculinity within society, and that sport defines only one of these, as well as interacting with the others. He quotes Connell (1995):

> Because gender is a way of structuring social practice in general, not a special type of practice, it is unavoidably involved with other social structures. It is now common to say that gender 'intersects' – better, interacts – with race and class. We might add that it constantly interacts with nationality or position in the world order . . . to understand gender, then, we must constantly go beyond gender. The same applies in reverse. We cannot understand class, race or global inequality without constantly moving towards gender.

7 The representation of race

On the face of it, the media construct positive representations in terms of sport and race. Carl Lewis or Michael Jordan or Tiger Woods are rich men whose faces have been all over product endorsements as well as the sports pages. In Britain, black footballers are on the TV every week helping clubs in the top flight to win matches, including in Europe. Ian Wright also had his own chat show on TV for a couple of series (1999–2001). And yet – where are the black sports commentators? Where are the black football managers? One does not wish to denigrate the achievements of individuals such as Lennox Lewis in the field of boxing. But – as well as the lack of Asian and oriental faces in western sports media – there is a relative prevalence of black faces in at least some high-profile sports such as football, and a distinct lack of them in the media as a whole. In other words, the representation of ethnic minorities in sports media neither endorses their status in the sports industries, nor does it add up to a general media stand on social equality. 'There are clear dangers that the media's projection of attractive images of black athletes and concentration on their financial success imply a generalisable solution to the "race problem" ' (Rowe, 2000).

Sport and Ethnic Representations
In one sense, images of achievement in a public space provide positive role models for a black identity. In another sense – and in the context of general news reporting, where images of ethnic groups are far less common in respect of politics or business – images of the black sportsperson may place them in a 'sports ghetto'.
Could one argue that such images serve to promote biased ideas about a given ethnic group being only 'naturally' good at physical (as opposed to intellectual) pursuits?
(Corbis)

Rowe has also pointed out (1999), that the use of black athletes to sell, for example, Nike commodities, does not deal with the broader issues of social inequality and racial difference: it is 'the commodification and expropriation of their difference and resistance'.

Brookes (2002) is direct in his criticism: 'sport has played a fundamental role in the reproduction of unequal power relations . . . in reinforcing regressive stereotypes, particularly through conservative ideologies around "natural" difference'. He sees a contradiction between legal and cultural moves against sexism and racism in society, and the ways in which black people and women are actually represented in sports media and targeted as consumers. He is not proposing that all representations are equally negative, or indeed always negative. But he does point out the contrast between the positive representation of someone like Tiger Woods in the field of golf and the negative depiction of Mike Tyson in boxing. One is a role model, the other is a racial 'other'. But both conspire to conceal real poverty and racism underneath, as it affects black people and communities in the USA.

One might also point to the interesting contrast between the two sports in terms of image. Golf has the image of a 'civilized' middle-class sport in which one whacks a ball, not someone else's head. It is a competition played outdoors, by the affluent and captains of industry. Some golf clubs have a reputation for social exclusiveness. Boxing, on the other hand, is a high contact working-class sport. It is a sport of physicality, half-naked bodies, of spectacle, of immediacy and the intense emotional involvement of spectators. It is more masculinized than golf, for all the existence of female boxers (as part of an exotic contest). In spite of efforts to brand it as 'the noble art', it is a sport with high-profile cases of serious injury and death, and with publicized connections between some managers and criminal activity. In spite of the veneer of rules and the scoring of points, its clear objective is to cause some degree of physical harm to the opponent. I suggest that the representation of sport has as much to do with the nature of the competition and its status, as it has to do with competitors.

Some commentators have observed kinds of ambivalence towards black athletes and expressions of national identity. Jim Pines (2001) comments on the fact that black American athletes will wave and wear the American flag almost as a matter of course. But the same is not true for British athletes and the Union Jack flag – with its uncomfortable connotations of empire. More explicit are the occasions when black football players endure abuse barracking from the terraces. He refers to the 1998 World Cup when saying that: 'The overall emphasis in terms of media representation – or, if you like, in terms of public relations – stressed the recognition and acceptance of (ethnic) diversity and inclusiveness within the broader framework of national teams.' But then, as he goes on to say, apparently positive images of 'black English-ness' in sport remain 'an awkward construction' because they attempt to 'play down or elide unresolved discourses of British race relations and multiculturalism'.

Issues surrounding ethnic identities and national identity remain intertwined. But race issues are not only to be linked with skin colour. Ferguson (1998) among many others, gives space to the notorious *Daily Mirror* coverage of the 1996 European football championship, in which anti-German sentiments were crude and rampant. As he says, whatever the backlash against the paper, the damage had been done. This is the power of negative representations.

Residual prejudices are confirmed. Racist representations in sport co-relate with racism elsewhere in the media. Images are intertextual. Meanings are mutually reinforced. 'All Germans had been confirmed, discursively, as sharing entirely negative characteristics, and the discursive reserve, carried in the memories of computers, editorials, readers and other members of the public, had been suitably replenished.'

It seems that too often representations of sport and sports people do confirm negative characteristics, though one should also recognize more positive current media celebrations of the success of such people as Paula Radcliffe, the British world class long-distance runner.

Clearly sport and its representations is an area where identities collide – national, ethnic, gendered: where discourses interact – the body standing for sexual distinction or sporting distinction: where cultural histories are renewed and revalued – past achievements by teams and individuals. Sport is not just the sum of its participants. But it is very much understood through them and how they are constructed by the media. It is relevant to a broader understanding of ideology and media that sports people are also, for instance, 'competitors'. They may stand for a degree of tension between the value placed on individualism and that placed on group commitment – a tension which we may read more widely into social institutions and social behaviours.

8 Discussion extract

The mediation of sport provides these very powerful insights into other aspects of our values just because these values are often expressed quite accidentally or innocently, as a half-conscious or unconscious by-product of our interest in the activity of sport itself. But this is not always so; sometimes what seems to be an article on a sporting theme – a newspaper piece, say, on Dutch or English fans, or African footballers – is either consciously or unconsciously a way of expressing views on another nationality or race, and only inform a piece about the world of sport. This means that media sport is not only very important *economically*, but also *politically* and *ideologically*: 'ideology' used here in both its senses, sometimes just neutrally as a 'view of the world', but more often negatively, as a 'distortion' of actual social or cultural life. There is a lot of such distortion in sports reporting, often apparently acceptable there where it would not be editorially possible elsewhere in a newspaper or broadcast.

And, since being a television or newspaper journalist or editor is a position of privilege, we should bear in mind that the ideologies the mainstream media produce or reproduce when giving us accounts of sports-related matters will tend to be those of socially dominant groups rather than those who may be disempowered: we are more likely to find out what men think about women than the other way around; more likely in Italy or France to find out what Whites think about Blacks than vice versa; more likely on British television networks to find out the English view of the next World Cup than the Welsh or Scottish expectations. Conversely, the accounts which we do *not* hear tell us a lot about the groups denied a voice on TV and radio or the press.

Blain and Boyle (1998)

1 In what ways may representations of sports events and sports persons be seen as doing ideological work?

2 In what ways do you think that media sport is important economically and politically?

3 Which groups can you identify as being absent or under-represented in media sports – and how does this matter?

9 Further reading

Brookes, R. (2002) *Representing Sport*. London: Arnold.

Creedon, P.J. (ed.) (1994) *Women, Media and Sport – Challenging Gender Values*. London: Sage.

Hall, M.A. (1996) *Feminism and Sporting Bodies*. Champaign, Illinois: Human Kinetics.

Maguire, J. (1999) *Global Sport – Identities, Societies, Civilisations*. Cambridge: Polity Press.

Rowe, D. (1999) *Sport, Culture and the Media*. Buckingham: Open University Press.

CHAPTER THIRTEEN

GLOBALIZATION AND THE MEDIA

Questions of power and of cultural exchange

“People are faced with an extending range of imagery and information involving models of citizenship, forms of production, styles of consumption, modes of communication, principles of world order . . .”

Spybey, A. (1996) *Globalisation and World Society*. Cambridge: Polity Press.

1 Introduction

Globalization is a contested concept which tries to make sense of a range of factors:

- the effects of technologies;

- the extension of corporate power;

- different kinds of cultural export and exchange;

- the arrival of new media and the creation of new kinds of media texts for both local and transnational audiences.

The contestation produces utopian and dystopian models for understanding what is happening. For example, there are pessimistic views such as those of Schiller (2000) and cautiously optimistic views such as those of Giddens (1990). There is a contrast between a view of a media world dominated by the products of trans-national businesses, and a view of media which facilitate information exchange and the creative interaction of cultures. 'The globalisation of capital also serves as a battering ram that relentlessly attacks working people's living standards' (Schiller, 2000). 'Globalisation . . . introduces new forms of world interdependence' (Giddens, 1990).

Giddens even argues that globalization is, in a positive sense, a sign of the declining grip of the West over the rest of the world, exemplified by phenomena such as the spread of the ubiquitous curry meal to the stream of immigration into the West.

This chapter will maintain a general focus on institution, text and audience. But you should note links with issues to do with the understanding of identity and cultural consumption. Media texts are produced and exchanged on a global scale. They continue to be cultural products. They continue to link with cultural practices. Media audiences are, as ever, simultaneously consumers of other cultural artefacts. In a social sense, they are practitioners, experimenters, generators of meaning and creators of culture. In this respect, globalization is not just about international politics or about kinds of media imperialism – it is about social practices, social institutions and about people's lives. This view would say that it is as much about the package holiday and the in-flight movie as it is about deals done with the global oil economy through OPEC.

Moran (1998) suggests that 'social life is shaped by world wide mechanisms'. This is certainly true for a number of countries. But how social life is being shaped and with what consequences is not so clear. Moran also talks about national cultures, economies and borders as disappearing. I would dispute this. Certainly one can see some examples of ways in which diasporic communities are linked worldwide via global technologies and regardless of national boundaries. But equally, national regulation of the media persists as a way of marking borders. I would propose a dynamic model in which the relationship between the global, the regional, the national and the specifically local is in a creative state of flux – in terms of production, consumption and textual features.

Although examples of media communication such as the Internet and satellites have contributed to the much talked about contraction of time and space on a global scale, I would suggest that globalization is about much more than this. It is also something of an illusion. Swathes of the planet do not have television. Many countries have very limited access to telephones. Reporters going in to remote areas with videolinks and satellite phones do not make for a truly contracted global space. Instant global communication is the privilege of the wealthy on this planet. I would argue that globalization is an idea, a way of conceiving the world, as much as being a material phenomenon. There are, indeed, those people, cultures and businesses that think global. But they comprise those whose material practices and cultural histories have encouraged them to think this way – what is loosely called 'the developed world'. There are still many peoples who do not think in this way.

Another point of debate recognizes that globalization may not be an intentional process. The global extension of capitalist practices, is not something that has been explicitly plotted in the business boardroom. It is, rather, an unsurprising consequence of

- the ideology of expansionism;

- the need to attract more investment to pay for that expansion;

- the continual feeding search for new markets;

- the belief in meeting and eliminating economic competition;

- the need to satisfy the unsatisfiable profit urge of shareholders.

The regional or global market is just an extension of the original local or national market. McQuail (2000) refers to 'the economic dynamics of global media markets that work blindly to shape the flows of media commodities' – dynamics which 'favour the free market model and in general promote capitalism'.

The American publisher Viking was not plotting to invade English culture when it took over Penguin books. It was seeking economic strength through acquisition. Amazon could not plan to be the pre-eminent online bookstore – in the sense that the technology that makes its business possible was not planned for commercial or social use in the first place. I am not saying that media businesses become globally powerful entirely by accident. But their intentions are not overtly political, social or cultural, even if these are some of the consequences of their existence. We are talking about opportunism and commercial impulses.

Of course, such comments place globalization within a dominantly economic context. And in this sense one would also comment on the selectiveness of economic globalization – the selection of certain audiences for certain media within certain countries or regions because they will make money. Latin America is attractive because 85 per cent of households have a television, and because many of the middle classes speak English.

But one also has to recognize that there is something unintentional about other features of globalization. Holiday companies did not intend to create a global problem with the transmission of diseases from one part of the planet to another. No one planned for media and their news operations to become information gatherers and million dollar fund raisers for disasters around the world – disasters which even fifty years ago ordinary people in the West would have hardly been aware of.

These last points remind us that, however one interprets globalization exactly, it operates at both a macro and micro level. It is not just some abstraction for economists or cultural critics. It is 'a transformation in the ways that we experience our everyday local lives as they are increasingly penetrated by distant global forces' (Tomlinson, 1997).

2 Major questions

1 In what ways are the media part of globalization, especially with relation to technologies?

2 What are key features of globalization, especially as they relate to media of communication?

3 What is the substance of debates about imperialism, global flows and hybridization?

4 How may we understand the relationship between notions of the global and of the local, with relation to texts, media use and identities?

5 How meaningful are concepts of global ownership, global audiences and global culture?

3 Globalization as history

One needs to be aware that globalization as we may now understand it, is not simply a product of late twentieth-century technology and of modernity. The notion of exploration for new markets and of global trafficking in goods goes back to the endeavours of such institutions as The East India Company in the seventeenth century. Today, the West brings back cheap DVD players, not spices. Politicking and shifting alliances between nation states in the eighteenth and nineteenth centuries, and the creation of empires, is a paradigm of shifting alliances and mergers between media corporations in the twentieth century. Again, the point is that these behaviours create ways of thinking global, of extending geography. Ideological bastions have fallen. The Berlin Wall fell. Chinese isolationism is melting. Consumerism is embraced. One way of looking at the history of globalization is to model it on the exploration of markets, the search for more consumers, the search for economies of production.

Our understanding of something called 'Japan' is one model for the historical dimensions of our understanding of this thing called 'globalization'. Japan has a geographical location because of exploration and maps of the nineteenth century. It has a political location because it was literally conquered by the USA in 1945, as part of western alliances. It has a cultural location and identity because its cultural goods were brought back to the West – see the stir cause by Hokusai's painting 'The Wave', in the late nineteenth century, or by Kurosawa's film *Rashomon* in 1953. It has an economic location because it embraced production-line Fordism, and in the 1960s began making the West its own market for motorcycles and cars.

The history of globalization is something that is still being made, so our understanding of it is shifting. Hamish McRae, in an article in the *Independent on Sunday* (27 April 2003) refers in economic terms to 'old' and 'new' globalization. He describes 'old globalization' as being about exporting goods and services (perhaps an old imperialism?). 'New globalization' is about local production based on foreign investment. This foreign investment happens within the developed world: it is not simply something which is done to the developing world. Either way, this kind of cross-border investment requires adjustment to local cultures and their values. McRae argues that this requires face-to-face contact – a global flow of people, as much as flows of trade and finance.

4 Global flows – imposition or exchange; global and local

Debates about the nature and development of globalization tend to centre around alternative views. One is about the imposition of (media) cultures by the West on the rest of the world – as opposed to a model of free cultural exchange and mutual benefits. The other is about the inevitable rise of global powers and formations, to the detriment of local cultures and differences (the spread of English, for instance).

Accounts of the global flow of information and entertainment texts tend to emphasize the apparent breaching of national boundaries by examples such as 24-hour stock markets or Hollywood high concept movies. But one needs to remember that there are many examples of texts that do not travel culturally – the British satirical chat-show performer Ali G was met by incomprehension in the USA (2002). It is also the case that nation states continue to regulate media and protect their cultures by invoking all sorts of controls. All European countries operate some sort of protectionism. For example, France demands a 60 per cent 'local' quota for its television programming.

Moran (1998) raises some interesting points in a discussion of television formats and copyright. Formats are copyrighted and licensed to different countries – although the evidence of legal cases is that this copyright is not global (cases asserting global copyright have been lost). But he suggests that television 'owners' go along with the notion of global copyright because it is a convenience – 'a format is a cultural technology which governs the flow of program ideas across time and space'. It helps 'to organise and regulate the exchange of program ideas between media producers'. By the same token, TV ratings do not really tell one anything about audiences, but serve usefully as a 'mechanism of exchange between broadcasters and advertisers'.

the global	v	regional and local
one-way flow	v	exchange
cultural imperialism	v	hybridization
imposition	v	resistance
technology/domination	v	technical appropriation
global audiences	v	local audiences and identities
loss of identity	v	extension of the diaspora
copyright	v	piracy
genre standardization	v	local innovation

Globalization as a Set of Oppositions
In critical terms, one might also see an opposition between a pessimistic political economy analysis and an optimistic pluralist view of what is happening globally, in respect of media ownership, media products, media audiences, and the preservation of cultures.
(*Graeme Burton*, 2004)

So one may say that a game show like *Wheel of Fortune* does represent a kind of media globalization – it turns up in various forms across many countries. But precisely because it is only the format that is licensed, because it is dubbed or adapted, then as a text it actually becomes 'nationalized'. So soaps or game shows may 'flow' around the planet to the benefit of media producers. But kinds of adaptation to local conditions represent a kind of cultural accommodation, rather than unalloyed cultural imperialism.

However, it should be recognized that some take a more pessimistic view of what is happening to national and local markets. For example, Frith (2000) comments on 'the increasing impossibility of a national (music) market the size of Britain sustaining the investment now needed to promote an act'.

Much the same might be said about the British film industry. However, it has to be pointed out that Britain historically has an unusually close cultural and economic relationship with the USA, which renders it especially susceptible to kinds of US dominance. It also depends on how one chooses to define a given media industry and its audience. In the case of music, it is true that if one looks to a model in which acts are nurtured expensively and groomed for performance and profit on the international stage, then it takes the resources of a Sony Corporation to sustain investment. But if one chooses to look at British popular music at a local level, then clubs, pubs and even national venues are bursting with performance. There is independent production. And companies such as World Music Network are producing, distributing and bringing performers to Britain who had hardly been heard of twenty years ago.

All this suggests that globalization produces simultaneous, different, and even contradictory effects. There is global control of the production and flow of some kind of music – even homogenization. And yet alternative music cultures develop locally, and even tap into a global flow. 'Globalisation does not mean imposing homogenous solutions in a pluralistic world' (Das, 2000). 'Globalisation and global cultural flows should not necessarily be understood on terms of a set of neat, linear determinations, but instead viewed as a series of overlapping, overdetermined, complex and "chaotic" conditions' (Barker, 1999).

There is an argument that market forces make global companies recognize and adapt to local media. Indeed Curran (2002) refers to the argument that, as global pressures erode national media, they actually promote something more local. There are those media which speak to, and for, a specifically Scottish or Basque identity and culture. It may also be said that global technologies enable local cultures to cross over, to create hybrid forms, to access new markets. The 1990s saw a surge of interest in Cuban music. In the same decade certain Australian soap operas took a firm hold on the British TV audience. From one point of view, we are back to a familiar argument about the media – determinism or pluralism? Do global media companies impose their production practices and products on local audiences – a one-way flow? Or are we seeing pluralistic globalization with cultural diversity, as practices, materials and ideas flow in many directions at once?

Sreberny (2000) would certainly think so, and rejects 'simplistic' imperialist models, without being happy either with the optimism of pluralists who see variety, diversity and choice in the global media landscape. She identifies four areas which she examines – media forms, media firms, media flows and media effects.

1 *Media forms* are discussed in terms of wide-ranging technical developments but with the critical comment that global does not mean universal with regard to technical 'reach' across the planet.

2 *Media firms* are discussed in terms of US company dominance, but with qualifications about the rapidly changing global scene, and about the true nature and extent of that dominance.

3 *Media flows* are discussed in terms of examples like the extraordinary penetration of audio and video recording to remote places, but also in terms of the complex and varied picture at a local level; also in terms of corporations' relative lack of interest in the developing world, not least because of the problems with piracy. This is significant because it draws attention to control of product and of copyright as underpinning much of capitalism and media businesses in particular. Piracy is, even unintentionally, a form of resistance. Media do not want their products to flow into areas where there is no return – but they may be appropriated anyway.

4 *Media effects* are discussed in terms of their ambiguity and unevenness, especially with relation to the developing world. There is evidence that global media affect leisure patterns and social lives, for instance, but not that they change beliefs. There are huge variations in consumption and assimilation because of factors such as illiteracy or the differences between urban and rural populations.

Sreberny discusses kinds of 'cultural bricolage', in which local audiences make selective and unexpected use of media and other cultural goods, rather than, for example, watching and making sense of television programmes in the way that a Western audience would. She argues that the exercise of global power, and the consumption of media goods and the effects of these, is complex. This is not to be understood in terms of comprehensive macro models of media imperialism or of audience resistance.

5 Facets of globalization

> The notion of globalisation is the assertion that a world-wide system of economic, cultural and political interdependence has come into being or is in the process of formation.
>
> **Moran (1998)**

Here, I am concerned with various ways in which globalization is described and understood. Its dimensions, so far as they are agreed, go beyond the flow of media texts or the global influence of multi-national corporations. Spybey (1996) talks about definitions in terms of 'polity, economy, communication and world order'. So the media context is one in which

- power is brokered on a global scale;

- the economies of nation states no longer stand alone;

- information and indirect social contact is available instantly between technologically developed societies across the planet;

● the interdependence of economies and societies is conceived of and discussed on a global scale.

Whether this adds up to anything like an identifiable global society or global cultures is another matter.

Moran is very sceptical about this and points out that in terms of the accessibility of media texts (TV in particular) and uses of media technology, one is talking about only about one third of the population of the planet, with a considerable bias towards the 'developed world'. In his view, the notion that there is some kind of internationalized economy does not add up to a global society, nor necessarily breaks down the nation state. What he does identify as both a feature of, and a context to, globalization is useful (my glosses in parenthesis).

● new trading blocks (in which for example, South East Asia and South America become both important markets for and (to some extent) producers of goods – Globo TV in Brazil);

● labour changes (in which for example, production is outsourced in Third World countries – telephone call centres relocated to India);

● mobility and tourism (in which the mobility of people around the planet may be linked with cultural interactions and the mobility of media goods);

● unemployment in the West (see outsourcing, the contraction of manufacturing, the growth of service industries and the growth of leisure industries (inc. media));

● new technologies (especially satellites, optic fibre cable and the Internet, which have enabled media convergence, digital systems and the global exchange of media texts).

Waters (1995) argues for broadly similar areas characterizing globalization as other commentators – economy, polity and culture. Behind these areas he posits kinds of exchange which work on different scales of geography. To summarize (with my glosses) –

● Material exchanges localize (the exchange of material goods has to be about production on a local level, even if their distribution is global – labour is material).

● Political exchanges internationalize (the exchange of political views (diplomacy) constructs a web of international relations and geographies among nation states).

● Symbolic exchanges globalize (the exchange of symbols – whether this is a piece of written text or the Nike tick – works on a global level. It is not confined by political borders or by material constraints – media texts or financial dealings are symbolic goods).

He also defines globalisation in social and geographical terms: 'a social process in which the constraints of geography and cultural arrangements recede and in which people become increasingly aware that they are receding'.

Here there is more than a touch of McCluhan's global village, and what one might call a populist view that globalization is all about the compression of time and space. This may be exemplified by the technologies of transport and electronic communication, which make it possible to reach the other side of the world in a day and to make contact with others in no time at all. However, you will see that throughout this chapter notions of what globalization is, let alone its causes and consequences, are more complex and questionable than the time/space model. Waters is as sceptical as others about the emergence of a genuine world society which threatens the nation state.

More interesting is his argument for four conditions that make globalization possible. These conditions would seem to be very much about western attitudes and development, and to some extent about modernity and materialism – (again, my glosses) –

- individualization – may be related to a belief in individual achievement and consumption (see the cult of celebrity in the media);

- internationalization – may be related to a politicized concept of the world as a network of alliances (see the view of the world expressed through news);

- societalization – may be related to the notion of something called 'society', which has global as much as national dimensions (see the directives of the European Union applying to a collection of member states; or see the assumptions behind international appeals for aid to the developing world);

- humanization – may be related to beliefs in human potential, in the individual, in achievement, in human morality and goodness, but apart from religion (see not only the content of media texts but also the very expansionism which is behind commercial and media global empires).

We are talking here about ways of modelling the world, of conceiving society, of constructing physical and cultural geographies, which make globalization possible, which influence how it has happened. One has to add in factors such as the notion of a market for goods, the assumptions with the kinds of rationalization that inform science and economics. Notions of science and economics are not shared by all cultures, though it may be true that they are being taken on board in some form. The example of younger generation Japanese is a good one in this case. They are embracing individualism and materialism (and even egalitarianism), whereas their grandparents thought more dominantly in terms of collectivism and kinds of spirituality.

In a material sense, globalization is about the traffic of people and goods around the planet. It is about worldwide commercial alliances. It is about the interchange of information which enables global financial arrangements. One could be talking about media businesses and the distribution of media texts. In an immaterial sense, globalization is about that sense of the world which is generated through representations in people's heads. The words and images may be shared by different people in different countries. But, inevitably, a sense of what the world is will not be shared identically. So one can argue that globalization means different things to different audiences. Our sense of the world may seem real enough, supplied as it is by television in particular. News and documentaries seem to bring us in touch with a global dimension of places, peoples, political events and so on. But as Morley (1996b) comments: – 'Television takes over from the real as the place where "real" things happen only if they are screened.' Here one might get into an argument which says that to some extent what we conceive of as globalization is just another media representation.

Appadurai (1993) posits a much quoted model of five connected and overlapping 'scapes' which describe global relations and processes. These are the mediascape, the financescape, the infoscape, the technoscape and the ethnoscape. Clearly these conceptions reinforce a general thinking about globalization in which technical innovations, information flow, finance, identities and media co-relate around the planet, albeit selectively, and with unpredictable consequences.

Barker (1999) proposes a similar map of globalization when, with reference to Giddens, he talks about

- a world capitalist economy;
- a nation state system;
- a world military order;
- a global information system.

6 Globalization and technologies

In talking about technology one needs to recognize the important role and effect of communicative media, and not be stuck in old mass-media models that emphasize entertainment and transmission. Indeed, the most significant technologies that underpin global exchange are to do with distribution, not content. It is cable and satellite that carries the material of telephone and the Web around the planet. One also needs to distinguish between those examples that are accessible to general populations, and those which are actually controlled by political, military or media elites. So you can access GPS positioning information to find out where you are on the planet, but you cannot use military channels to look into back gardens in Iran. You can pick up a telephone to talk around the world, but you are unlikely to have a satellite phone unless you are, for example part of a TV news team.

Control of the technology and understanding of globalization tends to be dominated by economic interpretations. One good example of this in Britain is the telephone. The core landline system was set up for national coverage as a public utility, though only those who could afford line rental would have had a phone. All the same, the country achieved saturation coverage, and the phone became a medium of social exchange and family bonding, as much as a commercial tool. But the mobile phone is entirely controlled by commercial interests. It is not available to everyone – there are still many rural places where signals do not reach. It is a cultural commodity as much as a social tool. Certain models are coveted as are certain makes of trainers. It is being re-engineered as a kind of portable games machine, as a link with commercial providers of information. This is also an example of convergence – in commercial interests. Globalization of this technology is defined by economic forces.

An interesting starting point for considering the characteristics of global technologies is a model provided by Waters (1995), which is now summarized with my own examples.

- miniaturization   the iPod portable music centre
- personalization   the handheld phone with picture messaging
- integration   the CD/DVD as a source for any example of audio-visual material, from films to 'encyclopedias'
- diffusion   satellite links or wireless to computer links

● autonomization

home recording studios or domestic computer editing programs for music and images

I have somewhat skewed the examples towards a domestic sphere, to make the point that global innovations in technology are not all about linking cultures, privileging global flow from West to the rest, or perhaps helping manufacture something called 'global society'. Technology may spread globally but it can be used locally. Camcorders can be used to preserve and even promote local forms of dance or music. Regionalized television can carry advertising images, or it can carry images which reaffirm religious practices and convictions.

There is a danger that one may become so 'excited' by the possibilities of technology, by visions of a harmonious world order, that one ignores the selectivity and limitations of such media technologies. Even in the West, domestic access to and familiar use of the Internet is by no means universal. The technology itself is not as reliable and user-friendly as commercial promoters would have us believe. So there are cultural divisions between elites that can afford the technology and its servicing, and those who cannot. Such divisions may be compounded by the nature of work. For some people it is in the interests of employers to supply technology and training; they may actually have access to global communication. Others never touch a keyboard, or need to talk to people in other countries. These divisions are magnified if one considers the world as a whole.

This technological elitism applies to other media – generally on grounds of cost, though there are also examples of regimes that control technology as a means of maintaining power (for example in Burma). There are still many households across the planet that do not own a telephone or a television (or running water for that matter). Technology has to be paid for, as well as make a profit for commercial enterprises, whether through purchase, installation or use. So in technological terms, the global map is selective, limited and drawn by political and commercial considerations. Indeed Curran (2002) comments that 'global regulation is heavily insulated from public influence' – in other words, it is pretty undemocratic.

7 Institutions and global ownership

The facts of global media ownership are indisputable. The significance of these facts is another matter. Clearly it raises issues of power – the power to manufacture and distribute representations on a global scale. There is the power to control certain views and understandings of the world through control of a few news agencies and news producers. There is the commodification of media goods. There is the categorization of media products. There is the setting up of global models for production and distribution that influence which films are made and how. And yet there is evidence against, as much as for, the homogenization of media texts. There are plenty of regional and local producers surviving. Audiences clearly prefer their own local cultural goods. And there is no evidence of a global and absolute control of meanings.

It is important to recognize that media institutions are merely some among others, on the global scale. In themselves they are often a part of corporations that have a complexity of material interests. They also coexist with, for instance, global mining

Balance of income on intellectual property: royalties and licence fees, $ billion (1999)

US
UK
Sweden
Ireland
Russia
France
China
Italy
Australia
Netherlands
Germany
Spain
Japan
South Korea

-2   0   2   4   6   8   10   12   14   16   18   20   22

Sources: IMF Balance of Payments Statistics Year Book 2000

America Dominates the Creative Industry
Culture translates into cash, as this chart shows. US royalty and licence income is disproportionately huge on a global scale.
(*The Independent*)

corporations or car manufacturers. In particular, one needs to recognize the importance of global financial systems which make possible the conduct of any kind of global business. So, for example, General Electric owns Primestar satellite and various cable companies. Three of the largest publishers in the world are owned by Bertelsmann (Germany), Viacom and AOL/TimeWarner (USA).

During (1999) provides an interesting case study of the film *Total Recall* (1990) and its star, Arnold Schwarzenegger. It was produced by Carolco, a company comprising French, Italian and Japanese backers. In 1993, TCI, the largest US cable operator, took a majority shareholding in Carolco (TCI itself was taken over by the telecommunications giant, AT&T, in 1998). The film was shot in Mexico City. It took $180 million of its $300 million gross from countries outside the USA. It was distributed by TriStar, which is an arm of Columbia Pictures, which itself is owned by Sony. This is a case study in global finance, production, distribution and markets (audiences).

The classic model for capitalist industries in the twentieth and twenty-first centuries has been that of vertical integration. The company seeks to control material sources, production, distribution and retailing. It eliminates competition by driving competitors out of business through undercutting on price, or through a takeover. Some media corporations have worked like that on a global scale.

But one needs to recognize that global industries may not preserve a vertically integrated model. There have been strong rumours that Ford will give up direct control of car production, but will retain its financial, distributive and marketing roles. It already owns production plants around the world. But Hollywood got there first. It was selling off fixed-cost production plant from the 1960s onwards. It has retained control of distribution and marketing. Hollywood majors are part of larger corporations and media alliances, and so can access huge amounts of capital to fund projects. As Malone and Laubacher (2000) put it: 'entire industries can evolve quite rapidly from centralised structures to network structures'. They cite the example of a fashion accessories company in the USA, *Topsy Tail*, which generated an $80 million a year income on the basis of having three employees and no contact with the products as such. Globalization moves in mysterious ways on the back of interactive technology.

8 Media imperialism

Although this has been a dominant model for understanding the reach of global media institutions and their products from the 1970s onwards, it no longer constitutes an adequate single explanation for what is going on globally. Such imperialistic models, including those for culture generally (Dorfman & Matterlart, 1975), tend to concentrate on consumption, and to miss production and the circulation of product. As fellow travellers in post-Marxism and inheritors of Adorno and Horkheimer, these models tend to assume that the text is a Trojan horse for the uncritical consumption of ideology.

I am not trying to bypass and ignore either effects or ideology, in some kind of postmodern sleight-of-hand. One may still argue for concern about the reach of global corporations and the possible effects of globally circulating texts. But such concerns have

The McGraw·Hill Companies

Global Leaders
Some companies are well-known world leaders in their businesses. Yet there are still many countries where most of the population would not have heard of them, or would not use their products.
    Where might this be, and why might it be so?
    These companies are mostly American. Yet it is, for instance, China that is the fastest growing economy in the world.
    So what may this fact, and other things you know about global media ownership, have to say about the nature of globalization and media power?
(BBC/McGraw-Hill)

also to take account of audience theories, of context, of an increasingly complex flow of cultural products.

David Rothkopf (2000) argues for cultural imperialism, though he does not see this as being entirely dominated by the US media owners. He points out that soap operas from Latin America do well in Russia. Nevertheless he also acknowledges US power. He sees the control of global markets by (media) corporations as a done deal. 'The global market-place is being institutionalised through the creation of a series of multi-lateral entities that establish common rules for international commerce.'

He makes a near moral argument for global imperialism, referring to cultural divisions which have fuelled war and genocide. Unfortunately, one cannot argue that an American dominated economic world order would be benign, non-violent or capable of alleviating division on the planet. He may be confusing division with difference: and difference is something which many would wish to preserve and to praise in the context of world media. Once more, globalization of the media is something which is evolving, and monolithic imperialist models seem outdated. Rothkopf talks about CNN as being a prime source of news in the Middle East. But the beginning of the twenty-first century has seen the inception of Al-Jazeera television news, which is both Arab and pretty independent in its coverage. It became a prime source of news in the war on Iraq (2003).

In trying to qualify the argument for US imperialism with regard to the media worldwide, I do not want to ignore imposing facts. Herman and McChesney (1999) quote a Disney executive as saying, 'The Disney strategy is to think global, act local.' Ownership and sales fit the strategy, even if one argues about what happens on the cultural ground.

In 2000 the USA had a television and film trade surplus with Europe of $5 billion. Also in 2000 US films accounted for 70 per cent of cinema admissions in Europe (Doyle, 2002). In the music industry, Polygram, TimeWarner, Disney, EMI and Bertelsmann account for 80 per cent of world sales. You will notice that the same names keep coming up. In the film industry, Disney, TimeWarner, Viacom (Paramount), Seagram (Universal), Sony (Columbia), Polygram, MGM and Newscorp (Fox) dominate world markets in which non US revenues represent 65 per cent of their income. Global media ownership is also fairly incestuous – Seagram/Universal owns 15 per cent of TimeWarner. Global media ownership is a very big poker game in which entry costs keep out all but the richest players. Newscorp was big enough to play the game in the USA, and, invoking the principle of synergy, has pieced together film, TV, cable and satellite interests (it owns DirecTV, Echostar and MCI, satellite and cable companies).

So there is a valid question about what space and influence is left either worldwide or locally for smaller companies. One may also ask whether anything like true competition is going to survive on the global media scale. Television news agency business is dominated by Reuters and Worldwide TV News. Advertising is dominated by WPP, Omnicom and Interpublic, who do more business outside the USA than in them.

Herman and McChesney (1999) also comment critically on US attitudes to what constitutes free world trade and legitimate national regulation and protection of culture industries, 'The US government aggressively insists upon a protection of intellectual property that provides maximum income to our industry, while displaying minimal interest in the concerns of anyone else.'

Media global commercialism has become marked by the synergy of mergers and associations between companies, and by the packaging of associated products for multiple audiences. Global consumption has become a five-course meal rather than a snack. In the case of Disney's 1996 ten-year deal with McDonald's worldwide (promoting jointly children's meals and Disney characters and product), we are talking literally about eating as well as cultural consumption. Disney business is not just about film. It owns or controls theme parks, Pay TV and a US TV network (control of distribution). It produces sound tracks and TV series, and has controlling interests in relevant distributors. Spin-offs and tie-ins to films make big money. In 1994 Disney's *The Lion King* took $300 million at the box office. But it took $1 billion through spin-offs.

In so far as the imperialism thesis still stands up, one should recognize that it is about more than the commercial imposition of goods on the many by the few, and about more than the covert export of ideology. It covers ways of doing things which in themselves assume ways of thinking about a combination of social relations and commercial practices. Negus and Roman-Velazquez (2000) talk about 'the pressure to conform to a series of aesthetic and commercial agendas, working practices, production routines and working codes'. This is about the corporations imposing their ways of doing things at a local level. It is about their power to allocate resources. It is about the dynamics of volume, where for little extra cost the local producer or market yields a good return on an original investment.

But one should recognize that there is resistance to forms of imperialism, especially at the level of government and regulation within the nation state. France has a law insisting that at least 40 per cent of pop radio output has to be about French product. Saudi Arabia has banned satellite dishes – though whether this is about freedom of speech rather than freedom of consumption is another matter.

If one looks at television schedules in any country, while it is evident that there is a lot of American product, prime time is still dominated by indigenous culture. Leading European TV channels import less than a third of their programmes from elsewhere, including the USA. Politicians will support, through regulation if necessary, the cultural preferences of those who vote them into power. In any case, genres such as news, chat shows, game shows and sport are usually cheap to generate – at least as cheap as imported product. There is some evidence of critical readings of US product – perhaps of audience pleasures that were not intended by the producers! (Liebes and Katz, 1993). In this respect one has to beware of generalizing about the global nature of entertainment media, and to recognize that television in particular is rather different from the film industry.

In terms of the 'conventional' media imperialism thesis, McQuail provides a useful summary of four kinds of effect of globalization:

- Global media promote relations of dependency rather than economic growth
- The imbalance in the flow of mass media content undermines cultural autonomy or holds back its development
- The unequal relationship in the flow of news increases the relative global power of large and wealthy news-producing countries and hinders the growth of an appropriate national identity and self image
- Global media flows give rise to a state of cultural homogenization or synchronization, leading to a dominant form of culture that has no specific connection with real experience for most people. (McQuail, 2000)

9 Global genres

In general, comments on media genres concentrate on film and television. They refer to forms such as the action thriller, soaps, news, sport and game shows. Within the imperialistic frame of understanding, much is made of the export of such generic programming, and of the ideologies that may be carried around the world within such texts. But while it is true that particular generic material has been especially successful, and while it is interesting that certain genres seem to be popular for many cultures, it is still dangerous to generalize about the transmission of meaning.

One may learn something from looking at points made about the licensing and adaptation of media texts, in respect of TV in particular. Moran refers to format licensors such as Globo TV and the show *Voce Decide*, and to devisor/producers such as Endemol and the programme *Casualty* when arguing that global texts actually change to meet local cultural conditions. Game shows appear to be especially adaptable. *American Pop Idol* (2004) has spun off its British original, making a celebrity of the imported British judge (Simon Cowell). *Big Brother* – in which contestants are observed in a studio-created house, confined, and are voted out by the audience – has versions in many countries, all with different emphases, on, for instance, the relationships between male and female and what is permitted to be shown on screen. The British presenter, Anne Robinson, has taken the game show *The Weakest Link* to the USA (2003) with some success, retaining an emphasis on humiliating the contestants. Once adapted, one may say that such shows reinforce national or local values and identities, not those of the culture of origin. The fact that chat shows are common to many TV systems, generically speaking, does not demonstrate that they are part of a global culture.

Global genres do not sell equally well in all countries. For example, it has been impossible to create a successful French soap, let alone one which appeals across Europe. In terms of top-rated programmes in most countries, it is clear that home grown productions predominate. Where programmes are syndicated, firstly language matters a great deal – dominantly concerning countries which share the English language. But then one also returns to the problem of audience interpretation: a romantic drama does not have the same meaning in every culture. And the material can be re-edited in different ways for export to take account of cultural sensibilities and interests.

Perhaps what is more interesting is the process of hybridization, in which generic materials interact and are adapted. There is Tarantino's *Kill Bill* (2003), in which the martial arts meet computer games, with post-modern irony. Japanese game shows have been notorious for an emphasis on physical challenge and suffering, with ritual humiliation. Only recently has the USA made something similar, in *Jackass*, in which painful, absurd and dangerous activities are highlighted – the kind of material that would make the *National Enquirer*.

10 Global audiences

An audience perspective on globalization throws into relief arguments between views which alternatively privilege centralization or localization. On the one hand there are the global texts of multi-nationals – the latest *Star Wars* movie, or CNN news, or a syndicated TV series. But then different audiences in different locations will read the same material in different ways, mainly because of differing cultural/ideological contexts. To take one obvious example, the reading of a representation of a female body will be different in Muslim cultures from its reading in the USA. The reading may affect perceptions of the motivation, credibility or responsibility of the subject concerned.

Lash and Urry (1994) talk about a contradiction between centralized production and decentralized reception. But one could point out that, apart from the fact that global production is not as centralized as some political economy interpretations would have us believe, reception studies even within national boundaries have shown that audiences are not passive victims of some kind of media textual determinism.

Technology may be global, but there is little or no evidence of anything that one can describe as a global audience or even a global culture. As always, the coherence of audiences as groups melts away when one tries to examine characteristics closely.

There is nothing meaningfully coherent about those watching CNN news in Washington and Jedda at the same time. Indeed it is the differences in reception that are most significant. There are ways in which one may identify global communities, especially in terms of diasporic cultures. Indian families in Britain may watch ZeeTV via satellite or rent videos of Bollywood films, which to some extent link their cultural and media experience with that of communities in India itself. The Internet links religious communities across the world. But again we have to recognize that the context of the experience is different. The participants cannot share the same quality of meaning production that might be the case if they were all living in one place for some time, sharing the same cultural and social rituals. Even websites such as *eelam.com* for worldwide Tamil communities must exist in a tension between shared beliefs and experiences from Sri Lanka, and disparate new contexts and experiences for those logging on.

The fact that television notoriously spills over national boundaries, and may indeed have some effects on its viewers, does not mean that those viewers constitute a coherent group or community, let alone experience a commonality of reactions and effects. So once again what evidence we have is ambivalent. It suggests that even having a world-wide audience sharing the same texts is not the same thing as having a culturally integrated global audience.

11 Cultures and identities

A globalised culture admits a continuous flow of ideas, information, commitment, values and tastes, mediated through mobile individuals, symbolic tokens and electronic simulations.

Waters (1995)

Globalization is also unavoidably about cultural interactions and both remaking and reaffirming identities. A positive take on globalization celebrates the hybrid music forms that appear in Brazil as hiphop or drum 'n' bass meets Latin; or the appearance of the telenovella as the form of TV soap is remade. There are simultaneous and apparently contradictory examples of globalization and localization. In north-east Spain both local media and cultural practices affirm more strongly than ever a separate Catalan identity. At the same time, the use of devices such as the ubiquitous mobile phone for social and business use also speaks of a Spanish and indeed a European identity.

There is a lot of truth in Waters' contention that 'consumption becomes the main form of self expression and the chief source of identity'. Commodification is global. Western corporations have effectively categorized the world as they see it into market areas. One may cite emblematic examples of commodity and identity such as a British TV ad for the Peugeot 205 car (2002–3). In this, one is supposed to be on the streets of an Indian city, where a young Indian guy physically batters and beats his old car into a semblance of the shape of the Peugeot. He wants to achieve cool-ness. He wants to own a cultural icon. It is a western product. His sense of his culture and identity is very different from that of his grandfather. And yet – middle-class Indian urban lifestyle does not simply clone that of western urban centres. People who can drop in to the new global territory of cyberspace, learn to use the increasingly global language of English, but do not abruptly abandon beliefs and cultural practices.

Daniel Yon (2000), in a study of Canadian high school students and their sense of identity, is in the end quite positive about the influence of the global: 'Globalisation opens up other ways of belonging.' It may 'transcend the idea of absolute national identity and culture in favour of a set of experiences that connect them'.

The effects of globalization on cultures are, put simply, complicated and unpredict-able. For example, outsourcing of production to the developing world, for media or other industries, may have unexpected effects in terms of gender identity. Just as the telephone exchange and the typewriter gave a non-domestic role to women in the West at the turn of the twentieth century, so also female factory labour in Asia may be changing women's sense of identity and of their relationship to family and society. Ong (2000) in surveying research into labour in the developing world asserts that 'factory women come to explore new concepts of self, female status, and human worth'.

At the same time as globalization seems to be a threat to the nation state and national identities, there are plenty of examples of how the media are part of new assertions of such identities. Indeed one could say that notions such as British national identity do not actually exist without the media to give them reality. A classic example of this would be the British nation apparently united in mourning by the death of Princess Diana (1997), but actually only really 'coming together' via television and the press.

Strange things may happen through global technologies such as the World Wide Web. Individuals may play with their online identities even as they join in virtual communities (not least because they are not seen). There are notorious examples discovered of participants changing their genders or their histories. Once more globalization is a process full of contradictions. It both develops communities and identities around the planet, and can also make them more ambiguous and fluid.

12 Discussion extract

66 99 The media landscape of the late twentieth century and early twenty first century has changed with the rise of a worldwide communications infrastructure and multinational corporations, the decline of the central power of the sovereign nation-state, and the resulting emergence of new forms of local and global cultures. Three central terms of these changes are *globalisation, convergence*, and *synergy*. With the wiring of the world, the rapid development of wireless communications, and the rise of multi-national corporations, many critics feel there has been a collapse of geographic distance and national boundaries – hence a globalisation of economics, technology and culture. The convergence of previously discrete media industries and technologies allows media to be integrated into the lives of people across geographic boundaries more smoothly and effortlessly. For example, the computer has moved in three decades from being a text-only instrument to integrating sound, image, and text, and will soon incorporate television and an increasing mobility of images. The ability to transmit text, image, and sound in one medium and through a network facilitates global interconnectivity. The growth of media conglomerates in the 1990s, with ownership across the realms of print media, television, radio, the music industry, and consumer products, amplifies the power of the corporation to influence cultural practices on a global scale. This creates a synergy in which programming, production, and distribution are all held together by single corporate entities that market globally. This set of conditions has promoted seemingly contradictory tendencies towards globally shared visual culture, on the one hand, and the rise of an abundance of local discourses and hybrid media cultures that defy categorisation according to geography and nationality, on the other.

1 What do you understand the terms 'convergence', 'synergy' and 'globalization' to mean?

2 What are the arguments for and against ideas about media imperialism, with relation to the conglomerates referred to?

3 In what ways can the Net be seen as a significant medium of social and cultural exchange?

13 Further reading

Barker, C. (1999) *Television, Globalisation and Cultural Identities.* Buckingham: Open University Press.

Herman, E. and McChesney, R. (1999) Global media in the late 1990s, in H. Mackay and T. O'Sullivan (eds) *The Media Reader – Continuity and Transformation.* London: Sage/Open University Press.

O'Meara, P., Mehlinger, H.D. and Krain, M. (eds) (2000) *Globalisation and the Challenges of a New Century.* Bloomington: Indiana University Press.

Waters, M. (1995) *Globalisation.* London: Routledge.

GLOSSARY

Binary oppositions: these appear in texts and in discourses (either implicitly or explicitly) as opposing sets of ideas, characters and plot elements. They are usually framed in terms of the positive and the negative: in effect, that which is approved by the dominant ideology, and that which is not.

Campaign: the organized use of adverts and publicity across media and over a period of time, for the purpose of promoting anything from goods to party political views.

Censorship: the suppression or rewriting of media material by those in power in order to deprive those in subordinate positions of any but a partial set of views which favour the powerful.

Classic realist text: describes the dominant form of narrative in our culture, in which a self-contained diegetic reality is constructed for and by the audience. This reality is bound up with character motivation, denouements at the end of the story, and an acceptance of a representation of time and space which does not match life experience.

Closure: identifies an aspect of popular narratives (classic realist text) in which at the end, problems are resolved, the story is closed off. One may distinguish between this kind of closure and ideological closure where what is shut down by the workings of dominant ideology is the possible range of understandings about the ideological significance of the text as narrative – for example, shutting down ways of understanding how masculinity is represented in a given text.

Code: a systematic combination of signs, bound by conventions or rules. Primary codes include those of speech, non-verbal communication and visual communication.

Cognitive dissonance: this describes an inconsistency or disagreement between two things which we believe that we 'know' about the world. Dissonance creates anxiety. Advertising plays on this by inducing a dissonance between that which we know we do, and what we know we believe in (and therefore ought to do). The 'problem' can be resolved by for example, buying the insurance which helps secure our family.

Commodities: these are goods. But – see Marxism – they may be more than material objects. For example, women may be turned into commodities if they are objectified through visual representations, and then 'sold' to us in an advert. The woman becomes a cultural commodity.

Commodification: is the process of creating commodities, of turning everything in a our culture into a commodity with a price on it. That price may be more than the 'goods' can possibly be worth in factual terms – see fetishism.

Commodity fetishism: Marxists' views envisage an alienated society dominated by commodity fetishism – the turning of goods such as cars into fetish objects with special meaning (e.g. sexual power), for which we pay far beyond their real material value as objects for transporting people.

Connotation: in semiotics, this is the meaning(s) that exist beneath the surface of that which is obviously represented through words or images. Connotations are implicit as much as explicit. They are culturally specific and/or not universal as meanings.

Consensus: that 'middle ground' of values and beliefs which it is assumed exist within a society. It implies the virtue of compromise. By definition it marginalizes alternative values and beliefs. See Chapter 9, News.

Consumption: refers to the process by which texts are decoded and used by people in everyday life, in material terms which suggest that texts (and mass culture) are commodities.

Conventions: these permeate the operation, the construction and deconstruction of the various languages which we use. These conventions govern and help make sense of our social lives, the words that we speak, the media texts that we experience. In a popular sense the term is familiar as a way of describing rules for social behaviour. In a formal sense the word has been borrowed into semiotics to describe, for example, the rules underlying the combining of words in terms of what we know as syntax or grammar.

These conventions govern the workings of media languages. There is a kind of 'understanding' between media producers and their audiences which absolutely depends on 'knowing' what these rules are. They are rules which enable us to decode the body language of the performer in a drama. They are rules which enable us to categorize media material by genre, and so adjust our expectations of how it will develop. They are rules about the mode of realism on offer, and therefore how we are to understand material.

Denotation: a semiotic term which (see connotation) describes those signs and meanings which are on the surface of a text – e.g. an image of a cow refers to cows, in the first place.

Deregulation: refers to a process which, from the late 1980s onwards, has affected the ownership of media in the USA, Britain and Europe. This process has been marked by various pieces of government legislation which have had the effect of allowing more cross-media ownership and of encouraging more companies to join the media market. It is linked to the arrival of digital media and to changes in broadcasting, in particular. From different perspectives, it has either removed protection from national media, or helped them to compete in a global marketplace. This process has not removed regulations so much as changed them (reregulation).

Determinism/determinist models: in this area one would look at post-Marxist and a political economy models. These would argue that there are determining forces at work on the media (essentially economic/market forces): the media then produce the texts influenced by these forces, which in this way go on to work on their audiences. Nevertheless, this position would not see audiences simply as victims of the media. It is a more pessimistic model which explicitly or otherwise retains the notion of ideology at work through the media. The determinist view might well see advertising as the Trojan horse of capitalism in the media sneaking in and endorsing a whole set of values to the advantage of the ideology of capitalism. Advertising is also the engine of media finance, appears as media text and is generally bound up with a dominant ideology. (See also technological determinism)

Deviancy: identifies social groups (or representatives of these) as varying from norms (see below) of appearance, behaviour and attitudes. Deviancy may glossed in terms which range from eccentricity to criminality. The representation of deviancy occurs through news as much as, say, drama.

Diegesis: describes that self-contained world of the text, whose existence and reality we tacitly agree to accept as, for instance, we watch the average feature film. Non-diegetic material is that which cannot exist in this reality, for example music which has no source in the world of a film.

Discourse: discourses are made apparent through particular uses of language to produce particular meanings. They are not peculiar to media. It could be said that myths are some of the meanings which they produce. It can be argued that media by their nature magnify and privilege certain discourses. This is another way of coming to the idea that media emphasize some ways of looking at the world and thinking about it, above others. One example of a discourse is the use of languages relating to babies. This refers not only to words but also to visual language – indeed, to all ways of communicating. The particular use of language is in the ways that we talk about babies. So, for example, words like 'sweet' and 'huggable' and even certain tones of voice, are selectively used. The media, especially adverts, magnify such words through pictures which in their language emphasize meanings such as 'adorable', 'to be protected', even 'clean and pure' (which babies without bowel control certainly are not!).

Discourses work together. So in the case of babies it can be interesting to see gender discourse in operation when male babies may be called 'a strong little chap' or female babies 'a sweet little thing' – when there is no discernable difference other than in genital detail.

Dominant ideology: that kind of ideology, set of values, view of the world and view of power relations in society, which dominates within a given culture. It prevails over other possible views, indeed, makes them difficult (if not impossible) to conceive of.

Ethnography: refers to kinds of audience research in which detailed studies are made on a small scale (such as that of the family). Such research may be carried out, for instance, in the family home, and through observations and directed conversations with respondents.

Feminist models: all feminist approaches to media and society pivot on an interest in how gender is represented through the media, in the connections between these representations and gender difference as it is lived in our society. But such approaches may be allied to different critical traditions. For example, a socialist feminist tradition would see gender inequality as a further evidence of ideology in action, of the oppression by the powerful of the powerless – in much the same way that Marx conceived of class oppression. Another strand draws on psychoanalysis, and critiques texts through Freudian or Lacanian readings, for example (Chapter 7). In the first case, comment might be made about patriarchal dominance or about fear of female sexuality on the part of males – many Hollywood action films may be read in this way. In the second case, comment might be made about 'the mirror self', about women seeing themselves in media images as being looked at by men. This is about the the subordination of women in society. Feminism would relate media representations to social practices, arguing that media narratives tell a story which often supports the idea of patriarchy.

Frankfurt school: describes a group of intellectuals and critics of society and culture, who originally came together in Frankfurt in the 1930s. Names include Walter Benjamin, Theodor Adorno, Max Horkheimer and Herbert Marcuse. They re-evaluated Marxist critiques, and to some extent criticized what they saw as the negative consequences of the development of mass media culture.

Fourth estate: is a term stemming from the eighteenth century, when it was used by Edmund Burke to identify the new influence of journalists and the press (in addition to that political power of the Commons, the Lords and the bishops).

Globalization: refers to a process by which cultural and economic forces have come to operate on global as much as national (or even continental) levels. It is also assumed to refer to the global extension of power of western corporations and to the increasing homogeneity of product on a global scale. But (see Chapter 13) this interpretation can be questioned.

Hegemony: in the view of Antoni Gramsci hegemony (the invisible exercise of power), is achieved through coercion and consent. The state exercises coercion through various kinds of institution such as the army and the police – a certain kind of law and social order is enforced through the explicit use of material power. But consent is obtained through less obviously instrumental institutions, such as education or the media.

So we acquire a naturalized and dominant view of how things should be, but indirectly, through formal learning and through media consumption. Gramsci also broke with the earlier models by arguing that in fact there is a continuous struggle for the dominance of one set of ideas over another. It may not even be an equal struggle, but it is there. He also proposed that 'intellectuals' were especially important in the struggle because they generated the ideas which inform ideologies. The media are one site for that struggle.

Hermeneutic code: hermenutics is about the theory and examination of the interpretation of texts. It assumes that texts have an essential meaning which may be discovered through interpretation, and which in that interpretation will reveal a certain view of the world. In Barthes's terms, the hermeneutic code is a structuring of narrative and meaning, which works to stop the text being interpreted in the range of ways that it might be. The code works to force interpretation in a particular way (see preferred reading).

Homogenization: describes a process by which the subject is made into a consistent whole. It is often applied to globalization and to that critical view which sees it as reducing media texts to a generalized set of characteristics (and genres), so reducing cultural distinctiveness.

Identity: is that sense of self-ness and belonging to a place and a history, belonging with certain others, which gives people a sense of 'who they are'. Identity comprises a mosaic of factors such as family background, sexual orientation and assumptions about personality traits. Identity is also about who we are not, about the dominance and subordination of certain social groups, and that process by which we may see ourselves or be seen as 'the other' (i.e. a subordinated group).

Ideological state apparatus: this phrase was devised by Louis Althusser to help explain how institutions operate to promote the dominant ideology. Again, one may see the media as an example of such an apparatus. Education and the family would be other examples. If the media reproduce certain kinds of social relations, and if media consumers see themselves in those relations, then they also see the ideology behind those relations as being acceptable, and they go along with it.

Ideology: this refers to that coherent set of beliefs and values which dominate in a society. This does not mean that everyone agrees with them. These are the beliefs of those who have economic, social and material power. Ideology is concerned with social and power relationships between differnt groups, and the means by which these are made apparent. Ideology is made evident through representations and discourses. Ideology becomes 'the truth' and 'common sense' through a process of naturalization (see below).

Interactionist models/dynamic models: this view of the relationship between media and society is one in which the two elements are seen as being in a dynamic and evolving relationship. It does not take on the deterministic approach of classic Marxism, in which something is done to large groups of people by economic forces or by institutions such as the media. Interactionism is interested in actions carried out by and conducted between people. It may be argued that these interactions give meanings and construct social relations.

Social interaction is a phrase commonly used to describe the complex dynamics of behaviours as between individuals and groups. It is just as clear that there is interactivity between media and media, between media and individual, between media and groups, between people after the media experience, and so on. Interactive or dynamic approaches, together with context, draw out the complexity of exploring influence.

Intertextuality: this describes the ways in which texts may refer to one other, especially within genres and across genres. It is about the production of meaning in that we understand one text by being able to refer to another.

Liberal pluralism/liberal pluralist model: this view and this model argues for freedom of the press in particular (as well as other media) and assumes that a belief in freedom is somehow associated with degrees of morality. This position was developed into a further pluralist theory of Social Responsibility, in which the obligation of the press (media) to be responsible for its utterances and its effects was made explicit.

66 99 The principal democratic role of the media, according to the liberal theory, is to act as a check on the state. The media should monitor the full range of state activity, and fearlessly expose abuses of official authority. Only by anchoring the media to the free market, in this view, is it possible to ensure the media's complete independence from government.

(Curran, 2000)

Macro and micro media perspectives: these stand for a general categorization of models (and critical views) of the media – society relationship into two kinds of critique. The one set takes a broad view of the relationship between media and society – macro perspectives. They may be interested in culture in general, as much as the media in particular. The other kind of critique – micro perspectives – may bear more directly on text and audience, for example, and be less direct in what they have to say about wider media – society connections. A general debate that is raised by most approaches to media is that which asks whether the media reflect or affect society. This question becomes sharp when, for instance, one is considering representations and the constructed views that these give us of social groups and social relationships.

Marxist models: broadly, Marxist approaches are characterized by a view of media and audience as collective and even coherent entities – mass media, mass audience. The classic Marxist view of the media–audience relationship is dominated by an assumption that the media do things to people. The media are part of capitalism and its interests, and inevitably promote views of the social elite – the ruling class – and promote the dominant ideology which serves to maintain the power of this elite. Capitalist ideology believes in the production and consumption of goods. Media programmes or magazines are examples of such goods. Goods may also be called commodities. Belief in materialism, in the importance of commodities, then affects the way that we value everything else in our lives. Even our social relationships could be valued in terms of these commodities. The process of defining social values and relationships in this way is called **commodification**. The energy which is behind capitalist media industries comes from the force of economic determinism – the behaviour of media institutions is determined by economic factors. The economic base of society is founded on the labour of workers. The media are run in the interests of the wealthy and of wealth creation, which remains the privilege of the few. The media may be seen as part of the Marxist superstructure of society, where ideology is at work. This ideology affects workers and their understanding of the exchange value of their labour and of the goods that they produce.

Marxist views have been much modified over the years, to explain for example why differences in power between social groups are evidently not set in concrete, and do change without revolution (see hegemony). They may be related to an argument that control over the means of production and distribution of goods leads to control over the ideas which are (in the case of media) within those goods. It is indisputable that control of media is concentrated in fewer and fewer hands (see Chapter 1). They produce ideas – through representations for instance – about status, power, class, which are made to seem true and valid when they are not. An unequal society is made to seem falsely, and yet naturally, acceptable. The manufacture of this false consciousness is part of the invisible exercise of power – or hegemony.

Mass culture: this a phrase used critically (see Frankfurt School) to identify the size and number of media products and audiences, based on a system of mass production, controlled by large institutions. The term is used pejoratively, and with the implicit assumption that real art, high culture and individualized production are the opposite of this and are more valuable. Of course, the distinction and the valuation do not necessarily hold true.

Mediation: this is about that inevitable operation and result of media work – that it comes between us and real experience. Therefore, it is not real experience. It is indeed only a representation of that experience. So mediation is inevitable but not obvious. It is not obvious because media in a number of forms (outside broadcasts) pretend to bring us reality – social, material, even truthful. But they do not, not least because they cannot. So any examination of a media text has to work on the knowledge that it is only an artifice. Any consideration of media production has to start with the realization that it is also the process of making an artifice – some kind of illusion.

Mode of address: this describes the 'voice' through which any media text addresses or talks to its audience. Most obviously, the audience is addressed through chat-show hosts or talk radio jocks, but also through other devices of style and engagement. The mode of address sets up a relationship between the text and the audience.

Modes of narrative: this refers to the variety of narrative approaches that we may recognize, characterized by factors such as narrative structure (circular narrative) and authorial position (autobiography).

Modes of realism: this refers to the variety of approaches to realism which are commonly recognized, along with their sets of of conventions (for example, documentary).

Moral panic: this term describes a collective and anxious response to given social events, as represented through the news media, and so passed on to the audience. Such panics are usually temporary, and are unjustified in their scale of reaction to, for example, kinds of crime or youth behaviour.

Myth/mythologies: these are ideas about culture and society which are essentially untrue, which are ideological, and which are very influential in the ways that they cause us to make meanings from texts and to think about our worlds. In some ways myths are also kinds of wish-fulfilment – things that we would like to be true. They may also be ideas which do not really work in our interests, but in the interests of those with power – hence the notion that they are ideological.

   Examples are, the myth that certain ethic groups are inherently superior to others, that science is always objective, that the best male is the strong, silent male.

Narrative: is about the representation of a structured reality which organizes place, events, characters, into a kind of order which makes it believable, and which gives rise to kinds of understanding and meaning about the world. It is what we refer to as 'the story', but is, for instance, about far more than just the plot. We make narratives through our engagement with media texts: they do not pre-exist, even though we are prone to believe that narratives exist independently of the teller, the telling and the audience (see also Chapter 2).

Narrowcasting: this term describes specialized media output for niche audiences (usually with reference to broadcast media).

Naturalization: this refers to a process by which certain kinds of meaning are made to seem natural and common sense and true, even though they are not. Ideological positions are accepted because they are naturalized. Discourses incorporate naturalized meanings. The very idea of 'common sense' is itself a discourse, and so has become naturalized into some kind of benchmark for the validity of beliefs and values.

Norms: are those kinds of social behaviour and belief which are understood to be 'normal' within a society, and so are held to be acceptable. What counts as 'normal' will differ over time, and from one group to another.

Paradigm: out of semiotics, this term describes our understanding of sets of signs as belonging together – the alphabet. Conventions organize such signs into a code – rules of spelling.

Political economy models: the political economy model is one which is concerned with ways in which the media exercise power over the society of which they are a part, and with the regulation and sources of that power. When applied to media, it is a view which (as with Marxism) proposes economic determinism in some form. It argues that the power and interests of the media corporations work against the interests of their audiences. This power is enhanced by global concentration of control of media. Consequently choice diminishes.

   'One can think about political economy as the study of the social relations, particularly the power relations, that mutually constitute the production, distribution and consumption of resources' (Mosco, 1996).

   Murdock and Golding (2000) identify three core tasks of political economy in practice

1 to examine the production of meaning as an exercise of power by institutions;

2 to approach textual analysis in terms of how institutions/production structure the discourses which inhabit texts (as opposed to looking at texts in isolation);

3 to deal with ideas about consumption in terms of a debate between sovereignty or struggle. This is in effect to look at the impact on audiences of institutions and their operations; at how far audiences have any power in this relationship. It is to contest culturalist views of audience autonomy in dealing with texts.

Pluralism/pluralist models: the optimism of the pluralist model extends to the notion of a variety of institutions producing a variety of products for a variety of audiences. In some cases a market model is invoked which is essentially self-regulating. In other cases it is accepted that the intervention of some regulation is needed to maintain this pluralism. In any case, the media provide opportunities to obtain information and to enjoy leisure. Pluralism would suggest that the media serve us by providing a variety of information and entertainment which represents a variety of points of view.

Polysemy: this literally means 'many signs', and refers to that quality of visual texts in particular, in which the image is packed with a variety of signs, and so with a range of meanings. It links with the fact that visual texts may be more complex and less specific in their meanings than are written texts.

Popular culture: this is commonly used to refer to a culture 'of the people', and is often conflated with mass culture. It becomes problematic when one questions how 'popular' is defined in terms of something being generally attractive to an audience, and how 'the people' are defined when one has such a variety of audiences within society.

Post-modernism: on the one hand this is concerned with the text (and not only media texts). It takes a positive view of the active audience having control of the text, and of the making of meanings. It is absorbed with form, fascinated by irony and it is squarely interested in popular culture, in one camp or the other – for example, John Fiske writing about jeans (1989), or Barbara Creed writing about cyberstars in film (2002).

It is characterized by a reaction against modernist interests in structures, in the big picture, in effects analysis. The view taken is that any possible relationship between media and society as a whole is so complex in its range of variables that nothing meaningful can be said about it. What relationships there are, work on a tighter level. The text and the audience are predominant. Post-modernism rejects teleology, or certainties about how society works – there are no absolute truths or meta-narratives (or overarching explanations about how society operates).

Preferred reading: this is that reading of or meaning to a text which is the dominant one. It is preferred because the text is so encoded through its conventions that this meaning is chosen by the audience above others. It is the meaning which the producer or encoder of the text would prefer the reader or audience to take from that text.

Reception studies: this kind of audience study examines the relationship between particular texts and specific audiences. These approaches also concentrate on the idea of context: the environment in which the reading of the text takes place. This environment – physical and cultural – may affect how a text is read or used. The emergence of interest in audience studies in the 1980s and in the idea of the active audience, naturally led to interest in the context in which the audience may read, watch and listen.

Regulation: this refers to those mechanisms, formal or informal, legal or economic or political, through media production and output is controlled and constrained. It defines how media may (as much as may not) operate.

Representation: this term refers to a process through which the media bring us constructions; manufacture versions of events, people and experiences. The nature of these constructions is predicated on beliefs and values – ideological positions. Representations – of different social groups, for example – are by definition untruthful, though not necessarily lacking any truth at all. Manufacturing representations is what media do. Critical interest is in how this happens, what is produced, how it may affect the conceptions of the audience.

Scopophilia: identifies 'the pleasure of looking' which we experience in our image-rich society. This pleasure is often associated with the production and reception of sexually stimulating images.

Semiotics/semiotic analysis: this is about the study and analysis of signs. The assumption is that all forms of communication are composed of signs. The purpose of the analysis is to identify signs, to consider possible meanings, to consider how those meanings are generated and how some meanings may be privileged above others.

Sign: in general, anything may be a sign if society agrees that it has a meaning. Specifically, semiotics tends to talk about signs which compose languages. Signs do not have any particular meanings attached to them (though it is often wrongly assumed that they do). Signs stand for something else. In this sense one might say that they are the raw material of representations, in that they help construct that 'something else', and suggest ideas about it. Signs may be iconic (look directly like what they suggest), or indexical (refer indirectly to what they suggest, as smoke refers to fire), or symbolic (are not direct at all, as in the case of writing).

Signifier: this is the part of the concept of 'sign' which identifies the fact that it has potential meaning – in a context. The signifier makes a word or a flick of the eyebrow active. We know from acquiring language that someone raising an eyebrow at us means something. We do not immediately know what it means – recognition, scepticism and so on.

Signified: this is the part of 'sign' which identifies a meaning. It is that meaning or mental concept to which the sign refers. All signs have many possible meanings, according to other signs used around them, among other factors. The interesting question is why some meanings are selected when we make sense of signs, and others are ignored.

Signification: this refers to that process through which meaning is generated by the use of signs.

Socio-linguistics: the study of language use in relation to social interaction.

Structuralism: this has a great deal to do with semiotic analysis in particular. Verbal and visual texts are understood as sets of signs organized according to conventions or rules. These signs, ranging from the spoken word to the camera shot, are combined to produce meanings shared between the producer and the audience. To this extent it might be said that the text is the interface between the institutional producers and the audience. Key debates revolve around how far meanings may be embedded in the text by producers so that texts can only be read one way, and how far the ambiguity of signs, especially in visual media, actually allows the audiences to make alternative or even oppositional readings to the one which is apparently to be preferred above all others.

Structuralist principles extend to narrative analysis, and ideas that there are organizing principles behind any 'story' in any medium. So, the notion of the classic realist text proposes that all conventional stories take the protagonist through difficulties which have to be overcome, until all is resolved at the end and order is restored. Discourse analysis is also structuralist to an extent: a discourse, or dominant set of meanings about the given subject, may be recognized through sets of oppositions – for example, opposing themes, or characters or sets of beliefs or even symbols. These oppositions – the negative and the positive – make clear in this 'either/or' structure what it is that we should approve or disapprove of – what it ideologically acceptable or not.

Syntagm: in semiotic terms, this is a string of signs within a code which add up to a recognizable small unit of meaning – a phrase in verbal language, or a sequence in film television codes (and narratives).

Technological determinism: the phrase describes that belief that technology determines certain kinds of development, possible social, but usually understood in terms of what shapes the growth of media.

Transmission models: these see meanings as being something which are sent out through media of communication, from institutions of the media. This simplistic notion of broadcasting messages as packages finds little favour in critical circles nowadays.

Writerly and readerly texts: are phrases used by Barthes (1972) to identify the relative accessibility of meanings in texts. The former are those examples where the reader has to work on the signs of the texts to make sense of the writer's intentions (because they may not be so easy to understand). The latter are easy to understand for the reader (for example, genres) because the use of 'language' is unambiguous and familiar.

BIBLIOGRAPHY

Adorno, T. (1991) *The Culture Industry*. London: Routledge.

Adorno, T. and Horkheimer, M. (1973) *The Dialectic of Enlightenment*. London: Allen Lane.

Allan, S. (1997) News and the public sphere, in M. Bromley and T. O'Malley (eds), *A Journalism Reader*. London: Routledge.

Allan, S. (1999) *News Culture*. Buckingham: Open University Press.

Allen, M. (1998) From Bwana devil to Batman forever: technology in contemporary Hollywood cinema, in S. Neale and M. Smith (eds), *Contemporary Hollywood Cinema*. London: Routledge.

Allen, R.C. (1989) Bursting bubbles – soap opera, audiences and the limits of genre, in E. Seiter, H. Borchers, G. Kreutzner and E. Warth, *Remote Control – Television, Audiences and Cultural Power*. London: Routledge.

Allen, R.C. (ed.) (1992) *Channels of Discourse Reassembled*. London: Routledge.

Allen, R.C. (ed.) (1995) *To be Continued, Soap Operas Around the World*. London: Routledge.

Althusser, L. (1969) *For Marx*. Oxford: Blackwell Verso.

Althusser, L. (1971) *Lenin, Philosophy and other Essays*. London: New Left Books.

Andersen, R. (1995) *Consumer Culture and Television Programming*. Oxford: Westview Press.

Anderson, B. and Tracey, K. (2001) Digital Living: The Impact (or otherwise) of the Internet on Everyday Life. Unpublished research report, Ipswich, Suffolk, Adastral Park: BTAXCT Research. In M. Castells (2002) *The Internet Galaxy*. Oxford: Oxford University Press.

Andison, F.S. (1977) TV Violence and Viewer Aggression – a cumulation of study results 1956–76. *Public Opinion Quarterly*, 41, 3.

Ang, I. (1985) *Watching Dallas: TV and the Melodramatic Imagination*. London: Routledge.

Ang, I. (1991) *Desperately Seeking the Audience*. London: Routledge.

Ang, I. and Stratton, J. (1995) The End of civilisation as we knew it, in R.C. Allen (ed.), *To be Continued, Soap Operas around the World*. London: Routledge.

Appadurai, A. (1993) Disjuncture and difference in the global cultural economy, in P. Williams and L. Chrisman (eds), *Colonial Discourse and Post-Colonial Theory*. London: Harvester Wheatsheaf.

Archer, J. (1992) The fate of the subject in the narrative without end, in S. Frentz (ed.), *Staying Tuned – Contemporary Soap Opera Criticism*. Ohio: Bowling Green State University Popular Press.

Atton, C. (2002) *Alternative Media*. London: Sage.

Auty, M. and Roddick, N. (1985) *British Cinema Now*. London: BFI.

Ballaster, R., Beetham, M., Frazer, E. and Hebron, S. (1991) *Women's Worlds – Ideology, Femininity and the Woman's Magazine*. Basingstoke: Macmillan.

Bandura, A. (1973) *Aggression – A Social Learning Analysis*. Englewood Cliffs, NJ: Prentice-Hall.

Bandura, A., Ross, D. and Ross, S.A. (1963) Imitation of film-mediated aggressive models. *Journal of Abnormal and Social Psychology*, 67(6): 601, 607. In J. Bryant and D. Zillmann (1994) *Media Effects, Advances in Theory and Research*. Hillsdale, NJ: Lawrence Erlbaum Associates.

Barker, C. (1999) *Television, Globalisation and Cultural Identities*. Buckingham: Open University Press.

Barker, M. and Petley, J. (eds) (2001) *Ill Effects* (2nd edn). London: Routledge.

Barnard, S. (2000) *Studying Radio*. London: Arnold.

Barsam, R. (1974) *Non Fiction Film*. London: George Allen & Unwin.

Barthes, R. (1973) *Mythologies* (trans. A. Lavers). London: Granada.

Barthes, R. (1977) *Image, Music, Text* (trans. S. Heath). London: Fontana.

Baudrillard, J. (1988) *Selected Writings* (ed. M. Poster). Cambridge: Polity Press.

Baym, N. (2000) *Tune in, Log On – Soaps, Fandom and Online Community*. London: Sage.

Bell, D. (1973) *The Coming of Post-Industrial Society*. New York: Basic Books.

Belson, W. (1978) *Television and the Adolescent Boy*. Farnborough: Saxon House.

Benjamin, W. ((1935) 1992) The work of art in the age of mechanical reproduction, in G. Mast and M. Cohen (eds), *Film Theory and Criticism* (4th edn). Oxford: Oxford University Press.

Bennett, A. (2001) *Cultures of Popular Music*. Buckingham: Open University Press.

Berger, A.A. (1997) *Narrative in Popular Culture, Media and Everyday Life*. London: Sage.

Berger, J. (1972) *Ways of Seeing*. London: BBC.

Berkowitz, D. (ed.) (1997) *The Social Meanings of News*. London: Sage.

Berkowitz, L. (1993) *Aggression – Its Causes, Consequences and Control*. Philadelphia: Temple University Press.

Beynon, J. (2002) *Masculinities and Culture*. Buckingham: Open University Press.

Bignell, J. (1997) *Media Semiotics*. Manchester: Manchester University Press.

Bird, S.E. and Dardenne, R.W. (1997) Myth, chronicle and story – exploring the narrative qualities of news, in D. Berkowitz (ed.), *The Social Meanings of News*. London: Sage.

Blain, N. and Boyle, R. (1998) Sport as real life: media sport and culture, in A. Briggs and P. Cobley, *The Media – An Introduction*. Harlow: Addison Wesley Longman.

Bolter, J. and Grusin, R. (2000) *Remediation – Understanding New Media*. Cambridge, MA: MIT Press.

Borchers, H. (1989) Towards an ethnography of soap opera viewers, in E. Seiter, H. Borchers, G. Kreutzner and E. Warth, *Remote Control – Television, Audiences and Cultural Power*. London: Routledge.

Bordwell, D. (1988) *Narrative in the Fiction Film*. London: Routledge.

Bordwell, D. and Carroll, N. (eds) (1996) *Post Theory – Reconstructing Film Studies*. Madison, Wisconsin: University of Wisconsin Press.

Born, G. and Hesmondhalgh, D. (eds) (2003) *Western Music and its Others*. London/Berkeley: University of California Press.

Bourdieu, P. (1984) *Distinction*. Cambridge, MA: Harvard University Press.

Boyd-Barrett, O. and Newbold, C. (eds) (1995) *Approaches to Media, A Reader*. London: Arnold.

Boyd-Barrett, O. and Rantanen, T. (1998) *The Globalisation of News*. London: Sage.

Brackett, D. (2002) Musical meaning: genres, categories and crossover, in D. Hesmondhalgh and K. Negus, *Popular Music Studies*. London: Arnold.

Braithwaite, B. (1998) Magazines, the bulging bookstores, in A. Briggs and P. Cobley (eds), *The Media, An Introduction*. Harlow: Longman.

Branston, G. (2000) *Cinema and Cultural Modernity*. Buckingham: Open University Press.

Brierley, S. (1995) *The Advertising Handbook*. London: Routledge.

Briggs, A and Cobley, P. (eds) (1998) *The Media – An Introduction*. Harlow: Addison Wesley Longman.

Bromley, M. and O'Malley, T. (eds) (1997) *A Journalism Reader*. London: Routledge.

Brookes, R. and Holbrook, B. (1998) Mad cows and Englishmen, in C. Carter, G. Branston and S. Allan (eds), *News, Gender and Power*. London: Routledge.

Brookes, R. (2002) *Representing Sport*. London: Arnold.

Brown, G. (2000) Something for everyone: British film culture in the nineties, in R. Murphy (ed.), *British Cinema of the Nineties*. London: BFI.

Brown, M.E. (1990) Motley moments: soap opera, carnival, gossip and the powers of utterance, in M.E. Brown (ed.), *Television and Women's Culture*. London: Sage.

Brown, M.E. (ed.) (1990) *Television and Women's Culture*. London: Sage.

Brown, M.E. (1994) *Soap Opera and Women's Talk – The Pleasure of Resistance*. London: Sage.

Buckingham, D. (1993) *Reading Audiences: Young People and the Media*. Manchester: Manchester University Press.

Burns, T. (1977) *The BBC – Public Institution and Private World*. London: Macmillan.

Burton, G. (1999) *Media & Popular Culture*. London: Hodder and Stoughton.

Burton, G. (2000) *Talking Television, An Introduction to Television Studies*. London: Arnold.

Burton, G. (2002) *More Than Meets the Eye – An Introduction to Media Studies* (3rd edn). London: Arnold.

Carter, C. and Kay Weaver, C. (2003) *Violence and the Media*. Buckingham: Open University Press.

Carter, C., Branston, G. and Allan, S. (eds) (1998) *News, Gender and Power*. London: Routledge.

Castells, M. (1997) *The Power of Identity – The Information Age: Economy, Society and Culture* (vol. 2). Oxford: Blackwell.

Castells, M. (2002) *The Internet Galaxy*. Oxford: Oxford University Press.

Chomsky, N. (1989) *Necessary Illusions*. London: Pluto Press.

Clover, C. (1992) *Men, Women and Chainsaws – Gender in the Modern Horror Film*. London: BFI.

Cohen, S. (1973) *Folk Devils and Moral Panics*. London: Paladin.

Cohen, S. (1991) *Rock Culture in Liverpool*. Oxford: Clarendon Press.

Cohen, S. and Young, J. (eds) (1973) *The Manufacture of News*. London: Constable.

Collins, J., Radner, H. and Collins, A.P. (eds) (1993) *Film Theory Goes to the Movies*. London: Routledge.

Collins, R., Garnham, N. and Locksley, G. (1999) The economics of television – UK case, in H. Mackay and T. O'Sullivan (eds), *The Media Reader – Continuity and Transformation*. London: Sage.

Congdon, T. (1995) The multimedia revolution and the open society, in T. Congdon, A. Graham, D. Green and B. Robinson, *The Cross Media Revolution – Ownership and Control*. London: John Libbey.

Connell, R. (1995) *Masculinities*. Cambridge: Polity Press.

Cook, P. and Bernink, M. (eds) (1999) *The Cinema Book* (2nd edn). London: BFI.

Corner, J. (1996) *The Art of Record*. Manchester: Manchester University Press.

Corner, J. and Harvey, S. (1996) *Television Times – A Reader*. London: Arnold.

Cornford, J. and Robins, K. (1999) New Media, in J. Stokes and A. Reading (eds), *The Media in Britain – Current Debates and Developments*. Basingstoke: Macmillan.

Creeber, G. (ed.) (2001) *The Television Genre Book*. London: BFI.

Creed, B. (2002) The cyberstar, digital pleasures and the end of the unconscious, in G. Turner (ed.), *The Film Cultures Reader*. London: Routledge.

Creedon, P.J. (ed.) (1994) *Women, Media and Sport – Challenging Gender Values*. London: Sage.

Cronin, A.M. (2000) *Advertising and Consumer Citizenship*. London: Routledge.

Croteau, D. and Hoynes, W. (1997) *Media/Society: Industry, Images and Audience*. London: Pine Forge Press/Sage.

Croteau, D. and Hoynes, W. (1999) *Media/Society: Industries, Images and Audiences* (2nd edn). London: Sage/Pine Forge Press.

Cullen, R. (2001) Addressing the digital divide, *Online Information Review*, 25 (5). In E. Devereux (2003), *Understanding the Media*. London: Sage.

Cumberbatch, G. (1989) *The portrayal of violence in BBC Television*. London: BBC Publications.

Curran, J. (1996) The new revisionism in mass communication research – a re-appraisal, in J. Curran, D. Morley and V. Walkerdine, *Cultural Studies and Communications*. London: Arnold.

Curran, J. (ed.) (1999) *Media Organisations in Society*. London: Arnold.

Curran, J. (2000) Rethinking media and democracy, in J. Curran and M. Gurevitch, *Mass Media and Society* (3rd edn). London: Arnold.

Curran, J. (2002) *Media and Power*. London: Routledge.

Curran, J. and Gurevitch, M. (2000) *Mass Media and Society* (3rd edn). London: Arnold.

Curran, J. and Seaton, J. (1997) *Power Without Responsibility – the Press and Broadcasting in Britain* (5th edn). London: Routledge.

Curran, J., Morley, D. and Walkerdine, V. (1996) *Cultural Studies and Communications*. London: Arnold.

D'Acci, J. (2000) Women characters and 'real world' femininity, in Horace Newcomb (ed.), *Television, the Critical View* (6th edn). New York: Oxford University Press.

Das, D. (2000) Local memoirs of a global manager, in P. O'Meara, H.D. Mehlinger and M. Krain (eds), *Globalisation and the Challenges of a New Century*. Bloomington: Indiana University Press.

Deacon, D., Pickering, R., Golding, P. and Murdock, G. (1999) *Researching Communications*. London: Arnold.

Deeming, C. (1990) For television centred criticism – lessons from feminism, in M.E. Brown (ed.), *Television and Women's Culture*. London: Sage.

Devereux, E. (2003) *Understanding the Media*. London: Sage.

Dickinson, M. (1983) The state and the consolidation of monopoly, in J. Curran and V. Porter (eds), *British Cinema History*. London: Weidenfeld and Nicolson.

Dickinson, R., Harindranath, R. and Linne, O. (eds) (1998) *Approaches to Audiences – A Reader*. London: Arnold.

Ditton, J. and Duffy, J. (1983) Bias in newspaper reporting of crime news. *British Journal of Criminology*, 23, 159–65. In P. Schlesinger and H. Tumber (1994) *Reporting Crime – The Media Politics of Criminal Justice*. Oxford: Oxford University Press.

Doane, M.A. (1982) Film and the masquerade – theorising the female spectator. *Screen*, 23, 3/4, Sept./Oct.

Dorfman, A. and Maltelart, A. (1975) *How to Read Donald Duck: Imperialist Ideology in the Disney Comic*. New York: International General.

Dougary, G. (1994) *The Executive Tart and other Myths*. London: Virago.

Doyle, G. (2002) *Understanding Media Economics*. London: Sage.

Du Gay, P. (ed.) (1997) *Production of Culture/Cultures of Production*. London: Sage.

During, S. (1999) Popular culture on a global scale: a challenge for cultural studies, in H. Mackay and T. O'Sullivan (eds), *The Media Reader – Continuity and Transformation*. London: Sage/Open University Press.

Dyer, R., Geraghty, C., Jordan, M. *et al.* (eds) (1981) *Coronation Street*. London: BFI.

Ellis, J. (1992) *Visible Fictions*, London: Routledge.

Ellis, J. (1999) Television as working through, in J. Gripsrud (ed.), *Television and Common Knowledge*. London: Routledge.

El-Nawawy, M. and Iskandar, A. (2002) *Al-Jazeera*. Cambridge, MA: Westview Press.

Elsaesser, T. and Buckland, W. (2002) *Studying Contemporary American Film, A Guide to Movie Analysis*. London: Arnold.

Ewen, S. (1977) *Captains of Consciousness*. New York: McGraw Hill.

Falk, P. (1996) The Benetton-Toscani effect, in M. Nava, A. Blake, I. MacRury and B. Richards, *Buy this Book – Studies in Advertising and Consumption*. London: Routledge.

Ferguson, M. (1983) *Forever Feminine – Women's Magazines and the Cult of Femininity*. London: Heinemann.

Ferguson, R. (1998) *Representing Race*. London: Arnold.

Feshback, S. and Singer, R. (1971) *Television and Aggression – An Experimental Field Study*. San Francisco: Jossey-Bass.

Feuer, J. (1992) Genre study and television, in R. Allen (ed.), *Channels of Discourse Reassembled*. London: Routledge.

Feuer, J. (1995) Narrative form in American network television, in O. Boyd-Barrett and C. Newbold, *Approaches to Media*. London: Arnold.

Fiske, J. (1987) *Television Culture*. London: Methuen.

Fiske, J. (1989) *Understanding Popular Culture*. London: Routledge.

Fiske, J. (1993) Television pleasures, in D. Graddol and O. Boyd-Barratt (eds), *Media Texts: Authors and Readers*. Clevedon: MultiLingual Matters/Open University Press.

Fiske, J. (1994) Television Pleasure, in D. Graddol and O. Boyd-Barrett, *Media Texts – Authors and Readers*. Clevedon: Multi Lingual Matters/Open University.

Flournoy, D. and Stewart, R. (1997) *CNN – Making News in the Global Market*. Luton: University of Luton Press/John Libbey Media.

Fowles, J. (1996) *Advertising and Popular Culture*. London: Sage.

Freeland, C.A. (1996) Feminist frameworks for horror films, in D. Bordwell and N. Carroll (eds), *Post Theory – Reconstructing Film Studies*. Madison, WI: University of Winsconsin Press.

Frentz, S. (ed.) (1992) *Staying Tuned – Contemporary Soap Opera Criticism*. Ohio: Bowling Green State University Popular Press.

Frith, S. (1992) The industrialisation of popular music, in J. Lull (ed.), *Popular Music and Communication*. London: Sage.

Frith, S. (1993) Popular music and the local state, in T. Bennet, S. Frith, L. Grossberg, J. Shepherd and G. Turner, *Rock and Popular Music*. London: Routledge.

Frith, S. (2000) Power and policy in the British music industry, in H. Tumber (ed.), *Media Power, Professionals and Policies*. London: Routledge.

Frith, S. and Goodwin, A. (eds) (1990) *On Record – Rock, Pop and the Written Word*. London: Routledge.

Fuery, P. (2000) *New Development in Film Theory*. Basingstoke: Macmillan.

Furst, L. (ed.) (1992) *Realism*. London: Longman.

Gabb, J. (1999) Consuming the garden: locating a feminist narrative, in J. Stokes and A. Reading (eds), *The Media in Britain*. Basingstoke: Macmillan.

Galtung, J. and Ruge, M. (1970) The structure of foreign news, in J. Tunstall, (ed.), *Media Sociology*. London: Constable.

Gans, H. (1980) *Deciding What's News*. New York: Vintage Books.

Garnham, N. (2000) *Emancipation, the Media and Modernity*. Oxford: Oxford University Press.

Garofalo, R. (1986) How autonomous is relative: Popular music, the social formation and cultural struggle. *Popular Music*, 6 (1). In D. Hesmondhalgh and K. Negus (eds) (2002), *Popular Music Studies*. London: Arnold.

Gauntlett, D. (1995) *Moving Experiences – Understanding Television's Influences and Effects*. London: John Libbey.

Gauntlett, D. and Hill, A. (1999) *Television Living – Television, Culture and Everyday Life*. London: Routledge.

Geraghty, C. (1991) *Women and Soap Opera – A Study of Prime Time Soaps*. Cambridge: Polity Press.

Geraghty, C. (1995) Social issues and realist soaps, in R.C. Allen (ed.), *To be Continued, Soap Operas around the World*. London: Routledge.

Geraghty, C. (1996a) Feminism and media consumption, in J. Curran, D. Morley and V. Walkerdine, *Cultural Studies and Communications*. London: Arnold.

Geraghty, C. (1996b) A woman's space, in H. Boehr and A. Gray, *Turning It On – A Reader in Women and the Media*. London: Arnold.

Geraghty, C. (1996c) Women in soap opera, in J. Corner, and S. Harvey, *Television Times – A Reader*. London: Arnold.

Geraghty, C. (2000) Representation and popular culture, in J. Curran and M. Gurevitch, *Mass Media and Society* (3rd edn). London: Arnold.

Gerbner, G., Gross, L., Morgan, M. and Signorelli, N. (1980) Living with television: The dynamics of the cultivation process, in J. Bryant and D. Zillman (eds), *Perspectives on Media Effects*. Hillsdale, NJ: Lawrence Erlbaum.

Giddens, A. (1990) *The Consequences of Modernity*. Cambridge: Polity Press.

Gilbert, J. and Pearson, E. (2002) *Discographies – Dance Music, Culture and the Politics of Sound*. London: Routledge.

Gilligan, C. (1982) *In a Different Voice*. Cambridge: Harvard University Press.

Gilroy, P. (1996) British cultural studies: the pitfalls of identity, in J. Curran, D. Morley and V. Walkerdine, *Cultural Studies and Communications*. London: Arnold.

Gitlin, G. (1980) *The Whole World is Watching – Mass Media in the Making and Un-making of the New Left*. Berkeley, CA: University of California Press.

Gledhill, C. and Williams, L. (2000) *Reinventing Film Studies*. London: Arnold.

Godard, A. (1998) *The Language of Advertising*. London: Routledge.

Goldman, R. (1992) *Reading Ads Socially*. London: Routledge.

Goldman, R. and Papson, S. (1998) *Nike Culture*. London: Sage.

Goldsmith's Media Group (1999) A radical political economic approach: central issues, in J. Curran (ed.), *Media Organisations in Society*. London: Arnold.

Goodwin, A. (1992) Rationalisation and democratisation, in J. Lull, *Popular Music and Communication*. London: Sage.

Gough-Yates, A. (2003) *Understanding Women's Magazines*. London: Routledge.

Graber, D. (1980) *Crime News and the Public*. New York: Praeger. In P. Schlesinger and H. Tumber (1994), *Reporting Crime – The Media Politics of Criminal Justice*. Oxford: Oxford University Press.

Graddol, D. and Boyd-Barrett, O. (1994) *Media Texts – Authors and Readers*. Clevedon: OU/ Multilingual Matters.

Gramsci, A. (1971) *Selections from the Prison Notebooks*. London: Lawrence & Wishart.

Green, D. (1995) Preserving pluralism in a digital world, in T. Congdon, A. Graham and D. Green, *The Cross Media Revolution: Ownership and Control*. London: John Libbey.

Greer, G. (1999) *The Whole Woman*. London and New York: Doubleday.

Gripsrud, J. (2002) *Understanding Media Culture*. London: Arnold.

Grossberg, L., Wartella, E. and Whitney, D.C. (1998) *Media Making: Mass Media in Popular Culture*. London: Sage.

Gunter, B. (1985) *Dimensions of Television Violence*. London: Gower Publishing.

Gunter, B. (1987) *Television and the Fear of Crime*. London: John Libbey.

Gunter, B. (1994) The question of media violence, in J. Bryant and D. Zillmann, *Media Effects, Advances in Theory and Research*. Hillsdale, NJ: Lawrence Erlbaum Associates.

Gunter, B. (1995a) *The Representation of Women on Television*. London: John Libbey.

Gunter, B. (1995b) *Television and Gender Representation*. London: John Libbey.

Gunter, B. and Furnham, A. (1998) *Children as Consumers – A Psychological Analysis of the Young People's Market*. London: Routledge.

Hall, M.A. (1996) *Feminism and Sporting Bodies*. Champaign, IL: Human Kinetics.

Hall, S. (ed.) (1997) *Representation – Cultural Representations and Signifying Practices*. London/ Buckingham: Sage/Open University Press.

Hall, S., Clarke, J., Critcher, C., Jefferson, T. and Roberts, B. (1978) *Policing the Crisis*. London: Macmillan.

Hallam, J. with Marshment, M. (2000) *Realism and Popular Cinema*. Manchester: Manchester University Press.

Halliday, M.A.K. (1996) Language as social semiotic, in P. Cobley (ed.), *The Communication Reader*. London: Routledge.

Hamilton, J.T. (1998) *Channelling Violence – The Economic Market for Violent Television Programming*. Chichester/Princeton: Princeton University Press.

Harrington, C. and Bielby, D. (1995) *Soap Fans*. Philadelphia: Temple University Press.

Harrison, J. (2000) *Terrestrial TV News in Britain, The Culture of Production*. Manchester: Manchester University Press.

Hartley, J. (1982) *Understanding News*. London: Methuen.

Hawkes, T. (1977) *Structuralism and Semiotics*. London: Methuen.

Hayward, S. (2000) *Cinema Studies* (2nd edn). London: Routledge.

Heath, S. (1981) *Questions of Cinema*. London: Macmillan.

Hebdige, D. (1979) *Subculture – The Meaning of Style*. London: Methuen.

Herbert, J. (2000) *Journalism in the Digital Age*. Oxford: Focal Press.

Herman, E. and McChesney, R. (1999) Global media in the late 1990s, in H. Mackay and T. O'Sullivan (eds), *The Media Reader – Continuity and Transformation*. London: Sage/Open University Press.

Herman, S. and Chomsky, N. (1988) *Manufacturing Consent*. New York: Pantheon.

Hermes, J. (1995) *Reading Women's Magazines*. Cambridge: Polity Press.

Hesmondhalgh, D. and Negus, K. (eds) (2002) *Popular Music Studies*. London: Arnold.

Hill, J. (1991) Issues of national cinema and British film production, in D.J. Petrie, *Creativity and Constraint in The British Film Industry*. New York: St Martins Press.

Hill, J. (1996) British film policy, in A. Moran (ed.), *Film Policy – International, National and Regional Perspectives*. London: Routledge.

Hill, J. and Gibson, P.C. (1998) *The Oxford Guide to Film Studies*. Oxford: Oxford University Press.

Hobson, D. (1982) *Crossroads – The Drama of a Soap Opera*. London: Methuen.

Hobson, D. (2003) *Soap Operas*. Cambridge: Polity Press.

Hoggart, R. (1957) *The Uses of Literacy*. Harmondsworth: Penguin.

Holland, P. (1998) The politics of the smile – soft news and the sexualisation of the popular press, in C. Carter, G. Branston and S. Allan (eds), *News, Gender and Power*. London: Routledge.

Hollows, J. and Jancovich, M. (1995) *Approaches to Popular Film*. Manchester: Manchester University Press.

Horvat, J. (2001) American news, global news, in T. Sylvia (ed.), *Global News, Perspectives on the Information Age*. Ames: Iowa State University Press.

Howarth, D. (2000) *Discourse*. Buckingham: Open University Press.

Howe, M. (1977) Television and Children. *New University Education*: 71–2. In B. Skegg and J. Mundy (1992) *The Media*. Walton-on-Thames: Nelson.

Jameson, J. (1990) *Late Marxism – Adorno, or, the Persistence of the Dialectic*. London: Verso.

Jameson, J. (1991) *Postmodernism, or the Cultural Logic of Late Capitalism*. London: Verso.

Jameson, J. (1992) Reification and utopia in mass culture, in J. Jameson, *Signatures of the Visible*. London: Verso.

Jameson, J. (1998) *The Cultural Turn – Selected Writings on the Postmodern*. London: Verso.

Jamieson, K. and Campbell, K. (2001) *The Interplay of Influence – News, Advertising, Politics and the Mass Media* (5th edn). Belmont, CA: Wadsworth/Thompson Learning.

Jancovich, J. (1995) Screen theory, in J. Hollows and M. Jancovich, *Approaches to Popular Film*. Manchester: Manchester University Press.

Jenkins, H. (1992) *Textual Poachers*. London: Routledge.

Jensen, K. (ed.) (1998) *News of the World – World Cultures Look at Television News*. London: Routledge.

Jhally, S. (1990) *The Codes of Advertising – Fetishism and the Political Economy of Meaning in the Consumer Society*. London: Routledge.

Johnson, F. (1996) Cyberpunks in the White House, in J. Dovey (ed.), *Fractal Dreams: New Media in Social Context*. London: Lawrence & Wishart.

Johnson, F. and Young, K. (2002) Gendered voices in children's television advertising. *Critical Studies in Media Communication*, Vol. 19, 4, December.

Jones, T. (2003) *The Dark Heart of Italy*. London: Faber & Faber.

Kane, M.J. and Greendorfer, S.L. (1994) The media's role in accommodating and resisting stereotyped images of women in sport, in P.J. Creedon (ed.), *Women, Media and Sport – Challenging Gender Values*. London: Sage.

Kaplan, E.A. (1992) Feminist criticism, in R.C. Allen (ed.), *Channels of Discourse Reassembled*. London: Routledge.

Katz, E. (1996) And deliver us from segmentation. *Annals of the American Academy of Political and Social Science*, 546.

Katz, E. and Lazarfield, P.F (1995) Between media and mass/the part played by people/the two step flow of mass communication, in O. Boyd Barrett and C. Newbold, *Approaches to Media: A Reader*. London: Arnold.

Keane, J. (1991) *The Media and Democracy*. Oxford: Polity Press.

Kenway, J. and Bullen, E. (2001) *Consuming Children – Education, Entertainment, Advertising*. Buckingham: Open University Press.

Kline, S. (1993) *Out of the Garden – Toys and Children's Culture in the Age of Television Marketing*. London: Verso.

Kolker, R. (1998) The film text and film form, in J. Hill and P.C. Gibson, *The Oxford Guide to Film Studies*. Oxford: Oxford University Press.

Lacan, J. (1993) The mirror stage as formative of the function of the I (trans. A. Sheridan (1989) *Ecrits, a Selection*. London: Routledge), in A. Easthope (ed.), *Contemporary Film Theory*. Harlow: Longman.

Lacey, N. (2000) *Narrative and Genre*. Basingstoke: Palgrave.

Langer, J. (1998) *Tabloid Television – Popular Journalism*. London: Routledge.

Lapsley, R. and Westlake, M. (1988) *Film Theory – An Introduction*. Manchester: Manchester University Press.

Larsen, M.S. (1997) The rise of professionalism – a sociological analysis, in D. Berkowitz (ed.), *The Social Meanings of News*. London: Sage.

Lash, S. and Urry, J. (1994) *The Economics of Signs and Space*. London: Sage.

Lax, S. (2000) The internet and democracy, in D. Gauntlett (ed.), *Web Studies*. London: Arnold.

Lee, M. (1993) *Consumer Culture Reborn – The Cultural Politics of Consumption*. London: Routledge.

Lister, M., Dovey, J., Giddings, S., Grant, I. and Kelly, K. (2003) *New Media – A Critical Introduction*. London: Routledge.

Liebes, T. and Katz, E. (1993) *The Export of Meaning – Cross Cultural Realities of Dallas* (2nd edn). Oxford: Polity Press.

Livingstone, S. (1990) *Making Sense of Television: The Psychology of Audience Interpretation*. Oxford: Pergamon Press.

Livingstone, S. (1996) On the continuing problem of media effects, in J. Curran and M. Gurevitch, *Mass Media & Society* (2nd edn). London: Arnold.

Longhurst, B. (1995) *Popular Music and Society*. Cambridge: Polity Press.

Lull, J. (1992) *Popular Music and Communication*. London: Sage.

Lyotard, J.-F. (1984) *The Post Modern Condition – A Report on Knowledge* (trans. Geoffrey Bennington and Brian Massumi). Manchester: Manchester University Press.

Macdonald, M. (1995) *Representing Women – Myths of Femininity in the Popular Media*. London: Edward Arnold.

Macdonald, M. (2003) *Exploring Media Discourses*. London: Arnold.

Mackay, H. (ed.) (1997) *Consumption and Everyday Life*. London: Sage/Open University Press.

Mackay, H. and O'Sullivan, T. (eds) (1999) *The Media Reader – Continuity and Transformation*. London: Sage/Open University Press.

Maguire, J. (1999) *Global Sport – Identities, Societies, Civilisations*. Cambridge: Polity Press.

Malone, T.W. and Laubacher, R.J. (2000) The dawn of the E-lance economy, in P. O'Meara, H.D. Mehlinger and M. Krain (eds), *Globalisation and the Challenges of a New Century*. Bloomington: Indiana University Press.

Manning, P. (2001) *News and News Sources – A Critical Introduction*. London: Sage.

Martin, A. (1992) – Mise en scène is dead, or the expressive, the excessive, the technical and the stylish. *Continuum*, 5r, 2: 87–140. In T. Elsaesser and W. Buckland (2002), *Studying Contemporary American Film, A Guide to Movie Analysis*. London: Arnold.

Matterlart, A. (1991) (trans. M. Chanan) *Advertising International – The Privatisation of Public Space*. London: Routledge.

Maxwell, I. (2002) The curse of fandom: insiders, outsiders and ethnography, in D. Hesmondhalgh and K. Negus (eds), *Popular Music Studies*. London: Arnold.

Mayne, J. (2002) Paradoxes of spectatorship, in G. Turner (ed.), *The Film Cultures Reader*. London: Routledge.

McCracken, E. (1993) *Decoding Women's Magazines*. Basingstoke: Macmillan.

McGregor, B. (1997) *Live, Direct and Biased? – Making Television News in the Satellite Age*. London: Arnold.

McKay, J. (2000) *The Magazines Handbook*. London: Routledge.

McLuhan, M. (1994) *Understanding Media – The Extensions of Man*. London: Routledge.

McLuhan, M. and Fiore, Q. (1967) *The Medium is the Message*. London: Penguin.

McNair, B. (1998) *The Sociology of Journalism*. London: Arnold.

McQuail, D. (1992) *Media Performance*. London: Sage.

McQuail, D. (2000) *McQuail's Mass Communication Theory* (4th edn). London: Sage.

Medved, M. (1992) *Hollywood versus America – Popular Culture and the War on Traditional Values*. New York: Zondervan Harper Collins.

Metz, C. (1974) *Film Language – A Semiotics of the Cinema*. New York: Oxford University Press.

Metz, C. (1982) *Psychoanalysis and the Cinema – The Imaginary Signifier*. London: Macmillan.

Meyer, T.P. (1976) The impact of 'all in the family' on children. *Journal of Broadcasting*, winter.

Middleton, R. (1990) *Studying Popular Music*. Buckingham: Open University Press.

Miller, T. (2000) The film industry and government – endless Mr Beans and Mr Bonds? in R. Murphy (ed.), *British Cinema of the Nineties*. London: BFI.

Modleski, T. (1984) *Loving with a Vengeance*. London: Methuen.

Moores, S. (1993) *Interpreting Audiences*. London: Sage.

Moran, A. (ed.) (1996) *Film Policy – International, National and Regional Perspectives*. London: Routledge.

Moran, A. (1998) *CopyCat TV – Globalisation, Programme Formats and Cultural Identity*. Luton: University of Luton Press.

Morley, D. (1989) Changing paradigms in audience research, in E. Seiter, H. Borchers, G. Kreutzner and E. Warth (eds), *Remote Control*. London: Routledge.

Morley, D. (1992) *Television Audiences & Cultural Studies*. London: Routledge.

Morley, D. (1996a) Postmodernism, the rough guide, in J. Curran, D. Morley and V. Walkerdine, (eds), *Cultural Studies and Communications*. London: Arnold.

Morley, D. (1996b) Populism, revisionism and the 'new' audience research, in J. Curran, D. Morley and V. Walkerdine, (eds), *Cultural Studies and Communications*. London: Arnold.

Mosco, V. (1996) *The Political Economy of Communication*. London: Sage.

Mulvey, L. (1989) Visual pleasure and narrative cinema, in L. Mulvey, *Visual and Other Pleasures*. Basingstoke: Macmillan.

Mumford, L.S. (1995) *Love and Ideology in the Afternoon*. Bloomington and Indianopolis: Indiana University Press.

Murdock, G. and Golding, P. (2000) Culture, communications and political economy, in J. Curran and M. Gurevitch, *Mass Media and Society* (3rd edn). London: Arnold.

Murphy, R. (ed.) (2000) *British Cinema of the Nineties*. London: BFI.

Nava, M., Blake, A., MacRury, I. and Richards, B. (1996) *Buy This Book – Studies in Advertising and Consumption*. London: Routledge.

Neale, S. (1995) Questions of genre, in O. Boyd-Barrett and C. Newbold (eds), *Approaches to Media, A Reader*. London: Arnold.

Neale, S. (2000) *Genre and Hollywood*. London: Routledge.

Negrine, R. (1994) *Politics and the Mass Media in Britain* (2nd edn). London: Routledge.

Negus, K. (1992) *Producing Pop*. London: Edward Arnold.

Negus, K. (1996) *Popular Music in Theory*. Cambridge: Polity Press.

Negus, K. (1999) *Music Genres and Corporate Cultures*. London: Routledge.

Negus, K. and Roman-Velazquez, P. (2000) Globalisation and cultural identities, in J. Curran and M. Gurevitch, *Mass Media and Society* (3rd edn). London: Arnold.

Neuman, R. (1991) *The Future of the Mass Audience*. New York: Cambridge University Press.

Nochimson, M. (1992) *No End to Her – Soap Opera and the Female Subject*. Oxford: University of California Press.

Nowell-Smith, G. (1985) But do we need it? in M. Auty and N. Roddick, *British Cinema Now*. London: BFI.

O'Barr, W.M. (1994) *Culture and the Advertisement – Exploring Otherness in the World of Advertising*. Oxford: Westview Press.

O'Donnell, H. (1999) *Good Times, Bad Times – Soap Operas and Society in Western Europe*. London: Leicester University Press.

O'Meara, P., Mehlinger, H.D. and Krain, M. (eds) (2000) *Globalisation and the Challenges of a New Century*. Bloomington: Indiana University Press.

Ong, A. (2000) The gender and labor politics of postmodernity, in P. O'Meara, H.D. Mehlinger and M. Krain (eds), *Globalisation and the Challenges of a New Century*. Bloomington: Indiana University Press.

Parkin, F. (1972) *Class Inequality and the Political Order*. St Albans: Paladin.

Paterson, C. (1998) Global battlefields, in O. Boyd-Barrett and T. Rantanen, *The Globalisation of News*. London: Sage.

Pavlik, J. (2001) *Journalism and the New Media*. New York: Columbia University Press.

Perkins, T. (2000) Who (and what) is it for? in C. Gledhill and L. Williams, *Reinventing Film Studies*. London: Arnold.

Peterson, R.A. and Berger, D.G. (1990) Cycles in symbol production – the case of popular music, in S. Frith and A. Goodwin (eds), *On Record – Rock, Pop and the Written Word*. London: Routledge.

Petley, J. (1992) Independent distribution in the UK, in D. Petrie (ed.), *New Questions of British Cinema*. London: BFI.

Petrie, D.J. (1991) *Creativity and Constraint in the British Film Industry*. New York: St Martins Press.

Petrie, D.J. (ed.) (1992) *New Questions of British Cinema*. London: BFI.

Philo, G. (1990) *Seeing and Believing – The Influence of Television*. London: Routledge.

Pines, J. (2001) Rituals and representations of black 'Britishness', in D. Morley and K. Robins, *British Cultural Studies*. Oxford: Oxford University Press.

Potter, R. (1998) Not the same: race, repetition and difference in hip hop and dance music, in T. Swiss, J. Sloop and J. Herman, *Mapping the Beat – Popular Music and Contemporary Theory*. Oxford: Blackwell.

Potter, W.J. (1999) *On Media Violence*. London: Sage.

Press, A.L. (2000) Recent developments in feminist communication theory, in J. Curran and M. Gurevich, *Mass Media and Society* (3rd edn). London: Arnold.

Preston, P. (2001) *Reshaping Communications*. London: Sage.

Prince, S. (1996) Psychoanalytic film theory, in D. Bordwell and N. Carroll (eds), *Post Theory – Reconstructing Film Studies*. Madison, WI: University of Wisconsin Press.

Protess, D.L. (1991) *The Journalism of Outrage – Investigative Reporting and Agenda Building in America*. London: The Guilford Press. In P. Manning (2001) *News and News Sources – A Critical Introduction*. London: Sage.

Radway, J. (1984) *Reading the Romance*. Chapel Hill, NC: University of North Carolina Press.

Real, M. (1989) *Super Media*. London: Sage.

Reese, S.W. (1997) The news paradigm and the ideology of objectivity, in D. Berkowitz, *The Social Meanings of News*. London: Sage.

Robinson, W. (1995) Market share as a measure of media concentration, in T. Congdon *et al.*, *The Cross Media Revolution – Ownership and Control*. London: John Libbey.

Rothkopf, D. (2000) In praise of cultural imperialism, in P. O'Meara, H.D. Mehlinger and M. Krain (eds), *Globalisation and the Challenges of a New Century*. Bloomington: Indiana University Press.

Rowe, D. (1999) *Sport, Culture and the Media*. Buckingham: Open University Press.

Rowe, D. (2000) No gain, no game? Media and sport, in J. Curran and M. Gurevitch, *Mass Media & Society* (3rd edn). London: Arnold.

Ruddock, A. (2001) *Understanding Audiences*. London: Sage.

Schiller, H. (1996) *Information Inequality – The Deepening Crisis of America*. London: Routledge.

Schiller, H. (2000) Digitised capitalism: What has changed? in H. Tumber (ed.), *Media Power – Professionals and Policies*. London: Routledge.

Schlesinger, P. and Tumber, H. (1994) *Reporting Crime – The Media Politics of Criminal Justice*. Oxford: Oxford University Press.

Schlesinger, P., Dobash, R. and Weaver, K. (1992) *Women Viewing Violence*. London: BFI.

Schudson, M. (1993) *Advertising, The Uneasy Persuasion*. London: Routledge.

Sconce, J. (1993) Spectacles of death, in J. Collins, H. Radner and A.P. Collins (eds), *Film Theory Goes to the Movies*. London: Routledge.

Seaton, J. (1997) The sociology of the mass media, in J. Curran and J. Seaton, *Power Without Responsibility* (5th edn). London: Routledge.

Seiter, E., Borchers, H., Kreutzner, G. and Warth, E. (1989) *Remote Control – Television, Audiences and Cultural Power*. London: Routledge.

Seymour-Ure, C. (1996) *The British Press and Broadcasting since 1945*. Oxford: Blackwell.

Shuker, R. (2001) *Understanding Popular Music* (2nd edn). London: Routledge.

Silverstone, R. (1994) *Television and Everyday Life*. London: Routledge.

Silverstone, R. (1999) *Why Study the Media?* London: Sage.

Sinclair, J. (1987) *Images Incorporated – Advertising as Industry and Ideology*. Beckenham: Croom Helm.

Skidmore, P. (1998) Gender and the agenda, in C. Carter, G. Branston and S. Allan (eds), *News, Gender and Power*. London: Routledge.

Sobchak, V. (2000) The scene of the screen: envisioning cinematic and electronic presence, in J.T. Caldwell (ed.), *Theories of the New Media – A Historical Perspective*. London: Athlone Press.

Soloski, J. (1997) News reporting and professionalism – some constraints on the reporting of news in D. Berkowitz, *The Social Meanings of News*. London: Sage.

Sparks, R. (1992) *Television and the Drama of Crime*. Buckingham: Open University Press.

Spybey, A. (1996) *Globalisation and World Society*. Cambridge: Polity Press.

Sreberny, A. (2000) The global and the local in international communications, in J. Curran and M. Gurevitch, *Mass Media and Society* (3rd edn). London: Arnold.

Sreberny-Mohammadi, A. *et al.* (1998) in K. Jensen (ed.), *News of the World-World Cultures Look at Television News*. London: Routledge.

Stacey, J. (2000) Hollywood cinema: the great escape, in G. Turner, *Film as Social Practice* (2nd end). London: Routledge.

Steemers, J. (1999) Broadcasting is dead. Long live digital choice, in H. Mackay and T. O'Sullivan, *The Media Reader*, pp. 243–4. London: Sage.

Steinem, G. (1995) Sex, lies and advertising, in R. Andersen, *Consumes Culture and Television Programming*. Oxford: Westview Press.

Sterling, C. (2000) US communications industry ownership and the 1996 Telecommunications Act, in H. Tumber, *Media Power, Professionals and Policies*. London: Routledge.

Stevenson, N. (2002) *Understanding Media Cultures* (2nd edn). London: Sage.

Stokes, J. and Reading, A. (eds) (1999) *The Media in Britain – Current Debates and Developments*. Basingstoke: Macmillan.

Street, J. (1999) Remote control? Politics, technology and 'electronic democracy', in H. Mackay and T. O'Sullivan, *The Media Reader – Continuity and Transformation*. London: Sage/Open University Press.

Street, S. (1997) *British National Cinema*. London: Routledge.

Sturken, M. and Cartwright, L. (2001) *Practices of Looking*. Oxford: Oxford University Press.

Sylvia, T. (ed.) (2001) *Global News, Perspectives on the Information Age*. Ames: Iowa State University Press.

Thompson, J. (1990) *Ideology and Modern Culture*. Cambridge: Polity Press.

Thompson, K. (1997) *Media and Cultural Regulation*. London: Sage/Open University Press.

Thussu, D. (2000) *International Communication*. London: Arnold.

Thwaites, T., Davies, L. and Mules, W. (1994) *Tools for Cultural Studies*. Melbourne: Macmillan.

Tinkler, P. (1995) *Constructing Girlhood – Popular Magazines for Girls Growing up in England, 1920–1950*. London: Taylor & Francis.

Tolson, A. (1996) *Mediations – Text and Discourse in Media Studies*. London: Arnold.

Tomlinson, A. (1999) *The Game's Up – Essays in the Cultural Analysis of Sport, Leisure and Popular Culture. Popular Cultural Studies*: 15. Aldershot: Ashgate Publishing.

Tomlinson, A. (2001) Sport, leisure and style, in D. Morley and K. Robins, *British Cultural Studies*. Oxford: Oxford University Press.

Tomlinson, J. (1997) Internationalism, globalisation and cultural imperialism, in K. Thompson, *Media and Cultural Regulation*. London: Sage/Open University Press.

Tomlinson, J. (1999) Cultural globalisation: placing and displacing the West, in H. Mackay and T. O'Sullivan, *The Media Reader – Continuity and Transformation*. London: Sage/Open University Press.

Toynbee, J. (2000) *Making Popular Music*. London: Arnold.

Tuchman, G. (1976) Telling stories. *Journal of Communication* 26 (Fall), 93–7. In J. Curran and M. Gurevitch (2000) *Mass Media & Society* (3rd edn) London: Arnold.

Tuchman, G. (1995) The news net, in O. Boyd-Barrett and C. Newbold (eds), *Approaches to Media, A Reader*. London: Arnold.

Tulloch, J. (2000) *Watching Television Audiences*. London: Arnold.

Tumber, H. (ed.) (2000) *Media Power, Professionals and Policies*. London: Routledge.

Turner, G. (1993) *Film as Social Practice* (2nd edn). London: Routledge.

Turner, G. (ed.) (2002) *The Film Cultures Reader*. London: Routledge.

Van Dijk, T.A. (1999) *The Network Society*. London: Sage.

Van Zoonen, L. (1994) *Feminist Media Studies*. London: Sage.

Van Zoonen, L. (1998) One of the girls? The changing gender of journalism, in C. Carter, G. Branston and S. Allan (eds), *News Gender and Power*. London: Routledge.

Velicer, W.F., Govia, J.M., Cherico, N.P. and Corriveau, D.P. (1985) Item format and structure of the Buss-Durkee Hostility Inventory. *Aggressive Behaviour*, 11, 65–82. In L. Berkowitz (1993) *Aggression – Its Causes, Consequences and Control*. Philadelphia: Temple University Press.

Volkmer, I. (1999) *CNN – News in the Global Sphere*. Luton: University of Luton Press.

Von Feilitzen, C. (1998) Media violence: four research perspectives, in R. Dickinson, H. Harindranath and O. Linne, *Approaches to Audiences – A Reader*. London: Arnold.

Von Ginneken, J. (1998) *Understanding Global News, A Critical Introduction*. London: Sage.

Waters, M. (1995) *Globalisation*. London: Routledge.

Wayne, M. (1994) Television, audiences and politics, in S. Hood (ed.), *Behind the Screens: The Structure of British Television in the 1990s*. London: Lawrence & Wishart.

Weber, M. ((1904) 1992) *The Protestant Ethic and the Spirit of Capitalism*. London: Routledge.

Webster, F. (1999) What Information Society? in H. Mackay and T. O'Sullivan, *The Media Reader – Continuity and Transformation*. London: Sage/Open University Press.

Wernick, A. (1991) *Promotional Culture – Advertising, Ideology, and Symbolic Expression*. London: Sage.

White, C. (1969) *Women's Magazines 1693–1968*. London: Michael Joseph.

Williams, C. (2000) After the classic, the classical and ideology: the differences of realism, in C. Gledhill and C. Williams, *Reinventing Film Studies*. London: Arnold.

Williams, K. (2003) *Understanding Media Theory*. London: Arnold.

Williams, P. and Chrisman, L. (eds) (1993) *Colonial Discourse and Post-Colonial Theory*. London: Harvester Wheatsheaf.

Williams, R. (1974) *Television, Technology and Cultural Form*. London: Fontana.

Williamson, J. (1978) *Decoding Advertisements*. London: Marion Boyars.

Woodward, K. (ed.) (1997) *Indentity and Difference*. London: Sage.

Yon, D. (2000) *Elusive Culture – Schooling, Race and Identity in Global Times*. New York: State University of New York Press.

Young, B.M. (1990) *Television Advertising and Children*. Oxford: Clarendon Press.

Selected Websites

This list of sites is intended to provide you with starting points for research into media, but certainly does not cover all possible topics. The range is across institutional sites and academic sites. There are of course any number of business/company sites which you can easily search for by name – e.g. Hollywood majors, or newspapers. I have added a comment in each case. These were all accessed in May 2004. Those marked with an asterisk I have not accessed so recently, but believe they are sound and worth including. If your favourites are not on this list, then this may be something I should know, or it may be that I have had repeated problems with accessing these sites.

abc.org.uk   Audit Bureau of Circulations
an industry site concerned with the press, which includes latest circulation figures

aber.ac.uk/media   Daniel Goldman's site at Aberystwyth
a considerable collection of material, covering a great range of topics, though perhaps uneven its usefulness

bbc.co.uk   The BBC's site
much information about the corporation, as well as many links to their various channels, and to specific programmes: needs to be browsed

bfi.org.uk   The British Film Institute
has useful links to other sites concerned with film industry and film study, as well as subsites for books and journals

byteachers.org.uk   Association of Teachers' sites
provides connection between sites and starting point for searches

cinemedia.org
is a film and media directory for the industries

cineuropa.org
is an industry front for European film

cpbf.org.uk   Campaign for Press and Broadcasting Freedom
the main benefit of this site lies in its database of articles: it also provides information about the work of the organization

cultsock.ndirect.co.uk/MUhome/csktml/   Mick Underwood's Australian site
has many summary items on various subjects, though it is uneven (nothing comes up for Representations, for instance)

*filmeducation.org
a useful wide range of resources and connections, covering many topics

http://vos.ucsb.edu/   University of California location
this the Voice of the Shuttle site which was being rebuilt when accessed, but still provided information on some topics: it has previously had useful links, obviously to other US sites, as well as having an unusual range of material

itv.com/about   ITV plc
provides useful background on the new commercial television giant

mediadesk.co.uk   UK Media Online
this is part of the EU media programme: it provides information about, for example, training, as well as links to other sites

media.guardian.co.uk   The *Guardian* newspaper's site
provides a useful range of current material about the media/media events, including a compilation of their own articles

* newmediastudies.com   David Gauntlett's site relating to new media
includes reference to resources, articles, reviews and more

popcultures.com   Sara Zupko's site: the Cultural Studies Centre
has useful links, general references, reviews, accounts of theorists, useful papers

startat/mediastudies   Steve Baker's A level site
this has a very useful range of links: obviously it is aimed at GCE level rather than degree, but it is a helpful starting point

theory.org.uk   David Gauntlett's site, now maintained by Bournemouth University
contains a mixture of reviews and articles: it is strong in some areas, such as identity and gender, offering some essays /dissertations

* wired.com/news
much news and information about almost anything to do with the Internet

INDEX

sport and national identity
317–19
sporting body 315–16
and television 313
sporting body 315–16
bio-medical body 316
commodified body 316
disciplined body 316
state surveillance 209
stereotypes 63–4
and ideologies 62–3
stereotyping 243
structuralist approach 55
subcultures and identities
168–70
resistance 168–70
subjects of representation 65
syntagm 51

taking pleasure 93–5
see also pleasure
technological determinism 201
technology
and globalization 337–8
and institutions 33–8
technology and media developments
200–3
remediation 202
technological determinism 201
terms and debates 200
see also impact of technology; new
technology (NT)
teen soaps 252
telenovellas 251–3
television drama *see* soaping
television industry, finance 14
television and new technology 218
television soaps 248–72
defining soaps 253–5
empowerment, resistance, ideology
and pleasure 268–71
gendered genre 263–8
key areas 250

narrative 255–6
nature 250–2
soaping of TV drama 259–62
social realism 257–9
teen soaps 252
telenovellas 251–2
text and contexts 48–9
environmental context 48
material context 48
social context 48–9
texts: violence 116–18
moral panics 117–18
mythologies and ideologies 117
texts and meanings 47–8
hermeneutic code 48
socio-linguistics 48
writerly and readerly text 47–8
texts and narration 54–8
diegesis 55
narrative modes 55
narrative structures 56–7
reader positioning 57–8
structuralist approach 55
texts and realism 58–61
ideological realism 59–60
intertextual motivation 60
material analysis 59
mediation 59
philosophical analysis 59
value analysis 59
texts, representations, ideology,
identity 61–7
identities through text 65–7
naturalization 64–5
representation subjects 65
social types 63–4
stereotypes and ideologies 62–3
subjects of representation 65
textual analysis 49
textual codes 49–50
transmission model 82
treatment 52
types 64

USA, globalization and economic
imperialism 185–7
utopias/dystopias 218–19
globalization 329–30

values, music 166–7
vertical integration 10
Video Recordings Act 1984 25
Video Standards Council 23
violence 301
see also audiences: violence; media
and violence
violence as representation 112–14
fact and fiction 113–14
severity of violence 112–13
viral marketing 234–5

web sites 3
when is the future present? 198–9
when is technology new? 198
women, strong 264
women's magazines 130–45
contradictions 142
genre features 133–5
guilt and pleasure 131–2
lads' mags 131
male gaze 131–2, 141–2
narrative strategies 138
pleasure and a woman's space
143–4
reader position 135–6
representations 137–8
roles 138–40
social interactions 140–1
and their readers 131–2
see also television soaps
World Wide Web 208–9
WPP 9
writerly and readerly text 47–8
WTN 288

Young Person's Harmful Publications
Act 1955 24–5